Large-Flowered Climbing Roses

ISBN 9781687303936
Independently published, 2019.

Cover photograph 'Ramira', title page 'Aloha'.
Both by Anne Belovich.

Dedication

This book is dedicated to Jeff Panciera, who drove me all over Europe to visit rose gardens where he also helped me photograph the roses. I could not have illustrated this book without his assistance and encouragement.

Acknowledgements

Thanks to Harald Enders for providing me with some of his own photographs and for helping me overcome the language barrier by contacting the staff of the Europa Rosarium in Sangerhausen, Germany with my request for photographs.

Thanks to Thomas Hawel, director of the Europa Rosarium for providing me with a large set of photographs of excellent quality that has helped me greatly to illustrate this book.

To Steve Jones, an American rosarian, for a similar gift of beautiful rose photographs.

Thanks to Keith Schneider for the initial layout and to Anne Basye and Pat Kevand Hutson for their extensive effort and use of their special skills in the completion and final polishing of this book.

Preface

If you think of climbing roses as an epicurean experience, then Ramblers are the entrée and the large-flowered climbing roses are the dessert, adding the gift of their beauty at the end of the rose story.

Large-flowered climbing roses are a rather heterogeneous group. We tend to think of them as large-flowered and repeat-blooming, but not all of them repeat reliably. The blooming duration and rhythm may be affected by the climate. Some of them are once-bloomers in cool or cold climates and bloom repeatedly in warm ones. Most of the roses included here are large-flowered, but you will also find entries for Climbing Miniatures and Climbing Polyanthas, both with smaller blooms. Basically, I'm including all the climbers that are not included in my book on Ramblers and other species hybrids. The largest groups are the Large-Flowered Climbers (ARS rose class) and the climbing sports of Teas, Hybrid Teas and Floribundas. To these I have added Noisettes, Hybrid Giganteas (omitted from the Rambler book), some of the more vigorous Old Garden Roses, and some of David Austin's English Roses that can be trained to climb. This is far from a perfect system since it is based on personal experience and observation rather than scientific criteria. If the roses I have chosen to include don't all grow as vigorously as you would like I hope you will still enjoy their beauty at a closer range.

Almost every description of a rose variety is accompanied by a photograph. This is an important feature in a book that may be used for identification of unknown specimens. I have taken some of the photographs during my extensive rose travels where I visited the great rose gardens of the world or in my own garden or in the gardens of friends and acquaintances. Many photographs have been kindly donated by rosarians in this country and in Europe. A large collection of photographs was sent to me for inclusion in the book by permission of the director of the Europa Rosarium at Sangerhausen, Germany. The photo credits on page 390 list the source of each photograph other than those taken by the author.

I have tried to check carefully the early descriptions of each rose to see if the rose presently grown under that name matches closely enough to be considered the original variety. In some cases all of the plants of a single variety fail to match and cannot be correct. Sometimes the right one is grown by one or more gardens or offered for sale by one or more nurseries and those grown elsewhere are imposters. I have included this information where it is known.

I have listed the roses alphabetically by the name usually considered to be the correct name, usually the one given by the breeder, followed by known synonyms in parentheses. I have included warnings in some cases about names that belong to more than one rose.

—Anne Belovich

A

'Abraham Darby'.

'A Shropshire Lad'.

'A SHROPSHIRE LAD'.

Breeder: David Austin, United Kingdom, 1997.
Parentage: 'Heritage' x Seedling. Leander is somewhere in the parentage.
Classification: Shrub, English Rose.
We think of the English Roses as shrubs, their assigned class, but many will climb nicely if given a small arbor or a low fence as support. 'A Shropshire Lad' may reach 8 to 10 ft (2.4-3 m) with these aids and can also be kept pruned as a shrub. Either way it will produce a multitude of fragrant, large, double, peachy-pink rosettes for the entire season. The outer petals fade as the flower matures, but the centers retain the darker color for longer. The plant is healthy in my usually temperate climate, almost thornless and has shown good hardiness by surviving a rare winter with a low temperature of 0 degrees F. The name of this rose commemorates an A. E. Houseman poem.

'ABOVE ALL'.

Breeder: Christopher H. Warner, United Kingdom, pre-2013.
Parentage: 'Westerland' x 'Sweet Magic'.
Classification: Large-Flowered Climber.
Orange color can appear harsh in roses, but not so in this beauty. The color is somehow brilliant and soft at the same time. The yellow-based petals fade with age to a more pinkish hue that adds to the charm of the plant. The fragrant blooms are medium–sized, double and held in large clusters. They start out cup-shaped and open out flat to show their stamens nestled into the flowers' yellow centers. The plant's climbing potential is about 10 to 14 ft (305 to 425 cm), perfect for an arbor. It has an excellent repeat blooming pattern and disease resistance and is rated for hardiness in USDA zone 5a.

'ABOVE AND BEYOND'.

Breeder: David C. Zlesak (United Stated, 2000).
Parentage: 'Lemon Puff' x (R. Virginia x R. laxa Retzius).
Classification: Large-Flowered Climber.
This light apricot-yellow rose will reward you with a plentiful display of lovely semi-double medium to large blooms in small to medium clusters if planted on a support like an arbor, a fence or a pillar. With a growth pattern of 10 to 13 ft (300 to 400 cm) it will not overwhelm a small support structure. It can also be grown as a shrub or a hedge. It is said to be hardy to USDA zone 3b. This is probably a trait inherited from Rosa laxa.

'Abraham Darby'.

'ABRAHAM DARBY'.

Breeder: David C. H. Austin (United Kingdom, 1985).
Parentage: 'Aloha' x 'Yellow Cushion'.
Classification: English Rose, Shrub.
The large buds, golden yellow with deep pink tips, open to reveal broad, pink outer petals surrounding numerous smaller apricot-colored, quartered petals. A nuance of yellow remains at the petal bases. The flowers are large, very full and arranged in small clusters. They bloom prolifically and continuously during the whole flowering season. The plants are well armed and have glossy, medium green foliage. With support, they will grow to about 10 ft (3 m). They are disease resistant except for a slight susceptibility for rust and are hardy to USDA zone 5b.

'Abraxas'.

'ABRAXAS'.

Breeder: VEG (S) Baumschulen Dresden (Germany, 1973).
Parentage: No information.
Classification: Shrub.
Although it is always classed as a shrub, 'Abraxas' will grow tall enough through repeated branching to be trained as a small climber. With its shrubby habit it will look best supported by a pillar or a small tree rather than an arbor where a rose with long, flexible canes is best. The flowers are full, large, shaped like a Hybrid Tea and produced in small clusters. They will brighten a garden with their brilliant dark red-vermilion color. They are mildly fragrant and rebloom well.

'ACIDALIE'.

Breeder: Rousseau (France, pre-1837).
Parentage: Unknown.
Classification: Bourbon.
The deep pink, rounded buds produce large, very full, light pink flowers that fade almost to white at the outer broad, reflexed petals. The smaller, darker inner petals have a roughly quartered form. There is a mild fragrance. The flowers bloom in repeated seasonal flushes. The canes have medium-sized, dark green foliage. The leaves are sometimes composed of seven leaflets rather than the usual five. The plant will grow to about 8 ft. (2.5 m) and is hardy to USDA zone 5b.

'Adam'.

'ADAM'.

Breeder: Adam (France, circa 1838).
Parentage: Thought to be 'Hume's Blush Tea-scented China' x 'Rose Edouard'.
Classification: Tea, Climbing Tea.
Adam is sometimes given the credit of being the first of the Tea roses, but this is questionable. A number of different plants are grown as 'Adam' today. Early descriptions specify a large, double flower with coppery/buff centers and light pink outer petals. Some plants of 'Adam' in Europe come close to this standard with the bloom color changing somewhat with the seasons: most pink when it is warm and light buff or cream during the colder months. This rose makes a lovely small climber. 'President' is no longer considered to be synonymous with 'Adam'.

'Adele Frey'.

'ADELE FREY'.

Breeder: Louis (Ludwig) Walter (France, 1911).
Parentage: Unknown.
Classification: Hybrid Tea, Cl.
This rose is not available commercially, but can be seen at Sangerhausen. The blooms are large, double, lightly fragrant and deep cerise pink. The plant blooms in flushes throughout the season. It is vigorous enough to be trained as a pillar rose or as a decoration for a low fence.

'Aëlita'.

'AËLITA'.

Breeder: Ivan I. Shtanko (former USSR, 1952).
Parentage: Seedling of 'New Dawn'.
Classification: Large-Flowered Climber.
The flowers of this lovely rose are pale pink fading to white with a reverse of a slightly deeper color. The petals roll back at the tips. The blooms are medium to large-sized, very full and very fragrant. They are carried singly (mostly) or in small clusters. The plants have small, shiny, dark green leaves and will reach a height of about 10 ft. (3 m).

'AGATHA CHRISTIE'.
See 'Ramira'.

'AGNES'.

Breeder: Dr. William Saunders (Canada, circa 1900).
Parentage: Rosa rugosa x Rosa foetida f. persiana hort.
Classification: Hybrid Rugosa.
'Agnes' has fragrant, soft light yellow flowers that fade, starting at the outer petals, to pale cream. The large-sized flowers are usually described as being very double, but the flowers on plants I have seen at Roseraie du Val-de-Marne (France) and Sangerhausen(Germany) are only double and are sometimes apricot rather than yellow, anomalies perhaps caused by hot weather. The flowers are borne singly (usually) or in small clusters and are primarily summer blooming, but in a warm climate, there may be some fall repeat. The plant is armed with prickles, has glossy, light green rugose (wrinkled) foliage, is hardy down to USDA zone 3b and will grow to about 8 ft. (2.5 m).

'Agnes'.

'AGRIPPINA, CL'.
See 'Cramoisi Supérieur, Cl.'

'Alain, Cl'., Roth Clone.

'ALAIN, CL.' ('Grimpant Alain').

Breeder: Discovered by Hippolyte Delforge (Belgium, 1957) and Konrad Roth (Germany, 1957).

Parentage: Sport of the Floribunda, 'Alain'.
Classification: Climbing Floribunda.
The flowers of this rose are very bright medium red, large, lightly scented and semi-double. The wavy petals arranged in an open form around the yellow stamens add to its charm. The blooms are carried in large clusters. Remontancy is a welcome bonus. The plant has glossy, dark green foliage and is reported to grow to as much as 25 ft. (7.6 m) if given adequate support. I have seen both clones and cannot detect any differences between them.

'Alaska'.

'ALASKA' ('Future').

Breeder: Hermann Kordes (Germany, 2005).
Parentage: KORklemol x Seedling.
Classification: Large-Flowered Climber.
I have seen this rose at Sangerhausen where it is being grown as a small climber with a potential of about 8 ft. (2.5 m). The flowers are mildly fragrant, medium to large, high-centered, very full and white with creamy centers. They are formed in medium to large clusters.

'ALBERT LA BLOTAIS'.

Breeder: Moreau-Robert (France, 1881).
Parentage: Unknown.
Classification: Cl. Hybrid Perpetual.
This old variety is graced with deep, bright red blooms nuanced with scarlet. The flowers are double with a globular form, a medium to large size and are strongly scented. They will repeat bloom in continuous flushes during the flowering season. The plant will grow to 10-16.5 ft. and looks beautiful on an arbor. There are several rose varieties with this name. The Bénard climbing rose of 1914 seems to no longer exist. This entry and the following entry are the remaining climbers of the group.

'Albert la Blotais', Moreau-Robert clone.

'ALBERT LA BLOTAIS'.

('Albert la Blotais, Cl.').
Breeder: Jean Pernet (France, 1887).
Parentage: 'Gloire de Dijon' x 'Général Jacqueminot'.
Classification: Cl. Hybrid Tea.
The flowers of this climbing Hybrid Tea are crimson/red aging to medium crimson, then finally to pink. They are lightly double and large. The center petals are wavy giving a muddled appearance. The height can reach at least 12 ft. (3.6 m).

'Albert Poyet'.

'Albert Poyet'.

'ALBERT POYET'.

Breeder: André Eve (France, 1979).
Parentage: 'Étendard' x 'Red Parfum'.
Classification: Large-flowered Climber.
Albert Poyet has a striking color combination. The pink of the petals is intensified to a crimson red at the tips and at the outer petals. The buds open in a Hybrid Tea shape and the outer petals curl down along each side to form triangular tips. The flowers are double, medium to large and carry little scent. The bloom is remontant. The plant is vigorous and healthy and will reach 10 to 16 ft. (3 to 5 m). 'Albert Poyet' received the Médaille d'Argent award at the 1978 Bagatelle Rose Trials.

'Alec's Red, Cl.'.

'ALEC'S RED, CL.'.

Breeder: Discovered by Robert Harkness (United Kingdom, 1975).
Parentage: Sport of 'Alec's Red'.
Classification: Climbing Hybrid Tea.
The flowers are bright crimson red (more pink in hot weather), very large, full, richly fragrant and have a classical Hybrid Tea high-centered form. They occur singly or in small clusters. The rose is summer blooming with a few flowers produced later. The showy flowers contrast well with the dark green foliage. Good vigor and upright growth allow it to be grown as a small climber of 7 to 8 ft. (2 to 2.5 m) if given support. The plant is moderately hardy.

'Alexander Mackensie'.

'ALEXANDER MACKENSIE'.

('A. Mackensie').
Breeder: Dr. Felicitas Svejda (Canada, 1970).
Parentage: 'Queen Elizabeth' x ('Red Dawn' x 'Suzanne').
Classification: Shrub.
The flowers of this unusually hardy rose (USDA zone 3b) are medium-sized, full, cherry red with a lighter reverse and are very pretty considering that they were bred primarily with cold resistance in mind as a specialty for the northern garden. They have a raspberry scent, a cupped form and grow in large clusters. The foliage is light green and glossy. There is some repeat in the fall. The disease and pest resistant plant will grow vigorously to about 8 ft. (2.4 m).

'Alexander Von Humboldt'.

'ALEXANDER VON HUMBOLDT'.

Breeder: Reimer Kordes.
Parentage: Rosa kordesii x 'Cleopatra'.

Classification: Hybrid Kordesii.

This rose produces large clusters of crimson, medium-sized, lightly double, mildly fragrant flowers with a flat, very open form that reveals the stamens and some small white streaks in the center. A little ruffling of the petals adds to the floral charm. There may be some repeat in the fall. The plant is quite vigorous, growing to 10 or 12 ft. (3 to 3.65 m).

'ALFRESCO'.

Breeder: Christopher H. Warner (U K, 2000.).
Parentage: 'Mary Sumner' x 'Summer Wine'.
Classification: Large-Flowered Climber.

The buds and new flowers are coral with a yellow center and a pink reverse. They become pinker and the yellow centers fade to cream as the flower ages. They are semi-double to lightly double, medium to large and open out flat to show the stamens. The bloom repeats all season in flushes. The plant bears healthy medium green, glossy foliage and will reach a height of 8-10 ft. There are no public gardens listed for this rose, but it is available in commerce.

'Ali Baba'.

'ALI BABA'.

('Schloss Bad Homburg', 'Sunset Glow')
Breeder: Christopher H. Warner (United Kingdom, pre-2006).
Parentage: Unknown.
Classification: Large-Flowered Climber.

The fragrance of this rose is fruity and moderate to strong. Opinions vary. The flowers are large, full and apricot-pink fading to mauve-pink from the outer petals inward. The petals are scalloped and beautifully ruffled. The rose is remontant with flushes of bloom throughout the season. The plant is disease resistant and will climb to about 8 ft. (2.5 m). It grows at Sangerhausen and some other European gardens under the name 'Schloss Bad Homburg'.

'Alister Stella Gray'.

'ALISTER STELLA GRAY'.

('Golden Rambler').
Breeder: Alexander Hill Gray (United Kingdom, 1894).
Parentage: 'William Allen Richardson' x 'Madame Pierre Guillot'.
Classification: Tea-Noisette.

Long, pointed buds open to double, medium-sized, fragrant, light yellow flowers with darker yellow centers. They soon fade to cream. They open out flat, but a center of shorter petals gives them a fluffy look. The flowers arrive in small clusters early in the season and large ones later in the fall. The plant is hardy to USDA zone 5b, but the plant blooms, grows and repeats best in a warm climate. The somewhat fragile petals need a dry climate as well for best appearance. The plant is tall enough at 16 ft. (5 m) to make a good display on an arbor.

'All Ablaze'.

'ALL ABLAZE'.

Breeder: Tom Carruth (USA, 2000).
Parentage: 'Don Juan' x ({'Zorina' x [Rosa soulieana x 'Europeana']} x 'Sunsprite').
Classification: Large-Flowered Climber.
You would probably never guess from the showy display of big clusters of medium to large, very double, bright red blooms that this rose has Rosa soulieana in its immediate background. The genetic influence of 'Don Juan', the dark red seed parent seems to be more influential. The flowers are slightly fragrant and have excellent remontance. The disease-resistant plant can be expected to grow to a height of 8 to 12 ft.

'Allegro'.

'ALLEGRO' (MEIleodevin).

Breeder: Meilland International (France, pre-2010).
Parentage: Unknown.
Classification: Large-Flowered Climber.
I have observed this rose at Sangerhausen where it is grown as a small climber with about an 8 ft. potential height. The magenta-pink flowers become more lavender with maturity. They are large, double and fragrant and are formed singly or in small clusters. The leaves are dark green and shiny. It is said to be disease resistant.

'Allen Chandler'.

'ALLEN CHANDLER'.

Breeder: Allen Chandler, 1923.
Parentage: 'Hugh Dickson' x unknown.
Classification: Climbing Hybrid Tea.
'Allen Chandler' has a color all of its own, between crimson and scarlet, but more toward the scarlet side. This is set off by a narrow ring of white in the center. The petals have a little twist that produces a wavy look. The flowers are semi-double (almost single at times) and range from large to very large. They grow singly or in small clusters. This is an excellent repeater, blooming in continuous flushes during the whole season. The plant has dark green, glossy foliage and few prickles. It is quite vigorous, reaching heights of around 16 ft. (5 m).

'ALLEN'S FRAGRANT PILLAR'.

Breeder: A. J. and C. Allen (United Kingdom, 1931).
Parentage: 'Paul's Lemon Pillar' x 'Souvenir de Claudius Denoyel'.
Classification: Large-Flowered Climber.
Large, double, bright cerise flowers open out to show a

yellow center that enhances the large bunch of golden stamens. True to its name it is strongly fragrant. The individual blooms are usually solitary, but may be seen in small clusters. At a height of 8 to 10 ft. (2.45 to 3 m) it will make a good pillar rose. It repeats well, blooming in flushes all season.

'Allen's Fragrant Pillar'. (above & below)

'ALLGOLD, CL.'.

Breeder: Discovered by Douglas L. Gandy (U K, 1961).
Parentage: Sport of 'Allgold' (LeGrice, 1956).
Classification: Climbing Floribunda.
The flowers of 'Allgold, Cl.' are medium-sized, semi-double to lightly double, mildly fragrant and an unfading, bright yellow. The plant takes a while to establish, but once that is done it is fairly remontant. Glossy, dark green foliage clothes the long arching canes with flowers produced singly or in small clusters along their lengths on lateral canes. The canes may grow to as much as 12 to 16 ft. (3.65 to 5 m).

'Allgold, CL.'.

'ALL IN ONE'. See 'Exploit'.

'ALOHA'.

Breeder: Eugene S. Boerner (United States, 1949).
Parentage: 'Mercedes Gallart' x' New Dawn'.
Classification: Large-Flowered Climber.
This longtime favorite of mine charmingly clothes a small trellis next to a house entry and spills down to cover a small retaining wall below with its large, full pink and coral blooms. The backs of the petals are darker and the coral turns to pink in the older flowers. This floral display is enhanced by the plant's dark, shiny, healthy foliage. The 6 to 8 ft. (1.8 to 2.4 m) of growth is perfect for covering small garden structures. I can always expect some repeat of bloom in the fall.

'Aloha'.

'Aloha Hawaii'.

'ALOHA HAWAII'.

('Aloha', Kordes Rose Aloha).
Breeder: Kordes & Sons (Germany, 2003).
Parentage: 'Westerland' x 'Rugelda'.
Classification: Large-Flowered Climber.
The buds of 'Aloha Hawaii' are deep apricot pink and open into moderately fragrant, large, very double, apricot flowers with outer petals more pink and touched with red and a darker petal reverse. With maturity, the flowers form low domes filled in the center with small petals and surrounded by fairly large outer petals. They are carried in large clusters. The plant's expected height is about 8 ft. (2.5 m). The summer bloom is very profuse with some repeat in the fall. Don't confuse this rose with the Boerner 'Aloha'.

'ALPIN'.

Breeder: Maurice Combe (France, 1960).
Parentage: 'Danse du Feu' ('Spectacular') x seedling.
Classification: Large-Flowered Climber.
'Alpin' produces well-shaped, medium-sized, full medium red flowers lightly touched and warmed with coral. They have a mild, but pleasant scent. The individual blooms occur singly or are carried in small clusters. The plants are fairly vigorous, reaching heights of 10 to 13 ft. (3 to 4 m). There may be an occasional repeat bloom late in the season.

'ALTISSIMO'.

('Altus', 'Sublimely Single').
Breeder: Delbard-Chabert (France, 1966).
Parentage: 'Ténor' x seedling.
Classification: Large-Flowered Climber.

'Altissimo'.

This beautiful variety grows about 15 ft. (4.5 m) into one of my fir trees. Its large, single, mildly fragrant, cupped to open formed scarlet flowers furnish a memorable contrast to the dark green, fuzzy fir boughs where they appear in single brilliant flashes or in small clusters. As the flowers age they become more crimson and open out flatter. There is little fading. The bloom repeats well in continuous flushes and is hardy to USDA zone 5b. It earned the Royal Horticultural Society Award of Garden Merit 1993.

'Amadeus'.

'AMADEUS'.

(Korlabriax, Super Conquerant).
Breeder: W. Kordes & Sons (Germany, 2003).
Parentage: Unknown.
Classification: Large-Flowered Climber.
This rose is usually described as bright red, but a more accurate description would be scarlet fading to a lighter

red of a cooler hue. The flowers are medium to large-sized, fully double and occur singly or are carried in small clusters. They open out as they age to allow a glimpse of stamens. The petals reflex at the tips and become slightly ruffled. 'Amadeus' is a good repeater, blooming in flushes during the whole season. The healthy plant has dark green, very glossy foliage and grows in a shrubby manner to about 8 to 15 ft. (2.5 to 4.5 m).

'Amaretto'.

'AMARETTO'.

Breeder: W. Kordes & Sons (Germany, 1994).
Parentage: Unknown.
Classification: Large-Flowered Climber.
'Amaretto' has lovely colors—very light cream outer petals touched with warm pink and progressively darker, more coral-hued petals toward the center. Fragrance is a welcome bonus. The flower is a regularly formed, medium to large-sized, very double Hybrid Tea-type rosette usually found singly, but sometimes in small clusters. It repeats well in continuous flushes. The plant will grow to about 8 ft. (2.5 m) and will serve well as a pillar rose.

'AMAZONE'.
See 'Spectacular'.

'AMBER CLOUD'.

Breeder: M.S. Viraraghavan (India, 2006).
Parentage: 'Rêve d'Or' x Rosa gigantea .
Classification: Hybrid Gigantea.
A blooming plant of 'Amber Cloud' looks more like a cloud of amber yellow tulips than a rose. The large, single flowers are cupped with pointed petals and about the same size as a typical tulip. The mostly single occurrence heightens this effect. They have a Tea rose fragrance. Reports vary on frequency of rebloom. Most say rebloom is good. The breeders describe the foliage with its large, long and pointed grey green leaves as incredibly beautiful.

'Amélie Gravereaux'.

'AMÉLIE GRAVEREAUX'.

Breeder: Gravereaux (France, 1900).
Parentage: (Rosa gallica L. x 'Eugène Fürst') x Rosa rugosa.
Classification: Hybrid Rugosa.
The richly fragrant, purple flowers are medium-sized, semi-double to double and are carried singly or in small clusters. As they mature they open out flat to reveal the stamens and the ruffled petals with irregularly shaped tips. The flowers are primarily summer blooming with an occasional bloom opening later. The plants are heavily armed with prickles, have rugose, bright green, 7-leaflet leaves and will grow to 6 or 8 ft. (2.5 m).

'AMERICA'.

Breeder: William A. Warriner (U S, pre-1975).
Parentage: 'Fragrant Cloud' x 'Tradition'.
Classification: Large-Flowered Climber.
'America' has flowers that are coral-salmon, medium to large-sized, double and carry a strong fragrance. They are borne mostly singly, or occasionally in small clusters and bloom in flushes during the whole season. The plant is very disease resistant and is quite hardy. It may reach a height of about 12 ft. (3.65 m) and can be grown on pillars, arbors and fences or it can be pruned lower and grown as a shrub. The

rose was named in honor of the country's bicentennial year. It was chosen for the All-America Rose Selection (1976). Color sports are 'Pearly Gates' (pink) and 'Royal America' (white).

'America'.

'AMY JOHNSON'.

Breeder: Alister Clark (Australia, 1931).
Parentage: 'Souvenir de Gustave Prat' x Seedling (possibly R. gigantea).
Classification: Large-Flowered Climber.
The name of the rose 'Amy Johnson' commemorates the landing of the brave English aviatrix by the same name who flew from England to Australia in 1930. The rose is a lovely shade of pink with lighter petal tips and lighter centers, sometimes with a touch of yellow. The flowers are large, semi-double to lightly double, very fragrant and have a cupped form with reflexed petal tips. The plants have somewhat wrinkled foliage. They freely grow to about 12 or 15 ft. (3.65 to 4.55 m).

'Andenken An J. Diering'.

'ANDENKEN AN J. DIERING'.

Translation: 'In Memory of J. Diering'.
Breeder: L. Wilhelm Hinner (Germany, 1902).
Parentage: Unknown.
Classification: Climbing Hybrid Tea.
The flowers of this German-bred rose are light pink with soft touches of yellow in the center. They are also large, double and moderately fragrant. The odd habit of the petals twisting this way and that gives them a rather irregular, but still attractive, form. They are borne mostly singly, but may also be seen in small clusters. This variety reblooms well, producing flowers steadily in flushes during the season. The plant is remarkably hardy to USDA zone 4b. It will grow tall enough to clothe a small pillar.

'Angel Face, Cl.'.

'ANGEL FACE, CL.'.

Breeder: Discovered by Haight (Unknown, 1981) and Rustin (1995, Australia).
Parentage: Sport of 'Angel Face'.
Classification: Climber, Floribunda, Cl.
The climbing sport of the highly regarded Floribunda, 'Angel Face' has been discovered and described by two separate parties, Haight and Ruston. There doesn't seem to be any significant difference between the two clones. 'Angel Face, Cl.' has flowers with a strong fragrance reminiscent of citrus. They are lavender-mauve, double, and large-sized with a ruffled bloom form, small petals in the center and a flattened shape. The bloom repeats in flushes during the flowering season. The foliage is dark green and glossy.

'ANGEL PINK'.

Breeder: Ralph Moore.
Parentage: 'Little Darling' x 'Eleanor'.
Classification: Climbing Miniature.
This very pretty little rose has small (2 in), coral pink, double blooms in small clusters, but lacks fragrance. The bloom repeats well in multiple flushes during the whole season. It will reach a height of about 7 ft. (2 m), enough to decorate a small trellis.

'Angela, Cl.'.

'ANGELA, CL'.

Breeder: The discoverer is unknown.
Parentage: Sport of 'Angela' (Floribunda, Kordes, 1984).
Classification: Climbing Floribunda.
The flowers open bright pink with lighter centers and fade to light pink. The petals have a darker reverse. The flower form is semi-double to lightly double and initially deeply cupped. The flowers open up more with maturity to form flattened cups. Mildly scented, they are carried in large clusters. An occasional repeat can be expected in the fall. The foliage is shiny, medium green and healthy. The potential height is about 16 ft. 5 in (5 m). It is sold in Japan.

'ANGELUS, CL.'.

Breeder: Discovered by the Dixie Rose Nursery (United States, 1933).
Parentage: Sport of Angelus (hybrid tea, Lemon, 1920).
Classification: Climbing Hybrid Tea.
Here is another beautiful, almost forgotten rose from the past. It seems to be grown only at Sangerhausen and is no longer in commerce. The flowers are large, double, fragrant and white with a touch of yellow in the center. The petals curl back strongly in the open flower. The foliage appears healthy and the growth is average for this class, about 10 ft. (3 m).

'Angelus, Cl.'.

'Anne Dakin'.

'ANNE DAKIN' (Mrs. Anne Dakin).

Breeder: Robert A. Holmes (United Kingdom, before 1972).
Parentage: Unknown.
Classification: Large-Flowered Climber.
On first opening, the very attractive double, medium-sized flowers are deep coral-pink with a pale yellow reverse. They soon fade and shift in hue to medium pink, then to light pink with a yellow petal base and a cream reverse. The petals are ruffled and may show some quartering in the centers. The tips are slightly scalloped and rather uneven. There is a mild

fragrance. The shiny, medium green leaves have seven leaflets. The plant can be expected to grow to about 10 ft. (3 m).

'Anne-Marie Côte'.

'ANNE-MARIE CÔTE'.

Breeder: Jean-Baptiste André (fils) Guillot (France, 1875).
Parentage: Unknown.
Classification: Noisette.
I observed this rose at Sangerhausen, but it also grows at Mottisfont Abbey and a few other European gardens. The flowers are medium-sized, lightly double and white and are sometimes flushed with pink. They are reported as having a pink petal reverse, but I did not observe that feature. The floral form is globular and opens to show the stamens. The petals fold back to form points that create a star-like effect. The flowers are borne singly or in small clusters and repeat their bloom in regular seasonal flushes. The plant will grow to 8 or 10 ft. (2.5 or 3 m).

'ANNE MARIE TRECHSLIN, CL.'

Breeder: David Ruston (Australia, 1972).
Parentage: Sport of 'Anne Marie Trechslin'.
Classification: Climbing Hybrid Tea.
I haven't seen this rose and know little about it, but I think it should be included here in order to record its existence. The Australian Rose Annual, 1997, described it as "a good climber or pillar rose in a rich orange-apricot color." The sport parent, 'Anna Marie Trechslin' which grows at Sangerhausen, appears identical except for the plant size. The richly scented, double, high-centered, apricot flowers with golden yellow centers become more lavender-pink with age. They retain the golden yellow in the center.

'Antique 89, Habit'.

'Antike '89'.

'ANTIKE '89'.

Breeder: W. Kordes & Sons (Germany, 1988).
Parentage: ('Grand Hotel' x 'Sympathie') x (seedling x 'Arthur Bell').
Classification: Large-Flowered Climber.
'Antike '89' is a two-toned rose featuring creamy white petals with broad crimson edges and a creamy white reverse. The general impression is of a light crimson rose. The large, full blooms are carried in large clusters. They repeat well in flushes during the whole season. They lack perfection only in their total lack of scent. The plant is well clothed in healthy glossy, dark green foliage and numerous prickles. It will reach a maximum height of about 14 ft. (4.25 m).

'APELES MESTRES'.

Breeder: Pedro (Pere) Dot (Spain, 1925).
Parentage: 'Frau Karl Druschki' x 'Souvenir de Claudius Pernet'.
Classification: Large-Flowered Climber.
'Apeles Mestres' seems to have inherited parent 'Frau Karl Druschki's very large, globular double flower form, but in a light yellow color. The moderately fragrant flowers can be found mainly as singles rather than in clusters. They bloom for one long late spring or early summer period only. The plant bears glossy, dark green foliage and will grow to a height of 12 ft. (3.65 m).

'Apollo XI'.

'APOLLO XI'.

Breeder: Jan Leenders (Netherlands, before 1970).
Parentage: Unknown.
Classification: Large-Flowered Climber.
The flowers are golden yellow, but fade at the outer petals to almost white while retaining traces of the reddish color from the buds. The large, double blooms reflex at the tips to form triangular shapes. The muddled center is filled with shorter petals.This rose is a generous bloomer. The potential height is about 10 ft. (3 m).

'Apotheker Georg Höfer, Cl.'

'APOTHEKER GEORG HÖFER, CL.'

Breeder: Found by Max Vogel (Germany, 1941).
Parentage: Sport of 'Apotheker Georg Höfer'.
Classification: Climbing Hybrid Tea.
Apotheker Georg Höfer, Cl. is a copper red rose with a lovely sweet fragrance and very large, very full, high-centered flowers that come in small clusters like a Hybrid Tea. It is fully remontant, blooming in flushes all season.

'APRICOT GLOW'.

Breeder: Dr. Walter D. Brownell and family, 1936, United States.
Parentage: ('Emily Gray' x 'Dr. W. Van Fleet') x 'Jacotte'.
Class: Large-flowered Climber, Hybrid Wichurana.
The large-sized, very full, roughly quartered, fragrant flowers open deep apricot and fade in time to light coral-pink. They are produced mostly as single blooms, but occasionally as small clusters. The foliage is dark green and glossy and the canes are well armed. It will grow to 10 ft. (3 m) or more in a temperate climate. It should have frost protection in colder weather.

'APRICOT IMPRESSIONIST'.

Breeder: John Clements (United States, 2006).
Parentage: Unknown.
Classification: Large-Flowered Climber.
This rose will impress you with its richly fragrant, deep apricot, large, very double flowers. They resemble the flowers of David Austin's old fashioned style English Roses with their broad outer petals enclosing the smaller,

'Apollo XI'.

numerous, quartered inner petals. Also similarly, they repeat their bloom in regular seasonal flushes. The plant is hardy to USDA zone 5b and will reach a height of 10 to 12 ft, enough to cover a lattice or an arbor.

'APTOS'.
See 'Dr. Robert Korns'.

'ARCHIDUC JOSEPH'.

Breeder: Gilbert Nabonnand (France, 1892).
Parentage: Seedling of 'Madame Lombard'.
Class: Tea.
Newly opened, the center of this rose is composed of short, folded, warm rose pink petals. They are packed into a cup of crimson-pink outer petals. The outer petals later reflex as well and become lighter in color. The inner petals age to crimson pink. The flowers are moderately fragrant, double and repeat blooming. The plant is well armed with prickles and is clothed in matte, grey-green foliage. A height of about 10' (3 m) can be expected.

'ARDS PILLAR'.

Breeder: Alexander Dickson II (United Kingdom, 1902).
Parentage: Unknown.
Classification: Hybrid Tea, Cl.
'Ards Pillar' has large, double (17-25 petals), light crimson, cupped flowers. It repeats in continuous flushes all through the season. Climbing capabilities are about 10 ft. (3m). The name refers to the Ards Peninsula, Ireland, where the A. Dickson nurseries were located.

'Ards Pillar'.

'ARDS RAMBLER'.

Breeder: Alexander Dickson II (United Kingdom, 1908).
Parentage: Unknown.
Classification. Climbing Hybrid Tea.
This rose is described as being orange-red or orange-pink, large, double and very fragrant, but the rose at Sangerhausen, the only public garden where it grows, is bright red and semi-double. It is probably the wrong variety.

'ARDS ROVER'.

Breeder: Alexander Dickson II (United Kingdom, 1898).
Parentage: Unknown.
Classification: Climbing Hybrid Perpetual. Early Large-Flowered Climber type.
The flowers are rich crimson, with slightly taupe nuances in the center. They are moderately fragrant, medium to large and double. Bloom form is shaped much like a Hybrid Tea. The rose blooms repeatedly in flushes. Expect a maximum height of up to 10' (3.05 m).

'Ards Rover'.

'ARIELE DOMBASLE'. (Lea Massari)

Breeder: Meilland International (France, 1991).
Parentage: Unknown.
Classification: Large-Flowered Climber.
Liven up your garden with this brightly colored rose. The petals are vermilion with yellow flushes and pure, bright yellow bases. The reverse is yellow. There is a mild fragrance. The flowers are medium-sized, semi-double or lightly double. There is an occasional repeat later in the season. It will grow to about 10 ft. (3 m).

'Ariele Dombasle'.

'Arrillaga'.

'ARRILLAGA'.

Breeder: Fr. George M.A. Schoener, (U S, 1929).
Parentage: Undisclosed, maybe (a Centifolia x' Mrs. John Laing') x 'Frau Karl Druschki'.
Classification: Climbing Hybrid Perpetual.
'Arrillaga' comes in light pink with yellow undertones. There is a moderate to pronounced fragrance. The flowers have very large, full, high-centered to cupped, old-fashioned bloom forms. They are summer blooming with an occasional repeat later in the season. There is an expected height of 8' to 10' (2.45 to 3.05 m). The potential is even taller with support. It was named for Don Jose Arrillaga, twice Spanish governor of California.

'Arthur Bell, Cl.'.

'ARTHUR BELL, CL.'.

Breeder: Discovered by Pearce (United Kingdom, 1979).
Parentage: a sport of 'Arthur Bell' (Floribunda, McGredy, 1964).
Classification: Climbing Floribunda.
This rose is an unusually beautiful bright golden yellow. The flowers are medium-sized, double and are carried in small clusters. A rich fragrance adds to the garden value. The rose repeats well, blooming in continuous flushes. The healthy plant grows somewhat stiffly and upright to about 10 ft. (3m).

'ASSO DI CUORI, CL.'.

Translates as 'Ace of Hearts'.
Breeder: Discovered by Vittorio Barni (Italy, pre-1990).
Parentage: Sport of 'Asso di Cuori'.
Classification: Climbing Hybrid Tea.
This beautiful dark red rose is the climbing sport of a highly regarded florist rose. The flowers are large, high-centered and double. It blooms generously, has dark green foliage and repeats in continuous seasonal flushes. The very mild fragrance is its only fault. It is commercially available in Italy.

'ASTRAL'.

Breeder: Paul Croix (France, 1982).
Parentage: Unknown.
Classification: Large-Flowered Climber.
This is a velvety dark crimson red rose with darker, almost blackish, veins in the petals. The flowers are large and double and very fragrant. The flower form is Hybrid Tea-like, high centered at first, then with cupped blooms at maturity. The plant is a modest climber to about 10 ft. (3 m), a good candidate for a pillar.

'Astrée, Cl'.

'ASTRÉE, CL'.

Breeder: Paul Croix (France, 1960).
Parentage: Sport of 'Astrée'.
Classification: Climbing Hybrid Tea.
Long shapely buds open to an apricot pink Hybrid Tea type flower with a strong fragrance. The outer petals fade to pink, but the centers remain more apricot. The flower opens to a wide cup form with regularly shaped, broad-tipped petals that show a touch of yellow at the base and a glimpse of the stamens.

'ASTRID LINDGREN'.

('Dream Sequence', 'Egon Schiele', Pouluf).
Breeder: L. Pernille and Mogens Nyegaard Oleson (Denmark, 1991).
Parentage: Unknown.
Classification: Shrub.
This pretty rose opens coral pink and soon fades to light pink. It has a fruity fragrance and medium-sized, lightly double flowers carried in small clusters. The bloom form is initially cupped, but opens out to a shallow cup with time. It is fully remontant, blooming throughout the season in continuous flushes. Decorative hips follow in the fall. The plant is tall, bushy and healthy and can be grown as an 8 ft. (2.45 m) climber, suitable for a small pillar or trellis. Hardiness to USDA zone 4b is a wonderful bonus for cold climate gardeners.

'Astrid Lindgren'.

'ATTLEBOROUGH'.

Breeder: Amanda Beales (United Kingdom)
Parentage: 'Paul's Scarlet Climber' x 'Parkdirektor Riggers'.
Classification: Large-Flowered Climber.
'Attleborough' comes in a very attractive shade of bright, medium red with a lighter petal reverse and occasional white streaks. The blooms are medium to large, full and scented of musk and are carried in large showy clusters. The repeat flowering is in continuous flushes during whole season. The foliage is medium green and glossy. The plants will grow in a bushy manner to about 10 to 13 ft. (3 to 4 m).

'AUGUSTE KORDES, CL.'.

('Lafayette, Cl.', 'Joseph Guy, Cl.').
Breeder: Discovered by Wilhelm J.H. Kordes II (Germany, 1928).
Parentage: Sport of 'Lafayette'.
Classification: Climbing Floribunda.
August Kordes is light rose red in color with very little fading. The petals twist a little as the flower opens up giving

'Auguste Kordes, Cl'.

it a pretty ruffled effect. The flowers are semi-double and medium to large in size and come in large clusters. There is very little fragrance, if any. The repeat blooming is good with flushes of bloom until fall. The thornless, or almost thornless, plant is clothed with glossy, dark green foliage. It may reach a height of up to 8 ft 2 in. (2.5 m).

'Augustus Hartmann, Cl.'.

'AUGUSTUS HARTMANN, CL.'.

Breeder: Discovered by Samuel McGredy III (Ireland, 1930). Discovered by Gianfranco Fineschi (Italy, 1980).
Parentage: Sport of 'Augustus Hartmann'.
Classification: Climbing Hybrid Perpetual, Climbing Hybrid Tea.
This rose is described in the older sources as being geranium-red with shadings of yellow or orange or even cerise, but the bush form of the rose I observed at Sangerhausen had crimson buds, opened deep crimson-pink and morphed to medium cerise-pink as the flower matured. The flowers are large and full and the petals are gently ruffled. The blooms are moderately scented and are carried mostly singly, but sometimes in small clusters. The plant will grow to about average climbing height.

'AURORA'.

Breeder: Reimer Kordes (Germany, 1956).
Parentage: R. kordesii hybrid.
Classification: Hybrid Kordesii.
Buds of 'Aurora' open salmon colored, an unusual color for a Hybrid Kordesii, and fade to pinker tones as the flower matures. The strongly fragrant, large, lightly double blooms start out cupped, then open up to show their stamens. The plant is summer blooming only, but has the benefit of forming decorative hips. The plants have dark green, glossy foliage and will grow to about 10 ft. (3 m).

'Aurora'.

'AURORE SAND'.

Breeder: Marcel Robichon (France, 1964).
Parentage: 'Madame Moisans' x 'Odette Joyeux'.
Classification: Large-Flowered Climber.
This strongly fragrant rose is large and double and has white petals with coral pink edges and a coral tinted center. The petal edges soon fade to plain pink, but the center remains somewhat coral. The flowers start out cupped and then open up wide enough to show their stamens. The plant will grow to 10 to 13 ft. (3 to 4 m).

'Aurore Sand'.

'AUSTRALIAN BEAUTY'.

Breeder: George H. T. Kerslake (Australia, 1907).
Parentage: 'Adam' x 'Lord Macaulay'.
Classification: Climbing Hybrid Perpetual.
True to its name, this deep blackish crimson, Hybrid Tea-type rose is beautiful. The white petal bases add a sparkle to the dark color and the pronounced fragrance adds a pleasurable element. The blooms are large, double and are borne singly or in small clusters. The plant grows to at least 10 ft. (3 m) and looks lovely on a pillar.

'Autumn Sunlight'.

'AUTUMN SUNLIGHT'.

Breeder: Charles Walter Gregory (United Kingdom, 1965).
Parentage: ' Danse du Feu' x 'Goldilocks, Cl.'
Classification: Large-Flowered Climber.
'Autumn Sunlight' opens bright orange and ages through vermilion to rose pink, resulting in a dramatic array of colors on a plant. The petal bases are lighter than the tips. The fragrant flowers are medium-sized, full, and rather globular and are carried in small clusters. The plant has shiny, dark green leaves and typically grows to about 8 ft.

'AUTUMN SUNSET'.

Breeder: Discovered by Malcolm (Mike) Lowe (United States, 1986).
Parentage: Sport of 'Westerland'.
Classification: Large-Flowered Climber.
This rose has been a good source of color for my garden, especially in the fall when some other roses have stopped blooming. The apricot and golden yellow blooms beautifully compliment the fall foliage color of the trees and their strong, sweet frgrance provides a closeup benefit. They are medium-sized, double and usually carried in small clusters on an upright plant of about 10 to 12 ft. (3 to 3.65 m). The very disease-resistant foliage is medium green and glossy. Decorative hips are formed in the fall.

'AWAKENING'.

See 'Probuzni'.

'Autumn Sunset'.

B

'Blossomtime'.

'BABY ROMANTICA'. (Meilivoine)

Breeder: Meilland Richardier (France, 2010).
Parentage: Unknown.
Classification: Large-Flowered Climber.
This rose has spectacular colors. The yellow-orange center of the newly opened flower is surrounded by a row of orange-crimson outer petals. As the flower ages, from the outer petals inward, it first becomes orange pink then more truly pink. The reverse is lighter. The flowers are medium-sized, very full and are carried in small clusters. The deeply cupped blooms tend to not open completely. The rose is fully remontant. It is moderately vigorous to a height of about 8 ft. (2.45 m).

'BACCARÁ, CL.'.

Breeder: Discovered by David Ruston (Austria, 1962) and Meilland (France, 1965).
Parentage: sport of 'Baccará' (Hybrid Tea, Meilland, 1954), a famous florist rose.
Classification: Climbing Hybrid Tea.
This rose is mildly fragrant, deep scarlet red, medium-sized, very full and is formed singly or in small clusters. It has good remontancy, blooming in flushes all season. The canes are clothed with dark green, leathery foliage. The bloom form starts cupped and opens up to a flattened dome that may have quartered petals. It is hardy to USDA zone 7b. It is best in a warm climate.

'Bad Neuenahr'.

'BAD NEUENAHR'.

Breeder: Reimer Kordes (Germany, 1958).
Parentage: Unknown.
Classification: Hybrid Kordesii.
'Bad Neuenahr' flowers are a lovely strong, clear crimson, large, very full and are carried in large clusters. The flower form is cupped and is often quartered. The foliage is dark green and leathery. The plant is very vigorous and will grow to about 16 ft. (5 m) if given support.

'Bajazzo'.

'BAJAZZO'.

Breeder: Tim Hermann Kordes (Germany, 2001).
Parentage: Unknown.
Classification: Large-Flowered Climber.
'Bajazzo' is a colorful rose, bright coral pink with a much lighter reverse and clear yellow stamens enhanced by yellow petal bases. It is medium-sized, semi-double with a very open cupped form and lacking in fragrance. Repeat bloom is in continuous seasonal flushes. The expected height is about 8 ft. (2.5 m). It can be pruned and grown as a shrub. The foliage is dark green and glossy.

'BALLERINA, CL'.

Breeder: Discovered by Ltd. Rearsby Roses (United Kingdom, 1997).
Parentage: Sport of 'Ballerina' (Bentall Hybrid Musk, 1937).
Classification: Climbing Hybrid Musk.
The small, single, very fragrant flowers open deep pink with a white eye. As they age the white eye gets larger and the pink petal borders fade until the flowers are nearly white. The large clusters are almost hydrangea-

like. Reports on remontancy are mixed, but mostly positive. The plant will grow vigorously to about 10 to 15 ft. (3 to 4.5 m). 'Ballerina', the sport parent, has identical characteristics except for plant size.

'Ballerina, Cl.'.

'Ballet, Cl.'.

'BALLET, CL.'

Breeder: Reimer Kordes (Germany, 1962).
Parentage: Sport of 'Ballet' (Kordes, 1958).
Classification: Climbing Hybrid Tea.
This rose has large, full, deep pink exhibition-quality flowers of Hybrid Tea high-centered form that are identical to those of the sport parent, but with the additional asset of being a fairly vigorous climber. There is a mild fragrance. The long, strong stems make it good for cutting. It repeats in continuous flushes during the growing season. This variety is becoming very rare. 'Ballet', the sport parent, has identical characteristics except for plant size.

'Bantry Bay'.

'BANTRY BAY'.

Breeder: Samuel Darragh McGredy IV (U K, 1967).
Parentage: 'New Dawn' x 'Korona'.
Classification: Large-Flowered Climber.
The flowers open slightly on the coral side of pink and are deeply cupped. They soon fade to clear pink with a darker reverse and open out to reveal their stamens. They are medium to large, semi-double to lightly double, lightly scented and carried in small clusters. The plant repeats its blooming well in flushes throughout the growing season. The plant is clothed with glossy, light green foliage and will grow to about 10 to 13 ft. (3 to 4 m).

'Bantry Bay'.

'BANZAI 83' ('Spectra').

Breeder: Marie-Louise Meilland (France, 1983).
Parentage: (MEIgold x 'Peer Gynt') x ([MEIalfi x MEIfan] x 'King's Ransom').

Classification: Large-Flowered Climber.
This rose is an excellent choice to brighten a dull corner of the garden. The flowers open yellow, but immediately begin to turn red, outer petal tips first, as they are exposed to the sun. Soon the whole rose turns red with light yellow petal bases. The flowers are large and very full with little fragrance and are carried singly or in small clusters. There is very good remontancy in continuous flushes during the growing season. The plant is almost thornless and is clothed with dark green, glossy, thick foliage. It will climb in a branching manner to about 16 ft. (5 m), a good size for an arbor.

'Banzai 83'.

'BARBARA ANNE'. See 'Scent From Heaven'.

'BAROCK'. (TANbak).

Breeder: Hans Jürgen Evers (Germany, 1999).
Parentage: Unknown.
Classification: Shrub, Large-Flowered Climber.
The colors of 'Barock' are complex and beautiful. The buds are deep coral and open to coral yellow blooms with deeper coral centers. They quickly fade to soft yellow with crimson flushes on the petal tips as they age. They are medium to large, full with a classical shape and strongly scented. They grow singly or in small clusters. The plant will climb in a bushy fashion to about 10 ft. (3 m). There is one main bloom with an occasional repeat later in the season.

'Barock'.

'BARONNE EDMOND DE ROTHSCHILD, CL.'.

Breeder: Discovered by Marie-Louise Meilland (France, 1974).
Parentage: Sport of 'Baronne Edmond de Rothschild'.
Classification: Climbing Hybrid Tea.
This rose blooms in bright cerise red with a lighter petal reverse that provides a striking contrast. The flowers are moderately fragrant, very large, and full and have a Hybrid Tea high-centered form. They are carried singly or in small clusters. The blooming is remontant in flushes throughout the growing season. The foliage is glossy and healthy.

'Baronne Edmond De Rothschild, Cl.'.

'BARONNE HENRIETTE SNOY'

('Baronne de Henriette Snoy').
Breeder: Alexandre Bernaix (France, 1897).
Parentage: 'Gloire de Dijon' x 'Madame Lombard'.

Classification: Tea.
The crimson flushed buds produce very attractive fragrant, medium to large, full, light pink flowers with a darker pink reverse. The initial form is a globular shape that opens out as a low dome packed with many petals reflexed at the tips, the outer ones folded to form points. The flowers are mostly produced singly, but may occur in small clusters. The plant is generally healthy except for a susceptibility to mildew. It will perform best in a really warm climate where it will grow to 10 or 12 ft. (3 to 4 m). In a cool climate it will be much shorter. It will repeat well in continuous seasonal flushes.

'Baronne Henriette de Snoy'.

'Barricade'.

'BARRICADE'.

Breeder: Maurice Combe (France, 1971).
Parentage: Unknown.
Classification: Large-Flowered Climber.
'Barricade' comes in a domed, medium to large, lightly double flower form and a spectacular vermilion color. The blooms are single or carried in small clusters. The leaves are dark green and glossy. The plant is healthy and will grow to about 10 ft. (3 m). Fragrance is all it lacks. It blooms in flushes throughout the growing season.

'BATHSHEBA'.

Breeder: David Austin (United Kingdom, 2016).
Parentage: Unknown.
Class: Shrub, English Rose.
This rose has large, very double, apricot-pink flowers with a soft yellow reverse. They fade to cream, starting at the outer petal as the flower ages and create a bicolor effect. The broad outer petals form a cup around the smaller, quartered, tightly packed inner petals. There is a rich fragrance of myrrh. The flowers repeat well. The plant has medium green foliage and can be trained as a climber of about 10 ft. (3 m). Bathsheba was the wife of King David and the mother of Solomon.

'BEAUTÉ DE L'EUROPE'.

Breeder: J.-M. Gonod (France, 1881).
Parentage: Seedling of 'Gloire de Dijon'.
Classification: Tea-Noisette.
Some of the old references say that the rose is bright or deep yellow with a copper reverse. Others mention salmon or pink-salmon with a darker reverse and darker centers, a range of color that more closely matches the flowers of plants being grown today. The flowers are also fragrant, large and double with a globular bloom form. The blooming is remontant. The present-day plants are probably not the original variety.

'Beauty Fairy'.

'BEAUTY FAIRY'.

Breeder: Odendahl (Germany, 1995).
Parentage: Seedling of 'The Fairy'.
Classification: Climbing Polyantha.
The flowers of this climbing rose look much like the flowers of 'The Fairy', but the rose is an offspring, not a climbing sport. Like 'The Fairy', the flowers are small, double and pink. The floral form is cupped and they are carried in clusters. The plant can be trained as a climber with an expected height of about 10 ft. (3 m).

'BEAUTY OF GLAZENWOOD'. See 'Fortune's Double Yellow'.

'BEAUTY OF ROSEMAWR'.

Breeder: Dr. Walter Van Fleet (United States, 1903).
Parentage: Unknown.
Classification: Hybrid China/Tea.
The opening buds are high-centered at first, then open further to form domed rosettes and finally become quite flat. The petals reflex at the tips and fold to form points. Initially, the color is crimson-pink, then starting with the outer petals, it darkens and becomes more crimson. The flowers are fragrant, double, medium-sized and are carried in small clusters. The plant blooms in flushes throughout the growing season, an asset that made it famous when it first appeared on the market. It is moderately vigorous, reaching about 7 ft. (2 m) under favorable conditions.

'Beauty of Rosemawr'.

'BELINDA'.

Breeder: Ann Bentall (United Kingdom, 1936). Named for her daughter.
Parentage: Unknown.
Classification: Hybrid Musk.
The flowers of this pretty rose are semi-double, small to medium-sized, moderately to strongly fragrant and medium rose-pink with small white petal bases. They bloom in continuous seasonal flushes. Given a mild climate and a support it will reach up about 8 ft. (2.5 m) enough to train as a pillar rose.

'Belinda'.

'BELKANTO'.

Breeder: Werner Noack (Germany, 2004).
Parentage: Unknown.
Classification: Large-Flowered Climber.
You can't help but notice this rose with its large, very double, fragrant, brilliant deep red flowers arranged singly or in small clusters. It is remontant in regular seasonal flushes. The foliage is healthy, shiny and dark

green. The plant can be expected to grow to about 10 ft. (3 m). It grows at Sangerhausen and several other European gardens.

'Belkanto'.

'BELLAVISTA'.

Breeder: Enrico Barni (Italy, before 2006).
Parentage: Unknown.
Classification: Large-Flowered Climber.
Long, well-formed buds open as medium-sized, double, light pink flowers with a touch of yellow at the petal bases and an open cupped form. They occur singly or in small clusters. The leaves are healthy, dark green and semi-glossy. The plant grows vigorously to almost 20 ft. (6 m) and is tall enough to decorate a small tree or a fence.

'BELLE BLANCA'.

Breeder: Unknown.
Parentage: Sport of 'Belle Portugaise'.
Classification: Hybrid Gigantea.
If you live in a warm climate, USDA zone 8b or warmer, you can grow this beautiful white-flowered giant. Except for its color, it is identical to 'Belle Portugaise', its sport parent. The fragrant flowers are large to very large and single or occasionally just semi-double. The cup-shaped form usually remains partially closed, but sometimes it opens enough to show a glimpse of the stamens and the heavy flowers often hang down. They are once-blooming early in the season, but the profuse display more than compensates for this shortcoming. The plants have foliage with a characteristic Gigantea look; long with attenuated tips, light green and drooping. They have the potential to grow to as much as 30 to 40 ft. (9 to 12 m).

'BELLE DE LONDRES'.
See 'Compassion'.

'BELLE D'ORLÉANS'.

Breeder: Marcel Robichon (France, 1958).
Parentage: Seedling x 'Independence'.
Classification: Large-Flowered Climber.
The flowers, seen in large clusters, are large, full and bright geranium red at first, a new color when this rose was bred. This was the result of pelargonidin, a biological pigment inherited from 'Independence' (Kordes, 1951), the first of the modern bush roses to have the pigment as the result of a mutation. Before this important event, all red rose flowers were crimson-red. As the flowers of 'Belle d'Orléans' age they become more crimson, then more lavender. There is one main bloom with occasional repeats. The plant is covered with shiny, healthy foliage and grows to about 16 ft. (5 m).

'Belle d'Orléans'.

'BELLE LYONNAISE'.

Breeder: Antoine Levet (père) (France, 1870).
Parentage: 'Gloire de Dijon' x Unknown Tea.
Classification: Tea-Noisette.
The flowers are soft yellow with a lighter yellow reverse. They fade with age to pale yellow starting at the petal tips. They are very large, double and cup-shaped with quartered petals. They have excellent remontancy in regular flushes during the flowering season. The plant has light green, shiny foliage and will reach a height of about 10 to 15 ft. (3 to 4.5 m). It reacts adversely to too much pruning.

'Belle Portugaise'.

'BELLE PORTUGAISE'.

Breeder: Henri Cayeux (Portugal, 1903).
Parentage: 'Souvenir de Madame Léonie Viennot' x Rosa gigantea.
Classification: Hybrid Gigantea.
This greatly vigorous rose can often be seen, in a favorable climate, cascading over fences, spilling out of trees or tumbling over roofs. It is capable of growing to as much as 40 ft. (12 m). The beautiful shell-pink and white, very large, semi-double flowers are borne mostly singly high up on the plant. They are richly fragrant of tea. Flowering occurs once in spring or summer. The foliage, in typical Gigantea form, is light green and semi-glossy. If you live in a climate of USDA zone 8b or warmer and have a tall, strong fence or a very large, sturdy tree in a lot of space you could grow this rose.

'BELLE SIEBRECHT, CL.'. See 'Mrs. W. J. Grant, Cl.'.

'BELLE VICHYSOISE' ('Cornélie').

Breeder: Robert and Moreau (France, 1858). An old rose found in Vichy, France and reintroduced by Louis Lévêque & Fils (France, 1897).
Parentage: Unknown.
Class: Noisette.
The fragrant, medium-sized, double blooms open from deep pink buds to soft pink flowers with lighter petal bases that soon fade to blush pink and then to white. The open cup-shaped flowers are arranged in large clusters. The plant can be trained as a climber of about 12 to 13 ft (3.5 to 4 m).

'Belle Vichysoise'.

'BELMONT' (Indica major, Cl.).

Breeder: Jean-Pierre Vibert (France, 1846).
Parentage: Unknown.
Classification: Climbing Hybrid China.
The flowers of 'Belmont' are very large, double, and sweetly fragrant and very light pink. The foliage is almost evergreen. Moderately vigorous, it is known to reach a height of about 10 ft. (3 m).

'Belmont'.

'BENJAMIN BRITTEN'.

Breeder: David Austin (United Kingdom, 1992).
Parentage: 'Charles Austin' x seedling.
Classification: Shrub (English rose type).
This has been one of my best Austin roses. The medium-sized, full flowers are red touched with orange and become more crimson with age. There is a strong fruit-like

'Benjamin Britten'.

fragrance. The form is a cupped rosette carried in small clusters. The blooming is fully remontant in flushes during the growing season. The foliage is semi-glossy and dark green. The plant is classed as a shrub, but it will reach a height of about 8 ft. (2.5 m) if given support and proper growing conditions, enough to be trained to a small trellis or pillar.

'Benvenuto'.

'BENVENUTO'.

Breeder: Meilland International (France, 1967).
Parentage: ('Alain' x 'Guinée') x 'Cocktail'.
Classification: Large-Flowered Climber.
'Benvenuto' produces deep, almost blackish red flowers with yellow petal bases. The petal reverse is lighter and yellowish. The flowers are medium, semi-double, and mildly fragrant and are carried in small clusters. The blooming is repeated in flushes throughout the growing period. The canes are covered with shiny, dark green foliage, are well armed and will branch while growing stiffly to a height of about 10 ft. (3 m).

'BERRIES 'N' CREAM'.

('Calypso', 'Concert', POUlclimb).
Breeder: L. Pernille Olesen and Mogens Nyegaard. Olesen (Denmark, 1997).
Parentage: 'Evita' (miniature, Olesen, 1984) x Seedling.
Classification: Large-Flowered Climber. Courtyard Climber.
The blooms of this rose are ruffled and white with deep pink stripes. They are medium-sized, double, strongly scented of apples and are carried in medium clusters. The remontancy is good with blooming repeated in flushes throughout the growing period. The healthy, almost thornless canes will grow to 12 or13 ft. (4 m) if given optimal conditions.

'Berries 'N' Cream'.

'BEST WISHES, CL.' ('Curiosity, Cl.').

Breeder: Discovered by Paul Chessum (United Kingdom, 1996).
Parentage: Sport of 'Curiosity' which was, in turn, a sport of 'Cleopatra'.
Classification: Climbing Hybrid Tea.
'Best Wishes' is an interesting rose with striking coloration. The petals are scarlet with yellow bases and a golden reverse that has scarlet petal edges. The flowers are medium to large-sized and high-centered like a Hybrid Tea. These features along with variegated foliage make it very decorative. The plant can be counted on to grow to about 8 or 10 ft. (2.45 or 3 m). Use as a pillar rose. 'Curiosity', the sport parent, is identical except for plant size.

'Curiosity Cocker'.

'Bettina, Cl.'

'BETTY PRIOR, CL.'.

Breeder: Discovered by Donell Cooper (Unknown, 1995).
Parentage: Sport of 'Betty Prior'.
Classification: Climbing Floribunda.
This climbing sport of 'Betty Prior' is medium crimson pink with small white centers and a darker reverse. It is single, medium-sized and blooms in large clusters. There is a prolific, almost continuous bloom all during the growing period. It is quite hardy, to as much as USDA zone 4b. There are no major public rose gardens listed for this rose and it is no longer in commerce. It is in danger of becoming extinct. 'Betty Prior', the sport parent is identical except for plant size.

'BETTINA, CL.' ('Grimpant Bettina')

Breeder: Discovered by Francis Meilland (France, 1958).
Parentage: Sport of 'Bettina' (Hybrid Tea, Meilland, 1953)
Classification: Climbing Hybrid Tea.
'Bettina, Cl.' has flowers of light coral pink with red veining that is especially prominent in the outer petals. The petal reverse is light yellow. The flowers are large, full and moderately fragrant. They have a classical high-centered Hybrid Tea shape. The flowering repeats in flushes during the whole growing period. The plants have glossy, dark green foliage, few thorns (prickles) and have the potential to grow stiffly to about 15 ft. (4.5 m). They are only hardy to USDA zone 7b so frost protection is needed.

'Betty Uprichard, Cl.'.

'Betty Prior, Cl.'.

'BETTY UPRICHARD, CL.'.

Breeder: Discovered by Max Krause (Germany, 1936).
Parentage: Sport of 'Betty Uprichard'.
Classification: Climbing Hybrid Tea.
The crimson-pink buds of 'Betty Uprichard, Cl.' open up salmon-pink with a crimson-pink reverse and center. The petals become more crimson-pink with sun exposure. The flowers are strongly scented, medium to large-sized, semi-double to lightly double and may be carried singly or in small clusters. The flowering is remontant in repeated flushes. There are no gardens or commercial sources for the climbing rose so it may be extinct. 'Betty Uprichard', the sport parent, is identical except for plant size.

'Bibiche, Cl.'.

'BIBICHE, CL.'.

Breeder: Discovered by Francois Dorieux I (France, 1980).
Parentage: Sport of 'Bibiche'.
Classification: Climbing Floribunda.
The flowers, as I observed them at Roseto Carla Fineschi, are large-sized and orange with shadings of vermilion on the outer petals and the petal reverses. The broadly wavy petals form shallow cups with the stamens revealed in the centers. They are borne in medium to large clusters. The plant grows sufficiently to be trained as a climber.

'BIENVENUE'. (Delbard).

Breeder: Bred by Delbard (France, 1999).
Parentage: Unknown.
Classification: Large-Flowered Climber.
Large, very full, deep pink flowers with darker centers and a rich fruity fragrance grace this rose. They are carried in medium clusters. The flower form is high-centered like a Hybrid Tea and the petal tips are deeply scalloped. The prolific bloom is fully remontant in repeated seasonal flushes. The plant grows to a height of 8 to 10 ft. (2.5 to 3 m).

'BIG SPLASH'.

Breeder: David L. Armstrong (United States, 1969).
Introduced in United States by Armstrong Nursery in 1969.
Parentage: 'Buccaneer' x 'Bravo'.
Classification: Climbing Hybrid Tea.
The climber, 'Big Splash', is the surprising result of a cross between two Hybrid Teas. It has the potential to grow to 8 or 10 ft. The richly fragrant flowers open medium-pink with some flushes of vermilion at the center and then become more crimson with age. The petal reverse is pale pink. The flowers are large, double and high-centered. They bloom in continuous seasonal flushes. The foliage is dark green and glossy.

'BILLARD ET BARRÉ'.

('Billiard et Barré').
Breeder: Joseph Pernet-Ducher (France, 1898).
Parentage: 'Mademoiselle Alice Furon' x 'Duchesse d'Auerstädt'.
Classification: Climbing Tea, Tea-Noisette.
This rose has large, semi-double to double, deep yellow flowers nuanced lightly with buff tones. The outer petals fade early to light yellow while the center remains more deeply colored. The floral form is an open cup. The flowers bloom in repeated seasonal flushes. The plant has large, dark green foliage and will grow to about 10 ft. (3 m).

'BILLY BOILER'.

Breeder: Alister Clark (Australia, 1927).
Parentage: 'Black Boy' x Unknown.
Classification: Climbing Hybrid Tea.
The long, narrow buds of this variety give rise to medium-sized, semi-double, strongly scented, brilliant dark red flowers. The flowering is remontant in repeated flushes. The potential height is about 10 ft. (3 m). The rose grown in Australia at the present time may not be the original variety.

'Birthday Present'.

'BIRTHDAY PRESENT'.

Breeder: Douglas Toogood (Australia, 1950).
Parentage: 'Guinee' x 'Rouge Mallerin'.
Classification: Large-Flowered Climber.
'Birthday Present' has medium to large-sized, lightly double dark velvety red flowers. There is one profuse blooming with an occasional bloom later. The almost thornless cans are covered with dark green foliage and will grow to about 10 to 13 ft. (3 to 4 m).

'Bischofsstadt Paderborn'.

'BISCHOFSSTADT PADERBORN'.

('Fire Pillar', 'Paderborn').
Breeder: Reimer Kordes (Germany, 1964).
Parentage: 'Korona' (floribunda, Kordes, 1955) x 'Spartan'.
Classification: Shrub.
The synonym 'Fire Pillar' clearly describes this rose with its large, semi-double flowers in brilliant orange-red with small cream-colored touches at the petal bases. The final flower form is very open and shows the stamens. The plant is classed as a shrub which will usually only grow to about 5 ft. (1.5 m), but if given support it will grow tall enough to be trained as a small climber with spectacular results.

'Black Boy'.

'BLACK BOY'.

Breeder: Alister Clark (Australia, before 1918).
Parentage: 'Étoile de France' x 'Bardou Job'.
Classification: Large-Flowered Climber.
This fragrant rose is an unusual color, very dark crimson nuanced with blackish tones that fades very little. The form is large, semi-double and open-cupped. The rose occurs singly or in small clusters. If sufficiently open, a few white flecks may be revealed. It is fully remontant in repeated flushes during the growing period. The plant may reach a height of 13 ft. (4 m).

'Blackberry Nip, Cl.'.

'BLACKBERRY NIP, CL.'.

Breeder: Discovered by Rob Somerfield (New Zealand, pre-2012).

Parentage: Sport of 'Blackberry Nip'.
Classification: Climbing Hybrid Tea.
I haven't seen this rose because it is quite new and grows only in New Zealand. It is reported on the Help Me Find web site to be dark purple, strongly fragrant, medium-sized and full with a cupped to flat, sometimes quartered bloom form. The flowers are produced mostly singly, but may occur in small clusters. It repeats in continuous flushes. The plant has semi-glossy, medium green foliage and is well armed with thorns (prickles). It can be trained as a moderate-sized climber.

'Blairii #1'.

'BLAIRII #1'.

Breeder: Blair (United Kingdom, 1837).
Parentage: 'Parks' Yellow Tea-scented China' x Unknown ('Tuscany' has been suggested).
Classification: Hybrid China. Hybrid Bourbon.
'Blairii #1' is rose pink with rapid fading of the outer petals to blush and then almost to white. The inner petals retain the color longer giving a two-toned effect. The flowers are moderately to strongly fragrant (opinions vary), large and double with a cupped bloom form. Quartering may occur. The flowers are mostly produced singly. The flowering occurs in continuous flushes during the blooming season (controversial). The plant has a potential height of about 12 ft. (3.5 m).

'BLAIRII #2' ('Blairii No. 2').

Breeder: Blair (United Kingdom, before 1843).
Parentage: 'Parks' Yellow Tea-scented China' x 'Tuscany'.
Classification: Hybrid China, Hybrid Bourbon.
The color of this rose is darker than that of 'Blairii #1'. It has deep pink centers and its outer petal are light pink as a result of fading. The flowers are strongly fragrant, very large and double with a flattened cup bloom form. It has one prolific flush of bloom in late spring or early summer and produces a few flowers later in the season. It will reach a height of about 10 to 15 ft. (3 to 5 m).

'Blairii #2'.

'BLANC PUR'.

Breeder: Mauget (France, 1827).
Parentage: Unknown.
Classification: Noisette.
The flowers are fragrant, medium-sized, double, globular to open cup and pure white, as the name implies. The petals roll back as the flower matures and form pointed tips on the outer petals. The plant will climb to about 10 ft. (3 m).

'Blanc Pur'.

'BLANCHE COLOMBE'.

Breeder: G. Delbard (France, 1995).
Parentage: Unknown.
Classification: Large-Flowered Climber.
'Blanche Colombe' translates fittingly as 'White Dove' since the rose is almost pure white with just a touch of yellow in the center and looks ready to fly away with its petals spread out. The flowers are scentless, double, medium-sized and formed like a Hybrid Tea with a high center. They are mostly produced singly on long stems suitable for cutting. Occasionally they are carried in small clusters. The potential height is about 10 ft. (3 m). They are remontant in regular flushes. It is grown only in private gardens so it is not easy to see, but it is commercially available in Europe.

'Blaze of Glory'.

'BLAZE OF GLORY'.

Breeder: Keith Zary (United States, pre-2005).
Parentage: 'Dynamite' x 'Dream Weaver'.
Classification: Large-Flowered Climber.
This attractive rose has medium orange flowers that are bright, but not a harsh color as orange can be. They are mildly fragrant of musk, medium-sized, semi-double to lightly double and bloom in large clusters. With maturity the petals reflex along the sides and can become almost quilled. Flowering is repeated in continuous flushes during the blooming season. The rose is hardy to USDA zone 5b and is heat tolerant as well. The plant has glossy, dark green foliage and grows vigorously to about 12 to 14 ft. (3.65 to 4.25 m).

'BLAZE SUPERIOR'.

See 'Demokracie'.

'Blessed Child'.

'BLESSED CHILD'.

Breeder: Rogue Valley Roses (United States, 2008).
Parentage: Unknown.
Classification: Shrub. Pillar rose in a mild to warm climate.
This lovely little known rose should be in more gardens. It is strongly scented like a wild rose, light pink with flushes of yellow at the petal bases, medium-sized and very double with a quartered petal arrangement. It blooms singly or in small clusters. The bloom is especially prolific and is regularly repeated in flushes through the blooming season. It will remain shrub height in a cool climate, but it will grow to 6 or 7 ft. (2 m) in a mild to warm climate, enough to train on a small pillar or trellis or to climb onto a porch railing.

'Blessings, Cl.'.

'BLESSINGS, CL.'.

Breeder: Discovered by Charles Walter Gregory (United Kingdom, 1967).
Parentage: Sport of 'Blessings'.
Classification: Climbing Hybrid Tea.
'Blessings, Cl.' has medium-sized, double, fragrant flowers in an unusual color of soft salmon-pink. The color shifts a little more toward pink with age. The flowers have a high-centered Hybrid Tea form and grow singly or in small clusters. They bloom only once in late spring or early summer. The plant is quite vigorous, reaching a height of about 15 ft. (4.5 m).

'Blossomtime'.

'BLOSSOMTIME'.

Breeder: Conrad O'Neal (United States, 1951).
Parentage: 'New Dawn' x Seedling.
Classification: Large-Flowered Climber.
The flowers of 'Blossomtime' are Hybrid Tea-like with high centers and quartered petal arrangements. They are light pink with darker centers and petal reverse, strongly scented, double and large. The petals reflex with maturity, often forming triangular tips. The flowers occur in small to medium clusters. The flowering repeats in regular flushes all during the blooming period. The plant is quite hardy to USDA zone 5a and is also shade tolerant and mildew resistant. The maximum expected height is about 15 ft. (4.5 m) under beneficial growing conditions.

'Blue Girl, Cl.'.

'BLUE GIRL, CL.'.

('Kölner Karneval, Cl.').
Breeder: Discovered by Thomas B. Kyle (United States, 1977).
Parentage: Sport of 'Blue Girl'.
Classification: Climbing Hybrid Tea.
This rose marks one more lost trail on the quest for a blue rose. The flowers are a mauve or purple blend, not blue as the name indicates wishfully, and fade to a silvery lilac hue. They are fragrant, large to very large, full, formed with a high center like a Hybrid Tea and are carried singly (usually) or sometimes in small clusters. The plant blooms in flushes throughout the season.

'BLUE MONDAY, CL'.

See 'Blue Moon, Cl.'

'Blue Moon, Cl.'.

'BLUE MOON, CL.'.

('Blue Monday, Cl.', 'Mainzer Fastnacht, Cl.', Sissi, Cl.').
Breeder: Discovered by Julie Jackson (Australia, 1978) and by Fred A. Mungia, Sr. (US, 1981).
Parentage: Sport of 'Blue Moon' (Hybrid Tea, Tantau, 1965, Germany).
Classification: Climbing Hybrid Tea.
Something that happens once in a blue moon is a very rare event, indeed, since moons don't come in blue. This one is actually lavender, strongly scented, large, double and beautifully shaped like a Hybrid Tea, but finally opening out enough to show the stamens. It is fully remontant in continual flushes. The plant is hardy only to USDA zone 7b so it will do best in a warm climate and should have frost protection in a cool one. It produces long arching canes of at least 10 ft. (3 m) with flowering laterals along the length.

'Blush Noisette'.

'BLUSH NOISETTE'.

('Noisette Carnée', Rosa indica var. noisettiana).
Breeder: Philippe Noisette (United States, 1814).
Parentage: seedling of 'Champneys' Pink Cluster'.
Classification: Noisette.
This is the Noisette that started it, the first of this class that was named for Philippe Noisette, the breeder. The buds are crimson, but the flowers, blush pink, are surprisingly light-colored and soon fade to become almost white. They are strongly scented of cloves, small to medium-sized, full and carried in large clusters. The plant is fully remontant. The foliage is glossy and the leaves may have seven leaflets. It will grow, in a shrubby manner, to 7 ft. (2 m) or more and is attractive tied to a small pillar, fence or trellis. Although it is fairly hardy, it will perform best in a mild to warm climate.

'Böhms Climber'.

'BÖHMS CLIMBER'.

Breeder: Jan Böhm (former Czechoslovakia, pre-1935).
Parentage: Unknown.
Classification: Large-Flowered Climber.
This attractive climber is crimson with a lighter petal reverse. The flowers are medium-sized, full and fragrant. The petal tips roll back as the flower matures. The foliage is large, medium green and has a matte surface.

'Bolero'.

'BOLERO'.

Breeder: Bred by Pernille and Mogens Olesen (Denmark, 1998).
Parentage: 'Morning Jewel' x Seedling.
Classification: Large-Flowered Climber.
'Bolero' is creamy white and blush pink, especially at the petal tips. The pink is most evident during cool weather, but fades in time to nearly white. The medium-sized, semi-double flowers have a spicy wild rose fragrance and are carried in small clusters. The flower form is cupped and becomes more flat with age. The plant has good remontancy, blooming in repeated flushes during the blooming season. The foliage is dark green and glossy. The plant will climb, in a bushy manner, to about 10 ft. (3 m).

'Bonn'.

'BONN'.

Breeder: Wilhelm J.H. Kordes II (Germany, 1950).
Parentage: 'Hamburg' x 'Independence'.
Classification: Shrub.
'Bonn' has scarlet flowers that age to a pinker hue. They are fragrant of musk, large, semi-double, rather loosely formed with wide petals that reflex at the tips as they age to form points, giving the flower the shape of a multi-pointed star. The plant is classed as a shrub, but it will grow to about 6.5 to 7 ft. (2 m), enough to train as a small climber.

'BOOGIE-WOOGIE'.

Breeder: Pernille and Mogens Olesen (Denmark, 2002).
Parentage: Unknown.
Classification: Large-Flowered Climber.
'Boogie-Woogie' is pink, scented of wild rose, medium-sized and semi-double to lightly double. The flowers seem to be fully double because of the perfectly imbricated form with which the petals are arranged. They spread out like shingles on a roof. The plant will climb in a bushy style to about 6.5 to 7 ft(2 m) and can be used as a small pillar rose or can be trained to a trellis or low fence.

'BOUGAINVILLE'.

Breeder: Pierre Cochet (France, 1822).
Parentage: Unknown.
Classification: Noisette.
This rose has fragrant, medium-sized, very double, lilac-pink flowers with a cup shape that opens widely to show the stamens. They bloom in continuous seasonal flushes. The plant is only moderately vigorous, but it will grow to 8 or 10 ft. (2.5 or 3 m) if given support.

'Bougainville'.

'BOUQUET D'OR'.

Breeder: Jean-Claude Ducher (France, 1872).
Parentage: 'Gloire de Dijon' x Seedling.
Classification: Tea-Noisette.
The flowers of this Tea-Noisette are large, full and buff-yellow and fade to cream. The flowers often have an irregular petal arrangement. The outer petals may reflex along their edges and can also be quartered. The flowering is remontant in flushes. The foliage is large and glossy. The plant will grow, with a branching style, to about 8 ft. (2.5 m).

'Bouquet D'Or'.

'BOUQUET PARFAIT'.

Breeder: Louis Lens (Belgium, 1989).
Parentage: (Rosa multiflora var. adenochaeta x 'Ballerina') x 'White Dream'.
Classification: Hybrid Musk.
This rose is creamy white, more yellow toward the center and each petal tipped with light pink. With maturity the colors fade and the flower becomes cream throughout. The flowers are fragrant, medium-sized, full and carried in large clusters. They are cupped and globular at first, and then they open out to flattened cups. The remontancy is good, occurring in flushes throughout the blooming season. The canes have glossy, dark green foliage and few thorns (prickles). The plant can be trained as an 8 ft. (2.45 m) climber.

'Bouquet Parfait'.

'BOUQUET TOUT FAIT'.

Breeder: Jean Laffay (France, pre-1836).
Parentage: Unknown.
Classification: Noisette.
The roses are richly fragrant, medium-sized, double and creamy white with pink centers fading to buff. They are borne in very large clusters. They are very remontant, blooming in continuous flushes during the flowering season. The plant is moderately vigorous and will grow as a 5 or 6 ft. (1.5 or 1.8 m) shrub or will reach about 10 ft. (3 m) if given support and allowed to climb. There seem to be several different roses grown under this name.

'Bouquet Tout Fait'.

'BRANDON'.

Breeder: Maurice Combe (France, 1964).
Parentage: Unknown.
Classification: Large-Flowered Climber.
I haven't seen this rose which grows at Bagatelle Park (France) and seemingly nowhere else. The flowers are described as being large, double, high-centered and dark red. It has one main spring-summer bloom with a few flowers opening later. It will make a good pillar rose.

'BRASÉRADE'.

Breeder: André Eve (France, 1979).
Parentage: Unknown.
Classification: Climber.
Fat buds open to deep scarlet (orange red), large, lightly double flowers. They have wide petals, an open, flat form and are carried singly or in small clusters. In time, the petal tips become more crimson. This rose blooms prolifically and repeats in regular flushes during the blooming season.

It is moderately vigorous, attaining a height of about 8 ft. (2.5 m).

'Braserade'.

'BREAK O' DAY, CL.'.

Breeder: Discovered by the Brownells (United States, 1944).
Parentage: Sport of 'Break o' Day'.
Classification: Climbing Hybrid Tea.
Plump buds with crimson-tipped guard petals produce apricot blooms that fade quickly to pale apricot and then pinkish apricot. The flowers are large and very full, often with quartered petals. With age, the petals reflex extensively and the flower opens out to reveal the stamens. Plants are slow to establish, but once a plant hits its stride it can grow to as much as 20 ft. (6 m). The foliage is very healthy. The plant flowers profusely in late spring or early summer with occasional blooms later in the year.

'Break O' Day, Cl.'.

'BREATH OF LIFE'.

Breeder: Harkness (United Kingdom, 1980).
Parentage: 'Red Dandy' x 'Alexander'.
Classification: Large-Flowered Climber.
This attractive apricot climber has large, full, strongly fragrant flowers with a classical Hybrid Tea form that come on long stems, making it good for cutting. With maturity the flowers open out fully and become somewhat more pinkish. There is one main bloom in late spring or early summer with an occasional flower produced later in the year. The plants are very healthy and moderately vigorous, reaching a height of about 10 ft. (3 m). The name was chosen as the winner in a naming contest sponsored by the The Royal College of Midwives in London, England.

'Breath of Life'.

'BRIDESMAID, CL.'.

Breeder: Discovered by Dingee & Conard (United States, 1897).
Parentage: Sport of 'Bridesmaid'.
Classification: Climbing Tea.
This is a climbing sport of a bush form that was a color sport of 'Katherine Mermet', a very light pink tea. 'Bridesmaid' has the same lovely flower form as 'Catherine Mermet', but it is a much richer color of pink. The color fades with time, but remains darker in the center and doesn't develop the unpleasant tones of yellow seen in the sport parent. The flower form is large, double, high-centered and scented strongly of tea. The flowering is fully remontant in regular flushes during the blooming season.

'BRIDGE OF SIGHS'.

Breeder: Harkness (United Kingdom, 2000).
Parentage: Unknown.
Classification: Large-Flowered Climber.
The flowers of this unusual rose are apricot, fading at the tips to pale apricot, and more yellow at the petal bases. They are strongly scented. The flower form is semi-double and the petals have scallops and mucronate (sharply pointed) tips. The flowers have the charming habit of closing up at night. The plant is not shade tolerant, but needs good sun exposure for best performance. It is moderately vigorous, attaining a height of about 10 ft. (3 m), good for a pillar rose.

'BRIGHT DAY' (Orange Keops).

Breeder: Christopher H. Warner (United Kingdom, 2001).
Parentage: 'Laura Ford' x 'Royal Baby'.
Classification: Climbing Miniature.
The flowers of 'Bright Day' live up to its name. They are bright vermilion with a lighter vermilion petal reverse and white petal bases. The individual flowers are small, double and are carried in medium clusters. The foliage is glossy and medium green. The plant grows in an upright manner to about 8 ft. (2.5 m), tall enough for training to a small trellis or low fence.

'BRIGHT FIRE' (Brightfire).

Breeder: Colin A. Pearce (United Kingdom, 1996).
Parentage: 'Parkdirector Riggers x Guinée.
Classification: Large-Flowered Climber.
The flowers of 'Bright Fire are bright vermilion, semi-double, large-sized, almost scentless and are shaped like a Hybrid Tea. The foliage is glossy, large, dark green and leathery. The canes will grow stiffly with some branching to about 12 ft. (3.65 m). The plant is fully remontant with continual flushes of bloom during the flowering season.

'BRIGHT FUTURE'.

Breeder: Gordon Kirkham (United Kingdom, 2007).
Parentage: Unknown.
Classification: Large-Flowered Climber.
This sweetly fragrant apricot climber appears to not fade rapidly, but maintains a fairly even color. The outer petals may acquire tinges of pink over time. The petals are wide and gently ruffled as seen when the flower opens up and becomes flattened. The bloom form is double, large and cluster-flowered. The plant grows to a height of about 10 ft. (3 m).

'BRIGHT IDEAS'.

Breeder: Colin P. Horner (United Kingdom, 2003).
Parentage: 'Lichterloh' x unnamed seedling.
Classification: Large-Flowered Climber.
The pink and white striped flowers of 'Bright Ideas' are medium to large, double and moderately fragrant and are carried in large clusters. The foliage is healthy, glossy, dark green and somewhat crinkled. The plant is known to reach a height of about 10 ft. (3 m) and will look very attractive on a small pillar, trellis or low fence.

'BRINDIS'.

Breeder: Simon (Simó) Dot (Spain, 1962).
Parentage: 'Orange Triumph, Cl'. x ('Phyllis Bide' x 'Baccará').
Classification: Large-Flowered Climber.
The flowers of 'Brindis' are scentless, single, medium-sized, and deep, brilliant crimson merging into the light yellow of the petal bases. The crimson fades and dulls and the centers become white as the flowers age. The flowers occur singly or are carried in small clusters spread out across the plant like a cloud of crimson butterflies. The plant has dark green foliage and will reach a height of at least 7 ft. (2 to 2.5 m) and a bit more under favorable conditions.

'Brindis'.

'BRITE EYES' (Radbrite).

Breeder: William J. Radler (United States, before 2002).
Parentage: RADtee x 'Abraham Darby'.
Classification: Large-Flowered Climber.
The opening flowers are salmon-pink with yellow centers and pale yellow reverse sides, then they become lighter and more pink and the centers fade to white. The flowers are semi-double, medium-sized, lightly scented of spice and carried singly or in small clusters. They tend to ball in wet weather. The foliage is very disease resistant, especially to blackspot and is medium green with a matte surface. The canes will grow to a height of about 8 ft. (2.45 m). The plant is hardy to USDA zone 5b. It is remontant in continuous flushes throughout the blooming season.

'BROTHER CADFAEL'.

Breeder: David C. H. Austin (United Kingdom, 1990).
Parentage: 'Charles Austin' x Seedling.
Classification: Shrub (English Rose).
The soft pink, large, very full flowers begin life deeply cupped and open out with time to low domes filled generously with reflexing, slightly ruffled petals. They are graced with an old rose scent. Long, strong, almost thornless stems make them useful as cut flowers. The foliage is very disease resistant and hardy to USDA zone 5b. My plant has grown in a bushy manner to at least 8 ft. (2.5 m) reaching up and along a porch rail. The rose was named for a character in a medieval novel by an English author.

'Brother Cadfael'.

'BUBBLE BATH'.

Breeder: Matson (1980).
Parentage: 'Kathleen' x 'Cécile Brunner, Cl.'
Classification: Hybrid Musk.
Newly opened flowers from bright pink buds are medium-sized, double and light pink with some yellow at the center. They are very fragrant and occur in large clusters. The sun fades the colors to blush pink, then to ivory, outer petals first. The plant is very shade tolerant so it is possible to preserve the colors better, without collateral damage to the plant, by providing some shade. The rose is fully remontant, repeating its bloom in regular flushes during the entire growing season. The plant is known to reach a height of 8 to 10 ft. (2.5 to 3 m).

'Bubble Bath'.

'BUFF BEAUTY'.

Breeder: Bentall (United Kingdom, 1939).
Parentage: 'William Allen Richardson' x Seedling.
Classification: Hybrid Musk.
The flowers of this rose are initially apricot and yellow with buff overtones, but the colors fade to cream with sun exposure. The flowers are medium, very full, strongly scented with a tea rose fragrance, and are carried in small clusters. The flowering is repeated in flushes throughout the blooming season. The plant is hardy with a rating of USDA zone 5b and is shade and heat tolerant. It will grow to about 10 ft. (3 m).

'Buff Beauty'.

'Burg Baden'.

'BURG BADEN'.

Breeder: Wilhelm J.H. Kordes II (Germany, 1955).
Parentage: Seedling of R. kordesii.
Classification: Hybrid Kordesii.
The deep pink flowers with pink stamens and creamy white petal bases are medium-sized, single and moderately scented. They are carried in large clusters on a plant that will grow to about 8 ft. in height (2.5 m) with long flexible canes. The flowering is remontant in flushes throughout the blooming season. The foliage is glossy and dark green. This rose is quite similar to Rosa kordesii, but with a brighter color.

'Butterscotch'.

'BUTTERSCOTCH'.

Breeder: William A. Warriner (United States, 1986).
Parentage: ('Buccaneer' x 'Zorina') x 'Royal Sunset'.
Classification: Large-Flowered Climber.
The unusual color of a newly opened flower of the rose 'Butterscotch' is very much like that of a piece of butterscotch candy, a strongly russeted yellow with subtle apricot overtones. As the flower ages it becomes cream colored. The flowers are large, lightly double, mildly fragrant, shallow cup formed and are carried in small clusters. The bloom is repeated in flushes all during the blooming season. It will usually grow to a height of about 10 ft. (3 m) with long arching canes.

'Butterflies'.

'BUTTERFLIES'.

Breeder: Dr. Anthony Casimir Mekdeci (Canada, circa 1981).
Parentage: 'Dornröschen' x 'Golden Wings'.
Classification: Shrub.
This is a rose of many brilliant colors, guaranteed to brighten up the garden. The orange buds open to single, small to medium-sized, strongly fragrant flowers with vermilion petals, bright yellow petal bases and a lighter reverse. They are carried in small to medium clusters. The flowers fade to scarlet, then to light crimson while the centers fade to cream. The effect is of a flock of brightly colored butterflies. The plant will grow in a shrubby fashion to about 10 ft. (3 m) and so it is best suited to a lattice or small fence. It is healthy and hardy to USDA zone 5b.

'Crown Princess Margarita'.

'CÄCILIE'.

Breeder: Lützow (Germany, 1999).
Parentage: Unknown.
Classification: Large-Flowered Climber.
'Cäcilie' is not a well known rose, but certainly merits wider use. The plant that grows at Sangerhausen has flowers that are moderately fragrant, very full and light yellow fading to white. The inner petals fold upward on a central line and show some quartering. They are produced singly or in small clusters. The plant appears to be a climber of average height.

'Cäcilie'.

'CADENZA'.

Breeder: David L. Armstrong (United States, 1967).
Parentage: 'New Dawn' x 'Embers, Cl.'
Classification: Large-Flowered Climber.
'Cadenza' provides a strong focal point in the garden with its beautifully formed, medium sized, double, gently ruffled dark red flowers held in very large clusters. The fragrant blooms are cupped at first, and then open out to low domes. There is one main bloom early in the season and an occasional repeat later in the season. The foliage is dark green, glossy, leathery and disease resistant. The plant is a shrubby climber and builds up by branching to a height of about 10 ft. (3 m).

'CALEDONIA, CL.'

Breeder: Jean Bel (France, 1936).
Parentage: A sport of 'Caledonia'.
Classification: Climbing Hybrid Tea.
'Caledonia, Cl.' is a sport of a lovely old Hybrid Tea. It produces large, very double, white, high-centered Hybrid Tea-type flowers with a warm touch of lemon-yellow in the center. They are moderately fragrant and are mainly carried singly. The stems are long and the blooms are lasting in the vase, making them good for cutting. The many petals may make them open poorly in wet weather. The plant reblooms in continuous flushes during the blooming season. The foliage is light green; the canes are almost thornless and long, growing about 10 ft. (3 m).

'Cadenza'.

'CALYPSO' (Poulsen, 1998).

There are many roses by this name. For the Poulsen climbing rose see 'Berries 'n' Cream'.

'CAMELOT'.

Breeder: Hans Jürgen Evers (Germany, 2005).
Introduced by Tantau, 2011.
Parentage: Unknown.
Classification: Large-Flowered Climber.
The very attractive flowers of 'Camelot' are bright medium pink with darker veining and reverse. They fade to light pink with time. They are moderately fragrant, medium-sized, very double and are carried singly or in small clusters. They are cupped at first, and then open out as a rosette with perfectly imbricated petals. The plant is healthy, hardy to USDA zone 5b and is shade tolerant. The blooming is fully remontant. The plant will grow to about 10 ft (3 m). It was the winner of the gold medal Baden Baden 2012 and gold medal Barcelona 2013.

'Campanile'.

'CAMPANELA'.
See 'Campanile'.

'CAMPANILE' ('Campanela').

Breeder: Delbard-Chabert (France, 1967).
Parentage: ('Queen Elizabeth' x 'Provence') x (seedling of 'Sultan' x 'Madame Joseph Perraud').
Classification: Large-Flowered Climber.
The flowers of 'Campanile' are deep magenta-pink, large, full, moderately fragrant and are produced singly or in small clusters. They open to a cupped form and then open out further to reveal the stamens. They can be used as cut flowers. This is a healthy rose with good heat tolerance, but it is only moderately winter hardy. It is remontant, blooming in continuous flushes during the blooming season. The expected height is about 10 ft (3 m).

'CANCAN'.

Breeder: William J. Radler (United States, 2001).
Parentage: RADcovery x RADcotee
Classification: Large-Flowered Climber.
This rose has unique and striking coloration. The petals are deep magenta-pink with irregularly shaped creamy white centers. The petal tips become dark purple with sun exposure resulting in a tricolor. The flowers are large, semi-double and lack fragrance. Rebloom is excellent in continuous flushes during the regular blooming season. The plant has very disease resistant semi-glossy foliage and will reach a height of about 10 ft (3 m). It is commercially available.

'CANDY CANE'.

Breeder: Ralph S. Moore (United States, 1958).
Parentage: (['Soeur Thérèse' x 'Skyrocket'] x [Seedling × 'Red Ripples']) x 'Zee'.
Classification: Climbing Miniature.
'Candy Cane' has deep pink flowers with fine white stripes and small white centers. They are semi-double (almost single), small and are carried in medium clusters. The petals sometimes have little pointed tips (mucronate). They are rather narrow and loosely spaced when mature. The flowering is remontant in flushes during the blooming season. This rose grows best in a warm climate reaching about 10 ft (3 m).

'Candy Cane'.

'CANDY LAND'.

Breeder: Bred by Tom Carruth (United States, 2006).
Parentage: 'Rosy Outlook' x 'Pretty Lady'.
Classification: Large-Flowered Climber.
'Candy Land' produces flowers of deep rosy pink with broad creamy white stripes and light yellow petal bases. They are large, semi-double to lightly double, moderately fragrant and carried in very large clusters. The bloom form is high centered like a Hybrid Tea. The whole effect is very decorative. The rose is fully remontant, blooming in flushes throughout the regular blooming season. The plant has healthy, light green, large, glossy foliage and is rated as hardy to USDA zone 5b. Under favorable conditions it will grow to about 15 ft (4.55 m).

'Candy Land'.

'CAPE DIAMOND'.

Breeder: Christian Bédard (United States, 2006).
Parentage: 'Marie-Victorin' x 'Louis Jolliet'.
Classification: Hybrid Kordesii.
This is a very hardy rose with a USDA zone rating of 4a and it is attractive as well, quite an accomplishment. The flowers are pink with a bit of lilac added. They are large, full, strongly scented and are carried in small clusters. There is one main bloom with an occasional repeat later in the season. The foliage is very disease resistant, glossy and light green. Even though it is hardy, the plant grows best in a warm climate where it will reach a height of about 10 ft (3 m). In a cold climate it may only reach about 6 ft.

'Captain Christy, Cl.'.

'CAPTAIN CHRISTY, CL.'.

Breeder: Discovered by Marie aka Veuve (widow) Ducher (France, 1881).
Parentage: Sport of 'Captain Christy' (hybrid tea, Lacharme, 1873).
Classification: Climbing Hybrid Tea.
This Hybrid Tea-type rose is medium pink and fades to light pink, usually with a darker center. The edges of the petals are sometimes scalloped. With maturity it opens to show a glimpse of the stamens. It is large, double and strongly fragrant of tea. It has an unfortunate tendancy to ball in wet weather so it is best in a dry climate. It is fully remontant, blooming in flushes throughout the blooming season. The plant is fairly vigorous, growing to heights of 8 to 10 ft (2.45 to 3 m).

'Captain Hayward, Cl.'.

'CAPTAIN HAYWARD, CL.'.

Breeder: George Paul (United Kingdom, 1906).
Parentage: Sport of 'Captain Hayward'.
Classification: Climbing Hybrid Perpetual.
The flowers of this lovely old Hybrid Perpetual sport are brilliant crimson-cerise with some narrow white streaks and a lighter reverse. They soon fade to a lighter tone. The flowers are large, moderately fragrant and semi-double to lightly double. The form is high-centered in the Hybrid Perpetual/Hybrid Tea mode with some quartering of the petals. They are single or in small clusters. There is very good remontancy in flushes during the blooming season. The plant can be expected to grow to about 8 ft (2.45 m).

'Captain Thomas'.

'CAPTAIN THOMAS'.

('George C. Thomas, Jr.').
Breeder: Captain George C. Thomas (United States, 1935).
Parentage: 'Bloomfield Completeness' x 'Attraction'.
Classification: Climbing Hybrid Tea.
'Captain Thomas' blooms in light, clear yellow which contrasts strongly with the dark orange of the stamen's filaments, but match the yellow anthers. The yellow soon fades to cream. The flowers are strongly fragrant, single and medium to large-sized with slightly wavy petals. They are carried singly or in small clusters. There is one main bloom with an occasional flower later. The foliage is medium green and glossy. The canes will grow, with much branching, to about 10 ft (3 m).

'Captaine Sisolet'.

'CAPITAINE SISOLET'.

Breeder: Unknown.
Parentage: Unknown.
Classification: Not certain. The American Rose Society considers it a Hybrid Perpetual. The Sangerhausen data base lists it as a Noisette Hybrid.
The flowers are large, double to very double and bright pink with white petal bases and a lighter reverse. The floral form is an open cup. There is one main spring-summer bloom follow later in the season by a few flowers. I was unable to detect a scent when I observed the rose at Sangerhausen. The plant is quite vigorous, reaching a height of 10 to 15 ft (3 to 4.5 m).

'Capitaine Soupa, Cl.'.

'CAPITAINE SOUPA, CL'.

Breeder: Max Vogel (Germany, 1938).
Parentage: sport of 'Capitaine Soupa'.
Classification: Climbing Hybrid Tea.
'Capitaine Soupa, Cl.' has bright rose pink (pink with a touch of coral), very large, full flowers that are carried singly or in small clusters. The plant is floriferous and repeats its bloom in regular flushes throughout the regular blooming season. The long, upright canes are almost thornless and will reach a height of about 10 ft (3 m).

'CAREFREE SUNSHINE, CL.'.

Breeder: Discovered by William Devor (United States, 2002).
Parentage: Sport of 'Carefree Sunshine'
Classification: Climbing Shrub.
This sport of a shrub known for its carefree qualities comes with light yellow single to semi-double blooms that fade to cream and are centered by golden yellow stamens. The

petals drop off cleanly at the the flower's end. There is a very light fragrance. The flowers are carried singly or in small clusters and are fully remontant in flushes. Bright orange hips develop in fall. The light green, matte foliage is highly disease resistant and the canes are hardy to at least USDA zone 5a. The plant is also heat tolerant. Expect growth to about 10 ft (3 m).

'Carina, Cl.'.

'CARINA , CL.' ('Grimpant Carina').

Breeder: Discovered by Meilland International (France, 1968).
Parentage: Sport of 'Carina'.
Classification: Climbing Hybrid Tea.
'Carina, Cl.' is a beautiful sport of a Hybrid Tea that has been much used as a florist's rose. The flowers are light pink with deeper pink centers, very large, very full, moderately fragrant and carried singly or in small clusters. They tend to ball in wet weather. The form is high-centered like a Hybrid Tea. The plant is somewhat tender and will do best in a warm, dry climate. Flowering repeats in flushes during the growing season. The disease resistant canes will grow to about 10 ft (3 m) in height.

'CARLA, CL'.

Breeder: Discovered by A. Ross & Son/Ross Roses (Australia, 1969).
Parentage: Sport of 'Carla'.
Classification: Climbing Hybrid Tea.
The flowers of this pretty rose are pink with just a touch of salmon, large, double and mildly fragrant. They are produced mostly singly or, sometimes, in small clusters. There is good remontancy in continuous seasonal flushes. The plant has dark green foliage and can be expected to grow to about 15 ft (4.5 m).

'Carla Fineschi'.

'CARLA FINESCHI'.

Breeder: André Eve (France, 2002).
Parentage: Unknown.
Classification: Large-Flowered Climber.
This floriferous deep scarlet-red climber has white petal bases and lighter petal reverses. The flowers are cup shaped and have gently wavy petals. The semi-double, medium-sized flowers are carried in small clusters on a tall shrubby, climbing plant that will grow to 10 to 13 ft (3 to 4 m) if given support. It can also be grown as a shrub.

'CAROLINE MARNIESSE'.

Breeder: Roeser (France, 1848).
Parentage: Unknown.
Classification: Noisette.
The flowers are fragrant, small to medium-sized, double and white with pale pink petal tips. They are borne in small clusters. The plant is fairly hardy for one of its class and can be trained as a shrubby climber of about 8 ft (2.5 m).

'Casa Blanca'.

'CASA BLANCA'.

Breeder: Edward P. Sima (United States, 1968).
Parentage: 'New Dawn' x 'Fashion'.
Classification: Large-Flowered Climber.
The bud is lightly tinged with pink, but that is the limit of any color for this lovely pure white rose. The flowers are mildly fragrant, medium-sized, semi-double with broad petals and are deeply cupped when they first open. They open out enough with maturity to show the stamens and finally become quite flat. They are carried in small clusters and are good as cut flowers. There is one main bloom with a few flowers produced later in the season. The canes are clothed with glossy, dark green foliage. They will grow to 10 to 13 ft (3 to 4 m).

'CASCADE'.

Breeder: Charles Mallerin (France, 1951).
Parentage: 'Holstein' x 'American Pillar'.
Classification: Large-Flowered Climber.
'Cascade' has bright crimson flowers with white petal bases and narrow white streaks along the petal midlines. The flowers are single to semi-double, medium-sized and are carried in large clusters. The plant will grow to a height of 12 to 13 ft (4 m).

'CASCADE'. (Poulskab, Nordina).

Breeder: L. Pernille and Mogens Nyegaard Olesen (Denmark, 1992).
Parentage: Unknown.
Classification: Large-Flowered Climber. Patio Climber, Courtyard Collection.
The Danish 'Cascade' rose (Olesen, 1992) is quite different from the French 'Cascade' rose (Mallerin, 1951) featured in the previous entry. The Olesen rose is peachy pink, fading to light pink and has a touch of soft yellow at the center that fades to white. It is semi-double to lightly double, medium to large-sized and is carried in small clusters. There

'Cascade' (Mallerin).

'Cascade' (Mallerin).

is a mild wild rose fragrance. The newly opened, cupped flower spreads out and become flat. The plant is covered with dark green foliage with flushes of reddish green. The growth is about 7 ft (2 m), enough for a small pillar or trellis.

'Casino'.

'CASINO' (Gerbe d'Or).

Breeder: Bred by Samuel Darragh McGredy IV (1963).
Parentage: 'Coral Dawn' x 'Buccaneer'.
Classification: Large-Flowered Climber.
'Casino' has deep yellow buds that open to light yellow flowers. The yellow soon fades to cream, remaining longer in the centers. The flowers are fragrant, large and double and are carried singly or in small clusters. The bloom form is flattened and the petals may be quartered. The plant is remontant in flushes. Glossy, dark green foliage covers the canes which will grow to about 12 ft (3.65 m). The best growth is in warm conditions; otherwise the plant may need frost protection.

'CASSANDRE'.

('Cassandre, Cl.', 'Cassandre, Grimpant').
Breeder: Meilland International (France, 1989).
Parentage: Unknown.
Classification: Climbing Hybrid Tea.
The ruffled flowers of 'Cassandre' are bright medium crimson and fade to lighter crimson pink. They are strongly fragrant, medium-sized, double and have an open form. The flowering is generous and repeats well in regular flushes through the regular blooming season. The canes are well armed and clothed with large, semi-glossy, medium green foliage. They have a potential height of about 12 to 13 ft (4 m).

'Cassandre'.

'CATALUNYA'.
See 'Gruss an Teplitz, Cl.'

'CATHRINE KORDES, CL.'.

Breeder: Discovered by Krohn (Unknown, 1938).
Parentage: Sport of 'Cathrine Kordes'.
Classification: Climbing Hybrid Tea.
The buds and the newly opened flowers of this fragrant climbing rose are dark crimson, sometimes with a flush of cerise. In time, they fade and become more pink. The flower form is large, double to very double and high-centered like a Hybrid Tea. The flowers are carried singly or in small clusters. The bloom repeats in flushes during the blooming season. The plant is reasonably cold hardy and is heat tolerant as well.

'Cathrine Kordes, Cl.'.

'CÉCILE BRUNNER, CL.'. See 'Mlle Cécile Brunner, Cl.'

'CÉLINE FORESTIER' ('Liésis').

Breeder: Victor Trouillard (France, 1842).
Parentage: Not certain. Perhaps 'Champney's Pink-Cluster' x 'Park's Yellow'.
Classification: Tea-Noisette.
'Celine Forestier' has light yellow flowers with deeper yellow centers. Sometimes there is a flush of pink associated with hot weather. The flowers are fragrant, large, full, low domed in form with petals that reflex along their lengths with creases down the centers. They are produced singly or in small clusters almost constantly during the blooming season. The growth is bushy and may reach 10 to 13 ft (3 to 4 m) if grown with a support for climbing.

'Céline Forestier'.

'CERVANKY' (Jan Böhm).

Breeder: Discovered by Jan Böhm (Czechoslovakia (former), circa 1935).
Parentage: Sport of 'Dr. Eckener'.
Classification: Large-Flowered Climber, Climbing Hybrid Rugosa.
Information on this rose is rather scant. It is sometimes listed as a Climbing Hybrid Tea which is rather odd since it is a sport of 'Dr. Eckener, a Hybrid Rugosa Shrub'. The flowers, which appear more or less identical on the two plants, are large, lightly double, and soft salmon-pink with soft, light cream-yellow centers fading to blush and cream. They are cup-shaped and have reflexed petal tips.

'Cervanky'.

'CÉSAR' (Romantic Occasion).

Breeder: Meilland International (France, 1993).
Parentage: Unknown.
Classification: Large-Flowered Climber (Romantica series).
Flowers start as plump cream-colored buds opening to very full, large blooms that are deep apricot pink in the center with yellow petal bases and light pink to almost white on the outermost rows of petals. They are carried mostly singly or in small clusters. There is one main bloom with a few repeats in late summer and early fall. The plant will grow to at least 10 ft (3 m) and more under beneficial conditions.

'César'.

'César'.

'CHAMPNEYS' PINK CLUSTER'.

(Champneyana, 'Champneys', Blush Cluster', 'Champney Rose').
Breeder: John Champneys (United States, circa 1811).
Parentage: Rosa moschata Herrm. x 'Parsons' Pink China'. Probably.
Classification: Noisette.
This rose is sometimes called the first Noisette even though Champney was the breeder and Noisette later used this variety to breed 'Blush Noisette', probably with the best claim to being called the first Noisette. The Champneys' rose has dark pink buds, but the opened flower is light pink with a mild fragrance. The flowers are very fragant of musk, small, double and are carried in large clusters. This rose is fully remontant in flushes. The plant is less vigorous than the Noisettes that came after it, growing to about 10 ft (3 m) with support. The rose by this name commonly sold in Europe appears to be a different variety.

'Champneys' Pink Cluster'.

'CHAMPS-ELYSÉES, CL.'.

Breeder: Discovered by Meilland International (France, 1969).
Parentage: Sport of 'Champs-Elysées'.
Classification: Climbing Hybrid Tea.
The flowers are dark, glowing crimson-red, large, double and mildly fragrant. The petals of the mature flower are rolled back at the tips. They bloom prolifically in continuous seasonal flushes. This variety is good as a pillar rose.

'Champs-Elysées, Cl.'.

'CHANTEBRISE'.

Breeder: Paul Croix (France, 1969).
Parentage: Unknown.
Classification: Large-Flowered Climber.
This rose has bright scarlet to crimson, large, lightly double flowers with broad petals that open out widely and reflex very little at the tips. They lack fragrance, but are fully remontant. The plant can be expected to grow tall enough to be trained as a climber of average size, about 10 ft (3 m). It grows at Roseto Carla Fineschi (Italy) and Sangerhausen (Germany).

'Chantebrise'.

'CHAPLIN'S PINK COMPANION'.

Breeder: H. J. Chaplin (1961).
Parentage: 'Chaplin's Pink Climber' x 'Opera'.

Classification: Large-Flowered Climber.
The richly fragrant flowers of this rose are pink with a hint of salmon, small, cupped and semi-double. They are held in medium to large clusters. The rose blooms prolifically during one long season only. The plant is very vigorous and will reach a height of about 15 ft (4, 5 m).

'CHARIVARI'.

Breeder: Reimer Kordes (Germany, 1971).
Parentage: 'Königin der Rosen' x 'Goldrausch'.
Classification: Shrub.
'Charivari' has dark pink buds. On opening, the flower colors begin as salmon yellow, then morph to golden yellow and finally the brilliant colors fade and the outer petals make a strong shift to cerise pink. The flower form is large, double and shaped like a low dome. There is a moderate fragrance. The plant has moderately vigorous shrubby growth to about 8 ft (2.5 m).

'Charivari'.

'CHARLES AUSTIN' (Charming Apricot).

Breeder: David C. H. Austin (United Kingdom, 1973).
Parentage: 'Chaucer' x 'Aloha'.
Classification: Shrub. English Rose.
Deep apricot buds open as apricot flowers with yellow petal bases that soon fade to light apricot yellow and then almost to white. They are strongly fragrant, cupped, medium to large, very full and carried singly or in small clusters on the ends of the canes. The rather rigid, bushy canes will grow vigorously in an up right manner to about 10 ft (3 m). Pruning will keep it as a shrub. The plant has one main bloom followed in the fall with a second. It is hardy to USDA zone 5b.

'Charles Austin'.

'CHARLES LEFÈBVRE'.

('Marguerite Brassac',' Paul Jamain').
Breeder: François Lacharme (France, 1861).
Parentage: 'Gén. Jacqueminot' x 'Victor Verdier'.
Classification: Hybrid Perpetual.
This rose opens to flowers of deep crimson which morphs to deep crimson purple with time. They are medium-sized, full, very fragrant, domed and are produced mostly singly or sometimes in small clusters. The petals are folded and twisted and the petal tips are slightly scalloped, giving the flowers a characteristic style. There is one main flowering with occasional repeats later. The almost thornless canes have light green foliage and will branch and grow to about 10 ft (3 m). There are reports of hardiness in USDA zone 4a.

'Charles Lefébvre'.

'CHARLES MALLERIN, CL.'.

Breeder: Baldacci & Figli (Italy, 1960).
Parentage: Sport of 'Charles Mallerin'.
Classification: Climbing Hybrid Tea.
This is an amazingly dark-colored rose, one of the so-called black roses, with black-red upper petal surfaces, deep crimson petal reverses and crimson petal tips. The flowers are very large, very full with a strong, fruity fragrance. They are shaped like Hybrid Teas, high-centered and aging to flattened cups. The flowers are borne singly or in small clusters. The blooming is remontant in flushes during the blooming season. The climbing canes are well armed and clothed with dark green, matte, foliage.

'Charles Mallerin, Cl.'.

'CHARLESTON, CL.'.

Breeder: Discovered by Roy H. Rumsey Pty. Ltd. (Australia, before 1966).
Parentage: Sport of 'Charleston'.
Classification: Climbing Floribunda.
'Charleston, Cl.' is a very showy rose. The large, double, lightly scented flowers open bright yellow and quickly turn vermilion, then pure red resulting in flowers with bright yellow centers and vermilion-red petal tips. Later, they fade to rose pink, white and creamy light yellow. The flower form is Floribunda-like, opening out very flat and held stiffly in small clusters. The foliage is dark green. The canes are healthy except for occasional blackspot and will reach heights of 16 to 20 ft (5 to 6 m).

'CHARLOTTE ARMSTRONG, CL.'

Breeder: Theodore J. Morris (United States, 1942).
Parentage: Sport of 'Charlotte Armstrong'.
Classification: Climbing Hybrid Tea.
This rose's sport parent was of one of the most important roses of the mid-20th century, for its own qualities and as a parent of 'Queen Elizabeth', 'Garden Party', 'Tiffany' and others. The climber shows the same excellence. The buds are long and pointed and the flowers are very fragrant, deep pink, very large and full with a Hybrid Tea shape. The foliage is dark green and very disease resistant. The plant reblooms in regular seasonal flushes. It grows to about 12 ft (3.65 m).

'Charlotte Armstrong, Cl.'

'CHARMIAN'.

Breeder: David C. H. Austin (United Kingdom, 1982).
Parentage: Seedling x 'Lilian Austin'.
Classification: Shrub (English Rose).
'Charmian' is a pretty rose with a strong old rose fragrance and large, double, pink, ruffled rosette-type flowers produced prolifically in one grand bloom and then a few flowers later

in the year. They are borne singly or in medium clusters on long, strong stems. The plant is disease resistant and hardy, rated to USDA zone 5b. It will grow to about 8 ft (2.5 m) as a climber or can be pruned and grown as a shrub. Charmian was Cleopatra's servant who committed suicide with her mistress.

'CHASTITY'.

Breeder: Frank Cant (United Kingdom, 1924).
Parentage: Unknown.
Classification: Climbing Hybrid Tea.
'Chastity', appropriately, is white with lemon yellow petal bases. The flowers are medium-sized, lightly double, moderately scented and Hybrid Tea-formed with high centers on opening. The mature flowers are loose cups, somewhat lacking in form and carried in small clusters. This is one of the earliest white roses to bloom, but only blooms once. The rose is disease resistant except for some mildew. The almost thornless canes, have glossy, light green foliage and will reach about 16 ft (5 m).

'Chastity'.

'CHATEAU DE CLOS VOUGEOT, CL.'.

Breeder: Henry Morse (United Kingdom, 1920).
Parentage: Sport of 'Château de Clos Vougeot'.
Classification: Climbing Hybrid Tea.
'Chateau de Clos Vougeot, Cl.', along with its sport parent honors the great wines of Burgundy. The colors are wine-like, deep crimson maturing to very dark purple-red. The flowers are large, double and very fragrant with a high-centered Hybrid Tea form that opens with large outside petals and a packed mass of smaller, reflexed petals in the center plus a glimpse of the stamens. The almost thornless canes will reach 8 to 10 ft (2.5 to 3 m), just right for a pillar rose. The rose is remontant in repeated flushes during the blooming season.

'Chateau Frontenac'.

'CHATEAU FRONTENAC'.

Breeder: Unknown (pre-2002).
Parentage: Unknown.
Classification: Shrub, Climber.
I have seen this rose only at Red Rose Ridge, a lovely privately owned garden in California where many of the Vintage Garden roses were moved for conservation when the nursery was shut down. It grows as a small climber producing large, double, deep crimson-pink blooms in repeated flushes during the flowering season. They have a licorice-like scent.

'Chatter, Cl.'

'CHATTER, CL.'

Breeder: Discovered by Karsten Schmidt (Germany, 1960).
Parentage: Sport of 'Chatter'.
Classification: Climbing Floribunda.
This rose has medium-sized, semi-double, deep velvety red blooms with a strong fragrance. It is fully remontant, blooming in flushes during the entire blooming season. The climber and bush can be observed at Sangerhausen (Germany).

'CHEEK TO CHEEK' (Poulslas).

Breeder: Introduced in Denmark by Poulsen Roser (2003).
Parentage: Unknown.
Classification: Large-Flowered Climber. Courtyard Collection.
'Cheek to Cheek' is a lovely addition to the existing white climbing roses. It is pure white with just a very light flush of pink in the center that soon fades away. There is little or no fragrance. The bloom form is medium-sized, double, broad petaled, cupped and carried singly or in small clusters. The canes have semi-glossy, dark green foliage and will grow in a bushy style to about 6 or 7 ft (2 m). Flowering is in continuous flushes during the blooming season.

'Cherry-Vanilla, Cl.'.

'CHERRY-VANILLA, CL.'.

Breeder: Discoverer unknown.
Parentage: Sport of 'Cherry-Vanilla'.
Classification: Climbing Grandiflora.
This is a very attractive climber with colors that are truly like cherry-vanilla ice cream, ivory-white with a band of cerise around the petal tips that spreads down the petals as the bloom matures. The center is flushed with warmer tones. The flowers are fragrant, full and very large, a quality enhanced considerably by culling a portion of the buds to allow a limited number of buds to open. The blooming is remontant in continuous flushes during the blooming season.

'Cherryade'.

'CHERRYADE'.

Breeder: De Ruiter Innovations BV (Netherlands, 1961).
Parentage: 'New Dawn' x 'Red Wonder'.
Classification: Shrub, Large-Flowered Climber.
Large, double, deep cerise colored flowers with a flattened cup form filled with swirled or quartered petals characterize this rose. The flowers are borne in small clusters. Their long stems make them good for cutting. The foliage is attractive and healthy. The plant will build up height with much branching, resulting in a bushy plant of about 10 ft (3 m) with flowers produced at the ends of the canes in continuous flushes during the blooming season.

'CHEYENNE'.

Breeder: Gordon J. Von Abrams (United States, 1962).
Parentage: 'Queen Elizabeth' x Seedling.
Classification: Climbing Hybrid Tea.
Cheyenne has flowers that are coral-pink to light pink, mildly fragrant, large, double and high-centered in Hybrid Tea style. It is remontant in regular seasonal flushes. The plant has the potential to climb to about 8 ft (2.5 m). ARS has ruled this rose extinct, but it still grows at Roseto Carla Fineschi (Italy).

'CHIANTI'.

Breeder: David C. H. Austin (United Kingdom, 1965).
Parentage: 'Dusky Maiden' x 'Tuscany'.
Classification: Shrub (English Rose).
This is one of my favorite roses. The flowers are deep crimson aging to purple-crimson, medium-sized, very full, cupped and strongly scented like an old rose. It blooms singly or in small clusters at the ends of the canes, the heavy blooms bending the canes outward. With support the canes grow to about 8 ft (2.5 m). It is hardy to USDA zone 5b and shade tolerant. There is only one bloom early in the season. All of the red Austin roses are descendants of this rose. The name 'Chianti' comes from the red wines of the Monte Chianti region of Tuscany.

'Chianti'.

'CHICAGO PEACE, CL.'.

Breeder: Discovered by S. Brundrett & Sons (Australia, 1978).
Parentage: Sport of 'Chicago Peace'.
Classification: Climbing Hybrid Tea.
This form of 'Peace' opens apricot pink with yellow petal bases and an apricot center. The outer petals quickly become more true pink resulting in striking bicolored flowers. The cupped, mildly fragrant flowers are very large, very full and are borne mostly solitary or in small clusters. They are produced in flushes throughout the blooming season. The plant has dark green, glossy foliage and is fairly vigorous, reaching to a height of about 13 ft (4 m).

'Chicago Peace, Cl.'.

'CHINA DOLL, CL.'.

('Weeping China Doll').
Breeder: Discovered by Robert Hardman Melville (Australia, 1965) and by O.L. "Ollie" Weeks (United States, pre-1977).
Parentage: Sport of 'China Doll'.
Classification: Climbing Polyantha.
This sport of 'China Doll' has large clusters of pink, small to medium, cupped, double flowers. The reflexed petals twist and turn a little giving the blooms a ruffled appearance. They are scented of spice and tea. Rebloom is good and occurs in continuous flushes all during the blooming season. The canes are almost thornless and have glossy foliage. They will reach a height of about 6 ft (1.85 m).

'China Doll, Cl.'.

'CHINATOWN' ('Ville de Chine').

Breeder: Niels Dines Poulsen (Denmark, 1962).
Parentage: 'Columbine' x 'Cläre Grammerstorf'.
Classification: Climbing Floribunda.
This rose is admired for its deep yellow, very fragrant, very large, double flowers with a classic high-centered Hybrid Tea form. The yellow color is usually pure in the young flower, but may become flushed with pink later. The flowers are held singly or in small clusters and blooms in continuous flushes. The plant, hardy to USDA zone 5b, will be a shrub in a cold climate, but will grow to 10 ft (3 m) or more in a warm climate if given support.

'Chinatown'.

'CHOCOLATE SUNDAE'.

Breeder: Meilland International (Fr, 2008).
Parentage: ('Delges' x 'Duc de Windsor') x 'Terracotta'.
Classification: Large-Flowered Climber.
Here is a climbing rose in a remarkable color of dark russet red with brown overtones in the petal tips and a lovely Hybrid Tea flower form as well. The flowers are small, double, scentless and are carried singly or in small clusters. The rose is fully remontant in continuous flushes during the blooming season. The Star Roses website states that it will give a good performance only in warm, dry climates, like California's. There it will grow to about 10 ft (3 m).

'CHORUS, CL.'.

Breeder: Discovered by Marie-Louise Meilland (France, 1983).
Parentage: Sport of 'Chorus'.
Classification: Climbing Floribunda.

'Chorus, Cl.'.

When I saw this rose at the Roseto Carla Fineschi in Italy I thought the vermilion color was very beautiful and unusually even-toned from the petal tips to the flower's center. The petal tips darken only a little over time. The flowers are lightly scented, large and double and open out Floribunda-like to flattened shapely rosettes held singly or in small clusters. Reblooming is in flushes during the blooming season. The plant has healthy medium green leaves and will climb to about 10 ft (3 m).

'Chris'.

'CHRIS'.

Breeder: Gordon Kirkham (United Kingdom, 1998).
Parentage: 'Morgengruss' x 'Whisky Mac'.
Classification: Large-Flowered Climber.
'Chris' has rich yellow, large, double flowers that fade, petal

tips first, to light yellow and then almost to white. The flowers remain darker in the center. They are very fragrant. The plant is moderately vigorous, climbing to a height of about 10 ft (3 m). The rose is commercially available in the United Kingdom. 'Chris' was named for the brother of the owner of C&K Jones Roses in Chester, England.

'CHRISTINE' ('Orange Altissimo')'

Breeder: Discovered by John Clements (United States, pre-1997).
Parentage: Sport of 'Altissimo'.
Classification: Large-Flowered Climber.
'Christine' shares all of the excellent qualities found in 'Altissimo', differing only in having a bright orange color instead of a red color. The blooms are single, large, mildly scented of cloves and carried mostly singly or in small clusters. They have the same evenness of color without the white center that is found in 'Altissimo'. The flowers begin in a cupped bloom form and then open out to very flat, the color harmonizing beautifully with the golden stamens in the center. The plant will reach a height of about 10 ft (3 m).

'Christine'.

'CHRISTINE, CL.'.

Breeder: Discovered by Willink (Ireland, 1936).
Parentage: Sport of 'Christine' (hybrid tea, McGredy, 1918)
Classification: Climbing Hybrid Tea.
This rose has small, lightly double, lightly scented, pure, deep yellow flowers with an elegant Hybrid Tea form. A lovely rose, but unfortunately nonremontant. The plant can be expected to grow to about 12 ft (3.65 m). Do not confuse this variety with 'Christine', the orange sport of 'Altissimo'.

'Christine, Cl.'.

'CHRISTOPHER STONE, CL'.

Breeder: Discovered by Edward Marsh (United States, 1942).
Parentage: Sport of 'Christopher Stone'.
Classification: Climbing Hybrid Tea.
This is a brilliant crimson red climber with very large, semi-double, scented flowers and an unusual capacity for growth, reputedly reaching heights of about 20 ft (6 m). The plant is remontant in repeated flushes during the blooming season. It performs best in a warm climate like that of California.

'Christopher Stone, Cl'.

'CHROMATELLA' ('Cloth of Gold').

Breeder: Coquereau (France, 1841).
Parentage: Seedling of 'Lamarque'.
Classification: Tea-Noisette.
'Chromatella' opens golden yellow with cream outer petals. The yellow fades to cream, outer petals first,

leaving the center a deeper color for longer. The petal reverse is light yellow. The flowers are large and double with a cupped, globular form and have a light scent of tea. The petals may be roughly quartered. The plant reaches its full potential in a warm, dry climate where it will bloom prolifically in continuous flushes during the blooming season and will grow to about 12 ft (3.65 m).

'Chromatella'.

'CHRYSLER IMPERIAL, CL.'.

('Grimpant Chrysler Imperial').
Breeder: Discovered by Paul B. Begonia (United States, 1956).
Parentage: Sport of 'Chrysler Imperial' (HT, Lammerts, 1952).
Classification: Climbing Hybrid Tea.
Imagine a rose named for an automobile. Well, here it is, or at least that was the intent with the name of the bush form of this rose. Fittingly it is an elegant dark, velvety crimson color with a rich fragrance and very large, double flowers formed like classic Hybrid Teas. This variety is remontant in continuous flushes during the blooming season. The plant has semi-glossy, dark green foliage and grows vigorously to about 12 ft (3.65 m). It can be observed at Roseraie du Val-de-Marne (France), Roseto Carla Fineschi (Italy) and Sangerhausen (Germany).

'Chrysler Imperial, Cl.'.

'CICILY LASCELLES'.

Breeder: Alister Clark (Australia, 1932).
Parentage: 'Frau Oberhofgärtner Singer' x 'Scorcher'.
Classification: Climbing Hybrid Tea according to the stated parentage, but the rose being grown at the present may be a Gigantea hybrid.
Dark pink buds open to light pink flowers lightly flushed with coral. They become more truly pink with age. The flower form is large, semi-double and flat. There are a couple of rows of large petals centered by golden yellow stamens and usually a small ring of petaloids that fold over to reveal the darker pink of the reverse. They bloom in flushes throughout the flowering season. The plant is well clothed in large, light green foliage and grows to at least 10 ft (3 m). The rose seems to be grown only in Australia and New Zealand.

'Cidade De Lisboa'.

'CIDADE DE LISBOA'.

Breeder: Moreira da Silva (Portugal, 1939).
Parentage: 'Belle Portugaise' x 'Madame Edouard Herriot'.
Classification: Large-Flowered Climber.
This rose carries many of the characteristics of its Hybrid

Gigantea seed parent. The flowers are mildly fragrant, salmon-pink fading to light pink, large, semi-double, high-centered and have mucronate tips on the broad outer petals. The leaves are large and light green. It grows vigorously. The rose can be seen at Roseto Carla Fineschi (Italy) and Sangerhausen (Germany).

'CINDERELLA, CL.'.

Breeder: Sequoia Nursery (United States, 1975).
Parentage: 'Cécile Brunner' x 'Peon'.
Classification: Climbing Miniature.
The flowers of this pretty little rose are very fragrant, small, very double and light pink fading at the outer petals to white. They are held singly or in small clusters and rebloom in continuous flushes during the flowering season. The rose can be trained as a small climber of 6 to 8 ft (1.8 to 2.5 m). It seems not to be grown in any public gardens, but it is commercially available.

'Circus, Cl.'.

'CIRCUS, CL.'.

Breeder: Discovered by House (Unknown, 1961).
Parentage: Sport of 'Circus'.
Classification: Climbing Floribunda.
The very full, medium-sized, high-centered flowers are initially yellow with flushes of coral. As they age, the petal tips turn deep pink and the yellow morphs to cream.The outer petals reflex into points giving the flowers a star-like outline. There is a moderate fragrance. The flowers are held in large clusters and bloom in continuous seasonal flushes. Dark green, semi-glossy foliage clothes the canes. They will reach up to about 8 ft (2.5 m).

'CITRUS BURST' (Radfifth).

Breeder: William J. Radler (United States, 2009).
Parentage: 'Fourth of July' x 'Johann Strauss'
Classification: Large-Flowered Climber.
There are pink and creamy white stripes on the outer to mid-part of the petals and yellow in the center of the flower. The stamens with their dark reddish filaments stand out against the delicate colors of the petals. The flowers are medium to large-sized, semi-double, cupped and are carried in small clusters. The plant is clothed in glossy, dark green foliage and will grow to about 12 ft (3.65 m).

'CITY GIRL' ('Country Cottage').

Breeder: Harkness (United Kingdom, 1985).
Parentage: 'Armada' x 'Compassion'
Classification: Large-Flowered Climber.
Deep coral pink buds open to mildly fragrant, salmon-colored, large, semi-double flowers with yellow petal bases that fade to light pink with darker centers, then to almost white. The flower form is cupped, petals reflexed at the tips. Blooming is remontant in continuous flushes during the blooming season. The foliage is dark green and glossy. My plant, probably typical, has never grown to more than about 8 ft (2.5 m). The habit is that of a shrubby climber. The name honors the centenary of The London School for Girls.

'City Girl'.

'CITY OF LONDON'.

Breeder: Harkness (United Kingdom, 1986).
Parentage: 'New Dawn' x 'Radox Bouquet'.

Classification: Floribunda or Shrub.
This is a rose of delicate coloring, fit for a bride's bouquet. The buds have light pink guard petals and deeper pink inner petals that can be seen in the high centered form. The petals fade as they open out wide and become almost white. The medium-sized, double flowers have a rich fragrance and are held in small clusters on long stems. They repeat their bloom in flushes. The foliage is medium green and glossy. A cool, mild climate (US Pacific NW or the United Kingdom) is best for this variety where it will grow to about 7 ft (2 m) and can be trained as a small climber.

'City of London'.

'CLAIR AUSTIN'.

Breeder: David C. H. Austin (United Kingdom, 2007).
Parentage: Unknown.
Classification: Shrub (English Rose).
The flowers of 'Clair Austin' look and smell like vanilla. The soft yellow buds begin to fade, on opening, to cream, then white while the centers remain darker. The flowers are medium to large-sized, very full and are produced mainly singly, but sometimes in small clusters as well. The flower form is globular with incurved, often quartered, petals. There are reports of flowers balling in wet weather. This rose repeats its flowering in flushes of seasonal bloom. The canes and their medium green foliage are healthy. The plant will grow to about 8 ft (2.5 m) according to the breeder.

'Clair Matin'.

'CLAIR MATIN'.

('Grimpant Clair Matin').
Breeder: Marie-Louise (Louisette) Meilland (France, 1960).
Parentage: 'Fashion' x (['Independence' x' Orange Triumph'] x 'Phyllis Bide')
Classification: Large-Flowered Climber.
The flowers begin as deep crimson buds, then crimson flowers that fade soon to light pink. They are medium-sized, semi-double and scented like a sweetbrier. The petals are gently ruffled at first, but flatten out as the flower opens out to form several orderly rows of petals within a circular outline. The blooms are carried in small clusters. They repeat well in flushes. The plant will grow to about 12 ft (3.65 m).

'Claire Jacquier'.

'CLAIRE JACQUIER'.

('Mademoiselle Claire Jacquier').
Breeder: Alexandre Bernaix (France, 1887).
Parentage: Polyantha x Tea.
Classification: This unusual cross doesn't easily fit into any known class. It is usually described as a Noisette, a decision probably based on its appearance.
Long, narrow, pointed yellow buds open to yellow-cream blooms that begin to fade quickly to cream while retaining the darker color in the centers for longer. The flowers are small, double and formed in medium clusters. There is one main bloom with an occasional repeat later in the season and hips may follow. The almost thornless canes are covered with large, glossy, dark green foliage and will grow to about 10 ft (3 m). The plant is shade tolerant.

'CLARENCE HOUSE'.

Breeder: Amanda Beales (United Kingdom, 2000).
Parentage: 'City of York' x 'Aloha'.
Classification: Large-Flowered Climber.
This rose is especially pretty when partially open and the cream outer petals contrast with the tightly cupped yellow inner petals. With time, the whole flower becomes white to cream and opens out flatter, but is still filled with many petals like an old rose. The flowers are strongly fragrant, medium-sized, full and are carried in small clusters. They repeat their bloom in regular flushes during the blooming season. The canes have medium-sized, dark green, glossy foliage and will grow to about 12 ft (3.65 m).

'CLINORA'.
See 'Landora, Cl.'

'CLOSER TO HEAVEN'.

Breeder: Ralph S. Moore (United States, 2005).
Parentage: 0-47-19 x MORqueencrest. 0-47-19 = Rosa wichurana x 'Floradora'.
Classification: Large-Flowered Climber.
The striking flowers are dark, velvety red with blackish-red petal tips, softly fragrant, semi-double, medium-sized and arranged in large clusters. They are centered by large bunches of light yellow stamens. The most distinguishing feature is the fringed and mossy (crested) sepals inherited from the pollen parent. They are once-blooming early in the season. The plants have dark green foliage and can grow to about 10 ft (3 m). The rose can be found only in a few private gardens.

'Clothilde Soupert, Cl.'.

'CLOTHILDE SOUPERT, CL.'.

Breeder: Dingee and Conard (1901, Luxembourg).
Parentage: Sport of 'Clothilde Soupert'
Classification: Climbing Polyantha.
The flowers are white with light pink centers, very fragrant, large and double. All of the petals reflex a little, inward in the center and outward at the edges, giving the flower a packed with curled petals look. The flowers are produced in small clusters. The bloom is fully remontant in regular seasonal flushes. The canes and foliage are healthy except for a tendency to mildew and they are hardy to USDA zone 5b. The rose is quite vigorous, growing to as much as 15 ft (4.55 m).

'CLOTH OF GOLD'.
See 'Chromatella'.

'Cloud 10'.

'CLOUD 10'.

Breeder: William J. Radler (United States, 2005).
Parentage: (Seedling x 'Pretty Lady') x unknown.
Classification: Large-Flowered Climber.
This is a very attractive white climber, added in 2005 and available commercially in the United States. When first opened the flowers have white outer petals and a soft creamy peach center. The color fades in time leaving a pure white rose. The flowers are medium-sized, very full, high-centered like a Hybrid Tea and are carried mostly singly or sometimes in small clusters. The canes are clothed with large, matte, dark green foliage and will grow to about 8 ft (2.45 m).

'Clytemnestra'.

'CLYTEMNESTRA'.

Breeder: Rev. Joseph Hardwick Pemberton (United Kingdom, 1915).
Parentage: 'Trier' x 'Liberty'.
Classification: Hybrid Musk.
The newly opened bloom is salmon-pink with salmon and yellow at the petal bases. The flowers are small, semi-double, strongly fragrant and are carried in large clusters. The salmon color fades very quickly to pink, but a touch of yellow remains in the center. The rather narrow petals reflex lengthwise and become quilled. The plant repeats its bloom regularly in continuous seasonal flushes. It will grow in a bushy form to about 10 ft (3 m) in a warm climate.

'Cochineal Glory, Cl.'.

'COCHINEAL GLORY, CL.'.

Breeder: Discovered by Max Vogel (Germany, 1945).
Parentage: Sport of 'Cochineal Glory'.
Classification: Climbing Hybrid Tea.
I have only seen this rose at Sangerhausen (Germany). The flowers are light red, large and semi-double to lightly double. They lack fragrance. The fully opened flowers have strongly curled back petals in a slightly ragged style. The plant grows to about 10 ft. (3 m).

'Cocktail'.

'COCKTAIL'.

Breeder: Francis Meilland (France, 1957).
Parentage: ('Independence' x 'Orange Triumph') x 'Phyllis Bide'.
Classification: Shrub.
'Cocktail' is a very showy rose when it first opens; bright red, medium-sized, single flowers with large, bright yellow centers. Unfortunately, these appealing colors soon fade, the red becoming crimson and the yellow changing to white. There is a mild scent of spice. The plant repeats its bloom in regular flushes all during the blooming season. The canes are well armed and covered with glossy foliage. They will grow to at least 8 ft (2.45 m). The plant is hardy to USDA zone 4b.

'Cocorico, Cl.'.

'COCORICO, CL.'.

Breeder: Discovered by David W. Ruston (Australia, 1964).
Parentage: Sport of 'Cocorico' (floribunda, Meilland, 1951).
Classification: Climbing Floribunda.
The medium-sized, single flowers are bright geranium red with deeper color on the petal tips and a lighter color on the petal bases. The center is set off by a crown of golden yellow stamens. Flowers are carried in small clusters. They are repeated in flushes throughout the blooming season. The foliage is dark green and glossy. The plant is described as a pillar rose and will grow to about 8 ft (2.5 m).

'COGNAC, CL.'.

Breeder: Discovered by Reimer Kordes (Germany, 1962).
Parentage: Sport of 'Cognac'.
Classification: Climbing Floribunda.
The newly opened flowers are apricot, fading to pale cream-pink and then to white. There is little scent. The flowers are large, lightly double and are produced in small clusters. The foliage is dark olive green and glossy. The plant will grow sufficiently to be trained as a climber.

'COLCESTRIA'.

Breeder: Benjamin R. Cant & Sons (United Kingdom, 1916).
Parentage: Unknown.
Classification: Climbing Hybrid Tea.
This is a beautiful rose in the classic sense. The color is silvery pink, fading to pale pink, but darker on the petal backs. The flowers are very fragrant, large, very full and high-centered in Hybrid Tea style, but tightly cupped when first opened like a ball of petals. With time, they open up some to wider cups and the outer petals roll outward at the tips. They are held singly or in small clusters and often hang down from their heavy weight. The plant will reach a height of 8 to 10 ft (2.45 to 3 m).

'Colcestria'.

'COLETTE' (Genevieve).

Breeder: Alain Meilland (France, 1994).
Parentage: ('Fiona' x 'Friesia') x 'Prairie Princess'.
Classification: Large-Flowered Climber (Romantica).
This rose is apricot-pink on first opening, but soon fades to pink. The flowers are large, full, sometimes quartered

and have a strong scent of tea. They are carried singly or in small clusters. The flowers may ball in wet conditions so it will do best in a warm, dry climate although I have grown it with some success in the rainy Pacific Northwest. The plant is healthy, hardy to USDA zone 5b and will grow to about 8 ft (2.45 m). Colette was a famous French novelist.

'COLIBRI 2010', 'COLIBRI FARBFESTIVAL' and 'COLIBRI'. See 'Raspberry Cream Twirl'.

'COLONIAL WHITE'. See 'Sombreuil'.

'Columbia, Cl.'.

'COLUMBIA, CL.'.

Breeder: Discovered by E. Gurney Hill Co. in 1920, Charles H. Totty Co., Inc. in 1920, Vestal in 1923, all in the United States. Victor Lens discovered a climbing sport in Belgium, 1929.
Parentage: Sport of 'Columbia' (E. G. Hill, 1916).
Classification: Climbing Hybrid Tea.
Long, pointed buds produce flowers with many superlatives: strong fragrance, very large, very double, rich rose-pink fading to light pink. The bloom has excellent remontancy in regular flushes throughout the blooming season. The foliage is dark green and glossy. The plant is a moderately vigorous climber reaching up to about 8 ft (2.45 m).

'Commandant Cousteau, Cl.'

'COMMANDANT COUSTEAU, CL.'

('Le Grand Huit, Cl.', 'Red Flame')
Breeder: Discovered by Michel Adam (France, 2001).
Parentage: Sport of 'Le Grand Huit'.
Classification: Climbing Hybrid Tea.
This rose is graced with flowers that are richly fragrant, large, double, high-centered and bright crimson-red. As they mature they fade little and don't develop bluish tints, but open into more of a cup-like form. They are carried mostly singly, occasionally in small clusters. There is an additional benefit of continuous flushes of bloom during the season. The plant has dark green, glossy foliage and will grow to 12 to 13 ft (3.65 to 4 m). It will perform best in a moderate to warm climate.

'Compassion'.

'COMPASSION' ('Belle de Londres').

Breeder: Harkness (United Kingdom, 1972).
Parentage: 'White Cockade' x 'Prima Ballerina' (Tantau, 1957).
Classification: Large-Flowered Climber.
'Compassion' has beautiful large, full, soft salmon-pink flowers in a high-centered Hybrid Tea form along with a rich fragrance. With time the colors fade to light creamy pink and then to buff-white with yellow tones at the center. The flowers are carried singly or in small clusters. The plant blooms in regular flushes during the blooming season. The foliage is dark green, glossy and disease resistant. The plant will climb, in a well branched, stiff fashion, to about 12 ft (3.65 m).

'Comte De Torres'.

'COMTE DE TORRES'.

Breeder: André (aka Schwartz Fils) Schwartz (France, 1906).
Parentage: 'Kaiserin Auguste Viktoria' x 'Madame Bérard'.
Classification: Large-Flowered Climber. Hybrid Tea type.
This rose has flowers that are large, double and light salmon-pink with a lighter reverse. They rebloom in continuous flushes during the flowering season. The plant is moderately vigorous, growing to about 8 ft (2.5 m) and is a good choice for decorating a pillar.

'COMTE F. DE CHAVAGNAC, CL.'.

Breeder: Siret-Pernet (France, 1929)
Parentage: Sport of 'Comte F. de Chavagnac'.
Classification: Climbing Hybrid Tea.
I observed this rose at Sangerhausen, the only garden where it seems to grow. The flowers are crimson-pink, medium-sized and double. It has none of the peach shading mentioned in the older references for the sport parent. I could not detect a scent. The potential height appears to be about 10 ft (3 m).

'Comte F. De Chavagnac, Cl.'.

'COMTESSE DE GALARD-BÉARN'.

Breeder: Alexandre Bernaix (France, 1893).
Parentage: Unknown.
Classification: Tea-Noisette.
The old references describe this rose as being large, double, very fragrant and light yellow with a pink tint in the center. The rose at Sangerhausen matches that description except that it is all pink. It is probably not the original variety. The rose commercially available at Roseraie du Désert appears to be correct. The flowers are very attractive and old fashioned with a button eye and reflexing outer petals that form a star shape. They are fully remontant in continuous flushes during the flowering season. The plant is fairly vigorous, growing to 10 or 12 ft (3 or 3.5 m), a good height for growing over an arbor.

'COMTESSE DE NOGHERA'.

Breeder: Gilbert Nabonnand (France, 1902).
Parentage: 'Reine Emma des Pays-Bas' x 'Paul Nabonnand'.
Classification: Tea.
This tall-growing Tea has attractive coloration. The petals are light salmon-pink with a darker, more pink center. The outer petals fade to vey light cream and with time the whole bloom fades as well. The flowers are very large and very double and are moderately fragrant. This

variety is fully remontant in regular flushes. The plant grows to about 10 ft (3 m) and can be trained as a climber.

'Comtesse De Noghera'.

'COMTESSE VANDAL, CL.'.

('Countess Vandal, Cl.', 'Grimpant Comtesse Vandal')
Breeder: Discovered by Jackson & Perkins (United States, 1936), Copas Rose Nursery (Australia, 1941).
Parentage: Sport of 'Comtesse Vandal'.
Classification: Climbing Hybrid Tea.
This variety has very large, double light salmon-pink petals with deep salmon-pink petal reverses. The flower has a high-centered Hybrid Tea form that shows off the colors beautifully, allowing a view of both petal surfaces at once. As the flower opens it fades to pale pink and then to white. The individual blooms are borne singly or in small clusters and are summer-flowering only. The disease-resistant plant is has moderate vigor and can be grown as a pillar rose.

'Comtesse Vandal, Cl.'.

'CONCERTO, CL.' (Mecertsar).

Breeder: Discovered by Georges Truffaut (France, 1968).
Parentage: Sport of 'Concerto' (Meilland, 1953).
Classification: Climbing Floribunda.
The flowers are mildly fragrant, medium-sized semi-double and geranium red, with an open form in medium clusters and bloom in great profusion. The blooming is repeated in regular flushes during the growing season. The red of the flowers contrasts attractively with the dark green, glossy foliage. The plant grows sufficiently tall to be trained to a pillar. The Floribunda sport parent, 'Concerto' (Meilland, 1953) is distinct from the buff/yellow Shrub (Meilland, 1994) or the Hybrid Tea (Meilland, 1988) both with the same name.

'Concerto, Cl.'.

'CONDESA DE SÁSTAGO, CL.'

Breeder: Discovered by Vestal (United States, 1936).
Parentage: Sport of 'Condesa de Sástago' (hybrid tea, Dot 1930)
Classification: Climbing Hybrid Tea.
Coral-red upper petals and deep yellow petal reverses, changing over time to crimson-cerise and soft yellow, creates a lovely bicolor effect. The flowers are cupped, large and very full and are carried in small clusters. They are moderately fragrant of spice. The rose is remontant in flushes of bloom during the flowering season. The canes are clothed with light green foliage and will grow in an upright fashion to cover a small trellis.

'Condesa De Sástago, Cl.'.

'CONFIDENCE, CL.'.

Breeder: Discovered by Ignace Hendrickx (Belgium, 1961).
Parentage: Sport of 'Confidence' (Hybrid Tea, Meilland, 1951).
Classification: Climbing Hybrid Tea.
With light pink outer petals, darker coral-pink centers and very large, double, high-centered blooms this pretty rose is formed very much in the Hybrid Tea mold. In hot weather it developes more coral tones. When fully open to a shallow cupped form it will reveal soft yellow petal bases. The petal reverses have flushes of yellow along with the pink. The canes are provided with dark green, leathery foliage and the capacity to grow tall enough to train to a small trellis or pillar.

'CONQUISTADOR' (FRYfocus).

Breeder: Gareth Fryer (United Kingdom, 2004).
Parentage: Unknown.
Classification: Large-Flowered Climber.
The flowers are fragrant, medium to large, very double and deep, brilliant red with rolled back petals. The plant has a growth potential to about 10 ft (3 m). It is remontant in continuous seasonal flushes and appears to be an outstanding garden rose.

'CONQUISTADOR'.

Breeder: Sean Pineau (Unknown, 1983).
Parentage: Unknown.
Classification: Large-Flowered Climber.
I was unable to find this rose in Bagatelle Park (France) or Roseto Carla Fineschi (Italy), the two public gardens where it is said to be grown. Photos on the HMF website show a lightly double, medium-sized, coral-pink rose with light cream reverse and petal bases. The leaves appear shiny. The rose received a silver medal in the Madrid Rose Trials of 1985.

'Conquistador' (Fryer.)

'CONSTANCE SPRY'.

Breeder: David C. H. Austin (United Kingdom, 1961).
Parentage: 'Belle Isis' x 'Dainty Maid'.
Classification: Shrub (English Rose).
Constance Spry was one of the earliest roses bred by Austin and served as a stepping stone to roses that would look and smell like old roses, but would be remontant. It had the first two reqirements with its large, full, deeply cupped pink flowers scented of myrrh, but it is only summer blooming. 'Chaucer', an offspring, succeeds in producing some additional blooms in the fall. 'Constance Spry' has a potential height of 15 ft (4.57 m) according to the breeder. It is very disease resistant and hardy to USDA zone 5b.

'Constance Spry'.

'Constanze'.

'CONSTANZE' ('Shogun').

Breeder: Hans Jürgen Evers (Germany, pre-2000).
Parentage: Unknown.
Classification: Large-Flowered Climber.
'Constanze' flowers are large, high-centered like a Hybrid Tea, double and deep pink with yellow petal bases. They are borne in small clusters. There is a mild fragrance. The flowering is remontant in flushes during the entire blooming season. The plant is known to climb to a height of about 10 to 13 ft (3 to 4 m).

'Constanze'.

'COOKIES'.

Breeder: Meilland International (France, 1999).
Parentage: Unknown.
Classification: Large-Flowered Climber.
The flowers are medium-sized, semi-double and orange-red. The reverse is less orange in tone and more red than the petal surface. I have seen it recently at the Fineschi garden in Italy and several years ago at Parc Floral de la Source in France. The plant has glossy, dark green foliage and will grow sufficiently to be trained as a small climber.

'Cookies'.

'COPACABANA'.

Breeder: Francois Dorieux I (France, 1966).
Parentage: 'Coup de Foudre' x Seedling.
Classification: Large-Flowered Climber.
This rose has mildly fragrant, double, medium-sized, vermilion flowers with a subtle flush of russet. They are carried in small clusters. The flowers open out to flattened domes filled with petals curled outward at their tips. The flowers repeat their bloom in regular seasonal flushes. The canes are clothed with disease resistant, dark green leaves. The plant will grow to a height of 10 ft or more.

'Copacabana'.

'COPENHAGEN' (Kobenhavn).

Breeder: Niels Dines Poulsen (Denmark, 1964).
Parentage: 'Hakuun' x 'Ena Harkness'.
Classification: Large-Flowered Climber.
'Copenhagen' has flowers that are moderately scented, large, lightly double, crimson (almost scarlet) and are borne singly or in small clusters. The repeat flowering is very good and occurs in regular flushes during the blooming season. The foliage is large and dark green. The plant has a potential height of about 10 ft (3 m). It can be pruned and grown as a shrub or given support and grown as a climber.

'Coral Dawn'.

'Coquette Des Blanches'.

'COQUETTE DES BLANCHES'.

Breeder: François Lacharme (France, 1871).
Parentage: 'Mademoiselle Blanche Lafitte' x 'Sappho'.
Classification: Hybrid Bourbon.
The old sources for this rose describe it as pure white. The rose as it is grown now may not be the original variety. It has pink buds and opens pale pink. When it fades to white the color is retained in the center. There is a moderate fragrance. The floral form is medium-sized, double and deeply cupped. The small inner petals are quartered and the outer ones roll back. There may be a green pip in the center of the flower. Blooming occurs in regular seasonal flushes. The plant is very disease resistant, has semi-shiny foliage and is vigorous enough to train as a small climber.

'CORAL DAWN'.

Breeder: Eugene S. "Gene" Boerner (United States, 1952).
Introduced in United States by Jackson & Perkins Co. in 1952.
Parentage: (seedling of 'New Dawn' x unnamed yellow Hybrid Tea) x unnamed orange-red Polyantha.
Classification: Large-Flowered Climber.
Deep coral-pink buds open to coral-pink, moderately fragrant, medium to large, cupped, full flowers carried singly or in small clusters. As the flowers open they become lighter and pinker. The repeat flowering is very good in continuous flushes all through the blooming season. The foliage is dark green and glossy. It is healthy except for a tendancy to blackspot. The plant is very hardy, rated to USDA zone 5b with unofficial reports of zone 3. It grows to about 12 ft (3.65 m).

'Coral Glow'.

'CORAL GLOW'.

Breeder: Paul Croix (France, 1964).
Parentage: 'Spectacular' x Seedling.
Classification: Large-Flowered Climber.
This rose has salmon-pink, semi-double (15 to 20 petals), mildly scented, large flowers carried in large clusters. It is very remontant and very floriferous. The plant can be expected to grow to about 10 ft (3 m).

'Coral Satin'.

'CORAL SATIN'.

Breeder: William and Sophia Zombory (United States, 1960).
Parentage: 'New Dawn' x 'Fashion'.
Classification: Large-Flowered Climber.
'Coral Satin' has coral-pink, large, double, richly scented flowers with a high-centered Hybrid Tea form. The color fades to more true pink. The flowers are carried singly or in small clusters. As the rose opens the petals reflex at the tips with the outer petals forming triangles. The canes are prickly and clothed with dark green glossy foliage. They are very hardy. The plant will grow to about 8 ft (2.45 m), enough to decorate a pillar.

'CORALINE' ('Opaline', 'Eveopa').

Breeder: André Eve (France, 1976).
Parentage: Unknown.
Classification: Large-Flowered Climber.
'Coraline' was the name originally given this rose by the breeder. It was later sold under the name 'Opaline'. 'Coraline' is a good fit since the flowers are coral-pink on opening. The inevitable fading is more toward true pink and lightens the outer petals first. The flowers are medium-sized and semi-double. The foliage is matte, dark green and healthy. Reblooming is in continuous flushes during the flowering season. The plant will climb to 12 or 13 ft (3.65 or 4 m).

'Coraline'.

'CORDON ROUGE'.

Breeder: Maurice Combe, Vilmorin-Andrieux (France, 1970).
Parentage: Unknown.
Classification: Large-Flowered Climber.
The flowers of this rose are bright orange-red (vermilion), large-sized, double and tend to not open enough to show their stamens. The petals reflex in triangular shapes at the tips giving a star-like appearance. The rose is remontant in regular seasonal flushes. The plant will grow sufficiently to be trained as a climber. It grows at Sangerhausen and Roseto Carla Fineschi.

'CORNELIA'.

Breeder: Rev. Joseph Hardwick Pemberton (United Kingdom, 1925).
Parentage: Unknown.
Classification: Hybrid Musk.
The buds are deep pink and the flowers start out apricot-pink with flushes of yellow at the center. They soon open out and fade, becoming lighter and more lavender-pink until nearly white. They are small, full, richly scented of musk and and have lightly wavy petals. Very large clusters are formed in the fall, smaller ones early in the year. The foliage is small, dark green and glossy and the canes are thornless or nearly so. Growth is to about 10 ft (3 m). The plant is hardy to USDA zone 5b and shade tolerant.

'Cordon Rouge'.

'Cornelia'.

This rose has apricot-orange flowers flushed yellow at the center that become more rose toned with time, outer petals first. The flowers are medium-sized, lightly double and are carried singly or in small clusters. The plant is remontant and will grow to about 7 ft (2 m).

'COROLLE'.

Breeder: Simon (Simó) Dot (Spain, 1962).
Parentage: 'Danse du Feu' x 'Cocktail' (shrub, Meilland, 1957)
Classification: Large-Flowered Climber.
I saw this climbing rose at the Europa Rosarium, Sangerhausen, Germany and was impressed with the decorative effect of its bright red flowers. They are mildly scented, semi-double, medium-sized and open out as a flat rostte to show the golden yellow stamens. The foliage is dark green and glossy.

'Corolle'.

'CORTÈGE'.

Breeder: Maurice Combe (France, 1976).
Parentage: Unknown.
Classification: Large-Flowered Climber.

'Cortège'.

'COSMOS'.

('Pluton', Poulcy007, POUlyc007).
Breeder: L. Pernille Olesen and Mogens Nyegaard Olesen (Denmark, 1994).
Parentage: Poulsint x Seedling.
Classification: Large-Flowered Climber.
This pretty rose has flowers that are small, double, fragrant of wild rose, cupped and coral-pink. The petals roll back at the tips in an attractive way. The plant has glossy, dark green foliage and will climb in a shrub-like manner to about 10 ft (3 m).

'COUNTESS OF STRADBROKE'.

Breeder: Alister Clark (Australia, 1928).
Parentage: Seedling of 'Walter C. Clark'.
Classification: Large-Flowered Climber.
This attractive dark red climber has strongly scented, large, double flowers usually carried singly, but also in small clusters. The flower form is globular at first, the opens out and flattens some. The plant is fully remontant in seasonal flushes. The canes are almost thornless and are covered with medium green wrinkled (rugose) foliage. They will grow to about 15 ft (4.55 m).

'Countess of Stradbroke'.

'COUP DE FOUDRE, CL.'.

Breeder: Discovered by Gianfranco Fineschi (Italy, 1976).
Parentage: Sport of 'Coup de Foudre'.
Classification: Climbing Floribunda.
This is a Floribunda type climber with its orange-red, large, ruffled, lightly double, cupped flowers produced singly or in small clusters. There is a mild fragrance. The bloom is remontant in seasonal flushes. The foliage is glossy bronze-green. 'Coup de Foudre' means a "flash of lightning".

'Coup De Foudre, Cl.'.

'COUPE D'HÉBÉ'.

Breeder: Jean Laffay (France, 1840).
Parentage: Bourbon hybrid x Rosa chinensis hybrid.
Classification: Climbing Bourbon.
'Coupe d'Hébé' has very fragrant, large, very double pink flowers with a touch of mauve. The form is deeply cupped and only partially opens with age. The main bloom occurs in the spring or early summer with a few flowers opening later in the season. The plant has dark green foliage and will climb to about 8 ft (2.5 m). It is hardy to USDA zone 5b.

'Coupe D'Hébé'.

'COURIER'.

Breeder: Alister Clark (Australia, pre-1930).
Parentage: Rosa gigantea x 'Archiduc Joseph'.
Classification: Hybrid Gigantea.
'Courier' has fragrant, medium-sized, double, light pink flowers fading almost to white. The reverse is a deeper pink that contrasts nicely with the light pink of the reflexed petal tips. The flowers are borne in small clusters and are once blooming early in the spring. The healthy foliage is typical Gigantea with large, light green, drooping leaflets. The plant will grow to a height of about 20 to 25 ft (6 to 8 m). It plant reacts negatively to much pruning. It will do best in a frost-free climate.

'CRAMOISI SUPÉRIEUR, CL.'.

('Agrippina, Cl.', James Sprunt, 'Lady Brisbane, Cl'.)
Breeder : Couturier fils (France, 1885). May have been earlier.
Parentage: seedling of 'Cramoisi Supérieur'.
Classification: Climbing China / Bengale.
Flowers are crimson with occasional white streaks, medium-sized, very double and have a mild fruity scent. The flower form begins deeply cupped with a globular shape and rolled-back petals. Then, it opens more as a flattened, shallow cup. The flowers are carried singly and in small clusters. There is one main summer bloom with occasional repeats later. The canes are armed and have

light green foliage. They will grow vigorously to about 20 ft (6 m). The plant is hardy only to USDA zone 7b and does best in a warm climate.

'Cramoisi Supérieur, Cl.'.

'CRAZY FOR YOU'.
See ' Fourth of July'.

'CRÈME DE LA CRÈME' (GANcre).

Breeder: Douglas L. Gandy (United Kingdom, before 1995).
Parentage: 'Morgengruss' x 'Whisky Mac'.
Classification: Large-Flowered Climber.
The color is cream which fades almost to white in time, but retains the color longer in the center. The flowers are moderately scented, large, double and have a high-centered Hybrid Tea form that opens out to a rosette with wavy petals. They are held singly or in small clusters. The bloom repeats well in seasonal flushes. The canes are covered with large, deep green leaves and will grow to about 10 ft (3 m).

'Crème De La Crème'.

'CREPESCULE'.

Breeder: Francis Dubreuil (France, 1904).
Parentage: Unknown.
Classification: Tea-Noisette.
The buds are deep apricot. They open as deep apricot flowers that fade to light apricot-buff, outer petals first. The flowers are medium-sized, semi-double and come in small clusters. They are most floriferous in warm climates, but are most colorful in cool climates like my own Pacific Northwest, US. They also need full sun for best color. The plant is said to be hardy to USDA zone 6b. It repeats in seasonal flushes. The height is about 12 ft (3.65 m).

'Crepescule'.

'CRESTED JEWEL'.

Breeder: Ralph S. Moore (United States, before 1964).
Parentage: 'Little Darling' x 'Crested Moss'.
Classification: Mossy Climber.
This is a small climber, only 5 ft (1.5 m) and could even be considered a shrub, but it is in proportion to the small, semi-double, bright pink flowers with their mossy sepals. The pink fades on the outer petals to pale pink leaving the stronger color in the center longer. There is a mild fragrance. The plant is rated hardy to USDA zone 5b. It repeats occasionally after the main bloom.

'Crested Jewel'.

'CRIMSON CONQUEST'.

Breeder: Discovered by Chaplin Bros., Ltd., United Kingdom, 1931).
Parentage: Sport of 'Red Letter Day' an old Hybrid Tea.
Class: Cl. Hybrid Tea.
The rose has semi-double, medium-sized, deep scarlet-crimson flowers that hold their color well as they age. The petal bases are white and there are some short white streaks radiating out. There is a slight fragrance. The flowers open wide with wavy petals. They bloom in flushes throughout the season. The foliage is glossy and bright green, unlike that of 'Red Letter Day', the supposed parent, which is matte and grey-green. The plant is a vigorous climber of 14 to 16 ft (4.27 to 4.8 m).

'Crimson Conquest'.

'CRIMSON CASCADE'.

('Fryclimbdown').
Breeder: Gareth Fryer (United Kingdom, before 1990).
Introduced in United Kingdom by Fryer's Roses/Fryer's Nurseries Ltd. in 1991
Parentage: Unknown.
Classification: Large-Flowered Climber.
The velvety dark red, Hybrid Tea-style flowers are medium to large-sized, lightly double and mildly fragrant. They are held in small clusters. The flowers are good for cutting because of a long vase life. Blooming is remontant in seasonal flushes. The foliage is dark green and glossy. The plant is shade tolerant, is susceptible to blackspot and has branching growth to about 10 ft (3 m).

'Crimson Cascade'.

'CRIMSON DESCANT'.

Breeder: Cants of Colchester (United Kingdom, 1972).
Parentage: 'Dortmund' x 'Étendard'.
Classification: Large-Flowered Climber.
This floriferous rose has large, double, lightly scented, bright crimson flowers carried singly or in small clusters. They are complimented by the deep green glossy foliage. The blooming is fully remontant in flushes during the blooming season. The plant is shade tolerant, healthy and will reach about 13 ft (4 m) in height, good for pillars and trellises.

'Crimson Descant'.

'CRIMSON PILLAR' (MEifulcen).

Breeder: Meilland International (France, 2003).
Parentage: Unknown.
Classification: Large-Flowered Climber.
The flowers open more scarlet than crimson, but soon become crimson with some very dark red flushes. The white petal reverse creates a rather surprising effect. The flowers are medium to large-sized, double and borne in small clusters. There is little or no fragrance. The bloom repeats well in seasonal flushes. The foliage is semi-glossy and dark green. The plant will climb to about 10 ft (3 m) and is hardy only to USDA zone 7b, so it is best for a warm climate.

'Crimson Pillar'.

'CRIMSON GLORY, CL.'.

('Grimpant Crimson Glory').
Breeder: Discovered by Millar Bros. (South Africa, 1941); Richardson (1944); Antonio Naungayan (U S, 1946).
Parentage: Sport of 'Crimson Glory'.
Classification: Climbing Hybrid Tea.
The long, pointed deep crimson buds open in a spiraled, high-centered Hybrid Tea form, becoming cupped as they open further. The flowers are deep velvety crimson, very large, double and carried mostly singly, but sometimes in small clusters. They have a rich damask scent. Flowering is remontant in flushes during the regular season. Growth is bushy with a height of about 10 to 12 ft (3 to 3.65 m). The plant is very hardy to USDA zone 4b.

'Crimson Glory, Cl.'.

'CRIMSON SKY.'

(MEIgrappo, ' Negresco').
Breeder: Alain Meilland (France, 2006).
Parentage: ('Cappa Magna' x 'Cassandre') x ('Ulmer Münster' x 'Altissimo').
Classification: Large-Flowered Climber.
Here is a rose with old-fashioned style flowers in a bright, modern color described by an admirer as unfading fire engine red. They are large, full, with a mild apple fragrance and are carried in small clusters. The plant will bloom in flushes all during the blooming season and will grow vigorously to about 12 ft (3.65 m). It is hardy to USDA zone 5b.

'Criterion, Cl.'.

'CRITERION, CL.'.

Breeder: Discovered by Gressard (1978).
Parentage: Sport of 'Criterion'.
Classification: Climbing Hybrid Tea.
This rose has deep rose pink, very large, double, moderately scented flowers with a classical Hybrid Tea form. They are held singly or in small clusters. The rebloom occurs in regular seasonal flushes. The plant has dark green foliage and will grow to about 10 ft (3 m).

'Croix Blanche'.

'CROIX BLANCHE'.

Breeder: Paul Croix France, 1982.
Parentage: Unknown.
Classification: Large-Flowered Climber.
'Croix Blanche' is a lovely white climber with cream-colored buds and very large, lightly scented, double flowers carried singly or in small clusters. The blooming pattern is plentiful and remontant in seasonal flushes. The flowers are damaged by wet conditions so the plant does best in a warm, dry climate. The canes are generously clothed with dark green foliage. They will grow to about 10 ft (3 m).

'CROIX D'OR'.

Breeder: Paul Croix (France, 1985).
Parentage: Unknown.
Classification: Large-Flowered Climber.
'Croix d'Or' translates as cross of gold and is also a play on the breeder's name. The flowers are an unusually rich, pure shade of yellow that is slow to fade. They are double, large and globose in shape, lightly scented and are held singly or in small clusters.

'Crown Princess Margarita'.

'CROWN PRINCESS MARGARITA'.

(AUSwinter).
Breeder: David C. H. Austin (United Kingdom, 1990).
Parentage: Seedling x Abraham Darby.
Classification: Shrub (English Rose).
The flowers of this rose are apricot, fading to pale apricot on the edges and remaining darker in the center. They are large, very full and cupped at first, then they open out to a flattened rosette. There is a rich, fruit-like fragrance. The individual blooms are mostly carried singly or sometimes in small clusters. The rebloom occurs in seasonal flushes. The plant will grow, in a bushy style, to at least 6 ft (1.85 m).

'ČSL. Legie'.

'ČSL. LEGIE' ('Corporal Legie').

Breeder: Jan Böhm (Czechoslovakia (former), 1933).
Parentage: 'Paul's Scarlet Climber' x 'Jan Böhm' (hybrid tea, Böhm, 1928).

Classification: Climbing Hybrid Tea, Large-Flowered Climber.
Jan Böhm has scored again with this garden worthy rose. According to the latest Rosenverzeichnis (catalogue of the collection) from Sangerhausen, the garden where it is grown, the flowers are double, very large and a dark crimson. It can be grown as a climber of average height.

'Cupid'.

'CUPID'.

Breeder: Benjamin R. Cant & Sons (United Kingdom, 1914).
Parentage: Unknown.
Classification: Large-Flowered Climber.
'Cupid' has light pink flowers with apricot shading in the centers that harmonizes with the large bunches of golden stamens. The colors soon fade to pale pink and white. The flowers are single, large, mildly fragrant, cupped, and held in small clusters. The plant is once-blooming, but has an added asset of forming hips. It is very vigorous, growing as much as 15 ft (4.55 m).

'CUPID'S KISSES' (WEKtriscala).

Breeder: Christian Bédard (United States, 2016).
Parentage: 'Tropical Twist' x ('Rosy Outlook' x 'Pretty Lady').
Classification: Climbing Miniature.
The flowers of this beautiful little climber are fragrant, small, semi-double to very lightly double and pure, bright cerise-pink with a lighter reverse. The ruffled petals have white bases that form a white eye. The flowers repeat well. The plant has small, glossy, medium green disease-resistant foliage and will grow to about 6 ft (1.8 m). It is commercially available in the United States.

'Cupid's Kisses'.

'CURIOSITY, CL.' See 'Best Wishes, Cl.'

'CYMBALINE'.

(AUSlean, AUSteen, Cymbeline).
Breeder: David C. H. Austin (United Kingdom, 1983).
Parentage: Seedling x 'Lilian Austin'
Classification: Shrub (English Rose).
This rose is an unusual shade of pink, rather muted and soft looking. The breeder says it is gray-pink. The centers are light yellow. The flowers are scented of myrrh, large, double and are held singly or in small clusters. There is one main bloom with an occasional repeat later in the season and it sets hips. The plant is hardy to USDA zone 5b. It will climb to at least 7 ft. I saw it on the wall at Grignon Castle in Southern France where it was even taller.

'Cymbaline'.

D

'Dr. W. Van Fleet' ('Daybreak').

'DAILY MAIL SCENTED ROSE, CL.'.

Breeder: Discovered by Wm. E.B. Archer & Daughter (United Kingdom, 1930).
Parentage: Sport of 'Daily Mail Scented Rose'.
Classification: Climbing Hybrid Tea.
This is a true sport of the exhibition-style Hybrid Tea and shares all of its virtues including large, double, rich blackish crimson, strongly fragrant flowers carried singly or in small clusters. Long stems make it good for cutting. It also shares a few faults like a tendency to mildew and problems with the flowers burning in the sun. Flowers bloom best in a moderate climate like that of England or Oregon, US. Rebloom occurs in flushes during the regular season.

'Dame De Coeur, Cl.'.

'DAME DE COEUR, CL.'.

Breeder: Discovered by Fred A. Mungia, Sr. (United States, 1984).
Parentage: Sport of 'Dame de Coeur'.
Classification: Climbing Hybrid Tea.
The flowers of this Hybrid Tea-type climber are crimson-red with flushes of cerise. They are scented like an old rose, large-sized, double, globular, then opening to a flattened cup form. They are carried singly (mostly) or in small clusters. The petals may be quartered and ruffled. The plant is well armed, has large, dark green, glossy foliage and will grow, in a branching manner, to about 10 ft (3 m).

'Dainty Bess, Cl.'.

'DAINTY BESS, CL.'.

Breeder: Discovered by Van Barneveld (Unknown, 1935).
Parentage: Sport of 'Dainty Bess'.
Classification: Climbing Hybrid Tea.
Roses with single flowers, such as this one, have a special appeal. Here, the appeal is enhanced by the combination of pink petals and contrasting dark reddish-brown stamens. The flowers are medium-sized, mildly scented and cupped, then opening to flat. They are carried in small clusters. The petals may be wavy. The flowering is remontant throughout the blooming season in regular flushes. The plant is hardy to USDA zone 4b and will grow to 10 or 12 ft (3 to 3.65 m).

'Dame Edith Helen, Cl.'.

'DAME EDITH HELEN, CL.'.

Breeder: Discovered by Howard & Smith (United States, 1930). Discovered by T.J. English & Son (United Kingdom, 1932).
Parentage: Sport of 'Dame Edith Helen'.

Classification: Climbing Hybrid Tea.
This beautiful rose has blooms that begin deep pink nuanced subtly with coral, then fade to light true pink. They are richly scented, very large and very double with a Hybrid Tea coiled, high center and rolled back tips on the outer petals. They occur mostly singly, but sometimes in small clusters. Remontancy is good with continuous flushes of bloom during the blooming season. The canes, well armed and well branched will grow to about 8 ft (2.5 m).

'Danaë'.

'DANAË'.

Breeder: Rev. Joseph Hardwick Pemberton (United Kingdom, 1913).
Parentage: 'Trier' x 'Gloire de Chédane-Guinoisseau'.
Classification: Hybrid Musk.
'Danaë' was one of Pemberton's earliest Hybrid Musks. Although it seems more cream than yellow today, in 1913 it was considered a good true yellow color. The name refers to a mythological shower of gold. The flowers are yellow in the bud, fading quickly to light yellow, then to cream and white. They are semi-double, medium-sized and held singly or in small clusters. The plant reblooms in repeated flushes during the growing season. The canes are clothed with dark green, glossy foliage and will grow to at least 6 ft (1.85 m) with support, enough for a small pillar or trellis.

'DANCING DOLL'.

Breeder: Ralph S. Moore (United States, 1952).
Parentage: 'Étoile Luisante' x 'Sierra Snowstorm'.
Classification: Climbing Floribunda.
This pretty rose has fragrant (wild rose), semi-double, medium-sized, bright rose-pink flowers with a flattened cup form. They occur in small clusters and bloom in continuous flushes during the flowering season. The plant has the potential to grow to about 10 ft (3 m). It can be observed at the San Jose Heritage Rose Garden.

'DANCING QUEEN' (Fryfestoon).

Breeder: Gareth Fryer (United Kingdom, 2004).
Parentage: Unknown.
Classification: Large-Flowered Climber.
This lovely pink Hybrid Tea-style climber has large, double, mildly fragrant flowers that open out from a high-centered bloom to a shallow cup that reveals the light yellow petal bases. The bloom repeats well in continuous flushes during the blooming season. In the fall it produces bright orange hips. The foliage is dark green. The plant will typically grow to about 10 ft (3 m).

'DANNY BOY'.

Breeder: Samuel Darragh McGredy IV (1969).
Parentage: 'Uncle Walter' x 'Milord'.
Classification: Large-Flowered Climber.
'Danny Boy' has flowers of scarlet-orange. In time, they fade to light coral-pink. They are large, double, mildly scented, high centered on first opening and are held singly or in small clusters. The plants have dark green foliage and will grow vigorously to about 16 ft (5 m).

'Danny Boy'.

'DANSE DES SYLPHES'.

('Danse des Sylves', 'Grimpant Danse des Sylphes', MALcair).
Breeder: Charles Mallerin (France, 1959).
Parentage: 'Spectacular' x ('Peace' x 'Independence').
Classification: Large-Flowered Climber, Climbing Floribunda.
This colorful, decorative climber has medium-sized, double, globular flowers of bright geranium-red that become flattened with maturity. They are carried singly or in small clusters. There is litle fragrance. The plant has medium green glossy foliage and will typically climb to about 10 ft (3 m).

'Danse Des Sylphes'.

'DANSE DU FEU'.
See 'Spectacular'.

'DAUPHINE, CL.'.

Breeder: Discovered by Jean-Marie Gaujard (France, 1959).
Parentage: Sport of 'Dauphine' (Floribunda, Gaujard, 1955).
Classification: Climbing Floribunda.
The flowers of this rose are scarlet-pink, large, full, moderately scented and held in small clusters. They begin cupped and end as an orderly rosette. The color becomes more crimson with time. The rebloom is in continuous flushes during the regular blooming season. The plant is almost thornless and grows vigorously to about 16 ft (5 m).

'DAYBREAK'.

('Dr W. Van Fleet').
Breeder: Bred by Dr W. Van Fleet (United States, 1899) and named modestly as 'Daybreak'. Introduced in the United States by Peter Henderson, in spite of the breeder's wishes, as 'Dr W. Van Fleet'.
Parentage: (Rosa wichurana x 'Safrano') x 'Souvenir du Président Carnot'.
Class: Large-Flowered Climber (one of the first).
This lovely rose has sweetly scented, medium to large-sized, open, light pink flowers that are carried singly (mostly) or in small clusters. They are produced once early in the season. The canes are armed with large prickles and clothed with large, glossy, bronze-green leaves. They are extremely vigorous. I once had a plant that grew at least 20 feet (6.1 meters) into a tree with lateral canes spreading out widely. It is hardy and disease resistant.

'DAYDREAM'.

Breeder: Alister Clark (Australia, 1925).
Parentage: 'Souvenir de Gustave Prat' x 'Rosy Morn'.
Classification: Climbing Hybrid Tea.
This is a rose of delicate appearance with mildly fragrant, large, single to semi-double, light pink flowers that open out flat and show their ruffled petals surrounding a large bunch of golden yellow stamens. It blooms in repeated seasonal flushes. The plant is predicted to grow to about 10 or 11 ft (3 to 3.5 m).

'Dearest, Cl.'.

'DEAREST, CL.'.

Breeder: Discovered by David W. Ruston (Australia, 1970).
Parentage: Sport of 'Dearest', (Dickson, 1960).
Classification: Climbing Floribunda.
Would you like to have a Floribunda on steroids? Here's your chance. The newly opened flowers of this rose are

pink with a hint of salmon, but change to pure pink with maturity. They are fragrant, medium to large-sized, lightly double and are grouped singly or in small clusters and repeat prolifically in flushes during the flowering season. The plant has dark green, glossy foliage and will grow to about 10 or 11 ft (3 or 3.5 m).

'DECLIC'.

Breeder: Dominique Croix (France, 1988).
Parentage: Unknown.
Classification: Large-Flowered Climber.
Cerise buds open to light cerise flowers with light petal bases fading to light lilac and white. They are medium-sized, semi-double to lightly double, cupped and are carried in large clusters. The breeder describes the fragrance as exceptional. The plant flowers early and repeats in flushes during the regular blooming season. The bloom is very floriferous. The expected height is about 16 ft (5 m).

'DÉCOR' ('Record').

Breeder: Charles Mallerin (France, 1950).
Parentage: ('Love' x 'Paul's Scarlet Climber') x 'Demain'.
Classification: Large-Flowered Climber.
The clustered flowers of 'Décor' are large, semi-double, scentless and bright scarlet. The bloom form is deeply cupped on opening, but ends up as a flattened cup that reveals the stamens. The roses occur singly or in small clusters. The plant will grow vigorously to about 12 ft (3.65 m). It is grown in the major rose gardens of Europe.

'DÉCOR ARLEQUIN'.

('Meilland Decor Arlequin', 'MEIzourayor').
Breeder: Marie-Louise Meilland (France, 1986).
Parentage: ('Zambra' selfed x 'Suspense' selfed) x 'Arthur Bell'.
Classification: Shrub.
The name of this rose refers to the strongly contrasting colors of the flowers. The upper surface of the petals is

bright cerise and the reverse is bright yellow. As the flowers age the cerise fades to pink and the yellow becomes cream. The cupped blooms are medium-sized, double and are carried singly or in small clusters. The flowering repeats in regular seasonal flushes. In a moderate to warm climate the plant will grow tall enough to be trained as a small climber.

'Décor'.

'Décor Arlequin'.

'DELBARD'S ORANGE CLIMBER'.

('DELpar, 'Grimpant Delbard').
Breeder: Delbard-Chabert (France, 1963).
Parentage: 'Spectacular' x ('Rome Glory' x 'La Vaudoise').
Classification: Large-Flowered Climber.
This showy rose has flowers that are bright orange-red, mildly scented, medium-sized, lightly full, high-centered aging to cupped and are produced in small clusters. The blooms are exhibition quality. Repeat flowering occurs in flushes throughout the blooming season. The plant has glossy, dark green, healthy foliage and grows, with much branching, to about 13 ft (4 m).

'Delbard's Orange Climber'.

'DELLA BALFOUR'.

('Desert Glo', HARblend, 'Royal Pageant').
Breeder: Harkness (United Kingdom, 1994).
Parentage: 'Rosemary Harkness' x 'Elina'.
Classification: Large-Flowered Climber.
This is a rose with apricot-buff, yellow-cream flowers nuanced with pink. They are strongly scented like lemon, double, medium to large-sized and high-centered. They become more cupped as they open out and show their wavy petals. There is one main bloom with some repeats later in the season. The plant grows to about 10 ft (3 m) and is hardy to USDA zone 5b. It is lovely grown as a climber or pruned and grown as a shrub.

'Della Balfour'.

'DEMOKRACIE'.

Breeder: Jan Böhm, 1935, Czechoslovakia (former). Introduced in the United States by Jackson and Perkins in 1950 as 'Blaze Improved'.
Class: Hybrid Multiflora (LCl per ARS).
The deep crimson flowers of this rose are medium to large-sized, double and occur singly or in small clusters. It is quite similar to 'Blaze', but it has a better color and the flowers are larger. The rose repeats well. It can be expected to reach a height of 12 to 15 ft (4-4.5 m).

'Demokracie'.

'DENISE DUCAS' ('Denyse Ducas').

Breeder: Paul Buatois (France, 1953).
Parentage: Unknown.
Classification: Large-Flowered Climber.
This rare rose has large, semi-double, yellow flowers that start out cupped and open out to reveal stamens with red filaments. The plant will reach a height as a climber of about 10 to 13 ft (3 to 4 m).

'DESCHAMPS'.

('Longworth Rambler', 'Madame Deschamps').
Breeder: Deschamps (France, 1877).
Parentage: Unknown.
Classification: Tea-Noisette.
This brightly colored rose is deep cerise-pink with white petal bases, medium-sized, double and is carried in small clusters. The canes are armed with thorns (prickles) and will climb to about 10 ft (3 m). The flowering repeats in regular flushes during the blooming season.

'DESERT GLO'. See 'Della Balfour'.

'Deschamps'.

'DESPREZ À FLEURS JAUNES' ('Desprez'). See 'Jaune Desprez'.

'DETROITER, CL.'.

(Schlösser Brillant, Cl.).
Breeder: Discovered by Jackson & Perkins (United States, 1960).
Parentage: Sport of 'Detroiter' which has 'Crimson Glory' as its pollen parent.
Classification: Climbing Hybrid Tea.
This lovely dark crimson-red Climbing Hybrid Tea has flowers that are fragrant, double, high-centered and large to very large. They are held singly or grouped in small clusters. The rose is remontant in continuous flushes during the blooming season. It is moderately vigorous with a height of about 10 ft (3 m).

'Detroiter, Cl.'.

'Deutsches Rosarium Dortmund'.

'DEUTSCHES ROSARIUM DORTMUND'.

Breeder: Reinhard Noack (Germany, 1994).
Parentage: Unknown.
Classification: Large-Flowered Climber.
This attractive light-pink climber is named for one of the world's most distinguished rose gardens located in Germany. The flowers are small, double and very flat when mature. The stamens are clearly visible. The flowers are arranged in large clusters and repeat their bloom in regular seasonal flushes. The canes are clothed with shiny, medium green foliage and will grow in a shrubby fashion to about 10 ft (3 m).

'DEVON MAID'.

Breeder: Christopher H. Warner (United Kingdom, 1982).
Parentage: 'Casino' x 'Elizabeth of Glamis'.
Classification: Large-Flowered Climber.
The flowers of 'Devon Maid' have a rich, fruity scent. They are large, full, and form small clusters. The rose is summer blooming with occasional repeat flowers later in the season. The plant grows to about 13 ft (4 m).

'Devoniensis, Cl'.

'DEVONIENSIS, CL'.

Breeder: Discovered by Pavitt (Unknown, 1858).
Parentage: Sport of 'Devoniensis' (Tea, Foster, 1838).
Classification: Climbing Tea.
This Tea sport has light yellow flowers aging to cream, then to ivory-white with an occasional pink blush in the center. They are strongly scented of tea, large, very double and carried singly or in small clusters. The petals may be quartered and the outer petals tend to fold up lengthwise with age. The bloom repeats in flushes during the regular flowering season. The plant is very vigorous and the long, strong, arching canes can grow to 16 to 20 ft (5 to 6 m) in a warm climate such as California's. An imposter is widely grown and may be 'Souvenir de la Malmaison, Cl.'.

'Diablotin, Cl.'

'DIABLOTIN, CL.'

(DELposar, 'Diablotin, Grimpant', 'Little Devil, Cl.').
Breeder: Discovered by G. Delbard (France, 1964).
Parentage: Sport of 'Diablotin'.
Classification: Climbing Floribunda.
The name of this rose makes reference to its very bright orange-red (devilish) color. The medium-sized, semi-double to lightly double flowers are solitary or in small clusters. The flower form is cupped at first, then becomes more flattened. There is no fragrance. The plant is fully remontant in flushes. It grows to about 10 ft (3 m).

'DISTINCTION, CL.'.

Breeder: Discovered by Victor Lens (Belgium, 1935).
Parentage: Sport of 'Distinction' which is a sport of 'Lafayette'.
Classification: Climbing Floribunda, Climbing Polyantha.
'Distinction, Cl.' has flowers in deep pink fading from the outer petals to light pink, medium to large-sized, lightly double. The reverse is more crimson in tone. The plant blooms in regular seasonal flushes.

'Dixieland Linda'.

'DIXIELAND LINDA'.

(BEAdix, Lady Ashe).
Breeder: Discovered by Gordon Bonnyman (1996).
Parentage: Sport of 'Aloha'.
Classification: Large-Flowered Climber.
'Dixieland Linda' is identical to its sport parent, 'Aloha' except for being apricot instead of pink. The flowers are very fragrant, large, very double, cupped and held in small clusters. They have old-style blooms with quartered petals. The plant will grow to about 10 ft (3 m).

'Dizzy Heights'.

'DIZZY HEIGHTS' (FRYblissful).

Breeder: Gareth Fryer (United Kingdom, 1999).
Parentage: Unknown.
Classification: Large-Flowered Climber.
This variety should go on a list of the best climbing red roses. The color of the flowers is rich scarlet-red becoming a little more crimson as it slowly fades. They are very fragrant, large, full, well formed and are carried in medium to large clusters. I have found them to be good for cutting. The blooming is repeated in regular seasonal flushes. The foliage is dark green and glossy. According to Heirloom Roses Nursery in Oregon, US, with a mild climate, the plant will grow to 10 or 12 ft (3 or 3.65 m). It needs full sun for best performance.

'Domaine De Courson'.

'DOMAINE DE COURSON' (MEIdrimy).

Breeder: Meilland International (France, 1993).
Parentage: Unknown.
Classification: Large-Flowered Climber, Romantica Group.
The flowers open mid pink with a touch of coral and soon start to fade to pale pink, outer petals first. The centers retain the full color longer. The initial form is cupped, then it opens out flat to show stamens with refexed petals. The flowers are large, double and carried singly or in small clusters. The bloom is very remontant in regular seasonal flushes. The plant can be grown as a shrub growing to about 5 ft (1.5 m) or as a small climber reaching to about 8 ft (2.5 m).

'DON JUAN'.

Breeder: Michele Malandrone (Italy, 1958).
Parentage: Seedling of 'New Dawn' x 'New Yorker'.
Classification: Large-Flowered Climber.
'Don Juan' is a beautiful dark red climber with exhibition-type, very fragrant, double, large, cupped to flat flowers with long stems that make them good for cutting. The flowers are held singly or in small clusters. They rebloom well in regular seasonal flushes, but are not very floriferous. The hardiness is rated for USDA zone 6b, but it may need a

little warmer climate to grow to full height and to bloom well. The glossy, dark green foliage is somewhat subject to blackspot and rust. The plant has a height potential of about 14 ft (4.25 m). The flowers are so lovely that they are worth any of the small shortcomings the plant has. 'Pink Don Juan' is a sport with deep pink, semi-double, medium to large-sized flowers.

'Don Juan'.

'DORIS DOWNES'.

Breeder: Alister Clark (Australia, 1932).
Parentage: Unknown.
Classification: Hybrid Gigantea.
The flowers of this rose are semi-double, very large, cup-shaped and pink turning darker with age. The opinions on fragrance range from moderate to strong. It is essentially a once-bloomer in the spring with an occasional flower opening later in the season. The expected height is about 8 to 10 ft (2.5 to 3 m).

'Dornröschen'.

'DORNRÖSCHEN'.

('Belle au Bois Dormant', 'Sleeping Beauty').
Breeder: Reimer Kordes (Germany, 1960).
Parentage: 'Pike's Peak' x 'Ballet'.
Classification: Shrub.
This rose features a rich fragrance and flowers that are large, double and a pretty pink. They are grouped singly or in small clusters and they bloom in repeated flushes during the flowering season. The plant is hardy to USDA zone 5b and, with support, can be trained as a small climber of up to 8 ft (2.5 m) or can be grown as a shrub. The Disney film "Sleeping Beauty" was premiered the year before this rose was introduced.

'Dortmund'.

'DORTMUND'.

Breeder: Wilhelm J.H. Kordes II (Germany, 1955).
Parentage: Seedling x Rosa kordesii.
Classification: Hybrid Kordesii.
The flowers of this excellent rose are blood red with a distinct white eye, light yellow stamens and a lighter reverse. The form is large, single, mildly fragrant, flat and held in large clusters. The plant blooms floriferously in mid-June and, if the hips are removed, it will flower

again in the fall. The foliage is dark green and shiny. The canes are well armed and will grow to as much as 12 ft (3.65 m) given favorable conditions. The plant is very disease resistant and very hardy (USDA zone 4b).

'DOUBLE CREAM'.

Breeder: Viru Viraraghavan. Sent to Helga Brichet (Italy, 2007).
Introduced in Italy by Le Rose di Piedimonte as 'Double Cream'.
Parentage: R. gigantea × Unknown.
Classification: Hybrid Gigantea (Indian form).
This plant has flowers that are far more yellow than you would expect from the name, but in time, the yellow does fade to cream. The flowers are very large, double, well scented of tea, opening out flat and borne singly (mostly) or in small clusters. The foliage is large, shiny, semi-glossy and medium green.

'Double Delight, Cl.'.

'DOUBLE DELIGHT, CL.'.

(AROclidd, 'Grimpant Double Delight').
Breeder: Discovered by John Nieuwesteeg (Australia, 1982) and by Jack E. Christensen (United States, 1982).
Parentage: Sport of 'Double Delight'.
Classification: Climbing Hybrid Tea.
This fragrant rose opens with yellow-cream petals having crimson-cerise tips. Fading causes the centers to become cream, then white and the petal tips become lighter and more cerise. This mixture of colors combined with very large and very double flowers is quite showy. The flower form is high centered. The individual blooms are borne singly or in small clusters. The remontancy occurs in seasonal flushes. The canes are covered with matte medium green foliage and will grow to at least 10 ft (3 m). They are not very hardy, rated to USDA zone 7b so they need frost protection. Watch for mildew.

'DR DOMINGOS PEREIRA'.

Breeder: De Magalhaes (Portugal, 1925).
Parentage: Unknown.
Classification: Climbing Tea or Tea-Noisette.
This beautiful rose should be more widely grown. The flowers are large, double and light pink with flushes of yellow at the center. When the flower is fully opened the small inner petals are quartered and the outer petals fold into points with a star-like effect. A glimpse of the stamens is revealed. There is a moderate fragrance. The rose can be seen at Sangerhausen (Germany). Domingos Leite Pereira (1882-1956) served in several government offices in Portugal in the early 20th century, including that of Prime Minister.

'Dr Eckener'.

'DR ECKENER' (Docteur Eckener).

Breeder: Vincenz Berger (Germany, 1928).
Parentage: 'Golden Emblem' x hybrid of Rosa rugosa.
Classification: Hybrid Rugosa, Shrub.
The flowers of 'Dr. Eckener' have a color that is hard to describe. The petals are basically apricot-buff with nuances of yellow increasing toward the petal bases. They fade to pink and cream. The form is large, semi-double and cupped with gently wavy petals and they are very fragrant. It shows

no indication of its Rugosa parentage. The excellent rebloom occurs in seasonal flushes. The plant will grow to about 10 ft (3 m). It is hardy to USDA zone 5b.

'DR F. DEBAT, CL.'.

Breeder: Vittorio Barni (Italy, 1955).
Parentage: Sport of 'Dr. Debat'.
Classification: Climbing Hybrid Tea.
This Hybrid Tea-type climber has very large, double, high-centered flowers that are quite variable in color. Sometimes they are more yellow, other times more apricot. Aging causes petal tips to turn pink. They are moderately scented of tea. They rebloom in seasonal flushes. The canes are almost thornless and bear glossy, dark green foliage. The plant grows at Roseraie du Val-de-Marne (France), Roseto Carla Fineschi (Italy), and Sangerhausen (Germany).

'DR J. H. NICOLAS'.

Breeder: J. H. Nicolas (US, 1940).
Parentage: 'Charles P. Kilham' x 'Georg Arends'.
Classification: Large-Flowered Climber.
The flowers are soft rose-pink with a lighter reverse, large, double and mildly fragrant of spice. It is very floriferous and reblooms in regular seasonal flushes. The plant will grow to about 10 ft (3 m). Jackson & Perkins honored the memory of Jean Henri Nicolas, their Director of Research, with the dedication of this rose.

'Dr Jackson'.

'DR JACKSON'

Breeder: David C. H. Austin.
Parentage: Seedling of 'Red Coat'.
Classification: Shrub, English Rose.
'Dr Jackson's' flowers are scarlet fading to more crimson, then adding some cerise. They lack scent. The form is medium, single with individual flowers borne solitary or in small clusters. The sepals are long, lovely and foliose, sometimes compound. There is one main, prolific late spring bloom with an occasional repeat later. Decorative hips are formed in the fall. The plant will grow to at least 10 ft (3 m) with support or can be grown as a large shrub.

'Dr Lande'.

'DR LANDE'.

Breeder: Adolf Berger (former Czechoslovakia, 1901).
Parentage: Unknown.
Classification: Climbing Tea.
The older records describe a rose that is salmon-pink and semi-double. The rose by this name that I have observed at Sangerhausen has flowers that are moderately fragrant, large, double and crimson-pink with magenta undertones and with lighter petal bases. They fade to light pink. They are deeply cupped at first, and then expand to an open cup filled with many petals. The plant is of average climbing height. The plant at San Jose Heritage Rose Garden in California appears to be the same variety. The original rose may be lost.

'Dream Girl'.

'DR RENATA TYRŠOVÁ'.

Breeder: Jan Böhm (Czechoslovakia, 1937).
Parentage: Unknown.
Classification: Climbing Hybrid Tea.
The rose grown at Sangerhausen does not fit the original description of a deep salmon-pink rose fading to pale pink with medium-sized, semi-double, globular flowers. The Sangerhausen rose has flowers that are large, double, medium pink fading to light pink and a shape much like a Hybrid Tea. They are borne singly or in very small clusters. The canes are clothed with dark green glossy foliage and will grow to about 12 ft (3.65 m).

'Dr Renata Tyršová'.

'DR ROBERT KORNS' ('Aptos', LETrob).

Breeder: Kleine Lettunich (United States, 1996).
Parentage: Unknown
Classification: Hybrid Musk.
Deep apricot pink buds open to pale apricot flowers with pale yellow centers. They soon fade to white. The small flowers are semi-double to lightly double. The plant is healthy and very vigorous. It will easily grow to 10 or 12 ft (3.05 to 3.65 m) in a mild climate if given support or it will form a large mound if allowed to grow freely.

'DR ROUGES'.

Breeder: Marie-Louise (aka Widow Schwartz or La Veuve) (France, 1893).
Parentage: Unknown.
Classification: Climbing Tea.
This rose has flowers of deep coral pink with a flush of yellow-apricot at the petal bases. They are spiral-centered, medium-sized, lightly filled and modestly scented. The petals reflex lengthwise and become quilled as the flower matures making it resemble a cactus dahlia. The plant can climb to about 10 ft (3 m).

'Dr Rouges'.

'DR W. VAN FLEET'.
See 'Daybreak'.

'DREAM GIRL'

Breeder: Martin R. Jacobus (United States, 1944).
Parentage: 'Dr. W. Van Fleet' x 'Señora Gari'.
Classification: Large-Flowered Climber.
'Dream Girl' flowers open deep salmon pink with a high centered Hybrid Tea shape, then expand to a lighter color and a more old-fashioned, low-domed form, often with much quartering. As the flowers age they become pinker. They are very fragrant, large-sized and double. There is one main summer bloom with occasional flowers later. The foliage is dark green and shiny. The plant may reach a height of 12 ft (3.65 m).

'Dr Robert Korns'.

'DREAM WEAVER' (JACpicl).

Breeder: Dr. Keith W. Zary (United States, 1998).
Introduced in United States by Bear Creek Gardens, Inc.

in 1997.
Parentage: 'Pink Polyanna' x 'Lady of the Dawn'.
Classification: Large-Flowered Climber.
The flowers are initially deep coral-pink and fade to lighter pink, outer petal tips first, leaving the centers and petal bases darker. The flowers are medium-sized, full and clustered in small groupings. They begin with a high-centered Hybrid Tea form and then flatten partially. The blooming is prolific in continuous seasonal flushes. The mildew and rust resistant foliage is dark green and glossy. The canes will grow in a branching manner to about 12 ft (3.65 m).

'Dream Weaver'.

'DREAMCOAT' (SEAcoat).

Breeder: Sean McCann (Ireland, 1996).
Parentage: 'Lady in Red' x 'Joseph's Coat'.
Classification: Miniature Climber.
'Dreamcoat' is yellow with flushes of red on the petal tips. This is a striking color combination, similar to that of the pollen parent, but it soon fades to white and pink. The flowering is so prolific that the effect is still attractive at any stage. The flowers are mildly fragrant, small to barely medium-sized, lightly double and cluster-flowered. The bloom is remontant in regular seasonal flushes. The plant grows to about 6 ft (1.85 m).

'DREAMING SPIRES'.

Breeder: John Mattock (United Kingdom, 1973).
Parentage: 'Buccaneer' x 'Arthur Bell'.
Classification: Large-Flowered Climber.
The name of this rose commemorates Oxford

'Dreaming Spires'.

University in England, near to the breeder's home. The flowers are bright golden-yellow, sometimes with an orange flush. They are very fragrant, medium-sized, double and carried in small clusters. The blooms are cupped at first, then open out to reveal the stamens with their reddish filaments. They are mainly summer blooming with occasional repeats later in the year. Potential growth is about 12 ft (3.65 m).

'DUARTE DE OLIVEIRA'.

Breeder: François Brassac (France, 1877).
Parentage: 'Ophirie' x 'Rêve d'Or'.
Classification: Tea-Noisette.
This Tea-Noisette has fragrant, medium to large-sized, double, salmon-pink flowers. The salmon is more dominant in the center and the outer petal tips are more of a pink hue. In time, the whole flower fades to light pink. The flowers are carried singly or in small clusters and repeat their bloom in continuous flushes during the flowering season. The plant will grow and bloom best in a warm climate, but it is hardy down to USDA zone 6b. It can be used as a 6 to 8 ft (1.8 to 2.5 m) pillar rose or as a climber for small trellises. 'Souvenir de Mme Ladvocat', a sport of this rose, is identical in all characteristics except for having variegated foliage.

'DUBLIN BAY' (MACdub).

Breeder: Samuel Darragh McGredy IV (before 1971).
Parentage: 'Bantry Bay' x 'Altissimo'.
Classification: Large-Flowered Climber.
This highly attractive rose is dark red with darker flushes on the petal tips. The red does not turn bluish. The flowers

'Dublin Bay'.

are mildly fragrant, medium to large-sized and full. The grouping is solitary or small clusters. They rebloom in regular seasonal flushes. The plant is very disease resistant and shade tolerant, but may be a little slow to establish. It has dark green, glossy foliage and will climb to about 10 ft (3 m).

'Duchesse d'Auerstaedt'.

'DUCHESSE D'AUERSTAEDT'.

('Duchesse d'Auerstädt', 'Madame la Duchesse d'Auerstädt', 'Madame la Duchesse d'Auerstaedt').
Breeder: Alexandre Bernaix (France, 1887).
Parentage: sport (or seedling?) of 'Rêve d'Or'.
Classification: Tea-Noisette.
This rose has pure golden yellow, large, very double, fragrant flowers borne singly (mostly) or in small clusters. The form is cupped, sometimes with quartered petals. There is little fading and very good rebloom in regular seasonal flushes. The foliage is dark green and semi-glossy. The plant is very vigorous and will reach a height of as much as 20 ft (6 m).

'Duchesse De Brabant, Cl.'

'DUCHESSE DE BRABANT, CL.'

('Comtesse de Labarthe, Cl.').
Breeder: Discovered by Lewis (Australia, circa 1900).
Parentage: Sport of 'Comtesse de Labarthe'.
Classification: Climbing Tea.
The flowers of this rose are pink with a slight coral tint that fades to pale, pure pink. They are medium-sized, very full, deeply cupped and fragrant of tea. They rebloom in continuous seasonal flushes. The plant will grow to about 13 ft (4 m).

'DUFTWOLKE'
See'Fragrant Cloud, Cl.'.

'DUKAT' ('Lancelot').

Breeder: Christian Evers (Germany, pre-2010). Introduced by Rosen Tantau.
Parentage: Unknown.
Classification: Large-Flowered Climber.
The flowers open deep yellow then fade to cream with flushes of pink on the petal tips. There is a moderate

fragrance. The bloom form is large and full with flowers occurring singly or in small clusters. Flowering is remontant in regular seasonal flushes. The plant has glossy, medium green foliage and can be expected to grow to as much as 16 ft (5 m).

'Dukat'.

'DUNE' (Delgrim).

Breeder: G. Delbard (France, 1993).
Parentage: Unknown.
Classification: Large-Flowered Climber.
'Dune' is a fragrant, bright yellow rose that fades a little with time, but remains attractive. The flower form is large, lightly double and deeply cupped, opening out later to a flattened cup. The remontancy is good and occurs in regular seasonal flushes. The plant is fairly vigorous, growing to about 10 ft (3 m).

'Dune'.

'DUQUESA DE PEÑARANDA, CL.'.

Breeder: Discovered by Germain Seed & Plant Co. (United States, 1940).
Parentage: Sport of 'Duquesa de Peñaranda'.
Classification: Climbing Hybrid Tea (Pernetiana).
This rose opens a fairly deep orange, but not a harsh tone. It soon fades, becoming a lighter salmon-pink harmonizing with the straw-colored stamens. The initial form is high-centered like its Hybrid Tea pollen parent, and then it opens out flatter to reveal its stamens. The flowers are large, double and occur singly or in small clusters. The blooming is repeated in continuous seasonal flushes. The foliage is large, dark green and glossy. Growing in a bushy manner, the plant will reach to about 10 ft (3 m).

'Duquesa De Peñaranda, Cl.'.

'DYNAMITE' ('High Flyer', JACsat).

Breeder: William A. Warriner (United States, 1992).
Parentage: Seedling x 'Sympathie'.
Classification: Large-Flowered Climber.
'Dynamite' reflects its Kordesii ancestors with its large, double, brilliant deep red flowers, broad, lightly wavy petals and its dark green, glossy foliage. The individual blooms are borne singly or in small clusters. They have a very mild scent of citrus. Repeat bloom occurs in regular seasonal flushes. The plant will reach a height of about 10 ft (3 m).

E

'Ellie Beauvillain'.

'E. G. HILL, CL.'.

Breeder: Discovered by G. Marlin (Australia, 1942).
Parentage: Sport of 'E. G. Hill'.
Classification: Climbing Hybrid Tea.
The flowers are deep scarlet-pink, very large, double and high-centered. The warm, scarlet color becomes more pure pink in the mature flower. The high-centered bloom opens to a low dome and the numerous inner petals twist a little causing it to look somewhat like a peony. There is a moderate fragrance of damask. The rose blooms in flushes throughout the season. The plant has glossy foliage and can be trained as a mid-sized climber. 'Rio Rita' is also a sport of 'E. G. Hill'.

'E. Veyrat Hermanos'.

'E.G. Hill, Cl.'.

'EARL OF ELDON'.

Breeder: Eldon-Coppin (United Kingdom, 1872).
Parentage: 'Cloth of Gold' x Seedling.
Classification: Tea-Noisette.
This is a very lovely rose with richly fragrant flowers that are medium large, double and coppery-orange fading to almost white. The form is old fashioned with quartered petals and sometimes with a button eye. The flowers are held in small clusters. They are fully remontant, blooming prolifically in repeated flushes during the flowering season. The plant will grow vigorously to about 15 ft (4.5 m).

'E. VEYRAT HERMANOS'.

('E. Veyrat Hermanos', 'Madame E. Veyrat Hermanos', 'Pillar of Gold').
Breeder: Alexandre Bernaix (France, 1895).
Parentage: Unknown.
Classification: Climbing Tea.
The color of the flowers is variable, but usually it is buff-yellow fading to cream with patches of apricot-pink to crimson-pink on the petal tips, especially in the centers. The form is cupped opening to a flattened cup, large, double, and borne mostly singly, or in small clusters. There is a strong, sweet scent. The flowers tend to ball in wet weather so the rose will flower best in a warm, dry climate. The plant grows to 10 ft (3 m) or more.

'Easlea's Golden Rambler'.

'EASLEA'S GOLDEN RAMBLER'.

Breeder: Walter Easlea and Sons, 1932, United Kingdom.
Parentage: Unknown.
Class: Hybrid Wichurana.
The flowers are apricot when they first open, but change to yellow, then to white as they mature. They are carried singly or in small clusters. Fragrance is an extra bonus. They bloom over a long stretch early in the season, but do not repeat. The plant is clothed with dark green, shiny foliage and will grow to about 12 ft (3.5 m).

'Eclipse, Cl.'.

'ECLIPSE, CL.'.

Breeder: Unknown.
Parentage: Sport of 'Eclipse'.
Classification: Climbing Hybrid Tea.
The flowers of this colorful, fragrant rose are large, lightly double, golden-yellow and are centered with red-gold stamens. The mature floral form is an open cup. The rose blooms in repeated flushes during the flowering season. The plant is susceptible to blackspot and should be protected from frost. It can be expected to reach a height of 8 to 10 ft (2.5 to 3 m).

'EDDA'.

Breeder: Massimiliano Lodi (Italy, pre-1929).
Parentage: ' Reine Marie Henriette' x 'Monsieur Boncenne'.
Classification: Large-Flowered Climber, Climbing Hybrid Tea.
'Edda' has flowers of mauve-pink with reddish flushes in the center and a lighter reverse. They are large, very double and are carried singly or in small clusters. The form is high-centered, Hybrid Tea style. The foliage is medium green with a matte surface. The plant will reach about 10 ft (3 m) in height.

'Edda'.

'EDEN'.
See 'Pierre de Ronsard'.

'EDEN CLIMBER'.
See 'Pierre de Ronsard'.

'EDEN ROSE 85'.
See 'Pierre de Ronsard'.

'EDEN ROSE, CL.'

Breeder : Alain Meilland (France, 1962).
Parentage : Sport of 'Eden Rose'.
Classification : Climbing Hybrid Tea.
This rose has scentless flowers of deep cerise-pink that are large to very large and very full. They are Hybrid Tea-style flowers with high, coiled centers and a spherical shape and typically occur singly or form small clusters. They rebloom well throughout the season in regular flushes. The plant will grow to about 10 ft (3 m). This Climbing Hybrid Tea should not be confused with 'Eden Rose 85' ('Pierre de Ronsard').

'EDITH DE MARTINELLI, CL.'

('Edith de Martinelli Grimpant', ORAdit).
Breeder: Discovered by Joseph Orard (France, 1981).
Parentage: Sport of 'Edith de Martinelli'.

Classification: Climbing Floribunda.
Initially, the flowers of this rose are orange-pink, but starting at the outside petals, they soon morph to pink. The form is cupped at first, then opens to a low rounded shape, the center filled with small petals. They are borne singly and in small clusters (mostly). The profuse bloom repeats in continuous seasonal flushes. The plant will grow 13 to 16 ft (3 to 4 m) and looks wonderful on an arbor.

'Edith De Martinelli, Cl.'

'EDITOR STEWART'.

Breeder: Alister Clark (Australia, 1939).
Parentage: Unknown.
Classification: Hybrid Gigantea or Climbing Hybrid Tea.
This attractive rose is quite different than most of the other Giganteas in having flowers of deep cerise-red instead of the usual pinks and creams. They are large, semi-double, very mildly fragrant and long stemmed. The petals develop a wave as they mature. The flowers bloom in repeated flushes during the regular flowering season. The plant has dark bronze-green foliage and will grow to about 8 or 10 ft (2.5 or 3 m).

'EFFECTIVE'.

Breeder: Hobbies (United Kingdom, 1912).
Parentage: Seedling of 'General MacArthur' x'Paul's Carmine Pillar'.
Classification: Large-Flowered Climber.
'Effective' has bright scarlet-red, large, cupped, lightly double flowers carried singly (mostly) or in small clusters. They are richly fragrant. There is one main summer bloom with occasional repeats later in the year. The rose grows at Roseraie du Val-de-Marne (France) and Sangerhausen (Germany).

'Effective'.

'EGLANTYNE'.

(AUSmak, 'Eglantyne Jebb').
Breeder: David C. H. Austin (United Kingdom, before 1994).
Parentage: Seedling x 'Mary Rose'.
Classification: Shrub. English Rose.
'Eglantine' has very pretty flowers with medium pink centers and lighter outer petals. They are medium-sized, very double and cupped, then more flat in maturity. The petals are gently ruffled and may be quartered. The flowers are carried in small clusters. The canes are well armed and covered with medium green, matte foliage. The rose is hardy, rated down to a low of USDA zone 5b. It can be grown as a shrub, or with support, it can be trained as a climber with a potential height of 10 ft (3 m).

'ELFE'.

See 'Pride of Venus'.

'Eglantyne'.

'ELIE BEAUVILLAIN' (Elie Beauvilain).

Breeder: Beauvilain/Beauvillain (France, 1887).
Parentage: 'Gloire de Dijon' x 'Ophirie'.
Classification: Tea-Noisette.
The flowers are coral-pink fading to lighter, pure pink with red veining. They are also large, double and blooming singly or in small clusters. They repeat in continuous seasonal flushes. The plant is disease resistant and will reach a height of about 10 ft (3 m).

'Elie Beauvillain'.

'ELINA' (DICjana, Peaudouce).

Breeder: Colin and Patrick Dickson (U K, 1984).
Parentage: 'Nana Mouskouri' x 'Lolita'.
Classification: Hybrid Tea.
'Elina' was my first rose many years ago and I have always maintained a special fondness for it. It is a beautiful, tall-growing Hybrid Tea, not a climbing sport. The color is pure yellow, fading to pale ivory at the petal tips, but darker at the bases and in the center. The form is high-centered, broad petaled, large and double. There is a mild fragrance. The flowers are borne singly or in small clusters. The repeat is good, occurring in regular seasonal flushes. My plant has shown good health and hardiness and has grown to about 8 ft (2.5 m).

'Elina'.

'ELIZABETH HARKNESS, CL.'

Breeder: Discovered by Harkness (United Kingdom, 1975).
Parentage: Sport of 'Elizabeth Harkness'.
Classification: Climbing Hybrid Tea.
The color of this rose is quite variable. Usually it is basically yellow fading to cream, then to white. It may have light yellow centers and petal bases or the same features may be more apricot with touches of pink. This seems to be an environmental influence. The flowers are richly scented, large to very large, double and high-centered in Hybrid Tea style. They are carried singly or in small clusters. The blooming is remontant in regular seasonal flushes. The foliage is medium green and shiny. The plant will grow to about 10 ft (3 m).

'ELLEN' (AUScup).

Breeder: David C. H. Austin (United Kingdom, 1984).
Parentage: 'Charles Austin' x Seedling.
Classification: Shrub. English Rose.

'Ellen'.

This is another one of the lovely Austin roses that can be grown as a climber. The flowers are apricot with a darker, more pink reverse. They are large, double and strongly fragrant with a cupped, old rose style form. They rebloom in regular seasonal flushes. The foliage is mid-green and semi-glossy. The plant can be grown as a shrub, their original intent, or it can be given support and trained as a climber. Mine has grown to about 10 ft (3 m) on my front porch.

'ELLIE KNAB, CL.'.

Breeder: Mathias Tantau (Germany, 1953).
Parentage: Sport of 'Elli Knab'.
Classification: Climbing Hybrid Tea.
This Hybrid Tea sport's very attractive flowers are light pink with a darker center, very large and double in a high-centered, coiled, broad-petaled Hybrid Tea style. They have a moderate scent. The petals reflex at the tips resulting in a curled look. The blooms are mostly carried singly, but may also be in small clusters. Their blooming is remontant in seasonal flushes. The expected height of growth is about 10 ft (3 m).

'ELLINOR LE GRICE, CL.'.

Breeder: Edward Burton Le Grice (United Kingdom, 1959).
Parentage: Sport of 'Ellinor Le Grice'.
Classification: Climbing Hybrid Tea.
The flowers are large and double and are yellow on opening, but quickly fade almost to white. There is a fruity fragrance. The inner petals form a cup around the golden-yellow stamens and the outer petals reflex at the tips to form points. The rose blooms in flushes throughout the season and will grow to 8 or 10 ft (2.5 or 3 m).

'ELVIRA ARAMAYO, CL.'.

Breeder: Discovered by Ingegnoli Bros. (Italy, 1933).
Parentage: Sport of 'Elvira Aramayo'.
Classification: Climbing Hybrid Tea, Climbing Pernetiana.
This rose will definitely add color to your garden. The flowers are bright orange-red with flushes of yellow, moderately scented, medium-sized and semi-double. They become more crimson with age and the petals become quilled. There is good remontancy in regular seasonal flushes. The plant grows at Sangerhausen (Germany).

'Emilia Plantier'.

'EMILIA PLANTIER'.

Breeder: Joseph Schwartz (France, 1878).
Parentage: Unknown.
Classification: Hybrid Noisette.
The flowers of this very old variety are medium to large-sized, double and soft yellow aging to cream. The newly opened flower is cupped, but as it matures the petals reflex inward along the center line giving it a starburst shape. The flowering is remontant in seasonal flushes. The plant will grow to about 10 ft (3 m).

'EMILIE DUPUY'.
See 'Mme Emily Dupuy'.

'EMILY RHODES'.

Breeder: Alister Clark (Australia, 1937).
Parentage: 'Golden Ophelia' x 'Zéphirine Drouhin'.
Classification: Large-Flowered Climber.
This rose is soft coral-pink, moderately scented, large-sized and double. It has a rather loosely cupped form. The plant will grow to about 10 ft (3 m) and makes a good pillar rose.

'EMIN PASCHA'.

Breeder: Heinrich Drögemüller (Germany, 1894).
Parentage: 'Gloire de Dijon' x 'Louis van Houtte'.
Classification: Hybrid Noisette.
'Emin Pascha' has large, double, scentless, deep crimson-pink flowers and blooms in regular flushes during the flowering season. It will grow to about 12 ft (3.65 m), a good size for an arbor or a pillar.

'Emin Pascha'.

'EMPRESS OF CHINA'.

Breeder: Discovered by Jackson (United States, 1896).
Parentage: Sport of 'Old Blush'.
Classification: Climbing China.
The flowers of this rose open very deep pink and soon fade to light pink. They are medium-sized, lightly double, scented of fruit and held singly or in small clusters. There is one long, profuse flowering with occasional repeats later in the year. The plant has average hardiness and is very vigorous with reports that indicate it may grow to 16 ft (5 m) or more.

'ENA HARKNESS, CL.'.

Breeder: Discovered by Gurteen & Ritson (Unknown, 1954).
Parentage: Sport of 'Ena Harkness'.
Classification: Climbing Hybrid Tea.
This rose is closely related to 'Crimson Glory', one of the world's best Hybrid Teas of all time which probably accounts for its beauty. The fragrant flowers are an intense, dark crimson. The form is large, full, high-centered like a Hybrid Tea and carried singly or in small clusters. The flowers fade very little and don't turn bluish like so many red roses. Its only fault is a tendency to hang its heavy head. The plant is vigorous, growing as high as 15 ft (4.55 m).

'EMMANUELLA DE MOUCHY'.

Breeder: Paul Nabonnand (France, 1922).
Parentage: Rosa gigantea Collett ex Crépin x 'Lady Waterlow'.
Classification: Hybrid Gigantea.
The flowers are light pink with a darker petal reverse. They are strongly fragrant, medium-sized, semi-double to double and have a globular bloom form. The plant has the potential to reach a height of up to 15 ft (up to 4.5 m). 'Irene Bonnet' is sometimes sold as 'Emmanuella de Mouchy'.

'Ena Harkness, Cl.'

'Emmanuella De Mouchy'.

'ERFURT'.

Breeder: Wilhelm J.H. Kordes II (Germany, 1939).
Parentage: 'Eva' x 'Réveil Dijonnais'.
Classification: Hybrid Musk.
The richly fragrant, single, medium to large-sized flowers of this rose are crimson-pink with a large white eye and flushes of yellow at the center. The color fades and becomes more

'Erfurt'.

cerise, then pale lavender and finally almost white. The flowers are produced singly or in small clusters. Reblooming is in regular seasonal flushes and decorative orange-red hips are formed after each flush. Growth can reach about 8 ft (2.45 m).

'Eric Taberly'.

'ERIC TABERLY'.

(MEIdrason, 'Red Eden', 'Red Eden Rose', 'Red Pierre', 'Rouge Pierre de Ronsard').
Breeder: Alain Meilland (France, 2002).
Parentage: Seedling of 'Cappa Magna' x 'Ulmer Münster'.
Classification: Large-Flowered Climber. Romantica Rose.
Deep crimson-red is the color of the richly fragrant, large, double flowers of this rose. Their flower form is initially deeply cupped then opens out more as an old-fashioned bloom with quartered petals. The flowers are grouped in small clusters. They bloom continuously in regular seasonal flushes. The foliage is medium green and semi-glossy. The plant will grow vigorously to about 15 ft. This variety is not related to 'Eden Rose 85' ('Pierre de Ronsard').

'Escalade'.

'ESCALADE'.

Breeder: Maurice Combe (France, 1962). Introduced by Vilmorin-Andrieux (France, 1962).
Parentage: 'Spectacular' x 'Charlotte Armstrong'.
Classification: Climbing Hybrid Tea, Large-Flowered Climber.
The large, semi-double flowers are described as red, but they looked scarlet to me when I observed the rose at Roseraie du Val-de-Marne, the only garden to feature it. It is remontant in regular seasonal flushes. The plant will grow to about 10 ft (3 m). It does not seem to be commercially available.

'ÉTENDARD'.

('New Dawn Red',' New Dawn Rouge', 'Red New Dawn').
Breeder: Marcel Robichon (France, 1956).
Parentage: 'New Dawn' (Large Flowered Climber, Dreer, 1930) x Seedling.
Classification: Large-Flowered Climber.
'Étendard' is a prolific bloomer with small clusters of lovely, deep crimson-red, lightly scented flowers. They are medium-sized, double and Hybrid Tea shaped when

first opened. The flowers are long lasting and good for cutting. There is one main summer bloom with occasional flowers produced later in the year. The plant will grow vigorously to about 12 ft (3.65 m).

'Étendard'.

'ÉTENDARD DE JEANNE D'ARC'.

Breeder: Armand Garçon (France, 1882).
Parentage: Seedling of 'Gloire de Dijon'.
Classification: Tea-Noisette.
The richly fragrant flowers are very large, very double, deeply cupped and cream fading to ivory white. The inner petals may be roughly quartered. The flowers bloom in repeated flushes during the flowering season. The plant is known to grow to as much as 15 ft (4.5 m). Jeanne d'Arc (Joan of Arc, La Pucelle, The Maid of Orleans) led the French army against the English troops. She was only 19 years old when she burned at the stake by the victorious English on 30 May 1431. She was canonized on 16 May 1920.

'Étoile De Hollande, Cl.'

'ÉTOILE DE HOLLANDE, CL.'.

('Climbing Étoile de Hollande', 'Grimpant Étoile de Hollande').
Breeder: Discovered by Mathias Leenders (Netherlands, 1931).
Parentage: Sport of 'Étoile de Hollande'.
Classification: Climbing Hybrid Tea.
The richly fragrant, large, double flowers have a classical Hybrid Tea shape with high coiled centers and broad petals that goes well with the crimson-red coloring. The red color seldom shows the often seen fault of blueing. The plant is remontant in seasonal flushes of bloom. It can reach a height of 18 ft (5.5 m).

'ÉTOILE DE LYON'.

Breeder: Guillot fils (France, 1876).
Parentage: Seedling of 'Madame Charles'.
Classification: Tea.
This lovely, fragrant Tea has very large, very double, yellow flowers that are borne singly or in small clusters. They fade quickly to light cream while retaining darker centers and petal reverses. The centers may have flushes of apricot. The receptacle roughly forms a square and the pedicels are glandular, valuable features for distinguishing this variety from the many other yellow Teas that exist. The flowers are produced in flushes during the whole blooming season. The plant will grow to 6 to 8 ft (1.85 to 2.5 m) or more in a warm climate and can be trained as a climber.

'ÉTOILE DE PORTUGAL'.

(Rosa Cayeuxii, var. 'Etoile de Portugal').
Breeder: Henri Cayeux (Portugal, 1898). It could have been a little later date.
Parentage: Rosa gigantea x 'Reine Marie Henriette'.
Classification: Hybrid Gigantea.
This rose was thought to be extinct until both Pamela Temple, a California rosarian, and John Hook, a nurseryman in France, discovered that the 'Vicomtesse Pierre le Feu' plants from the Beales nursery in their possessions are actually 'Etoile de Portugal". The flowers are fragrant, large, double and medium pink of a warm hue when opening and morphing to crimson pink with age, outer petals inward. There are small flushes of yellow at the petal bases. The large outer petals reflex outward and the much smaller inner petals curl inward. The flowers are produced mostly singly,

but can be found in small clusters as well. There is one prolific bloom early in the season. The plant has typical light green, droopy Gigantea-type foliage and will grow vigorously as a climber.

'Étude'.

'ÉTUDE'.

Breeder: Charles Walter Gregory (United Kingdom, 1965).
Parentage: 'Spectacular' x 'New Dawn'.
Classification: Large-Flowered Climber.
Deep pink flowers with darker petal reverses fade to lighter pink. They are cupped, large, lightly double and very fragrant. There is one main summer bloom with a few flowers later. The foliage is healthy, medium green and glossy. The plant is very hardy with reports of it growing in Norway, Russia and Sweden. It will grow to about 10 ft (3 m).

'EUROPEANA, CL.' (BUReuro).

Breeder: Joe Burks (United States, 1987).
Parentage: Sport of 'Europeana'.
Classification: Climbing Floribunda.
The flowers are dark, bright red, mildly fragrant, medium-sized and double. There is one main bloom early in the season with occasional flowers opening later. The plant can be trained as a lovely pillar rose of about 8 ft (2.5 m). It can also be grown on a fence or a small trellis. It is a beautiful rose that should be grown more.

'Europeana, Cl.'

'EUROROSE'.

Breeder: Paul Croix (France, 1997).
Parentage: Unknown.
Classification: Large-Flowered Climber.
I have observed this rose at Roseto Carla Fineschi in Italy and nowhere else. The flowers are mildly fragrant, semi-double, medium-sized and strikingly colored with broad, bright magenta-pink petal tips merging into white centers. The matte-surfaced foliage appears healthy and the plant has a potential for growth to about 10 ft (3 m).

'Eurorose'.

'EVA'.

Breeder: Wilhelm J.H. Kordes II (Germany, 1933).
Parentage: 'Robin Hood' x 'J.C. Thornton'.
Classification: Hybrid Musk.
The flowers are moderately scented, medium-sized and deep crimson-pink with a white eye. There is little fading. Deeply cupped on opening, they become flatter with

age. They are carried in large clusters. Remontancy is in regular seasonal flushes. The plant can be expected to grow to about 10' (3 m) with support or it can be pruned and grown as a shrub.

'Eva'.

'EVA TESCHENDORFF, CL.'.

Breeder: Discovered by A. Opdebeeck Fils, 1926 and by Teschendorff, 1932.
Parentage: Sport of 'Eva Teschendorff'. A

'Eva Teschendorff, Cl.'.

descendent, through a series of sports, from Tausendschön.
Classification: Climbing Polyantha.
The flowers are light cream to white with subtle green shading, small to medium-sized, lightly double to double, mildly fragrant and occur in small clusters. The wavy petals open out to show the stamens. They rebloom in regular seasonal flushes. The canes are almost thornless and are covered with small, glossy, light green foliage. They will grow in a bushy fashion to an average height of about 10 ft (3 m).

'EVELYN' ('Apricot Parfait', AUSsaucer).

Breeder: David C. H. Austin (United Kingdom, 1992).
Parentage: 'Graham Thomas' x 'Tamora'.
Classification: Shrub. English Rose.
I have always enjoyed having this lovely rose in my garden with its very full, medium-sized, richly fragrant flowers. They start out cupped and open out to old-style flat rosettes with quartered petals and are produced singly or in small clusters. The rebloom is good and comes in flushes during the blooming season. The canes are well armed and clothed with dark green foliage. The potential height as a climber is 10 to 12 ft (3 to 3.65 m).

'Evelyn'.

'EVENING LIGHT'.

Breeder: Christopher H. Warner (United Kingdom, 2001).
Parentage: 'Laura Ford' x ('Mary Sumner' x 'Kiskadee').
Classification: Large-Flowered Climber.
This rose has flowers of light peach fading to pink at the petal tips and yellow petal bases. The reverse is light pink. They will eventually fade to white, cream and pink. There is a big bunch

of russet-gold stamens at the center. The flower form is moderately fragrant, small, semi-double to lightly double with the flowers carried in small clusters. They bloom in regular seasonal flushes. The foliage is small, glossy and medium green. The rose may reach a height of 8 ft if given support and favorable conditions.

'EVERBLOOMING PILLAR NO. 82'.
See 'Show Garden'.

'EVERGREEN GENE' (VIRgene).

Breeder: M.S. Viraraghavan (India, 2006).
Parentage: 'Carmoisine' x Rosa gigantea .
Classification: Hybrid Gigantea.
The flowers of 'Evergreen Gene' are large to very large-sized, double and light yellow with touches of pink on the petal tips. There is very little fragrance if any. The flowers are formed like a Hybrid Tea with high, coiled centers and are held in small clusters. The plant has medium green, glossy foliage and is basically once-blooming with a few flowers later. The potential height is about 12 ft (3.65 m). This rose was named in honor of Gene Waering, a special American friend.

'Exploit'.

'EXPLOIT'.

(All In One, Colonia, Dorsland, Grimpant Exploit, MEIlider).
Breeder: Marie-Louise (Louisette) Meilland (France, 1984).
Parentage: 'Fugue' x 'Sparkling Scarlet'.
Classification: Large-Flowered Climber.
'Exploit' is a brilliant scarlet rose with double, medium-sized flowers carried singly or in small clusters. It has little fragrance if any. The canes are clothed with glossy, medium green foliage and will grow to about 10 to 13 ft (3 to 4 m).

'Express'.

'EXPRESS'.

Breeder: VEG (S) Baumschulen Dresden (Germany, 1984).
Parentage: Unknown.
Classification: Large-Flowered Climber.
This is a rose with lovely coral-pink, large, double, high-centered flowers borne mostly singly, but occasionally in small clusters. They are mildly scented. The rose repeats its bloom in regular seasonal flushes. The plant is fairly vigorous and will grow to about 12 to 13 ft (3.65 to 4 m).

F

'Fassadenzauber'.

'F. FERRER'.

Breeder: Lorenzo (Llorenç) Pahissa (Spain, 1935).
Parentage: Unknown.
Classification: Climbing Hybrid Tea.
The flowers of this rose are moderately fragrant, deep scarlet-red, semi-double, large and grow mostly singly, but sometimes in small clusters. The flowers open out very flat and look almost like single roses. They are once blooming with scattered flowers later.

'F.J. Grootendorst'.

'F. J. GROOTENDORST'.

('Grootendorst', 'Red Grootendorst', 'Nelkenrose').
Breeder: De Goey (Netherlands, 1918).
Parentage: R. rugosa rubra x 'Madame Norbert Levavasseur'.
Classification: Hybrid Rugosa.
This rose is sometimes called the Carnation Rose because its petals have fringed tips making it resemble the carnation. The small size, very double form and bright crimson color add to the illusion. The flowers occur in large clusters and bloom in continuous seasonal flushes. None of the Grootendorsts form hips. With a rating of hardiness to USDA zone 4b it is hardy enough for the Swedish Rose Society to have recommended it for northern Sweden. It struggles in a hot climate. The plant will grow to about 6 or 7 ft (2 m) and can be trained as a small climber.

'FALSTAFF' (AUSverse).

Breeder: David C. H. Austin (United Kingdom, 1990).
Parentage: Unknown.
Classification: English Rose.
The old fashioned flowers are large, full, cupped and dark crimson-red becoming more purple with age. They have a pronounced old rose fragrance. The plant has semi-glossy foliage, is hardy to USDA zone 5b and will climb to at least 8 ft (2.5 m).

'Falstaff'.

'FANDANGO' (MEIjade).

Breeder: Meilland International (France, 1989).
Parentage: Unknown.
Classification: Large-Flowered Climber.
The colors of this rose are pink with some coral-pink flushes, a rather delicate color for the imagery the name of the rose projects. The form is a better match having medium to large, lightly double, wide open flowers with scalloped petal tips and gently ruffled petals evoking the skirts of a fandango dancer. The plant has medium green, glossy foliage with a slight ruffling. There is a moderate scent. The height is about 10 ft (3 m).

'Fashion, Cl.'.

'FASHION, CL.'.

Breeder: Discovered by Eugene S. "Gene" Boerner (United States, 1951) and by John Mattock (United Kingdom, 1955).
Parentage: Sport of 'Fashion'.
Classification: Climbing Floribunda.
The flowers open deep coral-pink, then fade to light pink and finally to nearly white. The petal reverse is more yellow in color. The form is large, double with a strong wild-rose scent. The flowers are held singly or in small clusters. Blooming is remonstrant in regular seasonal flushes. Expected growth is about 15 ft (4.55 m).

'Fassadenzauber'.

'FASSADENZAUBER'.

Breeder: Noack (Germany, 1997).
Parentage: Unknown.
Classification: Large-Flowered Climber.
This rose has medium-pink flowers with a touch of coral fading to a light pink. They are medium to large-sized and double. They bloom in regular, continuous seasonal flushes. The plant has glossy, medium green foliage, a bushy habit and a potential height of about 8 ft (2.5 m).

'FÉE DES NEIGES, CL.'.
See 'Iceberg, Cl.'.

'FELICIA'.

Breeder: Rev. Joseph Hardwick Pemberton (United Kingdom, before 1926).
Parentage: 'Trier' x 'Ophelia'.
Classification: Hybrid Musk.
Coral-pink buds open to very fragrant, light pink flowers with a touch of coral and yellow petal bases. They fade to pale pink and finally almost to white. The flower form is medium-sized, semi-double, cupped to flattened rosette and they are held in large clusters. The flowers rebloom in regular seasonal flushes. The plant will grow with a bushy habit to about 9 ft (2.75 m).

'Felicia'.

'FELLEMBERG'.

('Fellenberg', 'Belle Marseillaise').
Breeder: Fellemberg (1835). Possibly a rediscovered rose.
Parentage: Unknown.
Classification: Noisette, Tea-Noisette. May be Hybrid China/ Noisette.
'Fellemberg' has bright crimson-pink, sweetly fragrant, medium-sized, double flowers borne in small clusters. With age the crimson fades to lighter pink with a hint of lavender. Flowering repeats in regular seasonal flushes. The canes are

covered with dark green foliage, are almost thornless and will reach a height of about 10 ft (3 m). Some authorities think that 'Belle Marseillaise' may be a distinct variety, not a synonym of 'Fellemberg'. The plant is hardy only to USDA zone 7b so it will do best in a warm climate.

'Fellemberg'.

'FELLENBERG'.
See 'Fellemberg'.

'Ferdy'.

'FERDY'.

Breeder: Seizo Suzuki (Japan, 1984). Introduced by Selection Meilland (France, pre-1985).
Parentage: Seedling x 'Petite Folie'.
Classification: Climbing Miniature.
The lovely decorative effect of this rose comes from the abundant blooming and the arrangement of the flowers in huge clusters. The individual flowers are small, lightly double, fragrant and coral pink. The bloom form is open and flattened. The plant is very disease resistant. It can be kept pruned and grown as a shrub, or in a warm climate, it will grow tall enough to be trained as a climber. It is excellent for hanging baskets and makes a good groundcover.

'FESTIVAL FANFARE' (BLEstogil).

Breeder: Discovered by W. D. Ogilvie (United Kingdom, 1982).
Parentage: Sport of 'Fred Loads' (Floribunda, Holmes, 1968).
Classification: Floribunda.
This rose is an unusual type of floral sport going from a solid color to a striped pattern with a ground of dark vermilion and pale pink stripes. The flowers are slightly fragrant, medium to large-sized and semi-double. They are remontant in regular seasonal flushes. The plant is hardy to USDA zone 4b. It can be grown as a shrub or given support and trained as a climber of about 10 ft (3 m).

'Festival Fanfare'.

'Feu D'Artifice'.

'FEU D'ARTIFICE' ('Fireworks, Cl.').

Breeder: Charles Mallerin (France, 1935).
Parentage: Hybrid of R. foetida x 'Colette Clémente'.
Classification: Large-Flowered Climber.
The buds are long and pointed and the flowers are scarlet with yellow petal bases, fading in time to crimson and white. They are mildly scented, large and semi-double (almost single) and cluster-flowered. There is one main bloom with a few flowers later in the season. The foliage is dark green and glossy. The plant will grow to about 8 ft (2.45 m) and can be grown as a climber on a small trellis or fence.

'Feuerschein, Cl.'.

'FEUERSCHEIN, CL.'.

Breeder: Discovered by Max Krause (Germany, 1936).
Parentage: Sport of 'Feuerschein' which, in turn, is sport of 'Lafayette' ('Joseph Guy').
Classification: Climbing Polyantha.
This is a sport of the scarlet-flowered Feurschein which, in turn, is a sport of the crimson-flowered Lafayette. The flowers are medium-sized, full and are carried in medium to large clusters. The plant has dark green foliage, many prickles and the potential to grow, in a bushy manner, to about 8 ft (2.5 m). It is very hardy. The plant that grows at Sangerhausen has crimson flowers that look like those of 'Lafayette'. It may have sported to 'Lafayette, Cl.'

'FEURIO, CL.'.

Breeder: Discovered by Reimer Kordes (Germany, 1963).
Parentage: Sport of 'Feurio'.
Classification: Climbing Floribunda.
This Climbing Floribunda has medium-sized, double, bright scarlet-vermilion flowers that come singly or in small clusters. The form is cupped becoming more open and flattened with age. Blooming is prolific and is repeated in continuous seasonal flushes. Long stems make it good for cutting. The plant is almost thornless, has light green, glossy foliage and is heat and rain tolerant. A plant can be seen at Sangerhausen (Germany).

'FIRE PILLAR'.
See 'Bischofsstadt Paderborn'.

'FIRECREST, CL.'.

Breeder: Discovered by Edward Burton Le Grice (United Kingdom, 1969).
Parentage: Sport of 'Firecrest'.
Classification: Climbing Floribunda.
This climbing version of 'Firecrest' has medium-sized, double, vermilion flowers that form in medium clusters. The petal reverse is more true red than the upper surface. The remontancy occurs in continuous flushes during the blooming season.

'FIRST PRIZE, CL.' (JACclist).

Breeder: Discovered by E. Reasoner (Unknown, 1976).
Parentage: Sport of 'First Prize' (Hybrid Tea, Boerner, 1970).
Classification: Climbing Hybrid Tea.
The flowers come from long, pointed buds and are very large, full, high-centered like a Hybrid Tea and moderately scented. The color is rose-pink with coral-pink centers fading to lighter cerise-pink, then pale lavender-pink. The reverse

is darker pink. The flowers are held singly or in small clusters. They rebloom in continuous seasonal flushes. The plant is prone to diseases so it will look best in a dry climate. The plant is armed, has dark green foliage and will grow to about 10 ft (3 m) in height.

'Flamenco'.

'FLAMENCO'.

(Northern Lights, POUltika).
Breeder: L. Pernille Olesen and Mogens Nyegaard Olesen (Denmark, 1998).
Parentage: Seedling x 'Brilliant' (shrub, Kordes, 1983).
Classification: Large-Flowered Climber. Courtyard collection.
'Flamenco' has medium pink, large, double flowers fading to light pink with a darker reverse and blooming abundantly in large clusters. They have a light citrus-like scent. They can be used as cut flowers. The plant is disease resistant and hardy in Denmark. It will grow in a bushy style to about 10 ft (3 m). There are other roses growing under the name 'Flamenco'— a Floribunda, a Hybrid Tea and a Shrub.

'FLASH'.

Breeder: Robert Marion Hatton (United States, 1938).
Parentage: 'Rosella' x 'Margaret McGredy'.
Classification: Climbing Hybrid Tea.
The flowers are orange-scarlet with yellow petal bases and reverses. They fade to crimson and ivory. The color was thought to be sensational when the plant was first introduced. The form is medium, lightly double, cup-shaped and carried singly or in small clusters. There is a light scent. There is one main summer bloom with very little repeat later. The plant has dark green, glossy foliage and will grow to a height of about 8 ft (2.45 m).

'Flash'.

'FLASHFIRE'.

Breeder: Lee W. Little (United States, 1992).
Parentage: 'Altissimo' x 'Playboy'.
Classification: Large-Flowered Climber.
This rose has single, medium-sized, bright vermilion flowers with broad, blunt-ended petals. They are borne singly or in small clusters. They have a mild fragrance. The plant will grow to 6.5 to 8 ft (2 to 2.5 m) and can be trained as a small climber for a short pillar or small trellis.

'Flashfire'.

'Flamenco'.

'Floradora, Cl.'.

'FLORADORA, CL.'

Breeder: Discovered by Paul Shamberger (United States, 1951).
Parentage: Sport of 'Floradora'.
Classification: Climbing Floribunda.
This Climbing Floribunda has flowers that are medium-sized, full and scarlet fading to pink. They are initially high-centered and deeply cupped, but when mature they open out into an orderly flattened rosette. The flowers are borne singly or in small clusters. There is a good rebloom in regular seasonal flushes. The foliage is dark green and glossy. The plant will grow in a branching manner to about 10 ft (3 m).

'Floralies De Valenciennoise'.

'FLORALIES DE VALENCIENNOISE'.

Breeder: Francois Dorieux I (France, 1954).
Parentage: Unknown.
Classification: Large-Flowered Climber.
This is a semi-double, almost single, rose with large petals, a gift for those who love this kind of simplicity. The color is bright crimson-pink with lighter petal bases, the flower size is large and the floral arrangement is single or small clusters. The plant has dark green, semi-glossy foliage. It will grow to about 8 ft (2.5 m).

'FLORENCE MARY MORSE, CL.'.

Breeder: Discovered by Gaujard (France, 1959).
Parentage: Sport of 'Florence Mary Morse'.
Classification: Climbing Floribunda.
This lucky find has flowers that are semi-double, medium-sized, lightly fragrant and a beautiful, bright scarlet. The floral form is cupped with softly rolled-back petals. The flowers are borne singly or in small clusters. They are produced in repeated flushes of bloom during the flowering season.

'Florence Mary Morse, Cl.'.

'FLORENTINA'.

Breeder: Tim Hermann Kordes (Germany, 2002).
Introduced by Kordes (Germany, 2011)
Parentage: Unknown.
Classification: Large Flowered Climber.
This most recent 'Florentina' has medium to large, very double scarlet-red flowers that are formed as deep cups in medium to large clusters. In time the flowers open out to shallow cups with an outer ring of broad enclosing petals and a center packed with smaller somewhat wavy petals. The color becomes more crimson with age. The flowers

rebloom in seasonal flushes. The canes are covered with healthy, dark green, shiny foliage and will grow with a bushy habit to about 10 ft (3 m). Do not confuse this Large-flowered Climber with the Kordes 1974 Hybrid Tea or the Leenders 1938 Hybrid Polyantha.

'Florentina'.

'FLORIAN, CL.'. See 'Tender Night, Cl.'.

'FLYING COLOURS'.

Breeder: Alister Clark (Australia, 1922).
Parentage: Seedling of Rosa gigantea.
Classification: Hybrid Gigantea.
Very large, single, softly fragrant, deep pink flowers with white petal bases open from long, slender buds. They are carried singly or in small clusters. The plant will produce flowers in a single prolific flush of bloom early in the season along with an abundance of drooping, light green, shiny leaves. It will grow to a height of about 26 ft (8 m). Flying Colors traditionally referred to the flags of a victorious ship after a battle and came to mean a great success of any kind. This rose is certainly a success and well earns its name.

'Folichonne'.

'FOLICHONNE'.

Breeder: Thierry Aubin (France, 2007).
Introduced by Roses Anciennes André Eve (France, 2008).
Parentage: Unknown.
Classification: Shrub, climber.
This rose is classed as a Shrub, but I saw it growing about 8 ft. (2.5 m) high on a trellis at Roseraie du Val-de-Marne in France. The flowers are single, large and deep crimson-pink with white petal bases and may have some additional white streaks. The plant I saw had the flowers arranged singly or in small clusters.

'Fortissima'.

'FORTISSIMA'.

Breeder: Louis Lens (Belgium, 1994).
Parentage: LLX8795 x 'Violet Hood'.
Classification: Hybrid Musk.
Typical of Hybrid Musks, 'Fortissima' can be grown as a modest climber to about 8 ft (2.5 m) or it can be pruned as a shrub. The flowers are small, single and pink with a white center. They are borne in large clusters and bloom in continuous flushes throughout the season.

'Fortune's Double Yellow'.

'FORTUNE'S DOUBLE YELLOW'.

('Beauty of Glazenwood', 'Gold of Ophir').
Breeder: Discovered by Robert Fortune (U K, 1844) in China in the garden of a rich mandarin.
Parentage: Unknown.
Classification: Tea hybrid, Hybrid Gigantea.
The newly opened flowers have deep yellow petals with salmon-pink bases. The petals soon develop coppery-pink tips that change to cerise as the rest of the flower fades to ivory and then to almost white. There is a light tea scent. The flower form is medium-sized, semi-double, borne in large clusters. They bloom profusely, but only once each spring or early summer. The canes are well armed with hooked prickles and in a warm climate, like California's, can grow to 30 or 40 ft (10 or 12 m). There is an enormous plant in the Rogue Valley Roses demonstration garden (Oregon, US).

'FORTY-NINER, CL.'.

Breeder: Discovered by William B. Moffet (United States, 1952).
Parentage: Sport of 'Forty-Niner'.
Classification: Climbing Hybrid Tea.
Newly opened flowers are rose-red with a yellow petal reverse. They fade to crimson, then cerise and pale yellow. They have a mild scent. The form is medium to large-sized, double and carried singly or in small clusters. The plant reblooms in continuous seasonal flushes. The foliage is dark green and glossy. The plant will grow to about 10 ft (3 m).

'FOURTH OF JULY'.

('Crazy for You', WEKroalt).
Breeder: Tom Carruth (United States, 1999).
Parentage: 'Roller Coaster' x 'Altissimo'.
Classification: Large-Flowered Climber.
This is a wonderfully colorful rose with its brilliant red and white stripes centered with a burst of golden stamens. The flowers are large, semi-double with ruffled petals, cup-shaped and carried in medium clusters. The flowers rebloom in seasonal flushes. They are scented of apple and rose. The plant can be slow getting established, especially in colder climates. In moderate to warm climates, once it has settled in, it can grow to about 15 ft (4.55 m). It is very disease resistant. This variety is known as 'Crazy for You' in the United Kingdom and 'Hanabi' in France.

'Fourth of July'.

'FRAGRANT CLOUD, CL.'.

('Climbing Nuage Parfumé', COLfragrasar, 'Duftwolke, Cl.', 'Nuage Parfumé, Cl.').
Breeder: Discovered by W.C. Collin (United Kingdom, 1973).
Parentage: Sport of 'Fragrant Cloud'.
Classification: Climbing Hybrid Tea.
The flowers open coral-red and become lighter and more pink with age. They are very large, full, high-centered like the Hybrid Tea they came from and are carried singly or in small clusters. There is a strong fragrance. The flowering is prolific and is repeated in regular seasonal flushes. The canes are armed with thorns, covered with dark green shiny foliage and will grow to about 10 ft (3 m).

'Fragrant Cloud, Cl.'

'FRANCESCA'.

Breeder: Rev. Joseph Hardwick Pemberton (United Kingdom, 1922).
Parentage: 'Danaë' x 'Sunburst'.
Classification: Hybrid Musk.
The flowers of 'Francesca' are apricot yellow fading to pale gold and finally to almost white with some color retained in the centers. They are also scented of tea, medium-sized, semi-double and are formed in large clusters. Weak stems may cause the flowers to hang their heads. The flowering is repeated in regular seasonal flushes. The plant is disease resistant and can be expected to grow to about 10 ft (3 m).

'Francesca'.

'FRANCINE AUSTIN' (AUSram).

Breeder: David C. H. Austin (United Kingdom, 1988).
Parentage: 'Alister Stella Gray' x 'Ballerina'.
Classification: Shrub. English Rose.
Pink, ovoid buds open to white, small, very full flowers with a flat rosette form. They are grouped in large clusters. There is a mild scent of musk. The flowers rebloom in regular seasonal flushes. Foliage is dark green and semi-glossy. The plant will climb, if given support, to about 10 ft (3 m).

'FRANCINE JORDI'.
See 'Pride of Venus'.

'FRAU ASTRID SPÄTH, CL.'

(Astrid Späth).
Breeder: Discovered by Victor Lens (Belgium, 1935).
Parentage: Sport of 'Frau Astrid Späth' which is a sport of 'Lafayette'.
Classification: Polyantha, Cl.
The flowers of this rose are light crimson, moderately scented, small to medium-sized, semi-double, cupped and are borne in small to medium clusters. They bloom continuously in regular seasonal flushes. The foliage is dark green and glossy. The plant can be seen at Roseto Carla Fineschi (Italy), San Jose

Heritage Rose Garden (California) and Sangerhausen (Germany).

'Frau Astrid Späth, Cl.'

'FRAU DR. HOOFTMAN'.

Breeder: G. A. H. Buisman (Netherlands, 1935).
Parentage: Unknown.
Classification: Climbing Polyantha.
The buds have touches of crimson on the outer petals, but the flower opens as coral-pink, and then fades from the outer petals inward to light cream-pink. The flowers are also large and double and are arranged singly or in small clusters. The rose is remontant in regular seasonal flushes. This is a moderately vigorous rose that can be trained as a small climber of about 8 ft. (2.5 m).

'Frau Dr. Hooftman'.

'FRAU IDA MÜNCH'.

Breeder: Wilhelm Beschnidt (Germany, 1919).
Parentage: 'Frau Karl Druschki' x 'Billard et Barré'.
Classification: Climbing Hybrid Tea.
The flowers are large, double, fragrant and light yellow with pale yellow reverse. The color fades to creamy-white. The floral form is globular with reflexed petal tips. The flowers are carried singly or in small clusters. The blooming is repeated in seasonal flushes. The plant is sometimes said to be about 4 ft (1.2 m), too short to be a climber, but it is reported in the Sangerhausen data base website as being about 11 ft in height (3.5 m). I observed it as a climber there.

'Frau Ida Münch'.

'FRAU KARL DRUSCHKI, CL.'

('Freedom', 'Grimpant Reine des Neiges', 'Snow Queen, Cl.', 'White American Beauty, Cl.').
Breeder: Discovered by Lawrenson (United Kingdom, 1906).
Parentage: Sport of 'Frau Karl Druschki'.
Classification: Hybrid Perpetual.
The long, pointed buds of this rose have touches of pink, but the flowers are pure white. They are also scentless, large-sized, double, high-centered and borne singly or in small clusters. There is one main summer bloom with an occasional repeat later in the season. The canes are well armed and are clothed with dark green foliage. The rose will climb, with much branching, to about 12 ft (3.65 m).

'Frau Karl Druschki, Cl.'.

'FRED LOADS'.

Breeder: Robert A. Holmes (United Kingdom, 1968).
Parentage: 'Dorothy Wheatcroft' x 'Orange Sensation'.
Classification: Climbing Floribunda (warm climates). Shrub (in cold climates).

Even by today's standards, 'Fred Loads' is a sensational color of brilliant orange-red. The flowers are single, medium to large-sized, open and gently ruffled and held in very large clusters. The plant is both hardy (USDA zone 4b) and shade tolerant. It will grow to about 10 ft (3 m), large enough to train as a small climber or it can be pruned and grown as a shrub. It makes an unforgettable hedge.

'Fred Loads'.

'FREIBURG II, CL.'.

Breeder: Discovered by L. Lindecke (Germany, 1953).
Parentage: A sport of 'Freiburg II'.
Classification: Climbing Hybrid Tea.

This light peachy-pink Climbing Hybrid Tea shows its ancestry plainly with its classic high-centered form. The outer petals spread out, reflex and fade while the center stays coiled up and remains a darker color for longer. The petal reverse is also a slightly darker shade. The flowers are large, double, moderately scented and are carried singly or in small clusters. They will rebloom in regular seasonal flushes. The plant grows only at Sangerhausen.

'Freiburg II, Cl.'.

'FREISINGER MORGENRÖTE'.

('Frisimo','KORmarter, 'Morgenröte', 'Sunrise').
Breeder: W. Kordes & Sons (Germany, 1988).
Parentage: Seedling x 'Lichtkönigin Lucia'.
Classification: Considered a Shrub, but grows and blooms like a Large-Flowered Climber.

This beautiful rose reminds me of the scenes from my childhood of the sun setting over the Pacific Ocean. The petals are basically copper-orange with more yellow on the petal reverse and toward the petal base and fading to pink at the tips, all part of a sunset or sunrise. The flowers are high-centered, large, double and are displayed in medium-sized clusters. They bloom in continuous seasonal flushes. The plant has dark green, glossy foliage that is healthy except for a tendency to blackspot. It will grow to about 8 ft and can be trained as a climber if given support and a reasonably warm climate or it can be grown as a shrub.

'Freisinger Morgenröte'.

'FRÉNÉSIE'.

Breeder: Maurice Combe (France, 1965).
Parentage: Unknown.
Classification: Large-Flowered Climber.
The flowers of this rose have an unusual color, vermilion subdued with a flush of taupe. The petal reverse is slightly lighter and more toward a crimson hue. The Sangerhausen catalogue calls it cinnabar-orange. The flowers are lightly fragrant, large, double and carried singly or in small clusters. The plant will grow to about 10 ft. (3 m).

'Frénésie'.

'FRITZ THIEDEMANN, CL.'

Breeder: Discovered by Reimer Kordes (Germany, 1961).
Parentage: Sport of 'Fritz Thiedemann'.
Classification: Climbing Hybrid Tea.
The flowers are large, double, moderately scented, high-centered and orange-red. They form an open cup in maturity. The roses rebloom in regular seasonal flushes. The plant is vigorous enough to be trained as a climber.

'Fugue'.

'FUGUE'. (MEItam).

Breeder: Marie-Louise Meilland (France, 1958).
Parentage: 'Alain' x 'Guinée'.
Classification: Large-Flowered Climber.
'Fugue' is only mildly scented, but is blessed with handsome deep, bright crimson-red, high-centered, medium-sized, double flowers that are profusely produced early in the season and repeat occasionally later. They open out well to a shallow cup with a glimpse of the stamens in the center of several orderly rows of reflexed petals. The plant will grow vigorously to about 10 ft (3 m).

'FULL MOON RISING'.

('Cyrano de Bergerac', Meivanery, 'Scouts Honour').
Breeder: Alain Meilland (France, 1999).
Parentage: Sport of 'Polka'.
Classification: Large-Flowered Climber (Romantica).
This rose is very ornamental with mildly scented, yellow flowers that fade to soft yellow and then to creamy yellow. The floral form is large, very full, with an old-fashioned shape, all borne singly or in small clusters. Remontancy is continuous in regular seasonl flushes.

The rose flowers look wonderful with perennials that have blue or purple flowers. The foliage is medium green and semi-glossy. The canes will grow to about 10 ft (3 m).

'Full Moon Rising'.

'FÜRST BISMARCK'.

Breeder: Heinrich Drögemüller (Germany, 1888).
Parentage: Seedling of 'Gloire de Dijon'.
Classification: Tea-Noisette.
This lovely rose has large, very double, golden-yellow flowers with quartered petals. The color is similar to that of 'Gloire de Dijon', but is more yellow and has smaller touches of pink on the outer petals. The rose blooms in continuous flushes during the flowering season. It is grown at 16-Eichen Rosenschätze Schaugarten (Germany), La Roseraie du Désert Display Garden (France) and Sangerhausen (Germany). The rose is sold in Europe. It was named for the German statesman who unified the German states and later, in 1871, became the first Chancellor.

'FÜRSTIN BISMARCK'.

Breeder: Heinrich Drögemüller (Germany, 1888).
Parentage: Gloire de Dijon (Tea Noisette, Jacotot 1850) × Comtesse d'Oxford.
Classification: Hybrid Tea-Noisette.
The large, double, scentless flowers open deep pink and fade to lighter pink. They bloom in flushes during the flowering season. The plant has dark green, glossy foliage and will grow to about 10 or 12 ft. (3 or 3.5 m). It can be seen at Sangerhausen and is commercially available in Europe.

'Fürst Bismarck'.

G

'Graham Thomas'.

'GAIL BORDEN, CL.'.

Breeder: Discovered by Jackson & Perkins (United States, 1960).
Parentage: Sport of 'Gail Borden'.
Class: Climbing Hybrid Tea.
'Gail Borden, Cl.' has deep, warm salmon pink flowers with yellow-cream petal bases and petal reverses. Their color fades to light pink with a white reverse. They are moderately fragrant. The flower form is high-centered in Hybrid Tea style, very large, double with reflexed petals at maturity. They are carried singly or in small clusters. The flowering repeats in regular seasonal flushes. The plants have glossy, medium green foliage and need frost protection since they are hardy only to USDA zone 7b. They will grow to about 10 ft (3 m).

'Gail Borden, Cl.'.

'GALWAY BAY' (MACba).

Breeder: Samuel Darragh McGredy IV (1966).
Parentage: 'Heidelberg' x 'Queen Elizabeth'.
Class: Large-Flowered Climber.
The flowers of 'Galway Bay' are a beautiful coral-pink, darker in the buds, petal reverses and the outer petal tips. The resulting color pattern with a lighter center is unusual since it is most common for roses to have darker centers. The newly opened bud is high centered like a Hybrid Tea, but soon becomes quite open and flattened, showing its stamens and reflexed petal tips. The flower form is medium to large-sized, semi-double and produced singly or in small clusters. The scent is mild. There is one main summer bloom with a few flowers later in the season. The canes have medium green, glossy foliage and will climb to 10 or 12 ft (3-3.65 m).

'Galway Bay'.

'GARDEJÄGER GRATZFELD'.

Breeder: Discovered by Gratzfeld (Germany, 1939).
Parentage: Sport of 'Rödhätte'. Trans: Red Riding Hood.
Class: Climbing Polyantha or Climbing Floribunda.
This rose has flowers that are lightly scented, medium-sized, semi-double to lightly double and deep crimson-pink. As they age they fade to lighter mauve-pink. They are carried singly or in small clusters on a plant that will grow to 6 or 8 ft (1.8 to 2.5 m).

'Gardejäger Gratzfeld'.

'GARDEN SUN'.

('Amber Glow', 'Göteborgs Rosarium', MEIvaleir, 'Michka', 'Valerie')
Breeder: Alain Meilland (France, circa 1996).
Parentage: 'Bettina, Cl.' x ('Westerland' x 'Circus').
Class: Large-Flowered Climber.
'Garden Sun' has large, high-centered, semi-double to double, yellow flowers with light flushes of apricot. They fade to light apricot-yellow and finally to ivory. In maturity the flower shape is cupped and filled with petals. There is a mild scent. The roses bloom in flushes all season. The foliage is medium green and glossy. The plant is a modest climber growing to about 7 ft (2.13 m).

'Garden Sun'.

'GARDENER'S GLORY' (Chewability).

Breeder: Christopher H. Warner (United Kingdom, pre-2005).
Parentage: 'Arcadian' x ('Baby Love' x ['Gingernut' x R. bella]).
Class: Large-Flowered Climber.
We don't often see a yellow rose that is really yellow. Most are light yellow to cream. Here is one that opens in a deep, bright yellow and fades slowly to a lighter tone. It is fragrant as well. The floral form is lightly double, medium to large-sized and is borne singly or in small clusters. The plant is clothed with foliage that is shiny, green, very disease resistant, shade and heat tolerant. It will grow to about 10 or 12 ft (3 or 3.65 m).

'GARTENDIREKTOR JULIUS SCHÜTZE'.

Breeder: Hermann Kiese (Germany, 1920).
Parentage: 'Madame Jules Gravereaux' x 'Pharisäer'.
Class: Climbing Hybrid Tea.
This is a very pretty climbing rose with pastel colors, good fragrance and an old-fashioned form. The flowers are light peach-pink with slightly darker centers and the tips of the quartered petals reflex strongly. The flower form is large, full and the flowers are carried singly or in small clusters. The plant is primarily summer-blooming with a few repeats later in the season. It is healthy other than being prone to rust.

'GASTON CHANDON'.

Breeder: Joseph Schwartz (France, 1884).
Parentage: Seedling of 'Gloire de Dijon'.
Class: Tea-Noisette.
The flowers of this rose are medium-sized, double and deep pink fading to light pink. There is a flush of yellow at the petal bases. The petal tips are strongly reflexed. The flowering occurs in continuous flushes during the entire blooming season. The plant will reach a height of about 8 ft (2.5 m). It will do best in a climate of USDA zone 7b or warmer.

'Gaston Chandon'.

'GAVROCHE'.

See 'Paprika'.

'GEHEIMRAT DUISBERG, CL.'.
See 'Golden Rapture, Cl.'

'GENERAL MACARTHUR, CL.'.
Breeder: Discovered by Hugh Dickson (United Kingdom, 1923).
Parentage: Sport of 'General MacArthur'.
Class: Climbing Hybrid Tea.
This rose is always described as scarlet, but it opens closer to pure red and then turns crimson very soon, an effect commonly known as bluing. The flowers have a strong damask fragrance and are semi-double to lightly double, large-sized, and borne singly or in small clusters. They have a classic Hybrid Tea shape and rebloom in regular seasonal flushes. The plant is healthy and quite vigorous, climbing to about 15 ft (4.55 m). It is a little tender and will grow best in a climate of USDA zone 7b or warmer. It was named in honor of the father of the WWII general by the same name.

'General MacArthur, Cl.'.

'GENERAL WASHINGTON'.
Breeder: Louis-Xavier Granger (France, 1860).
Parentage: Seedling of 'Triomphe de l'Exposition'.
Class: Hybrid Perpetual.
General Washington's flowers are pure crimson on opening, and then become more mauve with age. They are very large, very double and strongly scented. The floral form is a globular many-petaled rosette with reflexed petal tips and some quartering. There is good rebloom in regular seasonal flushes. The plant is usually described as a bush, but the long, arching canes make it easy to train as a climber of about 5 to 8 ft (1.5 to 2.5 m).

'General Washington'.

'GENERAL-SUPERIOR ARNOLD JANSSEN, CL.'.
Breeder: Discovered by Jan Böhm (Czechoslovakia (former), 1931).
Parentage: Sport of 'General-Superior Arnold Janssen'.
Class: Climbing Hybrid Tea.
This rose with the impressive name has flowers that are crimson with a strong touch of cerise, large, double and mildly fragrant. The flowers are carried singly (mostly) or in small clusters. The rose repeats its bloom in flushes during the flowering season.

'General-Superior Arnold Janssen, Cl.'.

'GEORGE DICKSON, CL.'.
Breeder: Discovered by F. J. Woodward (Unknown, 1949).
Parentage: Sport of 'George Dickson'.
Class: Climbing Hybrid Tea.
This rare rose has flowers that are very large, double, high-centered, very fragrant and bright crimson-red. They are

'Gertrude Jekyll'.

borne singly or in small clusters and rebloom in seasonal flushes. It seems to grow only at Roseto Carla Fineschi (Italy). It can be expected to grow sufficiently to be trained as a small climber.

'George Dickson, Cl.'.

'GERBE D'OR'. See 'Casino'.

'Gertrude Jekyll'.

'GERTRUDE JEKYLL' (AUSbord).

Breeder: David C. H. Austin (United Kingdom, 1986).
Parentage: 'Wife of Bath' x 'Comte de Chambord'.
Class: Shrub, English Rose.
'Gertrude Jekyll' is the perfect combination of old and new. From the old roses it gets a flower form of a very full flattened rosette full of quartered petals and the very rich old rose fragrance. They are held in small clusters. From the modern side comes the repeat bloom in continuous seasonal flushes. Add to that a lovely bright crimson color and you have quite a special rose. The canes are well armed with thorns (prickles) and covered with dark green leaves. They will grow much higher than usually stated. Mine has been about 10 ft (3 m) at times. 'Gertrude Jekyll' was a famous English gardener (1843-1932).

'Geschwind's Gorgeous'.

'GESCHWIND'S GORGEOUS'.

Breeder: Rudolf Geschwind (Austria-Hungary (former), before 1910).
Parentage: Unknown.
Class: Large-Flowered Climber.
'Geschwind's Gorgeous' is a pretty rose, but not exactly gorgeous. The flowers are light, bright crimson-red, semi-double, medium-sized and fragrant. There is a small white eye in the center and flushes of white on the petal reverse. The floral form is cupped, deep at first and opening out with maturity to reveal the stamens. The plant is sufficiently tall to be trained as a climber.

'GIARDINA'.

(L'Alhambra, RT 97-289, TAN97289.).
Breeder: Bred by Hans Jürgen Evers (Germany, 1997).
Parentage: Unknown.
Class: Large-Flowered Climber.
This handsome light pink climber has very full, medium to large-sized, fruit-scented flowers borne singly or in small clusters. The form is cupped with quartered petals. The rebloom is very good, occurring in regular seasonal flushes. The canes are covered with dark green, shiny leaves and will grow to about 10 to 13 ft (3 to 4 m).

'Giardina'.

'GINGER SYLLABUB' (HARjolly).

Breeder: Harkness (United Kingdom, 2000).
Parentage: 'Graham Thomas' x unnamed seedling.
Class: Large-Flowered Climber.
'Ginger Syllabub' nicely combines the old with the new.

'Ginger Syllabub'.

The flowers open apricot-yellow, but the outer petals fade very quickly with a flush of pink giving them a bicolored look. The form is old-fashioned—large, full and cupped with quartered petals. The blooming is modern—prolific and continuous in flushes during the regular season. The canes are clothed with dark green semi-glossy foliage and will climb to about 10 ft (3 m).

'GITES DE FRANCE'.

('Hagenbecks Tierpark', MEIwaton).
Breeder: Meilland International (France, 1995).
Parentage: Unknown.
Class: Large-Flowered Climber, Shrub.
This rose has flowers that are bright neon pink, semi-double and medium-sized. Initially they are deeply cupped, but with time they open out as a shallow cup with stamens clearly visible. They bloom prolifically in small to medium clusters and in continuous flushes during the regular season. The plant can be expected to climb to about 10 ft (3 m).

'Gites De France'.

'GLADIATOR'.

Breeder: Michele Malandrone (Italy, 1955).
Parentage: 'Charlotte Armstrong' x ('Pink Delight' x seedling of 'New Dawn').
Class: Large-Flowered Climber.
'Gladiator' has flowers of bright cerise-pink that are large, double, fragrant and have a high-centered bloom like a Hybrid Tea. They are carried singly or in small clusters. The foliage is dark green. There is one main flush of bloom in the early summer with a few flowers later in the season. The plant will reach a height of about 10 to 12 ft (3 to 3.65 m).

'Gladiator'.

'GLARONA'.

Breeder: Dr. Georg August Christian Krüger (Germany, before 1913).
Parentage: 'Sunset' x 'Madame Verrier Cachet'.
Class: Large-Flowered Climber.
The flowers of 'Glarona' are medium-sized, full, cupped with a globular shape and light rose-pink with outer petals fading to almost white. They are strongly fragrant. They are borne singly (mostly) or in very small clusters and hang their heads from the weight of the blossoms. There is one main bloom with an occasional repeat later in the season.

'Glarona'.

'GLENARA'.

Breeder: Alister Clark (Australia, before 1949).
Parentage: Unknown.
Class: Usually described as a Hybrid Tea, but could be classed as a Large-Flowered Climber.
'Glenara' has semi-double, medium to large-sized, lightly fragrant, deep pink flowers that fade to lighter pink. The form is an open, shallow cup. There is continuous bloom in flushes during the entire flowering season. The plant can be grown as a shrub or given support and grown as a climber of about 6 to 8 ft (1.8 to 2.5 m).

'GLORIA DEI, CL.'.
See 'Peace, Cl.'.

'Gloire De Dijon'.

'GLOIRE DE DIJON'.

('Glory John', 'Old Glory').
Breeder: Pierre and Henri Jacotot (France, 1850).
Parentage: 'Desprez à Fleur Jaune' x 'Souvenir de la Malmaison'.
Class: Tea-Noisette.
The buds are pale salmon (almost white) and open to buff-salmon flowers that fade quickly, starting at the outer petals, to light buff-salmon, sometimes with flushes of pink. The flowers are very full, large, fragrant and have a somewhat quartered form. They bloom in continuous seasonal flushes. The foliage is glossy and dark green. The plants are a little tender and will do best in a USDA zone of 7b or warmer. They are shade tolerant and very vigorous, growing to as much as 16 ft (4.9 m) in a warm climate.

'Gloire De Ducher'.

'GLOIRE DE DUCHER'.

('Germania' is sometimes given as a synonym.).
Breeder: Jean-Claude Ducher (France, 1865).
Parentage: 'Baron de Bonstetten' x 'Jean Soupert'.
Class: Hybrid Perpetual.
The very large, double flowers, opening from fat buds, are crimson at first. As they mature they become purpler and finally almost blue at the outer edges. The flowers are formed with the outer large petals arranged as a cup that holds the smaller, quartered inner petals. There may be a button-eye at the center. The flowers are carried singly or in small clusters. They repeat in flushes throughout the growing period. The potential height of the rose is modest at about 6 to 8 ft (1.8 to 2.5 m), but it will beautifully decorate a small trellis, a porch rail or a short fence.

'GLORIA DI ROMA, CL.'.

Breeder: P. Vially-Reymond (France, before 1966).
Parentage: Sport of 'Gloria di Roma'.
Class: Climbing Hybrid Tea.
This rose is described as having scarlet flowers, but I see more crimson than scarlet. They are large, very full, very fragrant and bloom once early in the summer with a few repeat flowers later in the season. The plant has dark green foliage and will grow to about 10 ft (3 m).

'GLORIA MUNDI, CL.'.
See 'Princess van Orange'.

'GLORIANA'.

(CHEwpope, 'Gloriana 97', 'Sugar Plum').
Breeder: Christopher H. Warner (United Kingdom, 1997).
Parentage: 'Laura Ford' x 'Big Purple'.
Class: Climbing Miniature (Patio Rose).
'Gloriana' is one of the wonderful series of Patio Roses by Chris Warner. This one is deep glowing purple with small, double, well-formed cupped flowers borne singly (mostly) or in very small clusters. They are said to have a scent of violets. The plant blooms in continuous seasonal flushes and will grow to about 8 ft (2.5 m).

'Gloriana'.

'GLORY OF CALIFORNIA'.

Breeder: Fr. George M.A. Schoener (United States, 1935).
Parentage: Unknown.
Class: Hybrid Gigantea.
There is much confusion in the literature about this rose. It is often wrongly attributed to Alister Clark, perhaps because it is a Gigantea hybrid. It is said by some sources to be fragrant and yellow, but most sources list it as a pink rose. The plant with this name at Sangerhausen has pink flowers, but the plant label reads yellow. It is the only plant we know of at the present so there is nothing to compare it with.

'Glory of Waltham'.

'GLORY OF WALTHAM'.

Breeder: Jacques Vigneron (France, 1865).
Parentage: seedling of 'Souvenir de Leweson Gower'.
Class: Hybrid Perpetual.
The flowers of this rose are very fragrant, large, double, old fashioned in form and deep crimson. Starting with the outer petals, it becomes more mauve with age. The inner petals are roughly quartered. The rose repeats well in continuous flushes during the flowering season. The plant can be trained as a pillar rose or as a climber for a small lattice or fence.

'Gold Badge, Cl.'

'GOLD BADGE, CL.'

('Gold Bunny, Cl.', 'Grimpant Rimosa', MEIgronurisar, 'Rimosa, Cl.').
Breeder: Meilland International (France, before 1991).
Parentage: Sport of 'Gold Badge'.
Class: Climbing Floribunda.
The flowers are medium to large, very full, deep pure yellow fading to light yellow with time. They are cupped, globose and filled with ruffled petals, a beautiful effect. The only asset they lack is fragrance. The individual blooms are held singly or in small clusters. They bloom prolifically in continuous seasonal flushes. The plant may climb to 8 ft (2.5 m).

'GOLD BUNNY, CL.'.
See 'Gold Badge, Cl.'.

'GOLD RUSH.' ('Goldrush').

Breeder: Carl G. Duehrsen (United States, 1941).
Parentage: Unknown.
Class: Large-Flowered Climber.
'Gold Rush' is well named with its brilliant golden-yellow flowers that fade to light yellow. They are medium to large-sized and double with a high-centered floral form that may reflect a Hybrid Tea in their ancestry. They are borne singly or in small clusters and have one main summer bloom with a few repeats later in the season. The canes are clothed with dark green, glossy foliage and will grow to about 10 ft (3 m).

'Golden Arctic'.

'GOLDEN ARCTIC'.

('Everblooming Pillar No. 84').
Breeder: Brownell Family (United States, 1954).
Parentage: Unnamed seedling x 'Free Gold' (hybrid tea, Brownell, 1948).
Class: Large-Flowered Climber (Sub-zero Rose collection).
This deep yellow climber with a strong fragrance, medium to large-sized and double flowers borne singly or in small clusters. The yellow color fades in time through light yellow to nearly white, outer petals first. The form is cupped with the outer petals reflexing to form triangular tips. This gives

the flowers a star-like appearance. They rebloom in continuous seasonal flushes. The plant is susceptible to blackspot, but healthy otherwise and can be expected to grow with much branching to about 8 ft (2.5 m).

'Golden Cascade'.

'GOLDEN CASCADE'.

Breeder: Dr. Dennison H. Morey (US, 1962).
Parentage: ('Captain Thomas' x 'Joanna Hill') x 'Lydia'.
Class: Large-Flowered Climber.
I have always liked this rose and have wondered why it has not been more popular. The color is a really good yellow and the flowers are large, double and held in small clusters. They open with a high-centered form, Hybrid Tea style, and finish with a domed shape filled with many short, slightly twisted petals. They have a moderate fruity fragrance. There is good repeat. The canes are provided with healthy, glossy, dark green foliage and will grow vigorously to about 13 ft (4 m).

'GOLDEN CLIMBER'.
See 'Mrs. Arthur Curtis James'.

'Golden Celebration'.

'GOLDEN CELEBRATION' (AUSgold).

Breeder: David C. H. Austin (United Kingdom, 1992).
Parentage: 'Charles Austin' x 'Abraham Darby'
Class: Shrub, English Rose.
The flowers are deep golden yellow, large, very full with an old-fashioned globular form and sometimes with roughly quartered petals. They are very fragrant and are held singly (mostly) or in small clusters. The repeat is good, occurring in continuous seasonal flushes. The plant is hardy to USDA zone 5b. The canes are healthy with semi-glossy, dark green foliage and will grow in a branching manner to about 10 ft (3 m) in a moderate to warm climate. The plant can be given support and trained as a climber or kept pruned and grown as a shrub.

'Golden Dawn, Cl.'

'GOLDEN DAWN, CL.'

Breeder: Discovered by J. A. Armstrong (United States US, 1935), George Knight & Sons (Australia, 1937), Edward Burton Le Grice / LeGrice (United Kingdom, 1947).

Parentage: Sport of 'Golden Dawn'.
Class: Climbing Hybrid Tea.
The Australian Hybrid Tea, 'Golden Dawn', has sported to a climbing form three times as shown above. The LeGrice sport is the one most frequently referred to in the literature, but they all have enough in common that one description will suffice for all with the exception of the paler color found with the Knight sport. The yellow buds may have touches of pink. The flowers are yellow and are also sometimes flushed with pink. They are large, double, very fragrant and globular in shape. The plant is mainly summer flowering with a few repeat blooms later in the season. It is healthy, shade tolerant and quite vigorous, growing to about 12 ft (3.65 m).

'GOLDEN FUTURE' (HORanymoll).

Breeder: Colin P. Horner (United Kingdom, 1999)
Parentage: Seed: 'Anytime' x ['Liverpool Echo' x ('Flamenco' x Rosa bella)].
Pollen: KORresia x 'Kiskadee'.
Class: Large-Flowered Climber.
It was not a simple breeding that produced this very attractive rose. The flowers are very fragrant, large, double, high-centered and medium yellow fading to cream, then to almost white. The petal reverse is also lighter. The plant has a potential height of about 10 to 12 ft (3 to 3.65 m).

'GOLDEN GATE'.

(KO 95/1858-07, KORgolgat).
Breeder: Tim Hermann Kordes (Germany, 1995).
Parentage: 'Postillion' x unnamed seedling
Class: Large-Flowered Climber.
'Golden Gate' has medium golden yellow flowers that are also medium to large-sized, double and cupped opening out to a flattened cup with wavy petals. A cluster of reddish stamens provides a center contrast to the yellow petals. There is a moderate citrus-like scent. The flowers are borne singly or in small clusters. The remontancy is good, occurring in continuous seasonal flushes. The canes are covered with very healthy, semi-glossy, medium green foliage and will grow to about 8 ft (2.5 m).

'Golden Gate'.

'GOLDEN OPHELIA, CL.'.

Breeder: Discovered by W. C. Hage (Holland 1924).
Parentage: Sport of 'Golden Ophelia'.
Class: Climbing Hybrid Tea.
This rose opens with medium yellow centers and light yellow outer petals. The flowers soon fade to cream, then almost white. The floral form is large, double and high-centered like its Hybrid Tea parent and is borne singly or in small clusters. There is a moderate fragrance. The bloom repeats in continuous seasonal flushes. The plant is a little tender and will grow best in a USDA zone of 7b or warmer. It is known to reach to about 10 ft (3 m).

'GOLDEN ORANGE CLIMBER'.

Breeder: Discovered by the Brownell Family (United States, 1937).
Parentage: Sport of Mrs. Arthur Curtis James.
Class: Large-Flowered Climber.
This rose matches its sport parent in every way except

for the color which is golden orange instead of pure yellow and it is lightly double instead of fully double. The flowers are fragrant and large and the broad petals open out sufficiently to show the stamens. If it grows as vigorously as 'Mrs. Arthur Curtis James' it can reach 15 or 16 ft. (5 m).

'Golden Orange Climber'.

'GOLDEN RAMBLER'. See 'Alister Stella Gray'.

'Golden Rapture, Cl.'.

'GOLDEN RAPTURE, CL.'

('Geheimrat Duisberg, Cl.').
Breeder: Discovered by Herbert C. Swim (United States, 1941). Also discovered by Knackfuss (Germany, 1954).
Parentage: Sport of 'Geheimrat Duisberg'.
Class: Climbing Hybrid Tea.
The flowers of this rose are medium yellow fading to pale yellow with centers remaining darker longer. They are large, double and have a moderate fragrance. The plant has glossy, medium green foliage and is vigorous enough to be trained as a climber.

'Golden Scepter, Cl.'.

'GOLDEN SCEPTER, CL.'

('Climbing Spek's Yellow', 'Spek's Yellow, Cl'.).
Breeder: Discovered by Walters (Unknown, 1956).
Parentage: Sport of 'Golden Scepter'.
Class: Climbing Hybrid Tea.
'Golden Scepter, Cl.' has deep yellow flowers that fade little, are moderately fragrant, lightly double and large with a high-centered bloom like a Hybrid Tea that opens out to reveal the golden stamens. Blooming is repeated in continuous seasonal flushes. The foliage is dark green and glossy. The plant is very vigorous, growing to about 16 ft (5 m).

'Golden Showers'.

'GOLDEN SHOWERS'.

Breeder: Dr. Walter E. Lammerts (United States, circa 1950).
Parentage: 'Charlotte Armstrong' x 'Captain Thomas'.
Class: Large-Flowered Climber.
'Golden Showers' has flowers in a good yellow with a wonderfully profuse bloom. They are large, double and carried singly or in small clusters. The form is open, rather loose and is centered by a bunch of reddish stamens. There is a tea fragrance. The plant blooms early and repeats in continuous seasonal flushes. The plant is healthy except for a tendency to blackspot, shade tolerant and very hardy down to USDA zone 3b. It will climb to about 10 to 14 ft (3 to 4.25 m).

'Golden Threshold'.

'GOLDEN THRESHOLD' (Virhold).

Breeder: M.S. Viraraghavan (India, 2005).
Parentage: 'Golden Showers' x 'Sirohi Sunrise'.
Class: Hybrid Gigantea.
This rose has flowers of deep, bright yellow rather than gold, but they are treasures, nevertheless. They are medium to large-sized and single with rounded petal tips. Reddish stamens contrast attractively with the yellow petals and produce red pollen. The flowers are formed mostly singly or sometimes in small clusters. There is one main summer flowering with a few repeats in the fall followed by a crop of large, round hips. The canes are well clothed with large, shiny, medium green foliage. They will grow stiffly to at least 10 ft (3 m), enough for a pillar or half an arbor. The name comes from the poetry anthology of Sarojini Naidu, a famous Indian poet and independence freedom fighter.

'GOLDEN VISION'.

Breeder: Alister Clark (Australia, before 1922).
Parentage: 'Maréchal Niel' x Rosa gigantea.
Class: Hybrid Gigantea.
The flowers of this rose are richly fragrant, medium-sized, semi-double and sometimes an unusually brilliant yellow. More often they are a softer color. Either way, the petal tips soon fade to cream or almost white. They are attractive in the newly opened bud, but become ragged in appearance with age. There is one main bloom very early in the season. The plant will grow with much vigor to about 30 ft (10 m).

'GOLDENER OLYMP'.

('Golden Olymp', KORschnuppe, 'Olympic Gold').
Breeder: Reimer Kordes (Germany, before pre-1984).
Parentage: Unnamed seedling x 'Goldstern'.
Class: Large-Flowered Climber.
The flowers of 'Goldener Olymp' are deep golden yellow with a hint of bronze, large, double and borne singly or in small clusters. The golden yellow fades to ivory. Wavy petals with scalloped petal tips give the rose a fluffy, open look. There is a strong, rich scent. There is one main summer bloom with a few flowers opening in the fall. The foliage is dark green with a matte surface. The plant will grow to about 8 ft (2.5 m) and will clothe a small pillar or a low fence.

'Goldener Olymp'.

'Goldfassade'.

'GOLDFASSADE'.

Breeder: Karl Baum (Germany, 1967).
Parentage: Unknown.
Class: Large-Flowered Climber.
This is a golden yellow rose that fades with age and develops flushes of red on the petal tips. The flowers are large, full and borne singly or in small clusters. As flower ages the outer petal tips reflex in an angular manner forming sharp triangular points and giving a star-like appearance. The petals open out to reveal the stamens. The foliage is dark green and glossy. The plant is fully remontant in seasonal flushes and will grow to about 10 ft (3 m).

'Goldilocks, Cl.'.

'GOLDILOCKS, CL.'.

Breeder: Discovered by Frederick L. Caluya (United States, 1951).
Parentage: Sport of 'Goldilocks'.
Class: Climbing Floribunda.

'Goldilocks, Cl.' has high-centered yellow buds with red tips that open to small, double yellow flowers held singly or in small clusters. With age the nice yellow color fades almost to white and the flowers open out and reflex, becoming roughly quilled. They have a sweet, moderate fruity scent. The rose reblooms well in continuous seasonal flushes. The foliage is dark green and glossy. Growth of 10 to 12 ft (3 to 3.65 m) can be expected.

'Goldmarie, Cl.'.

'GOLDMARIE, CL.'

('Climbing Goldmarie', KORkuma).
Breeder: Martens (Germany, 1998).
Parentage: Sport of 'Goldmarie'.
Class: Climbing Floribunda.
This Climbing Floribunda has mildly fragrant (fruity) medium-sized, semi-double, deep yellow-gold flowers formed singly or in small clusters that may have red flushes on the petal tips. The flowers open out as a flat rosette and show the stamens. The plant has dark, shiny foliage and will climb to about 8 ft (2.5 m).

'GOLDREGEN'.

Breeder: Werner Noack (Germany, 1986).
Parentage: Unknown.

'Goldregen'.

Class: Large-Flowered Climber.
'Goldregen' has flowers that are large, lightly double, high-centered, fragrant and deep yellow that fades to light yellow. They are borne singly or in small clusters and bloom in continuous seasonal flushes. The foliage is dark green and semi-glossy. It is healthy and hardy to USDA zone 5b. The vigorous plant will get as high as 16 ft (5 m).

'Goldstern'.

'GOLDSTERN'.

('Gold Star', 'Stella Dorata', TANtern).
Breeder: Mathias Tantau, Jr. (Germany, 1966).
Parentage: Unknown.
Class: Hybrid Kordesii, Shrub.
This 'Gold Star' will shine brightly in the garden when it opens from red-tipped, long, pointed buds to form large, double, fragrant, golden-yellow flowers. They are centered with reddish-gold stamens. In maturity, they spread out to flattened, rather loose rosettes that are carried singly or in small clusters. The plants are bushy, provided with dark green, glossy foliage and will grow to about 8 ft 2.5 m).

'Goldzauber'.

'GOLDZAUBER'.

Breeder: Franz Wänninger (Germany, 2013).
Parentage: Unknown
Class: Large-Flowered Climber.
This new and little known rose is bound to be a winner when people learn of its excellent qualities. The flowers are fragrant, large, double and bright yellow fading to cream from the outer petals inward. They repeat their bloom in repeated seasonal flushes. The plant I observed at Sangerhausen appeared very healthy. It will grow to about 8 ft (2.5 m).

'GOOD AS GOLD' (CHEWsunbeam).

Breeder: Christopher H. Warner (United Kingdom, 1994).
Introduced in United Kingdom by Warner's Roses in 1995 as 'Good as Gold'.
Parentage: 'Anne Harkness' x 'Laura Ford'.
Class: Climbing Patio Rose, Patio Climber (Warner's preference).
This Patio Climber from Warner has small, lightly double, sweetly scented, deep yellow flowers that look like small Hybrid Teas. They are borne in large clusters that repeat in continuous seasonal flushes. They have red stems, and

small, dark, shiny foliage and will grow rather stiffly to 7 or 8 ft (2.2 or 2.5 m).

'Graciosa'.

'GRACIOSA'.

Breeder: Werner Noack (Germany, 2002).
Parentage: Unknown.
Class: Large-Flowered Climber.
This is a beautiful rose with large, double, fragrant, high-centered pale pink flowers. The petals are softly ruffled. Flowers are borne singly or in small clusters. The plant is fully remontant in seasonal flushes. When I saw the plant at Sangerhausen the dark green, semi-glossy foliage appeared healthy. The plant grows to about 10 ft (3 m).

'Graham Thomas'.

'GRAHAM THOMAS'.

(AUSmas, 'Lemon Parody').
Breeder: David C. H. Austin (United Kingdom, 1983).
Parentage: 'Charles Austin' x ('Iceberg' x unnamed seedling).
Class: Shrub, English Rose.
Classed as a shrub, but climbing readily, this rose can get quite tall, 10 to 12 ft (3 to 3.65 m) according to the breeder. Mine has reached a height of about 10 ft (3 m) several times while covering itself with large, double, deeply cupped, very fragrant, deep yellow flowers and dark green shiny foliage. The plant is disease resistant and hardy down to USDA zone 5b.

'Granada, Cl.'.

'GRANADA, CL.'.

Breeder: Discovered independently by Rob Comley Roses (Australia, 1968), Herb Swim (United States, before 1969) and O. L. "Ollie" Weeks (United States, before 1969). All of these sports look much the same and the flowers closely resemble those of the sport parent.
Parentage: Sport of 'Granada'.
Class: Climbing Hybrid Tea.
The outer petals of this rose rapidly turn from yellow to orange-pink, then deep rose-pink, a result of sun exposure. The center remains more yellow, giving a bicolor effect. The flowers are high-centered in Hybrid Teas style, semi-double, large, strongly fragrant of spicy rose and held singly or in small clusters. The bloom is repeated in continuous seasonal flushes. The plant will grow to about 10 ft (3 m).

'GRAND HOTEL' (MACtel).

Breeder: Samuel Darragh McGredy IV (Northern Ireland, 1972).
Parentage: 'Schlösser's Brilliant' x 'Heidelberg'.
Class: Large-Flowered Climber.
'Grand Hotel' is a lovely bright red climber with medium

to large, high-centered, strongly fragrant, double flowers that open their wavy petals out to show the stamens. They occur singly or in small clusters and repeat their bloom in continuous seasonal flushes. The glossy, dark green foliage is healthy except for a tendency to blackspot. The plant will climb to about 13 ft (4 m).

'Grand Hotel'.

'GRANDESSA'.
See 'Messire Delbard'.

'Grand'mère Jenny, Cl.'

'GRAND'MÈRE JENNY, CL.'

(Gremsar, 'Grimpant Grand'mère Jenny').
Breeder: Discovered by Francis Meilland (France, 1958).
Parentage: Sport of 'Grand'mère Jenny'.
Class: Climbing Hybrid Tea.
The flowers of this Climbing Hybrid Tea are apricot-yellow with outer petals fading to light yellow and petal edges turning pink. The colors reflect those of 'Peace', a close ancestor. They are also very large, double, fragrant and have a high-centered shape, Hybrid Tea style. The plant reblooms in continuous seasonal flushes. It is very vigorous, growing to as much as 18 ft (5.5 m).

'GREAT WESTERN'.

Breeder: Jean Laffay (France, 1838).
Parentage: Seedling of 'Céline'.
Class: Bourbon. Sometimes classed as a China.
Even though it is usually classed as a Bourbon I have always thought 'Great Western' had something Gallica-like about it. Perhaps it is the color which is crimson with progressive aging to deep magenta and, finally, to purple. Or it is the strong fragrance. Or the way the petals fold up along the sides and sometimes show quartering. The flowers are very large-sized, double and globular in shape. They occur singly or in small clusters. The plants will grow to about 8 ft (2.5 m), enough to be trained as a small climber. It is hardy to USDA zone 5b and is once-blooming early in the season. The original Great Western was a steamship that carried the mail across the Atlantic Ocean in the early nineteenth century.

'Great Western'.

'GRETA LOUISA'.

Breeder: Bernhard Bührmann (Germany, 2009).
Parentage: Unknown.
Class: Large-Flowered Climber.
The flowers of this rose are large, very double and fragrant. The buds are deep yellow which lightens and becomes more coral, then more pink as the flower opens. The fully open flower is pink with cream edges and finally fades to cream. The plant grows tall enough to be trained as a moderately vigorous climber.

'Greta Louisa'.

'GRIBALDO NICOLA'.

Breeder: Soupert & Notting (Luxembourg, 1890).
Parentage: 'Bouquet d'Or' x 'La Sylphide'.
Class: Tea-Noisette.
The older references describe a rose with silvery white flowers having a light pink reverse and a yellow center. The rose by this name grown today is light pink fading to white. The photographs do not reveal a yellow center. The current Sangerhausen catalogue reports very large, double flowers and a moderate fragrance. The floral form is initially globose becoming flattened with age. There is one main bloom with occasional repeats later in the season. The plant grows to about 8 ft (2.5 m).

'Gribaldo Nicola'.

'GRIMPANT DELBARD'.
See 'Delbard's Orange Climber'.

'GRISELDIS'.

Breeder: Rudolf Geschwind, pre-1894.
Parentage: (Rosa canina x unknown Tea or Hybrid Tea) x (Rosa canina x unknown Bourbon).
Class: Bourbon.
This rose was originally described as having flowers that were large, full and bright pink. It was said to be reblooming. The rose labeled 'Griseldis' that I saw at Sangerhausen has flowers that are semi-double, medium-sized, and fragrant. I was told that it produced some flowers in the fall. It is doubtful that the rose by this name being grown today is the authentic Geschwind variety.

'Griseldis'.

'GRUSS AN AACHEN, CL.'.

Breeder: Wilhelm J. H. Kordes II (Germany, 1937).
Parentage: Sport of 'Gruss an Aachen'.
Class: Climbing Floribunda.
The flowers of this rose are light pink with a hint of apricot and a slightly darker center. They are large, very full, mildly fragrant and borne singly or in small clusters. The floral form is an old-fashioned rosette and the flowers are so heavy with many petals that they tend to bend their heads. The profuse bloom is repeated in continuous seasonal flushes. The foliage is large and medium green. The plant can be expected to grow to 12 ft (3.65 m).

'Gruss An Aachen, Cl.'.

'Gruss An Baden Baden'.

'GRUSS AN BADEN BADEN'.

(CHEwrubyramb).
Breeder: Christopher H. Warner (United Kingdom, 2000).
Parentage: Unknown.
Class: Miniature Climber.
This miniature Climber has small, scentless, semi-double, deep scarlet-red flowers that open out into flat rosettes and show a small white eye topped by a bunch of golden stamens. They are formed in medium clusters. The plants have small, dark green foliage and will grow to about 8 ft (2.5 m).

'GRUSS AN FRIEDBERG'.

Breeder: Discovered by Rogmanns (Germany, 1902).
Parentage: Sport of 'Duarte de Oliveira'.
Class: Tea-Noisette.
This climbing sport is identical to its sport parent in form, but quite a big change in color, going from salmon-pink to yellow. The flowers are medium to large, moderately fragrant, double, deeply cupped on opening, then expanding into old-fashioned quartered blooms. They are formed singly or in small clusters. They are not rain tolerant so they will bloom best in a warm, dry climate. They will rebloom in continuous seasonal flushes. The plant will grow to at least 6.5 ft (2 m).

'Gruss An Friedberg'.

'GRUSS AN HEIDELBERG' (KORbe).

Breeder: Reimer Kordes (Germany, 1959).
Parentage: 'World's Fair' x 'Floradora'. Some sources maintain the breeding was 'Minna Kordes' x 'Floradora'.
Class: Climbing Floribunda. Not a Kordesii as is sometimes reported.
The deep, bright crimson flowers of this rose have a lighter rose-red reverse. They are large, double with a mild fragrance and a high-centered bloom like a Hybrid Tea. They are borne singly or in small clusters. The flowering is

repeated in continuous seasonal flushes. The foliage is medium green and glossy. The plant will reach up to at least 8 ft (2.45 m).

'Gruss An Teplitz, Cl'.

'GRUSS AN TEPLITZ, CL.' ('Catalunya').

Breeder: Discovered by Storrs & Harrison Co. (United States, 1911).
Parentage: Sport of 'Gruss an Teplitz'.
Class: Bourbon, Cl.
This rose has medium-sized, double, very fragrant, cupped, deep bright crimson blooms with small white petal bases and a lighter reverse. The flower form is tightly cupped at first and opens out to show the stamens. The flowers are borne in small clusters, usually in threes. This is the reason for the English nickname, "Grows in Triplets". The rose has excellent remontancy, blooming in continuous seasonal flushes. The nearly thornless plant will grow to 10 or 13 ft (3 or 4 m). The bush form grows to about 6.5 ft (2 m) and can be grown as a small climber.

'GUINÉE'.

Breeder: Charles Mallerin (France, 1938).
Parentage: 'Souvenir de Claudius Denoyel' x 'Henri Quinard'.
Class: Climbing Hybrid Tea, Large-Flowered Climber.
'Guinée' has beautiful dark, velvety, garnet-red flowers turning a little more crimson with age. The red color does not develop bluish tones as occurs in some red roses. The flowers are medium to large-sized, full, high-centered, very fragrant and carried singly or in small clusters. The plants repeat their bloom in continuous seasonal flushes. The foliage is large and dark green on vigorous canes that will climb to 16 ft (5 m).

'Guinée'.

'GUIRLANDE FLEURIE'.

Breeder: Marcel Robichon (France, 1968).
Parentage: Unknown.
Class: Large-Flowered Climber.
The flowers are bright pure red, semi-double to lightly double, medium-sized and Hybrid Tea shaped in large clusters. Some people say they can detect a mild fragrance, others say there is none. The plant blooms in continuous flushes throughout the season. It is very vigorous, climbing to 19 or 20 ft (6 m).

'Guirlande Fleurie'.

'GWEN NASH'.

Breeder: Alister Clark (Australia, 1920).
Parentage: 'Rosy Morn' x unnamed seedling.
Class: Large-Flowered Climber.
'Gwen Nash' is pink with a light touch of coral and has light yellow petal bases that gently reflect the yellow stamens. It fades to pale lavender-pink and white. The flowers are large, semi-double and cupped with wavy petals adding a decorative touch. They are borne singly or in small clusters. The rose has one main summer bloom with a few repeats later in the season. The foliage is gray-green and rugose. The plant is sufficiently tall to be trained as a climber. It will grow and bloom best in a warm climate.

'GWYNNE CARR, CL.'.

Breeder: Discovered by Lomans (1932). Discovered by Walter Easlea & Sons (United Kingdom, 1934).
Parentage: Sport of 'Gwynne Carr'.
Class: Climbing Hybrid Tea.
This rose is very light pink with slightly darker centers, fragrant, large, double and carried singly (mostly) or in small clusters. The outer petals are large, open and reflex to form triangular tips. The inner ones are quartered. The rose reblooms in continuous seasonal flushes. The bushy plant bears light green foliage and is tall enough to be trained as a climber.

H

'Handel'.

'H. V. Machin, Cl.'.

'H. V. MACHIN, CL.'.

('Herbert Vessey Machin, Cl.').
Breeder: Discovered by Hugh Dickson (United Kingdom, 1919), Howard & Smith (United States, 1922).
Parentage: Sport of 'H. V. Machin'.
Class: Climbing Hybrid Tea.
The flowers of this rose are dark red, large, double and formed with a high center like an exhibition Hybrid Tea. The bloom repeats in regular seasonal flushes. Erich Unmuth has confirmed that 'H. V. Machin, Clg.' at Sangerhausen is identical with Geschwind's 'Meteor'. It is possible that all of the plants in commerce are incorrect.

'Hadley, Cl.'.

'HADLEY, CL.'.

Breeder: Discovered by Heizmann (Switzerland, 1927) and Teschendorff (Germany, 1927).
Parentage: Sport of 'Hadley'.
Class: Climbing Hybrid Tea.
This Climbing Hybrid Tea has dark crimson flowers that are very fragrant, large and double with a typical high-centered Hybrid Tea form. They are borne singly (mostly) or in small clusters. The flowers are weak-necked so they will look down on you from their climbing height of about 10 ft. They have a tendency to blue (become more purple) and may burn in the sun of a hot climate. The rose repeats in continuous seasonal flushes.

'Haldensleben'.

'HALDENSLEBEN'.

Breeder: Hans Jürgen Weihrauch (Germany, 2005).
Parentage: Unknown.
Class: Shrub. Climber.
The opening bud is yellow with nuances of scarlet and coral, but the opened flower shows only the yellow. The bright colors fade quickly leaving a cream-colored rose. The flowers are large and lightly double, not very double as is sometimes reported. The plant can be trained as a shrubby climber of about 8 ft (2.5 m).

'HAMBURG' ('Hambourg').

Breeder: Wilhelm J. H. Kordes II (Germany, 1935).
Parentage: 'Eva' x 'Daily Mail Scented Rose'.
Class: Lambertiana.
'Hamburg' has deep, bright crimson flowers that are large, semi-double, mildly scented and borne in very large clusters. The plant has one main summer bloom with a few flowers produced later in the season. The foliage is glossy and medium green. The plant will grow sufficiently tall to be trained as a small climber.

'HAMBURGER PHOENIX'.

('Hamburg Rising', 'Hamburger Phönix')
Breeder: Wilhelm J. H. Kordes II (ca. 1918 - 1955) (Germany, 1954).
Parentage: Rosa kordesii x unnamed seedling.

'Hamburger Phoenix'.

Class: Hybrid Kordesii.

The name of this rose can be roughly translated as "The Bird of Fire from Hamburg", a fitting description of the medium-sized, semi-double, unfading, brilliant, dark red-cupped flowers. They are carried in large clusters and they have a mild fragrance. The plant is a moderate climber to about 8 or 9 ft (2.45 to 2.75 m). The foliage is disease resistant, shiny and dark green. The rose is fully remontant, repeating its bloom in continuous seasonal flushes.

'Hamburg'.

'Handel'.

'HANDEL'.

('Haendel', MACha, ,McGredy's Händel').

Breeder: Samuel Darragh McGredy IV, Northern Ireland (1965).

Parentage: 'Columbine' x 'Heidelberg'.

Class: Large-Flowered Climber.

This rose has cream-colored flowers with deep pink petal edges that fade to white and light pink. They are also medium to large-sized, double, mildly fragrant and cupped. The petals reflex strongly at the tips giving a rolled up appearance. The flowers are carried singly or in small clusters. The rose reblooms with continuous seasonal flushes. The plant has glossy, dark green foliage and will climb vigorously to 13 to 16 ft (4 to 5 m).

'Hansa'.

'HANSA' (Rosa rugosa 'Hansa').

Breeder: Schaum & Van Tol (Netherlands, 1905).

Parentage: Unknown.

Class: Hybrid Rugosa, Shrub.

'Hansa' has flowers that are large, double, fragrant and an unusual violet-red color. They are produced singly (mostly) or in small clusters. The heavy blooms are weak-necked and tend to nod. The rose reblooms in continuous seasonal flushes and forms large, decorative hips. The plant is thorny, very disease resistant, drought tolerant, very hardy (USDA zone 3b) and is recommended by the Swedish Rose Society for growing in northern Sweden. 'Hansa' is sensitive to pesticide sprays and may drop its leaves if sprayed. The foliage is medium green and rugose (wrinkled). The plant can be grown as a large shrub, a hedge or as a small climber of about 7 or 8 ft (2.15 to 2.5 m), but beware. It tends to sucker.

'Happy, Cl.'.

'HAPPY, CL.'.

('Climbing Alberich', GORhappy, 'Happy Wanderer').
Breeder: Discovered by Barbara A. K. Gordon (United States, 2000).
Parentage: Sport of 'Happy' (Polyantha, de Ruiter, 1954)
Class: Climbing Polyantha.
'Happy, Cl.' is a climbing sport of one of De Ruiter's seven dwarfs (without Snow White). Originally, they were named with the German equivalents of the English names, 'Happy' being known as 'Alberich'. The flowers are crimson with a mild fragrance and are small, semi-double to lightly double and cupped. They are reported as blooming in continuous seasonal flushes by some people and as having one main summer blooming with a few repeats later by others. The foliage is dark green and shiny and the canes are very vigorous, climbing 10 to 12 ft (3 to 3.65 m). Don't confuse this rose with McGredy's 1966 Floribunda.

'Happy Child'.

'HAPPY CHILD' (AUScomp).

Breeder: David Austin (United Kingdom, before 1992).
Parentage: (Seedling of 'Iceberg' x unnamed seedling) x 'Hero'.
Class: Shrub, English Rose.
The flowers have a Tea Rose fragrance and are large, very full and deep, brilliant yellow. They are formed singly or in small clusters. The plant has few thorns and will grow sufficiently to be trained as a small climber in a warm climate. This variety has been discontinued by David Austin Ltd., but it is available from numerous commercial sources.

'HARBINGER' ('Herald of Spring').

Breeder: Alister Clark (Australia, before 1923). Introduced in Australia by E. & W. Hackett Ltd. in 1923.
Parentage: Hybrid of Rosa gigantea.
Class: Hybrid Gigantea.
The plant by this name now being offered for sale is quite beautiful, but may not be Clark's original rose. It has flowers that are large, single and pink fading to light pink. The white petal bases form a white eye. There is a light fragrance. The blooming period begins in the early spring along with 'Tonner's Fancy' and 'Jessie Clark'. The medium green, large,

drooping foliage is typical of Rosa gigantea. The plant will grow vigorously to 20 ft (6 m) or more in a warm climate.

'Harlekin'.

'HARLEKIN'.

('Arlequin', 'Harlequin', 'Kiss of Desire', KORlupo)
Breeder: Reimer Kordes (Germany, before 1986).
Parentage: Unknown.
Class: Large-Flowered Climber.
'Harlekin's' white flowers look as though the petal tips have been dipped in a wash of deep crimson-pink. They are large, well shaped, cupped, full, blessed with a rich wild rose scent and occur singly or in small clusters. Blooming is prolific in continuous seasonal flushes. The canes bear dark green, shiny foliage and will climb in a bushy manner to about 12 ft (3.65 m). They are hardy to USDA zone 4b.

'HARLEQUIN'.
See 'Harlekin'.

'HARRY WHEATCROFT, CL.' (Caribia, Cl.)

Breeder: Discovered by Fred A. Mungia, Sr. (United States, 1980), David W. Ruston (Australia, 1990).
Parentage: Sport of 'Harry Wheatcroft'.
Class: Climbing Hybrid Tea.
This rose has spectacular colors with yellow stripes and flecks on an orange-vermilion ground. The center and reverse are plain yellow. This decorative effect is enhanced by the flowers being large and double. They are borne singly or in small clusters. Blooming occurs in continuous seasonal flushes. The plant has glossy dark green leaves and grows sufficiently tall to be trained as a pillar rose. It is becoming very rare.

'Harry Wheatcroft, Cl.'.

'HASSI-MESSAOUD'.

Breeder: Hemeray-Aubert (France, 1961).
Parentage: Unknown.
Class: Large-Flowered Climber.
This Large-Flowered climber has medium-sized, double, vermilion flowers borne singly or in small clusters. They have a classical high-centered Hybrid Tea form. The plant has one main bloom with occasional flowers opening later and grows vigorously to about 15 ft (4.5 m).

'HEIDELBERG'.
See 'Gruss an Heidelberg'.

'HEIN EVERS, CL.'.

Breeder: Discovered by Reimer Kordes (Germany, 1963).
Parentage: Sport of 'Hein Evers'.
Class: Climbing Floribunda.
This is a pure red rose that is medium-sized, semi-double or lightly double, mildly fragrant and held singly or in small clusters. It blooms in continuous seasonal flushes. The plant has glossy, medium green foliage and can be trained as a climber.

'HEINRICH BLANC' (HELklewei).

Breeder: Karl Hetzel (Germany, 1994).
Parentage: Unknown.
Class: Large-Flowered Climber.
The flowers of this rose open light pink and soon fade to white giving a lovely pastel effect. The pink remains longest in the center. The flowers are medium-sized, full with reflexed petal tips and are borne in small clusters. The bloom is fully remontant. The plant can be trained as a short climber of about 10 ft (3 m).

'Helen Traubel, Cl.'.

'HELEN TRAUBEL, CL.'.

Breeder: Discovered by Jack Miller (Australia, 1970).
Parentage: Sport of 'Helen Traubel'.
Class: Climbing Hybrid Tea.
This attractive rose opens from long buds to apricot, high-centered, very large, double flowers born singly (mostly) or in very small clusters. The apricot color morphs to pink in time, and then fades completely to cream. The flowers are too heavy for the floral stems so they nod and look down on the viewer from their climbing support. They repeat their prolific bloom in continuous seasonal flushes. The foliage is medium green with a matte surface. The plant can be trained as a climber.

'Hella'.

'HELLA' (KO 03/2053-01, KORditwol).

Breeder: Tim Hermann Kordes (Germany, 2003).
Parentage: Unnamed seedling x unnamed seedling.
Class: Large-Flowered Climber.
The opening buds reveal white flowers with centers of pale coral. The coral fades and disappears soon, leaving the flowers totally white. They are medium to large-sized, semi-double to lightly double, slightly wavy, initially open cupped, then become flattened and are borne singly or in small clusters. There is very little fragrance, if any. The blooming is repeated in continuous seasonal flushes. The foliage is semi-glossy and dark green. The plant is hardy to USDA zone 5b and will grow with much branching to about 8 ft (2.5 m). This rose honors Hella Brumme, former director of the Europa Rosarium at Sangerhausen, Germany.

'HENRY IRVING'.

Breeder: Conard & Jones Co. (United States, 1907).
Parentage: Unknown.
Class: Climbing Hybrid Perpetual.
The flowers are crimson, strongly fragrant, medium-sized, full and deeply cupped with a globose shape. They are held singly or in small clusters. There is one main bloom with some repeats later in the season. The plant's expected height is about 10 ft (3 m). Sir Henry Irving was a highly regarded English actor who was knighted.

'Henry Kelsey'.

'HENRY KELSEY'.

Breeder: Dr. Felicitas Svejda (Canada, before pre-1984).
Parentage: R. Kordesii × seedling of D02.

Class: Hybrid Kordesii.

This rose is not only very hardy (USDA zone 3a), but is quite pretty as well. The flowers are crimson red, moderately fragrant, medium-sized, and semi-double to lightly double. They are borne in large clusters. The petals are cupped at first then open out widely and reveal a contrasting bunch of golden yellow stamens at maturity. There is one main, extended bloom in spring or early summer with a small rebloom in the fall. The plant has shiny, dark green, disease resistant foliage. In a moderate climate, with support, it will grow to at least 10 ft (3 m), but less in a cold climate.

'Hermann Löns'.

'Heritage'.

'HERITAGE' (AUSblush, 'Roberta').

Breeder: David C. H. Austin (United Kingdom, 1984).
Parentage: Unnamed seedling x 'Iceberg'.
Class: Shrub. English Rose
This is a delicate, pastel pink rose with flowers that are medium to large-sized, very full, and strongly fragrant. They are grouped in small clusters or grow singly. The inner petals are often quartered and are held in a cup formed by the outer petals. It blooms in continuous seasonal flushes. The nearly thornless canes are bushy, are clothed with small, semi-glossy, dark green foliage and will climb to about 7 ft (2 m), a sufficient height for a small pillar or trellis. The plant is hardy to USDA zone 5b and is disease resistant.

'HERMANN LÖNS'.

Breeder: Mathias Tantau (Germany, 1931).
Parentage: 'Ulrich Brunner Fils' x 'Red-Letter Day'.
Class: Described variously as a Climbing Hybrid Tea or a Climbing Hybrid Perpetual. Large-Flowered Climber seems like a better fit. This rose is beautiful in its simplicity. The flowers are bright dark blood-red with matching stamens and a small white eye. They are also single, large, slightly cupped or flat and carried in large clusters. There is a moderate fragrance. The plant has one main summer bloom with an occasional repeat later. It can be trained as a climber of 10 to 13 ft (3 to 4 m).

'Hermann Robinow, Cl.'.

'HERMANN ROBINOW, CL.'.

Breeder: Discovered by Peter Lambert (Germany, 1934).
Parentage: Sport of 'Hermann Robinow'.
Class: Climbing Hybrid Tea.
This Climbing Hybrid Tea has flowers that are medium pink with lighter petal edges, large, double, very fragrant and borne singly (mostly) or in small clusters. There is one main bloom with a few repeats later in the season. The plant can be trained as a climber of about 8 ft (2.5 m).

'High Hopes'.

'Hero'.

'HERO' (AUShero).

Breeder: David C. H. Austin (United Kingdom, 1982).
Parentage: 'The Prioress' x unnamed seedling.
Class: Shrub. English Rose.
The flowers of 'Hero' are deeply cupped at first, and then open out to form rosettes with wavy inner petals. They are large, double, very fragrant of myrrh and cluster-flowered. The outer petals are light pink, the center darker. The foliage is medium green and semi-glossy. The plant will grow, with repeated branching, to about 7 ft (2 m) with support in a warm climate. It is hardy to USDA zone 5b, but it will be smaller there. Leander swam the Hellespont for Hero, a priestess of Aphrodite.

'High Hopes'.

'HIGH HOPES' (HARyup, Karlesrube).

Breeder: Harkness (United Kingdom, 1992).
Parentage: 'Compassion' x 'Congratulations'.
Class: Large-Flowered Climber.
'High Hopes' has light pink, medium to large-sized, semi-double to lightly double flowers carried singly (mostly) or in small clusters. There is a moderate, spicy fragrance. The flowers form an open cup with rolled back petals. The plant blooms in continuous seasonal flushes. It has semi-glossy, medium green foliage. The potential height is about 10 to 12 ft (3 to 3.65 m).

'HIgh Noon'.

'HIGH NOON'.

('Legacy of Iola Maule').
Breeder: Dr. Walter E. Lammerts (United States, 1946).
Parentage: 'Soeur Thérèse' x 'Captain Thomas'.
Class: Large-Flowered Climber.
'High Noon' has golden yellow buds flushed with red and bright yellow flowers that soon fade to cream, then to ivory. The dark, reddish stamens add interest. The flowers are also medium to large-sized, lightly double. They are initially cupped, and then become flattened. They are borne singly or in small clusters. The petals reflex along the sides leaving rather square tips. They have a moderate fragrance. The plant blooms in continuous seasonal flushes. The canes are very hardy, have glossy, dark green foliage and will climb to a height of 10 or 12 ft (3 or 3.65 m).

'HIGH SOCIETY' (JACadyna).

Breeder: Dr. Keith W. Zary (United States, 2005).
Parentage: 'Dynamite' x 'America'.
Class: Large-Flowered Climber.
'High Society' has flowers of unfading light red that are large, full, scented of damask and are borne singly (mostly) or in small clusters. They rebloom in continuous

'High Society'.

seasonal flushes. The foliage is shiny, dark green and disease resistant. The plant will grow to about 12 or 14 ft (3.65 or 4.25 m). It is somewhat tender and will grow and bloom best in USDA zone 7a or warmer.

'Highfield'.

'HIGHFIELD'.

(HARcomp, 'Lemon Sunbeam').
Breeder: Discovered by Harkness (United Kingdom, 1980).
Parentage: Sport of 'Compassion'.
Class: Large-Flowered Climber.
'Highfield' has sported as a light yellow, semi-double rose from 'Compassion', a medium pink, fully double rose that is also larger. The result is simply a less attractive flower, but one that can be grown for personal preference. Other characteristics are shared by parent and offspring such as large size, strong, sweet fragrance and repeat bloom in continuous seasonal flushes. The plant has a climbing potential of about 10 ft (3 m).

'HIGH FLYER'.
See 'Dynamite'.

'Holstein, Cl.'.

'HOLSTEIN, CL.'.

Breeder: Discovered by Wilhelm J. H. Kordes II (Germany, 1947).
Parentage: Sport of 'Holstein'.
Class: Climbing Floribunda.
The flowers of this rose are colored deep, bright red with small white petal bases, mildly scented, large, single and grouped in large clusters, reminding me of red poppies. They will bloom prolifically in continuous seasonal flushes. The foliage is healthy and bronze-green. The plant can be trained as a climber.

'HOME SWEET HOME, CL.'.

Breeder: Unknown.
Parentage: Sport of 'Home Sweet Home'.
Class: Climbing Hybrid Tea.
This rose has flowers in a very pretty medium pink color. They have a strong damask fragrance and are large and double with a globular floral form. The rebloom is good and occurs in regular seasonal flushes. The plant is covered with glossy, dark green foliage and is quite vigorous, climbing to about 15 ft (4.55 m). It is commercially available in the United Kingdom.

'HONEYMOON'.

(KO 02/1705-99, KORhemtra, 'Vanilla').
Breeder: W. Kordes & Sons (Germany, 2002).
Parentage: Unknown.
Class: Large-Flowered Climber.
'Honeymoon' is as romantic in appearance as its name. The flowers are large, very double and creamy white with pink centers. They fade to white in time. The broad outer petals reflex at the tips and the small inner petals fold lengthwise and reflex along the sides. They are globular in form and are held singly or in small clusters. Expect growth of about 10 ft (3 m).

'Honor Bright'.

'HONOR BRIGHT'.

Breeder: S. Eacott (United Kingdom, 1950).
Parentage: ('New Dawn' x 'Allen Chandler') x ('Mrs. W. J. Grant, Cl.' x 'Richmond, Cl.').
Class: Large-Flowered Climber.
This is a cheerful rose with bright crimson, strongly fragrant, medium-sized, semi-double flowers. There is a main summer bloom followed by an occasional repeat later in the season. The plant can be trained as a climber of about 10 ft (3 m).

'HUGH DICKSON CL.'.

Breeder: Discovered by the California Rose Company, (United States, 1914).
Parentage: Sport of 'Hugh Dickson'.
Class: Climbing Hybrid Perpetual.
I recently saw this lovely old rose at the Roseraie du Val-de-Marne in France. It has flowers that are richly fragrant, high-centered, large, very full and crimson red. The form is cupped with petals that reflex into points and

'Hugh Dickson Cl.'.

open widely to show the stamens. They are carried singly or in small clusters and bloom in regular seasonal flushes. The plant can be trained as a climber of about 10 ft (3 m).

'HUME'S BLUSH TEA-SCENTED ROSE'.

('Odorata').
Breeder: Unknown. First collected by Dr. Dieck (Germany) in China late in the nineteenth century.
Parentage: Unknown.
Class: Tea, China.
The flowers are pale pink, fading almost to white at the petal edges, double, large and tea-scented. The plant can be trained as a small climber of about 7 or 8 ft (2 or 2.5 m). There are several clones in existence. The one at Sangerhausen (Germany), originally from China, is called the Beales form. It matches quite well with Redoute's illustration. There is also a clone from Laos and the rose 'Spice' from the Bermuda collection has been identified as 'Hume's Blush'.

'HUNTINGTON'S HERO'.

Breeder: Discovered by Huntington Botanic Gardens Trustees (United States, 1995). Commemorates the 75th anniversary of the garden.
Parentage: Sport of 'Hero'.
Class: Shrub. English Rose.
Whereas the Austin rose 'Hero' is medium pink and lightly double, its sport, 'Huntington's Hero' is light apricot, fading to blush pink and then white, and is semi-double. Both roses are sweetly fragrant, have large, deeply cupped flowers and one main bloom with some repeats later. They will both grow to about 6 or 7 ft (1.8 to 2 m) with the benefits of a support and a warm climate.

'Intervilles'.

'Ice White, Cl.'.

'ICE WHITE, CL.'.

(MACvisar, Vision Blanc, Cl.).
Breeder: Discovered by Samuel Darragh McGredy IV (circa 1966).
Parentage: Sport of 'Ice White'.
Class: Climbing Floribunda.
The flowers are pure white except for a hint of cream in the centers or blotches of crimson from rain damage. They are medium-sized, lightly double and borne singly or in small clusters. The floral form is an open, orderly rosette with stamens fully visible. Rebloom occurs in continuous seasonal flushes. Well-armed canes with thorns have semi-glossy, dark green foliage. Grows to about 10 ft (3 m).

'Iceberg, Cl.'.

'ICEBERG, CL.'.

('Fée des Neiges, Cl.', 'Schneewittchen, Cl.').
Breeder: Discovered by Cants of Colchester (United Kingdom, 1968).
Parentage: Sport of 'Iceberg'.
Class: Climbing Floribunda.
'Iceberg, Cl.' opens from white buds with a faint flush of pink to medium to large, mildly fragrant, semi-double to double, open-cupped flowers. There is a hint of yellow in the centers. There is nothing unique or exciting about this solid, dependable white garden rose, but when you view a well-grown plant of 'Iceberg, Cl.' you are bound to be impressed by the profuse snow white roses in large clusters. The plant is fully remontant in continuous seasonal flushes. It is almost thornless, has light green foliage and will grow vigorously to about 15 ft (4.55 m).

'Illusion'.

'ILLUSION'.

Breeder: Reimer Kordes (Germany, 1961).
Parentage: Unknown.
Class: Hybrid Kordesii, Large-Flowered Climber.
This pretty bright red rose has large, double, moderately fragrant flowers held in large clusters that repeat well in seasonal flushes. It is iron-clad in typical Kordesii fashion; hardy to USDA zone 5b, heat tolerant and disease resistant. The rather thorny plant has medium green glossy leaves and will grow to about 10 ft (3 m).

'ILSE KROHN'.

Breeder: Reimer Kordes (Germany, 1957).
Parentage: 'Golden Glow' x Rosa kordesii.
Class: Hybrid Kordesii.
'Ilsa Krohn' has white flowers with buff-yellow centers. They are large, very double, mildly fragrant, high-

'Ilse Krohn'.

centered and borne singly or in small clusters. There is one main bloom followed by a few flowers later in the season. The foliage is large, dark green and glossy. The plant is cold hardy and disease resistant and will grow vigorously to about 16 ft (5 m).

'Ilse Krohn Superior'.

'ILSE KROHN SUPERIOR'.

Breeder: Discovered by Reimer Kordes (Germany, 1964).
Parentage: Sport of 'Ilse Krohn'.
Class: Hybrid Kordesii.
This rose is, in some ways, an improvement on its sport parent. The flowers are larger, but double rather than very double, and they are more fragrant. The remontancy is superior, occurring in continuous seasonal flushes. Most other features are the same in both varieties. The white flowers with buff-yellow centers are carried singly or in small clusters. The plant has dark green, shiny foliage and is cold hardy and disease resistant. It is a little shorter than 'Ilsa Krohn', growing to about 10 ft (3 m). Because of its hardiness it is widely grown in Scandinavia.

'IMPÉRATRICE ROUGE'.
See 'Red Empress'.

'INDEPENDENCE, CL.'.

('Kordes' Sondermeldung, Cl.').
Breeder: Discovered by Baldacci & Figli (Italy, 1960).
Parentage: Sport of 'Independence'.
Class: Climbing Floribunda.
The flowers of this rose are deep, bright vermilion-red, moderately fragrant, large, double and borne singly (mostly) or in small clusters. The floral form is cupped at first, then opens widely to reveal the stamens. The petals reflex to form pointed petal tips, giving the flower a star-like appearance. The rose repeat blooms in regular flushes during the season. It has large dark-green, glossy foliage and will grow to about 13 ft (4 m).

'Independence Day, Cl.'.

'INDEPENDENCE DAY, CL.'.

Breeder: Discovered by W. & J. Brown (Unknown, 1930).
Parentage: Sport of 'Independence Day'.
Class: Climbing Hybrid Tea, Climbing Pernetiana.
This rose is an unusual and beautiful color, golden yellow flushed with orange, especially toward the petal bases. The flowers are medium to large-sized, strongly fragrant, semi-

'Independence, Cl.'.

double to double, high-centered like a Hybrid Tea and held singly or in small clusters. They are remontant in continuous seasonal flushes. The plant is very disease resistant and can be trained as a climber.

'Indra'.

'INDRA'.

Breeder: Tantau (Germany, before pre-1936).
Parentage: ('Ophelia' x Rosa multiflora) x 'Florex'.
Class: Large-flowered Climber, Hybrid Multiflora.
'Indra' has flowers that are mildly scented, medium to large-sized, semi-double and medium pink fading to light pink, then to white. The floral form is a flattened cup made up of wavy petals that reflex at the tips and are carried in large clusters. The rose is once-blooming early in the season. The plant will grow to 10 ft (3 m) or more, enough to decorate a small arbor.

'Inspiration'.

'INEZ SASTRE'.

See 'Raspberry Cream Twirl'.

'INSPIRATION'.

Breeder: Martin R. Jacobus (United States, 1946).
Parentage: 'New Dawn' x 'Crimson Glory'.
Class: Large-Flowered Climber.
Initially, the flowers of 'Inspiration' are medium pink with small white petal bases and then fade to light pink. They are strongly fragrant, large and semi-double and are carried singly (mostly) or in small clusters. The bloom is repeated in continuous seasonal flushes. Large, dark green, shiny foliage covers the branching upright canes. The height is potentially about 10 ft (3 m). There is a Hybrid Tea and also a Floribunda by the same name as this rose.

'Intervilles'.

'INTERVILLES'.

Breeder: Marcel Robichon (France, 1968).
Parentage: 'Étendard' x unnamed seedling.
Class: Large-Flowered Climber.
'Intervilles' has flowers that are brilliant scarlet, medium-sized, semi-double to lightly double and lacking in fragrance. They open with a high-centered form that matures to a cup shape. Individual flowers are held singly or in small clusters. There is one, main, profuse bloom followed by occasional flowers later in the season. The foliage is dark green and glossy. Growth can be expected to reach about 10 ft (3 m).

'INTRÉPIDE'.

Breeder: Maurice Combe (France, 1972).
Parentage: Unknown.
Class: Climbing Hybrid Tea.
This Climbing Hybrid Tea should be better known for its large, double, brilliant scarlet-orange flowers that open out into classic, well shaped rosettes. They are produced singly or in small clusters and are remontant. The plant is a modest climber, reaching up to about 7 ft (2 m), but tall enough for a small pillar or trellis.

'Intrèpide'.

'Irène Bonnet'.

'IRÈNE BONNET'.

Breeder: Clément Nabonnand (France, 1920).
Parentage: Unknown.
Class: Climbing Hybrid Tea.
This rose clearly shows its Hybrid Tea heritage with its high-centered bloom form. The flowers are medium-sized, full, moderately fragrant and pale pink with darker centers and a darker reverse. It blooms in continuous seasonal flushes. The plant will climb, in a branching style, to about 8 ft (2.5 m).

'IRENE MARIE' (Morlindsey).

Breeder: Ralph S. Moore (United States, 2006).
Parentage: 'Golden Gardens' x 'Playboy'.
Class: Climbing Miniature.
Climbing miniatures make wonderful contributions to pots or window box plantings where a full-sized rose would be overwhelming as well as finding their value in the rose border. 'Irene Marie' will make a strong statement with its brilliant gold petals edged with orange. With age, the colors morph to pink petal edges and white centers. The flowers are small, single and grouped in small clusters. There is no fragrance. The prolific bloom is repeated in continuous seasonal flushes. The plant is almost thornless and has semi-glossy, medium green foliage. It will grow to about 6 ft (1.85 m).

'ISKRA'.

See 'Sparkling Scarlet'.

'IVORY FASHION, CL.'.

Breeder: Discovered by J. Benjamin Williams (United States, 1964).
Parentage: Sport of 'Ivory Fashion'.
Class: Climbing Floribunda.
This rose has flowers of ivory with light yellow centers that fade to cream. The stamens have golden anthers and dark scarlet styles that add interest to the light colors. The flowers are large and semi-double to lightly double and are strongly fragrant. They bloom in continuous seasonal flushes. The plant is healthy, fairly hardy and heat tolerant as well. It can be trained as an average climber of about 10 ft (3 m).

J

'Jeanne Lajoie'.

'J. B. CLARK, CL.'.

Breeder: Discovered by Max Vogel (Germany, 1939).
Parentage: Sport of 'J.B. Clark'.
Class: Climbing Hybrid Tea. Climbing Hybrid Perpetual.
Crimson-red flowers that are fragrant, very large, full and Hybrid Tea-shaped with high centers opening to a cupped form and carried singly (mostly) or in small clusters characterize this rose. It reblooms well in continuous seasonal flushes. In a hot climate it will have the best color if grown in partial shade. The plant is armed with thorns and grows in a bushy manner to about 15 ft (4.55 m).

'J. OTTO THILOW, CL.'.

Breeder: Discovered by Howard Rose Co. (United States, 1933).
Parentage: Sport of 'J. Otto Thilow'.
Class: Climbing Hybrid Tea.
This pretty rose has flowers of deep rose-pink, darkest in the centers. They are moderately fragrant, large-sized, double, well formed like Hybrid Teas and borne singly (mostly) or in small clusters. They bloom in continuous seasonal flushes. The plant can be trained as a small climber of about 10 ft (3 m).

'J. Otto Thilow, Cl.'.

'JACKIE, CL.'.

Breeder: Ralph S. Moore (United States, 1957).
Parentage: 'Golden Glow' x 'Zee'.
Class: Climbing Miniature.
The flowers of 'Jackie, Cl.' are mildly fragrant, small, very full and soft yellow with a darker center aging to cream. The petals reflex strongly lengthwise to become quilled. The flowers are borne in large clusters. There is a good rebloom in continuous seasonal flushes. The plant has medium green foliage and will reach a height of about 10 ft (3 m).

'Jackie, Cl.'.

'JACOB'S LADDER'.

('The Schofield Rose', WEKsacsodor).
Breeder: Tom Carruth (United States, 2003).
Parentage: 'Santa Claus' x (Hybrid of R. soulieana x 'Dortmund').
Class: Large-Flowered Climber.
'Jacob's Ladder' has flowers that are scarlet-vermilion, moderately fragrant, semi-double and medium-sized. The petals are arranged in an orderly rosette form. The flowers are formed singly or in small clusters. The plant has large, glossy, dark green foliage and will grow to 9 or 10 ft (2.75 m to 3 m).

'Jacob's Ladder'.

'JACOB'S ROBE' (Wekausboy).

Breeder: Tom Carruth (United States, 2006).
Parentage: 'Autumn Sunset' x 'Playboy'.
Class: Large-Flowered Climber.

When the flowers first open they are very showy, mainly yellow with scarlet flushes and broad stripes on the tips of the outer petals. As they mature the stripes become more extensive and more pure pink, especially on the outer petals, until it becomes the dominant color. The petals open out wide and flattened to show the stamens. The flowers are borne in small clusters and repeat well in continuous seasonal flushes. The plants have large, glossy, medium green foliage and will grow to about 8 ft (2.5 m).

'James Galway'.

'JAMES GALWAY' (AUScrystal).

Breeder: David C. H. Austin (United Kingdom, 2000).
Parentage: 'Heritage' x unnamed seedling.
Class: Shrub. English Rose.
'James Galway' has flowers that are large, very full and deep coral pink on opening. They fade and become more mauve with age. They are carried singly or in small clusters and rebloom in regular seasonal flushes. The plant has large, semi-glossy medium green foliage and can be trained as a climber of about 10 ft (3 m). This rose was named for the talented Irish flautist, James Galway, in commemoration of his 60th birthday.

'JAMES SPRUNT'.

Breeder: Discovered by Rev. James M. Sprunt (United States, 1858).
Parentage: Sport of 'Cramoisi Supérieur'.
Class: Climbing China.
This Climbing China, named for its discoverer, has bright crimson, medium-sized, double, fragrant flowers with a few white spots or streaks. They are

'James Sprunt'.

fuller and larger than those of the sport parent. The form is globose rosettes with rolled back petals that occur singly or in small clusters. Flowering is repeated in continuous flushes during the warm season. The plant is armed with thorns and may grow to as much as 20 ft (6 m). This is not the same plant as 'Cramoisi Supérieur, Cl.' which is a seedling rather than a sport of 'Cramoisi Supérieur'.

'Janet'.

'JANET' (AUSpishus).

Breeder: David C. H. Austin (United Kingdom, 2003).
Parentage: 'Golden Celebration' x unnamed seedling.
Class: Shrub. English Rose.
'Janet' has ivory outer petals and deep pink centers with light yellow petal bases and petal reverses. The flowers are large, very full, globose in form and borne singly or in small clusters. There is one main early bloom with some repeats later in the season. The plant is healthy, but not entirely rain proof so it will do best in a warm, dry climate. If given support

and favorable conditions the plant will grow to about 10 ft (3 m). The flowers are heavy and the supporting canes are somewhat thin so they tend to hang their heads.

'JANET INADA' (Ardinada).

Breeder: Paul Barden (United States, 2007).
Parentage: 'Westerland' x 'Abraham Darby'.
Class: Large-Flowered Climber.
Janet Inada is the co-owner of Rogue Valley Roses, a rose nursery in Oregon, United States. Her decorative namesake flower is golden yellow-orange becoming lighter with age, medium-sized, very double, strongly fragrant of fruit and borne singly or in small clusters. The rebloom is in continuous flushes throughout the season. The plant has healthy, hardy (USDA zone 5), glossy, dark green foliage and can be trained as a small climber of about 8 ft (2.5 m). The flowers are good for cutting.

'JANET MORRISON'.

Breeder: Alister Clark (Australia, 1936).
Parentage: 'Black Boy' x Seedling.
Class: Large-Flowered Climber.
The flowers of this rose are large, semi-double and borne singly or in small clusters. They are bright cerise-pink with a lighter reverse and have a spicy fragrance. There is one main bloom followed by an occasional flower later in the season. The plant will grow to at least 10 ft (3 m). It is a very good rose and should be more widely available.

'Jasmina'.

'JASMINA'.

('Climbing Jasmina', Korcentex).
Breeder: Tim Hermann Kordes (Germany, 1996).
Introduced in Germany (Kordes, 2005), Canada (Palantine Roses, 2007), Australia (Treloar Roses, 2010).
Parentage: Unnamed seedling x 'Centenaire de Lourdes'.
Class: Large-Flowered Climber.
The flowers open mid-pink and fade to light violet and then almost to white. They are medium-sized, very full, sweetly fragrant, cupped and quartered like an old-style rose and carried in large clusters. The remontancy is good and takes place in continuous seasonal flushes. The plant has semi-glossy, medium green, disease resistant, hardy foliage (USDA zone 5) and is well armed with thorns. It can be trained as a climber of about 10 ft (3 m).

'Jaune Desprez'.

'JAUNE DESPREZ'.

('Desprez à Fleur Jaune').
Breeder: Jean Desprez (France, 1830).
Parentage: 'Blush Noisette' x 'Parks' Yellow Tea-scented China'.
Class: Noisette, Tea-Noisette.
'Jaune Deprez' was an attempt to create a yellow rose before rose breeders had been able to introduce the genes for strong yellow from Rosa foetida into the garden roses of the day. It is soft buff-yellow with a touch of gold that fades to pale coral-pink and is medium to

large, double, and fragrant with a fruit-like scent, cupped, quartered and borne in small clusters. It sometimes has a button eye. There is good rebloom in continuous flushes during the flowering season. The plant is very vigorous, climbing to as much as 20 ft (6.1 m).

'Jazz'.

'JAZZ'.

('Naheglut', POUlnorm, Pulnor, 'That's Jazz').
Breeder: L. Pernille and Mogens Nyegaard Olesen (Denmark, 1986).
Parentage: unnamed seedling x 'Norita'.
Class: Large-Flowered Climber.
This is a good rose with large, very full, dark bright red, high-centered Hybrid Tea-style flowers having a strong spicy scent. As the flowers mature they open out to a cup shape and then become more flattened. They are carried singly or in small clusters. Rebloom occurs in continuous seasonal flushes. The plant has semi-glossy, medium green foliage and will grow to about 13 ft (4 m).

'JEANNE D'ARC'.

Breeder: Victor Verdier (France, 1848).
Parentage: Unknown.
Class: Noisette.
The medium-sized, semi-double blooms of the rose are pure white, very fragrant, cupped, then open and flat. Individually they are rather ordinary, but create a pretty, delicate effect en masse. They are fully remontant, blooming in continuous seasonal flushes. The plant will grow to a height of about 8 ft (2.5 m) and can be trained as a small climber. Growth and

'Jeanne D'Arc'.

flowering will be best in a warm climate. There are many other roses by this name—an Alba, a Polyantha, a Tea, a Moss and a Hybrid Perpetual. Jeanne d'Arc (Joan of Arc) was a French general who led the troops in a war with England. She was burned at the stake at age 19 on May 30, 1431 by the victorious English forces. This remarkable woman is honored in France with a yearly national feast day on the second Sunday in May.

'Jeanne Lajoie'.

'JEANNE LAJOIE' (Jeanne La Joie).

Breeder: Edward P. Sima (United States, 1975).
Parentage: ('Casa Blanca' x 'Independence') x 'Midget'.
Class: Climbing Miniature, Climbing Patio Rose.
The flowers of 'Jeanne Lajoie' are a lovely shade of medium pink with a darker pink reverse. They are small, double, and

mildly fragrant. They are carried in medium to large-sized clusters. They rebloom in very prolific, continuous seasonal flushes described by one gardener as sheets of bloom. The plant drops its old flowers nicely. The canes branch vigorously and can reach a height of about 10 ft (3 m).

'JERI JENNINGS' (ARDjeri).

Breeder: Paul Barden (United States, before 2007).
Parentage: 'Joycie' x 'Trier'.
Class: Hybrid Musk.
'Jeri Jennings' is a very attractive rose, both in color and form. The color is soft medium yellow with hints of buff and gold fading to cream from the outer petals inward. The flowers are small, very double, strongly scented of musk, globular in shape with an old rose form and are borne in medium-sized clusters. The plant reblooms in prolific, regular, continuous seasonal flushes. The canes have very healthy semi-glossy, medium green foliage and will grow, in a graceful arching style, to about 7 ft (2.13 m), enough for training as a small climber for a low fence or a small trellis or pillar.

'JESSIE CLARK'.

Breeder: Alister Clark (Australia, 1915).
Parentage: Rosa gigantea x 'Madame Martignier'.
Class: Hybrid Gigantea.
The flowers are large and single with softly wavy petals. They open medium pink with a white center and fade to pale pink. There is a light fragrance. The floral arrangement is single or small clusters. The plant has one prolific bloom very early in the season. In a warm climate it will grow vigorously to as much as 25 ft (7.62 m).

'JOHN GROOMS'.

Breeder: Peter Beales (United Kingdom, 1993).
Parentage: Unknown.
Class: Large-Flowered Climber.
'John Groom's' flowers are deep salmon-pink in the bud then lighten some to medium pink on opening. The petal bases have flushes of soft yellow. The blooms are medium to large-sized and lightly double and are held singly (mostly) or in small clusters. There is little or no fragrance. The rose is summer flowering with scattered blooms later in the season. The plant will do best in a warm climate where it will grow to about 10 ft (3 m). The name of this rose honors the John Grooms Charity, an organization that helps disabled people.

'John Russell, Cl.'.

'JOHN RUSSELL, CL.'.

Breeder: Discovered by Ketten Frères/Bros./Gebrüder (Luxembourg, 1930).
Parentage: Sport of 'John Russell'.
Class: Climbing Hybrid Tea.
The flowers of this rose are deep crimson with flushes of purple, especially on the outer petals. They are very large, full and high-centered like the flowers of the parent. The outer petals open out and gently reflex while the inner petals remain in a closed cup. There is no fragrance, unfortunately, but the plant reblooms in continuous seasonal flushes, a bonus. The canes are armed with thorns and tend to get mildew, but are healthy otherwise and will grow to about 10 ft (3 m).

'Jolly Dance'.

'JOLLY DANCE'.

('Heester Jolly Dance').
Breeder: Discovered by W. Kordes & Sons (Germany).
Parentage: Sport of 'Leverkusen'.

Class: Hybrid Kordesii.
'Jolly Dance' has flowers that are apricot with yellow petal bases. The apricot color is deepest in the center and fades to pink as the flower ages. The floral form is double, medium to large, cupped and opens flat with maturity. There is a mild lemon scent. The rebloom occurs in continuous flushes during the blooming season. Much like other Kordesiis, this plant has shiny, dark green foliage and is hardy to USDA zone 5b. It can be given support and trained as an 8 to 10 ft climber (2.45 to 3 m).

'Jonkheer J. L. Mock, Cl.'.

'JONKHEER J. L. MOCK, CL.'.

Breeder: Discovered by Jos. Timmermans (Netherlands, 1910).
Parentage: Sport of 'Jonkheer J. L. Mock'.
Class: Climbing Hybrid Tea.
This rose has flowers that open medium pink with a hint of coral. They fade to light pink that blues a little. The reverse is slightly darker crimson-pink. They are also strongly fragrant of tea, large, and double with a high-centered, Hybrid Tea form. The rebloom is in repeated flushes during the blooming season. The plant has dark green foliage and will grow vigorously to about 15 to 20 ft (5 to 6 m).

'JOSEPH'S COAT'.

Breeder: David L. Armstrong and Herbert C. Swim (United States, 1964).
Parentage: 'Buccaneer' x 'Circus'.
Class: Large-Flowered Climber.
'Joseph's Coat' is a real show stopper with its brilliant colors. The bright red buds open to orange flowers that become yellow with scarlet tips on the outermost

'Joseph's Coat'.

petals and then morph to totally deep scarlet with yellow petal bases. Since there are flowers in different stages of development on the plant at the same time, the effect is reminiscent of the coat of many colors worn by Joseph in the bible story. The flowers are mildly fragrant, large-sized, double and borne in small clusters. They rebloom in regular flushes during the whole blooming season. The plant is armed with thorns and covered with shiny dark green foliage that is somewhat susceptible to rust and blackspot, but has the merit of being hardy down to USDA zone 4b. It will climb stiffly to about 12 ft (3.65 m).

'Josephine Baker, Cl.'.

'JOSEPHINE BAKER, CL.'.

Breeder: Discovered by Joseph Orard (France, 1983).
Parentage: Sport of 'Josephine Baker'.
Class: Climbing Hybrid Tea.
This lovely rose has flowers that are dark red, large, double,

mildly fragrant and high-centered like its Hybrid Tea sport parent. They are carried singly on long stems. It repeats well in continuous seasonal flushes. The plant is slightly tender and will do best in a climate of USDA zone 7b or more. It can be trained as a climber or grown as a bush rose. Josephine Baker was a beautiful Afro-American woman who became a night club entertainer in Paris during the 1930's. She was decorated for her work with the French resistance during WWII including being given the Chevalier of the Légion d'honneur by General Charles de Gaulle.

'Josephine Bruce, Cl.'.

'JOSEPHINE BRUCE, CL.'.

Breeder: Discovered by Bees (United Kingdom, 1954).
Parentage: Sport of 'Josephine Bruce'.
Class: Climbing Hybrid Tea.
This is an excellent red climbing rose with a beautiful color and good vigor. The flowers are very dark, velvety crimson with blackish overtones, large, full, high-centered, moderately fragrant and held singly or in small clusters. They rebloom in continuous seasonal flushes. The plant is quite vigorous, growing to as much as 15 ft (4.55 m). It will perform best in a climate of USDA zone 7b or warmer.

'JUDE THE OBSCURE'.

(AUSjo, N22B89).
Breeder: David C. H. Austin (United Kingdom, 1989).
Parentage: 'Abraham Darby' x 'Windrush'.
Class: Shrub. English Rose.
The flowers of 'Jude the Obscure' are initially apricot, but fade to light apricot yellow, then to pale cream. Their form is double, large, cupped in a globular fashion and they are carried singly or in small clusters. The plant reblooms in repeating flushes during the flowering season. It is hardy to USDA zone 5b, armed with thorns and has semi-glossy, medium green foliage. It will grow to about 10 ft (3 m) if given support and beneficial conditions or it can be grown as a shrub. The rose received the Corona Regina Teodelinda Perfume Award in Monza, Italy.

'Jude the Obscure'.

'JULES'.

Breeder: Paul E. Jerabek (United States, 1997).
Parentage: Unknown.
Class: Large-Flowered Climber.
This is a beautiful dark red rose with large, very double, but very mildly scented flowers. Initially it has a cupped bloom form, but finally opens out to look more like a Floribunda. It is reported to be disease resistant and hardy to zone 5b.

'Jules Margottin, Cl.'.

'JULES MARGOTTIN, CL.'.

Breeder: Discovered by John Cranston & Company (United Kingdom, 1874).
Parentage: Sport of 'Jules Margottin'.
Class: Climbing Hybrid Perpetual.

The flowers of this rose open cherry-red and become more cerise with age. They are large, double, and fragrant. They have an old-fashioned form, and are borne singly or in small clusters. The bloom repeats in continuous seasonal flushes. The plant is well armed with many reddish thorns and is noted for having dense foliage. It can be trained as a climber or pruned and grown as a shrub.

'Jules Margottin, Cl.'.

'JULIEN POTIN, CL.'.

Breeder: Discovered by J. A. Bostick (United States, 1935).
Parentage: Sport of 'Julien Potin'.
Class: Climbing Hybrid Tea.

This Climbing Hybrid Tea has flowers that open in bright, deep, rich golden yellow and fade to light yellow, then to cream. The reverse is lighter. The form is large, double, and high-centered in Hybrid Tea style, opening to show the stamens. The flowers

'Julien Potin, Cl.'.

are borne singly or in small clusters. They have a moderate fragrance. The rose blooms in continuous flushes during the flowering season. It has glossy, medium green foliage and can be trained as a climber.

'Juliette Greco'.

'JULIETTE GRECO' (Delblabe).

Breeder: G. Delbard (France 1999).
Parentage: Unknown.
Class: Shrub.

This rose has flowers that are light yellow fading to light cream, medium-sized, very double, and strongly fragrant. They are deeply cupped and globose at first, and then open out to form a rosette. They are long stemmed and good for cutting. The plant will grow to as much as 15 ft (4.57 m).

'Julius Fabianics De Misefa'.

'JULIUS FABIANICS DE MISEFA'.

Breeder: Rudolf Geschwind (Austria-Hungary (former), 1902).
Parentage: 'Bardou Job' x 'Souvenir du Dr. Passot'.
Class: Tea. Tea Hybrid.
The flowers of this rose are bright crimson with flushes of scarlet, large, double, cup formed and moderately fragrant. John Hook, a nurseryman in France, reports the canes as being very thorny. It is said to grow to about 8 ft (2.5 m) and can be trained as a climber. Erich Unmuth, a prominent European rosarian, questions whether 'Julius Fabianics de Misefa' in gardens and in commerce is the original Geschwind rose. Martin Weingart, a German nurseryman, has identified 'Eugenie E. Marlitt', another Geschwind rose, and "Maggie", an American found rose, as being identical to 'Julius Fabianics de Misefa'.

'June Morn'.

'JUNE MORN'.

Breeder: Jean Henri (J. H.) Nicolas (United States, 1939).
Parentage: 'Madame Grégoire Staechelin' x 'Souvenir de Claudius Pernet, Cl.'.
Class: Large-Flowered Climber.
Initially the flowers are a very pretty light crimson with yellow centers and a lighter yellowish reverse, but change with age to an unattractive mauve pink with white centers. They are large, double, high-centered and borne singly or in small clusters. There is one main bloom followed by occasional repeats later in the season. The plant can be trained as a small climber of about 8 ft (2.45 m). The foliage has a tendency to blackspot.

K

'Kir Royal'.

'Kaiser Wilhelm'.

'KAISER WILHELM'.

('Kaiser Wilhelm der Siegreiche', 'Empereur Wilhelm').
Breeder: Heinrich Drögemüller (Germany, 1889).
Parentage: 'Madame Bérard' x 'Perle des Jardins'.
Class: Climbing Tea.
I was unable to see this rose when I last visited the Europa Rosarium at Sangerhausen. The Rosenverzeichnis (catalog) of the collection describes it as having large, very full, moderately fragrant flowers of light yellow with a deeper yellow center that has flushes of pink. The plant has glossy foliage and can be trained as a climber of average height. The rose is remontant. "Siegreiche" means victorious.

'Kaiserin August Victoria, Cl.'.

'KAISERIN AUGUST VICTORIA, CL.'.

('Climbing Kaiserin', 'Climbing Kaiserin Auguste Viktoria', 'Mrs. Robert Peary').
Breeder: Discovered by Alexander Dickson II (United Kingdom, 1897).
Parentage: Sport of 'Kaiserin Auguste Viktoria'.
Class: Climbing Hybrid Tea.
This beautiful Climbing Hybrid Tea opens from green-flushed buds to ivory-white flowers with pale yellow centers. They are large, very double, moderately fragrant and high-centered like the Hybrid Tea sport parent. They bloom in continuous flushes all during the growing season, but not prolifically. The canes are armed with thorns, hardy to USDA zone 5b, and covered with healthy, rich, medium green foliage. They will climb to about 10 ft (3 m).

'Kaiserin Friedrich'.

'KAISERIN FRIEDRICH'.

Breeder: Heinrich Drögemüller (Germany, 1885).
Parentage: 'Gloire de Dijon' x 'Perle des Jardins'.
Class: Tea-Noisette.
The flowers of this rose are large, very double and have light pink petal tips and pale yellow petal bases. The outer petals fade to almost white. The broad outer petals reflex at the tips and the numerous inner petals may be roughly quartered. The plant blooms in continuous seasonal flushes. It will reach a height of about 10 ft (3 m), enough to be trained as a small climber. Kaiserin Friedrich, born in 1840, was the eldest child of Queen Victoria and Prince Albert of England and the wife of Kaiser Friedrich III of Germany.

'KALINKA, CL.'.

see 'Pink Wonder, Cl.'.

'KARDINAL SCHULTE, CL.'.

Breeder: Unknown (before 1936).
Parentage: Sport of 'Kardinal Schulte'.
Class: Climbing Hybrid Tea.
The large, double bright, rich red flowers with a moderate fragrance are produced singly (mostly) or in small clusters on this rose. They have one main bloom with a few flowers opening later in the season. The plant is bushy, but can be trained as a small climber.

'Karl Herbst, Cl.'.

'KARL HERBST, CL.'.

Breeder: Unknown.
Parentage: Sport of 'Karl Herbst'.
Class: Climbing Hybrid Tea.
This rose has flowers of brilliant deep red with a darker reverse. They are large, double, strongly fragrant, high-centered in Hybrid Tea style and borne singly or in small clusters on long stems. The plant will grow to 10 or 13 ft (3 or 4 m). 'Karl Herbst', the sport parent was named for a German nurseryman who was interned by the British, along with Wilhelm Kordes, on the Isle of Man during World War I. They became lifelong friends and worked together in Kordes' nursery.

'KARLSRUHE'.

Breeder: Reimer Kordes (Germany, 1957).
Parentage: Seedling of Rosa kordesii H. Wulff.
Class: Hybrid Kordesii.
The flowers of 'Karlsruhe' are medium pink, mildly fragrant, large and double with an old-fashioned quarter-petaled form that is slightly convex. They are grouped in large clusters and rebloom in continuous flushes during the flowering season. The plant has the potential to reach 15 ft (4.55 m) in height. Karlsruhe is the name of a city in Germany.

'Karlsruhe'.

'KASSEL'.

Breeder: Reimer Kordes (Germany, 1957).
Parentage: 'Hamburg' x 'Scarlet Else'.
Class: Large-Flowered Climber.
'Kassel' has flowers that are scarlet-red, double, large, mildly fragrant and borne in small to medium clusters. They bloom in continuous seasonal flushes. The leaves have a matte surface and are reddish when immature. The plant is large enough to be trained as a climber for a small trellis or pillar. The rose is named for a German city.

'Kassel'.

'KATHARINA VON BORA' (PinkEIS).

Breeder: Heinrich Schultheis (Germany, before 2006).
Parentage: 'Pink Cloud' x unnamed seedling.
Class: Large-Flowered Climber.

'Katharina Von Bora'.

This lovely climber has flowers that open medium pink, but soon fade, starting at the outside petals resulting in a rose with pale pink edges and a darker pink center. The flowers are large, very double, moderately fragrant and open out to flattened, roughly quartered blooms. The foliage is dark green and the canes will grow to as much as 16.5 ft (5.m).

'Kathleen'.

'KATHLEEN'.

Breeder: Rev. Joseph Hardwick Pemberton (United Kingdom, 1922).
Parentage: 'Daphne' x 'Perle des Jardins'.
Class: Hybrid Musk.
'Kathleen', one of the famous Pemberton Hybrid Musks, has small, single, blush pink flowers that fade to white. They are borne in large clusters. The remontancy is very good with continuous bloom during the flowering season. The plant is very vigorous, reaching a height of about 15 ft (4.5 m).

'Kathleen Ferrier, Cl.'.

'KATHLEEN FERRIER, CL.'.

Breeder: Unknown.
Parentage: Sport of 'Kathleen Ferrier'.
Class: Climbing Floribunda.
When newly opened, the fragrant flowers are pink with a hint of salmon and the petals pale to white at the center. They become more rosy pink as the flower matures. The flower form is semi-double, medium-sized with flowers grouped in large clusters. There is one main bloom with a few flowers opening later. The plant has semi-glossy foliage, good disease resistance, heat tolerance and hardiness to USDA zone 4b.

'Kathleen Harrop'.

'KATHLEEN HARROP'.

Breeder: Discovered by Alexander Dickson II (United Kingdom, 1919).
Parentage: Sport of 'Zéphirine Drouhin'.
Class: Bourbon. Few thorns may indicate a Boursault ancestor as well.
This rose differs from 'Zéphirine Drouhin', the sport parent in having light rose-pink flowers with a darker pink reverse instead of deep cerise-pink and in being less full and having slightly shorter canes that the sport parent. They are large, lightly double, moderately fragrant and cupped to flat with reflexed petal tips. The individual flowers are held singly (mostly) or in small clusters and bloom in continuous seasonal flushes. The canes are almost thornless, have matte, light green foliage, are hardy to USDA zone 5b and will grow to about 10 ft (3 m).

'Kathryn Morley'.

'KATHRYN MORLEY'.

Breeder: David C. H. Austin (United Kingdom, 1990).
Parentage: 'Mary Rose' x 'Chaucer'.
Class: Shrub. English Rose.
This beautiful English Rose has very double, large, mildly fragrant, light pink flowers fading to pale pink and borne singly or in small clusters. They will bloom in continuous flushes during the flowering season. The plant is susceptible to black spot, but is healthy otherwise and is hardy to USDA zone 5b. It is classified as a shrub, but it will grow to about 8 ft (2.5 m) if given support and favorable conditions.

'KATIE'.

Breeder: O'Neal (1959). Introduced by Wyant (United States, 1959).

'Katie'.

Parentage: 'New Dawn' x 'Crimson Glory'.
Class: Large-Flowered Climber.
The large, semi-double, softly ruffled pink flowers make me think of a woman's flounced skirt. The petals are squared off at the tips and open out flat. The stamens with reddish filaments add to the decorative effect. There is a rich fragrance. The rose has one main spring-summer bloom with a few repeats later in the season. The plant will grow to about 8 ft (2.5 m).

'Kimono, Cl.'.

'KIMONO, CL.'.

Breeder: Unknown.
Parentage: Sport of 'Kimono'.
Class: Climbing Floribunda.
In the early stages of bloom these salmon-pink, very large, double flowers have inner petals that are quartered while the outer petals form a cup around them. This interesting

pattern becomes obscured with maturity. The flowers also quickly fade around the edges leaving the centers a deeper color. They are arranged in large clusters and bloom prolifically in continuous seasonal flushes. The plant is fairly vigorous, climbing to about 13 ft (4 m).

'King Midas'.

'KING MIDAS'.

Breeder: Jean Henri (J. H.) Nicolas (United States, 1942).
Parentage: 'Rochester' x 'Mary Hart'.
Class: Large-Flowered Climber.
This rose has yellow flowers where we might expect golden-yellow with the name King Midas, the mythical gentleman who counted his golden treasure over and over. They are also medium to large, double, fragrant and carried singly or in small clusters. There is one main bloom with intermittent flowering later. The plant will grow vigorously to as much as 16 ft (5 m).

'KING TUT'.
See 'Laura Ford'.

'KIR ROYAL' (MEInibur).

Breeder: Meilland International (France, before 1995).
Parentage: Unknown.
Class: Large-Flowered Climber.
'Kir Royal' opens as a dark pink rosette, but soon fades to light pink with a darker center. The flowers are medium-sized, lightly double and mildly fragrant. The repeat is very good. The plant is healthy and will grow to about 10 ft (3 m). It grows at Sangerhausen.

'KISS OF DESIRE'.
See 'Harlekin'.

'Kir Royal'.

'KITTY KININMONTH'.

Breeder: Alister Clark (Australia, before 1920).
Parentage: Seedling x Rosa gigantea.
Class: Hybrid Gigantea.
Kitty's flowers are fragrant, large to very large, semi-double and deep crimson-pink with a somewhat lighter reverse. In time, they fade to light pink. The cupped form becomes shallowly cupped as the flowers age. They are born singly or in small clusters and bloom profusely early in the season with an occasional flower produced later. The almost thornless plant will grow to 20 ft or so (6 to 7 m).

'Köln Am Rhein'.

'KÖLN AM RHEIN'.

('Cologne', 'Kölln').
Breeder: Reimer Kordes (Germany, 1956).
Parentage: Unknown.
Class: Hybrid Kordesii.
The flowers are deep pink, lightly to moderately scented, large, semi-double and carried in large clusters. They open out flat to show the stamens. Blooming is prolific and occurs in continuous seasonal flushes. The plant is quite hardy, has healthy, dark green, glossy foliage and can be expected to grow to about 8 ft (2.5 m).

'KÖLNER KARNEVAL, CL.'. See 'Blue Girl, Cl.'.

'KORDES PERFECTA, CL.'

Breeder: Discovered by the Japan Rose Society (Japan, 1962).
Parentage: Sport of 'Kordes' Perfecta'.
Class: Climbing Hybrid Tea.
This rose has flowers that are large, very full, strongly fragrant, high-centered like a Hybrid Tea and very light pink with darker pink petal edges. It blooms in continuous seasonal flushes. The foliage is dark green and glossy. The plant grows sufficiently to be trained as a climber.

'KORDES ROBUSTA'. See 'Robusta'.

'KORDES ROSE ALOHA'. See 'Aloha Hawaii'.

'KORDES ROSE MOONLIGHT'. See 'Moonlight'.

'KORDES SONDERMELDUNG'. See 'Independence, Cl.'

'KORONA, CL.'

Breeder: Reimer Kordes (Germany, 1957).
Parentage: Sport of 'Korona' (floribunda, Kordes, 1955)
Class: Climbing Floribunda.
Here is a rose with semi-double, medium-sized, mildly fragrant, vermilion flowers that age to lighter coral-pink. It blooms in flushes during the flowering season and is sufficiently tall to be trained as a climber.

'KRISTIN, CL.' (Benkricl).

Breeder: Discovered by Frank A. Benardella (United States, 2008).
Introduced in United States by Nor' East Miniature Roses in 2008.
Parentage: Sport of 'Kristin'.
Class: Climbing Miniature, Climbing Patio Rose.
The newly opened flowers of 'Kristin, Cl.' are white with strongly contrasting bright cherry-red tips. As they age the cherry-red takes over giving the impression of a red rose with white petal bases. The flowers are fragrant, medium-sized, double and are borne singly (mostly) or in small clusters. They bloom in continuous flushes during the flowering season. The plant has glossy, dark green foliage, is hardy to USDA climate zone 5a, and will reach a height of about 10 ft (3 m).

'Kronenbourg, Cl.'.

'KRONENBOURG, CL.'.

Breeder: Discovered by G. Kasturi Rangan (India, 1973).
Parentage: Sport of 'Kronenbourg'.
Class: Climbing Hybrid Tea.
This is a rose with memorable colors, crimson petals with a light yellow reverse. The crimson reflexing petal tips of the partially opened bud forms a striking pattern with the yellow petal backs. The flowers are fragrant, very large, double, high-centered and borne singly or in small clusters. They bloom in flushes during the flowering season. The plant grows vigorously to about 16.5 ft (5 m).

'La France, Cl.'.

'L'Abondance'.

'L'ABONDANCE'.

Breeder: Moreau-Robert (France, 1887).
Parentage: Unknown.
Class: Noisette.
The buds are white flushed with pink. The delicately beautiful flowers open medium-sized, double and pale pink, then become pure white as they age. They form large clusters of bloom and repeat continuously during the entire flowering season. The plant can be expected to reach a height of 10 ft (3 m).

'L'AFRICAINE'.

Breeder: Charles Mallerin (France, 1953).
Parentage: 'Guinée' x 'Crimson Glory'.
Class: Large-Flowered Climber.
The flowers are very dark red with flushes of crimson toward the petal tips, large-sized, double, mildly fragrant, and high-centered as seen in Hybrid Teas. It is once blooming, late spring or early summer. The plant can be trained as a climber of 10 ft or more (3 m). A plant grows at Roseraie du Val-de-Marne in France.

'LA BICHE'.

(Translation: 'The Doe').
Breeder: Toullier (France, before pre-1832).
Parentage: Unknown.
Class: Noisette.
The flowers of this lovely old rose open from white buds flushed with pink. They are very fragrant of tea, large-sized, double and white, often with pale pink centers. The flowers are born singly or in small clusters. They repeat their bloom in regular seasonal flushes. The plant has glossy leaves with seven lanceolate leaflets that have long, narrow tips. It will reach about 8 ft (2.5 m) in height and makes a good pillar rose. Some of the roses in commerce under this name have been identified as 'Mademoiselle de Sombreuil', a Tea.

'La Biche'.

'LA FOLLETTE'.

('Folette', 'Follette',' Lafollette', 'Senateur Follette', 'Senateur Lafollette'). 'Follette' is the earliest name according to Bill Grant.
Breeder: Jesse Busby (France, circa 1910).
Parentage: Rosa gigantea x Seedling.
Class: Hybrid Gigantea.
Here is a rose that really earns the designation as a climber, growing to as much as 30 ft (10 m) in a warm climate. The flowers are large, double, lightly fragrant and initially high-centered in Tea Rose style, then opening out loosely formed with angular reflexing at the petal tips. The color varies with the season, light coral-pink early in the season, darker and more crimson in warmer weather. The petals fade to pale pink at the tips leaving darker centers. The foliage is light green and semi-glossy.

'LA FRANCE, CL.'.

Breeder: Peter Henderson (United States, 1893).
Parentage: Sport of 'La France'.
Class: Climbing Hybrid Tea.
This Climbing Hybrid Tea has light pink flowers with slightly darker centers and a darker pink reverse. They are very fragrant, large, full, high-centered (Hybrid Tea style), with a globular flower form and are borne singly (mostly) or in small clusters. The flowers have a tendency to not open in wet weather. They bloom in flushes during the regular flowering season. The plant can grow to about 12 ft (3.65 m).

'La France, Cl.'.

'LA FRANCE DE '89'.

Breeder: Robert and Moreau (France, 1883).
Parentage: 'Reine Marie Henriette' x 'La France'.
Class: Large-Flowered Climber.
The flowers of this rose are medium crimson with flushes of cerise at the petal tips or may be entirely crimson-cerise. The petal reverse is light pink. They are richly scented, large, double. Their heaviness causes them to hang down. The plant is remontant and will grow to about 10 ft (3 m).

'La France De '89'.

'LA SEVILLANA, CL.'.

('Grimpant La Sevillana', MEIge-kanusar).
Breeder: Discovered by Meilland International (France, 1997).
Parentage: Sport of 'La Sevillana'.
Class: Climbing Floribunda.
A name like this one evokes the brilliant and romantic colors associated with Spain and in this case our expectations are rewarded with flowers of the brightest orange-red. They are medium to large-sized, semi-double or lightly double. The flower form is initially cupped, and then opens out more to form rosettes with rolled back petal tips. The flowers are formed singly or in small clusters. There is either no fragrance or a very light fragrance. The flowers rebloom in continuous seasonal flushes. The plant can be expected to reach a height of about 10 ft (3 m).

'La Sevillana, Cl.'.

'LACE CASCADE' (JACarch).

Breeder: William A. Warriner (United States, 1993).
Parentage: 'Iceberg' x 'Prairie Fire'.
Class: Large-Flowered Climber.
'Lace Cascade' is a pure white rose with just a touch of creamy white in the center. It is medium-sized, double, and moderately fragrant. The flowers are cupped at first and then open flat to show the stamens with a form less formal than 'Iceberg's, this variety's seed parent. The flowers are held singly or in small clusters and bloom prolifically in regular seasonal flushes. The plant has medium, dark green glossy foliage and grows to about 12 ft (3.65 m). It is hardy to USDA zone 5b, a trait inherited from Rosa arkansana, through 'Prairie Fire', its pollen parent.

'Lace Cascade'.

'LADY ANN KIDWELL'.

Breeder: Alfred Krebs (United States, 1948).
Parentage: seedling of 'Cécile Brunner'.
Class: Poly-Tea.
This rose has flowers that are deep pink or cerise-pink, mildly fragrant, medium-sized, double, borne singly (mostly) or in small clusters. Weak stems cause the flowers to nod their heads. The petals reflex along their sides to form sharp angles at the tips creating a starburst effect. The height of the plant is usually given as 6 ft (1.85 m), but in a warm climate it can be trained as a small climber.

'Lady Ann Kidwell'.

'LADY ASHE'. See 'Dixieland Linda'.

'LADY BARBARA' (CHEWba).

Breeder: Christopher H. Warner (United Kingdom, 1990).
Parentage: 'Red Planet' x ('Elizabeth of Glamis' x ['Galway Bay' x 'Sutter's Gold']).
Class: Large-Flowered Climber.
This is a rose with striking colors of apricot-orange with a deep golden yellow reverse. The flowers are moderately fragrant, medium-sized, and double and have a high-centered floral form. They are borne singly or in small clusters. There is one main bloom with a few flowers later in the season. The plant has medium green, semi-glossy foliage and will grow to about 10 ft (3 m). It makes a good pillar rose with its upright growth.

'LADY BRISBANE, CL.'. See 'Cramoisi Supérieur, Cl.'.

'Lady Emily Peel'.

'LADY EMILY PEEL'.

Breeder: François Lacharme (France, 1862).
Parentage: 'Mademoiselle Blanche Lafitte' x' Sappho'.
Class: Hybrid Bourbon (Noisette per ARS).
This "noble" rose has pink buds and flowers that are fragrant, double, and medium-sized, deeply cupped, held in small clusters and are white flushed with pink. Blooming occurs in regular seasonal flushes. The plant is very disease resistant, has semi-shiny foliage and is vigorous enough to train as a small climber.

'LADY FORTEVIOT, CL.'.

Breeder: Discovered by Howard Rose Co. (United States, 1935).

'Lady Forteviot, Cl.'.

Parentage: Sport of 'Lady Forteviot'.
Class: Climbing Hybrid Tea.
This Climbing Hybrid Tea is a real eye-catcher with its flowers of golden yellow and flushes of vermilion. The flowers are strongly fragrant, large, semi-double, and high-centered like a Hybrid Tea and are carried in small clusters. They are produced on the lateral canes of the long main canes. The rose blooms in continuous seasonal flushes. The plant is well armed with thorns and has glossy foliage. It will grow, somewhat stiffly, to about 10 ft (3 m).

'Lady Hillingdon, Cl.'.

'LADY HILLINGDON, CL.'.

Breeder: Elisha J. Hicks (United Kingdom, 1917).
Parentage: Sport of 'Lady Hillingdon'.
Class: Climbing Tea.
This lovely rose has flowers that are apricot yellow, moderately fragrant of tea, large, semi-double and carried singly or in small clusters. The rose is remontant in repeating seasonal flushes. The plant has green foliage with a hint of bronze and will grow in an upright, bushy style to about 16 ft (5 m).

'LADY OF SHALOTT' (AUSnyson).

Breeder: David C. H. Austin (United Kingdom, 2009).
Parentage: Unknown.
Class: English Rose.
The flowers are scented of tea, medium-sized, double, salmon-pink with a golden-yellow reverse and deeply globular in shape. They are borne in small clusters. The rose blooms in continuous seasonal flushes. The plant has semi-glossy, dark green foliage and can be grown as a small climber of about 8 ft (2.5 m).

'Lady Penelope'.

'LADY PENELOPE' (CHEWdor).

Breeder: Christopher H. Warner (United Kingdom, before 1993).
Parentage: 'Laura Ford' x 'Royal Baby'.
Class: Large-Flowered Climber.
The flowers of this rose begin salmon-pink with a pink reverse and fade to pink, starting at the outer petals. The petals are regularly arranged in an orderly imbricated form with a button eye in the center. They reflex to form a low dome, giving the flower a pompon appearance. The flowers are medium-sized, double, mildly fragrant and borne in small clusters. The plant has few thorns, medium green glossy foliage and will grow 8 to 10 ft (2.5 to 3 m).

'LADY SYLVIA, CL.'.

Breeder: Discovered by Walter Stevens, Ltd. (United Kingdom, 1933).
Parentage: Sport of 'Lady Sylvia'.

'Lady Waterlow'.

Class: Climbing Hybrid Tea.
The sport parent of this rose, 'Lady Sylvia' was, in turn, a sport of 'Ophelia', a pale salmon-colored rose with darker salmon-yellow centers. 'Lady Sylvia' and its climbing sport differ from 'Ophelia' in having pale pink outer petals with slightly darker centers. The form is a large, double, high-centered bloom borne singly (mostly) or in small clusters. The rose reblooms in continuous seasonal flushes. The potential height is as much as 20 ft (6 m).

'Lady Silvia, Cl.'.

'LADY WATERLOW'.

('Climbing Lady Waterlow'.).
Breeder: Clément and Paul Nabonnand (France, 1902).
Parentage: 'La France de '89' x 'Madame Marie Lavalley'.
Class: Climbing Hybrid Tea. There is some Noisette in the ancestry.
This lovely rose has always been one of my favorites. The flowers open from yellow buds with flushes of crimson to pink flowers with a hint of salmon, yellow petal bases and touches of crimson on the petal edges. They are

'Lady Waterlow'.

very large, semi-double, richly fragrant and are borne singly or in small clusters. The rose is remontant in regular flushes during the blooming season. The plant is resistant to fungus diseases except blackspot and may grow to 18 ft (5.5 m).

'Lady X, Cl.'.

'LADY X, CL.'.

Breeder: Discovered by David W. Ruston (Australia, 1970). Discovered by Yoshiho Takatori (Japan, 1976). Introduced by Japan Rose Nursery (Japan, 1976).
Parentage: Sport of 'Lady X'.
Class: Climbing Hybrid Tea.
'Lady X, Cl.' is a beautiful rose with mauve-pink flowers that are large, full, high-centered with a lovely shape, mildly fragrant and held singly or in small clusters.

The nearly thornless plant blooms prolifically in continuous flushes throughout the season. The foliage is susceptible to rust and burns easily in the sun. It will need frost protection in USDA zone 6 and below.

'LAFAYETTE, CL.' See 'August Kordes'.

'Laguna'.

'LAGUNA'.

('KO 94/2394-01, KORadigel).
Breeder: Tim Hermann Kordes (Germany, 1994).
Introduced by Kordes & Sons (Germany, 2004).
Parentage: ('La Sevillana' x 'Sympathie') x unnamed seedling.
Class: Large-Flowered Climber.

'Laguna' has deep pink flowers that are medium to large-sized, very full, strongly fragrant (fruity, spicy), and are borne singly or in small clusters. The outer petals reflex in an orderly, imbricated form and the centers are filled with many small, straight petals. Rebloom is very good, occurring in regular seasonal flushes. The plant has many thorns, dark green glossy foliage, is hardy to USDA zone 5b and grows with a bushy habit to about 8 to 10 ft (2.5 to 3 m). It has very good resistance to black spot and mildew.

'LAL, CL.'.

Breeder: Discovered by Max Vogel (Germany, 1937).
Parentage: Sport of 'Lal'.
Class: Climbing Hybrid Tea.

This attractive Climbing Hybrid Tea blooms in salmon-pink with touches of yellow in the centers. The flowers age to plain pink and are very large, double, richly fragrant of damask, strongly reflexed at the petal tips and long-stemmed. They are carried singly or in small clusters and tend to nod. It blooms in continuous seasonal flushes. The plant grows tall enough to be used as a climber.

'L'ALCAZAR'. See 'Pride of Venus'.

'LAMARQUE'.

('General Lamarque', "Glengallon Rose", 'Maréchal').
Breeder: Maréchal (France, 1830).
Parentage: 'Blush Noisette' x 'Parks' Yellow Tea-scented China'
Class: Tea-Noisette.

The flowers of 'Lamarque' are large, double, moderately fragrant of lemon and tea, globular in form and white with light yellow centers and petal bases. The flowers are carried singly (mostly) or in small clusters. The rose blooms in continuous seasonal flushes. The plant is not hardy and will grow and bloom best at USDA zone 7b and warmer climates. It is very vigorous and will grow to at least 20 ft (6 m) in a warm climate.

'Lamarque'.

'LANCELOT'. See 'Dukat'.

'LANDORA, CL.'

(ClinORA, 'Sunblest, Cl.').
Breeder: Discovered by Joseph Orard (France, 1978).
Parentage: Sport of 'Sunblest'.
Class: Climbing Hybrid Tea.

'Landora, Cl.'

If you want a climbing yellow rose, this rose offers everything to be wished for. The flowers are large, double, richly scented and beautifully shaped in a high-centered style. The color is deep, pure, brilliant yellow, no buff or gold. The remontancy is excellent in continuous seasonal flushes. The plant is clothed with dark green, glossy foliage and will climb to about 13 ft (4 m).

'Laura Ford'.

'LAURA FORD'.

(CHEWarvel, 'King Tut', 'Normandie').
Breeder: Christopher H. Warner (United Kingdom, 1989).
Parentage: ('Anna Ford' x 'Elizabeth of Glamis') x ('Galway Bay' x 'Sutter's Gold').
Class: Climbing Miniature.
'Laura Ford's flowers are medium yellow with a lighter yellow reverse fading to ivory white and sometimes developing pink flushes on the petal tips. They are small to medium, mildly fragrant, lightly double and borne singly or in small clusters. The rose reblooms in continuous flushes during the regular flowering season. The plant has small, light green, glossy foliage and will grow in a bushy, upright style to about 12 ft (3.65 m).

'LAURA LOUISA'.

Breeder: Discovered by Roy Riches (United Kingdom, 1995).
Parentage: Sport of 'Leverkusen'.
Class: Hybrid Kordesii.
'Laura Louisa', a sport of the yellow 'Leverkusen', is medium coral-pink with yellow flushes in the center on opening. It becomes lighter and truer pink with age. Except for the color, the characteristics of 'Laura Louisa' closely match those of 'Leverkusen'. The flowers are double, medium to large-sized, mildly fragrant and borne singly or in small clusters. This rose has one main summer bloom with a few flowers opening later in the season. The plant has dark green, shiny foliage, is healthy, hardy to USDA zone 5b and will grow to about 12 ft (3.65 m).

'LAURENT CARLE, CL.'.

Breeder: Discovered by L. P. Rosen and Son (Australia, 1923). Discovered by Louis Mermet (France, 1924).
Parentage: Sport of 'Laurent Carle'.
Class: Climbing Hybrid Tea.
The flowers of this rose are large, double, richly fragrant, high-centered and deep crimson. The flowers are borne singly or in small clusters. They rebloom in regular repeating flushes during the flowering season. The plant is resistant to mildew and has glossy dark green foliage. It has the potential to reach a height of about 13 ft (4 m).

'Laurent Carle, Cl.'.

'LA VANOIS PARC NATIONAL'.
See 'Rosanna' (Kordes, 2006).

'Lavender Lassie'.

'LAVENDER LASSIE'.
Breeder: Reimer Kordes (Germany, 1960).
Parentage: 'Hamburg' x 'Madame Norbert Levavasseur'.
Class: Hybrid Musk, Lambertiana.
My 'Lavender Lassie' has survived many years of my casual gardening and one winter with a spell of 0 degrees, Fahrenheit. I can always count on it to add its lovely lilac-pink color to a corner of the garden. The flowers are medium to large-sized, strongly fragrant, double and held in small to medium clusters. They are remontant in regular seasonal flushes. The plant is disease resistant, shade tolerant and will climb to about 12 ft (3.65 m).

'Lawinia'.

'LAWINIA'.
(TANklewi; TANklevi; 'Lavinia').
Breeder: Mathias Tantau, Jr. (Germany, 1980).
Parentage: Unknown.
Class: Large-Flowered Climber.
The flowers of 'Lawinia' are bright, medium pink initially, but fade to light pink from the outer petals inward with age. They are large, double, strongly fragrant and borne in medium to large clusters. There is one prolific summer bloom followed in the fall with a few flowers. The plant has dark green leaves and will grow to about 10 ft (3 m).

'LEANDER'.
(AUSlea, Lovely Apricot).
Breeder: David C. H. Austin (United Kingdom, 1982).
Parentage: 'Charles Austin' x unnamed seedling.
Class: Shrub. English Rose.
Leander's flowers open deep apricot and change to light pink with age. They are medium-sized, very double, fragrant

and carried singly or in small clusters. There is one main summer bloom followed by a few flowers later in the season. The plant has dark green, glossy, disease resistant foliage and will grow to about 10 ft (3 m).

'Leander'.

'LEAPING SALMON'.

(PEAmight, Salmon Scentsation).
Breeder: Colin A. Pearce (United Kingdom, 1983).
Parentage: [('Vesper' x 'Aloha') x ('Paddy McGredy' x 'Maigold')] x 'Prima Ballerina'.
Class: Large-Flowered Climber.
The flowers of this rose are double, very large, richly fragrant, high-centered and bright salmon-pink fading from the edges to a lighter and pinker color. They bloom prolifically, have excellent remontancy, but tend to ball in the rain. The plant has healthy, thick, glossy green foliage and will climb to 20 ft (6 m).

'Leaping Salmon'.

'LE GRAND HUIT, CL.'.
See 'Commandant Cousteau, Cl.'

'LEMON MERINGUE'.

(WEKradler).
Breeder: Discovered by William J. Radler (United States, 2003).
Parentage: Sport of 'Autumn Sunset'.
Class: Climber, Shrub.
This is a light yellow sport of the apricot 'Autumn Sunset'. Other than color it closely matches the sport parent. The flowers are medium-sized, double, strongly fragrant of spicy fruit, and born in small clusters. The outer petals are fairly large and become increasingly smaller toward the center. The rose blooms in regular flushes during the flowering season. The plant has dark green, glossy foliage and will grow in a bushy manner to 10 or 12 ft (3 or 3.65 m).

'Lemon Meringue'.

'LEVERKUSSEN'.

Breeder: Wilhelm J. H. Kordes II (Germany, 1954).
Parentage: Rosa kordesii H. Wulff x 'Golden Glow'.
Class: Hybrid Kordesii.
'Leverkussen' is the only yellow Kordesii. The color is medium lemon yellow fading from the edges inward to light yellow, then to white. The flowers are large, double with ruffled petals, mildly fragrant of lemon and are carried singly or in small clusters. They have one main flush of summer bloom with a few flowers produced later in the season. The flowers are followed by yellow hips in the fall. The bushy plant is disease resistant, hardy to USDA zone 5b and will grow to about 13 ft (4 m).

'Ley's Perpetual'.

'LEY'S PERPETUAL'.

Breeder: Unknown (before 1900). Discovered by F. Ley (United Kingdom, before pre- 1937) and reintroduced by Sunningdale Nursery (United Kingdom, circa 1958).
Parentage: Unknown. Shows a relationship to 'Gloire de Dijon'.
Class: Tea-Noisette.
This rose has flowers that are large, double, fragrant of tea and light yellow fading to buff-white. When the flowers are fully mature the outer petals reflex in points forming a star-like pattern, but the inner petals have a more rolled-back form. The flowers bloom in continuous seasonal flushes. The leaves are unusually orbicular (round). The plant is quite vigorous and can be trained to climb to 15 or 16 ft (5 m).

'Liane'.

'LIANE'.

Breeder: Anne G. Cocker (Scotland, 1989).
Parentage: Unknown.
Class: Large-Flowered Climber.
'Liane' has flowers that are large, double, mildly fragrant and borne singly or in small clusters. They are very colorful with medium orange petals and golden yellow petal bases aging to pink and yellow. The rose has one main summer bloom followed by a few less colorful flowers later in the season. The plants have dark green, glossy leaves and will grow to about 8 ft (2.5 m).

'LIBERTY, CL.'.

Breeder: Discovered by H.B. May (United States, 1908).
Parentage: Sport of 'Liberty'.
Class: Climbing Hybrid Tea.
'Liberty, Cl.' has medium-sized, richly fragrant, double, bright crimson flowers that bloom in continuous seasonal flushes. They are borne singly (mostly) or in small clusters. The plant can be trained as a small climber of about 10 ft (3 m).

'Lichtkönigin Lucia'.

'LICHTKÖNIGIN LUCIA'.

(KORlilub, 'Lucia', 'Reine Lucia').
Breeder: Reimer Kordes (Germany, 1966).
Parentage: 'Zitronenfalter' x 'Cläre Grammerstorf'.
Class: Shrub.
This rose is medium yellow, large, loosely double with ruffled petals and moderately fragrant. The buds are deep yellow with crimson flushes. It has one main summer bloom with a few flowers later in the season. The plant is hardy to USDA zone 5b. It can be grown as a shrub or as a climber of about 8 ft (2.5 m).

'Lijiang Rose'.

'LIJIANG ROSE'.

('Lijiang Road Climber').
Breeder: Discovered in China and brought back to Italy by Gianlupo Osti in 1995. Also seen before 1993 by Roger Phillips and Martin Rix during their trip to China.
Parentage: Probably a hybrid between R.gigantea and cultivated Rosa x odorata.
Class: Hybrid Gigantea; Tea, Cl.
The flowers are medium pink fading to light pink, large, semi-double to lightly double and fragrant of fruit and of tea. The stamens have yellow anthers and pink filaments. There is one main bloom with a scattering of flowers later in the season. The rose blooms in the spring in my USDA zone 7b climate. In a warm climate, there may be a better repeat pattern and more vigorous growth. It may need frost protection in a cold climate. The plant is very vigorous, growing to about 16 ft (5 m). Mine is always overgrowing its allotted space and threatening passersby with its large hooked thorns.

'Lilli Marleen, Cl.'

'LILLI MARLEEN, CL.'

('Lili Marlene Cl.', 'Lilli Marleen Grimpant', PEKlimasar).
Breeder: Discovered by Paul Pekmez (France, 1982).
Parentage: Sport of 'Lilli Marleen'.
Class: Climbing Floribunda.
This rose has flowers that are deep, bright red, medium-sized, double, cupped and carried singly (mostly) or in small clusters. The rebloom is excellent in continuous seasonal flushes. The plant has matte, medium green foliage and can be trained as a climber of about 13 ft (4 m).

'Lilliput'.

'LILLIPUT'.

Breeder: George Paul (United Kingdom, 1897).
Parentage: Unknown.
Class: Climbing Polyantha.
'Lilliput' has flowers that open from fat buds to form small, double, cerise to crimson rosettes with white petal bases. The plant can be grown as a small climber. Named for Lilliput, land of the diminutive and the timid, from Swift's *Gulliver's Travels*.

'LILY MESTCHERSKY'.

Breeder: Gilbert Nabonnand (France, 1877).
Parentage: Unknown.
Class: Hybrid Noisette.
The flowers are medium-sized, very full and deep mauve-pink fading to a lighter color with the same hue. They have very little fragrance. They occur singly or in small clusters and repeat bloom in continuous flushes during the flowering season. The very prickly plant will climb to about 10 ft (3 m). Lily was the nickname of Princess

Natalia "Natascha" Aleksandrovna Meshcherskaya, a Russian noble woman.

'Lily Mestchersky'.

'LINDERHOF'.

('KORelasting, 'Summer Breeze').
Breeder: Reimer Kordes (Germany, 1983).
Parentage: Unknown.
Class: Shrub.
Here is a very pretty, fragrant, single pink rose with a yellow center made for single rose lovers. The floral form is medium-sized with gently ruffled petals. The flowers are borne singly or in small clusters. They bloom in continuous seasonal flushes. The bushy plant has glossy, dark green foliage and can be grown as a shrub or as a climber of about 8 ft (2.5 m) with support.

'Linderhof'.

'LITTLE RAMBLER'.

('Baby Rambler', CHEWramb).
Breeder: Christopher H. Warner (United Kingdom, 1994).
Parentage: ('Cecile Brunner' x 'Baby Faurax') x ('Marjorie Fair' x 'Nozomi').
Class: Climbing Miniature.
'Little Rambler' has bright pink buds that open as light pink, strongly fragrant, double, small-sized, cupped, clustered flowers. As the flowers mature they become pale pink to white and develop a flat floral form. They are remontant in continuous seasonal flushes. The plant has easily trained pliable canes, is hardy to USDA zone 5b, very disease resistant and will grow to about 8 ft (4.45 m). The synonym for this rose, 'Baby Rambler', is also the name of several other rose varieties.

'Little Rambler'.

'LITTLE SHOWOFF'.

Breeder: Ralph Moore (United States, 1960).
Parentage: 'Golden Glow' x 'Zee'.
Class: Climbing Miniature.
Small, double bright yellow flowers with broad bands of red at the petal tips enhance the beauty of this miniature rose. They open high-centered then reflex strongly and spread out quite flat. The petals have mucronate tips. The colors fade in time. The flowers are borne singly or in small clusters

and bloom prolifically in continuous seasonal flushes. The plant has shiny green foliage, an average number of prickles and will attain sufficient height to be used as a climber.

'Looping'.

'LOOPING' (MEIrovonex).

Breeder: Marie-Louise (Louisette) Meilland (France, 1977).
Parentage: Seed parent: ('Zambra' x 'Zambra') x [(MALcair x 'Danse des Sylphes') x ('Cocktail' x 'Cocktail')]. Pollen parent: 'Royal Gold'.
Class: Large-Flowered Climber.
This fragrant rose opens peach colored and soon fades to pink with a touch of coral. The flower form is medium to large-sized, double and cupped with reflexed petals. The flowers eventually open out fairly flat to reveal a glimpse of the stamens with their red filaments. The bloom is remontant contrary to reports of being once-blooming. The plant is healthy except for a tendency to get blackspot. It can be trained as a climber of about 13 ft (4m).

'LORDLY OBERON' (Aaron).

Breeder: David C. H. Austin (United Kingdom, 1983).
Parentage: 'Chaucer' x 'Chaucer'.
Class: Shrub. English Rose.
This is an early variety that David Austin considers inferior and does not recommend growing unless you're a collector, but I see it as a rose with much beauty and vigor and one that should still be grown. The flowers are large, very double, fragrant of anise and damask, globular and light pink fading to pale pink. They have excellent remontancy. The foliage is matte, large and medium green. Kim Rupert reports that the rose can be grown as a climber of 15 or 20 ft in a warm climate.

'Lordly Oberon'.

'LORENZO PAHISSA'.

(Laurenzo Pahissa).
Breeder: Lorenzo (Llorenç) Pahissa (Spain, before 1940).
Parentage: unnamed seedling x 'Marí Dot'.
Class: Large-Flowered Climber.
The flowers are moderately fragrant, very large, semi-double, light coral fading to pale pink and borne singly (mostly) or in small clusters. The plant can be trained as a climber of about 13 ft (4 m).

'Lorenzo Pahissa'.

'LORRAINE LEE, CL.'.

Breeder: Discovered by Ninian Bow Mackay (Australia, 1932).
Parentage: Sport of 'Lorraine Lee'.
Class: Hybrid Gigantea.
This rose has very fragrant, large, semi-double, coral

'Lorraine Lee, Cl.'.

pink flowers with a high-centered shape opening into a cupped floral form. The petal tips are lighter and a cooler pink hue than the center. The petal bases are yellow. The plant has a plentiful supply of the usual attractive Gigantea foliage with deep green, glossy, drooping leaves. It will grow to at least 16 to 20 ft (5 to 6 m) in a warm climate. The bush form, 'Lorraine Lee', can be trained as a small, shrubby climber to about 10 ft (3 m) if given proper support.

'Los Angeles, Cl.'.

'LOS ANGELES, CL.'.

Breeder: Howard & Smith (United States, 1925).
Parentage: Sport of 'Los Angeles'.
Class: Climbing Hybrid Tea, Climbing Pernetiana.
This rose has flowers that are large, double, strongly fragrant and coral-pink with yellow petal bases, fading to light pink with cream petal bases. They are held singly or in small clusters. The petal tips become strongly reflexed with age. The rose blooms in continuous seasonal flushes. The plant can be trained as a small climber of about 8 ft (2.5 m).

'LOUIS BARBIER'.

Breeder: Barbier Frères & Compagnie (France, 1909).
Parentage: 'Madame Bérard' x R. foetida 'Bicolor'.
Class: Climbing Pernetiana.
The flowers are medium pink with a touch of copper and yellow petal bases. The reverse is light buff-yellow. The petals may have little yellow streaks. The colors fade and shift to mauve tones. The floral form is medium-sized, double and borne in small clusters. There is one main bloom with little repeat. The plant can be trained as a small climber of about 10 ft (3 m).

'Louis Barbier'.

'LOUIS BRUYÈRE'.

Breeder: Paul Buatois (France, 1941).
Parentage: Unknown.
Class: Climbing Hybrid Tea.
This attractive French rose has medium-sized, double, high-centered, deeply cupped, pink flowers with a touch of cerise. As the flowers mature they open out flatter and the outer petal tips reflex. The plant makes a nice pillar rose, growing to about 10 or 13 ft (3 or 4 m).

'LOUISE CATHERINE BRESLAU, CL.'.

Breeder: Discovered by Wilhelm J. H. Kordes II (Germany, 1917).
Parentage: Sport of 'Louise Catherine Breslau'.
Class: Climbing Hybrid Tea, Climbing Pernetiana.
This rose is graced by having very large, double, fragrant, coppery-pink flowers with yellow petal bases and flushes of yellow on the petal reverse. As the petals fade they lose their rich hues and become just plain pink. The floral form is cupped and the petals are wavy. The flowers are borne singly or in small clusters and bloom in continuous seasonal flushes. The plant will climb moderately to about 10 ft (3 m).

'LOUIS JOLLIET'.

Breeder: Dr. Felicitas Svejda (Canada, 1984).
Parentage: Hybrid Kordesii on both sides.
Class: Hybrid Kordesii, Explorer Series.
This Explorer rose has flowers that are medium pink, fading to lighter more mauve-pink. They are mildly fragrant, medium, double and borne singly or in small

clusters. The plant has semi-glossy, medium green foliage that is remarkably hardy to USDA zone 3b. It can be grown as a ground cover or a small climber of about 8 ft (2.5 m).

'Louis Jolliet'.

'LOUIS PAJOTIN, CL.'.

Breeder: Introduced in France by Pajotin / Pajotin-Chédane in France 1959.
Parentage: Sport of 'Louis Pajotin'.
Class: Climbing Hybrid Tea.
This rose's flowers are deep coral-pink with a light yellow-buff reverse. The coral-pink fades with age to a less attractive light pink with a touch of mauve. The flowers are large, very full and bloom in continuous seasonal flushes. They are borne singly or in small clusters. The plant is reported by the Loubert nursery to grow to about 13 ft (4 m).

'Louis Pajotin, Cl.'.

'LOVE'.

Breeder: Berthe Caron (France, 1935).
Parentage: 'Hadley' x 'Ami Quinard'.
Class: Large-Flowered Climber.
'Love' has flowers that are deep scarlet-red, strongly fragrant, medium to large and semi-double. They open out into a flattened rosette and reveal their stamens. The flowers bloom in continuous seasonal flushes. The plant has dark green, thick foliage and can be trained as a climber of about 12 ft (3.65 m).

'LOVE KNOT' ('Chewglorious').

Breeder: Christopher H. Warner (United Kingdom, 1999).
Introduced by Warner's Roses (United Kingdom, 2000).
Parentage: 'Laura Ford' x 'Ingrid Bergman'
Class: Climbing Miniature, Patio Rose.
'Love Knot' blooms profusely in regular seasonal flushes with flowers that are fragrant, small to medium, double, Hybrid Tea shaped and brilliant, deep scarlet-red. The canes are disease resistant, have medium green, glossy foliage and will grow stiffly to about 8 ft (2.5 m).

'Love Knot'.

'LUCETTA' (AUSemi).

Breeder: David C. H. Austin (United Kingdom, 1983).
Parentage: Unknown.
Class: Shrub. English Rose.
I have a plant of this rose that I have grown for at least 20 years. It has never failed to produce a bountiful crop of lovely apricot-pink, fragrant, large, semi-double, cupped flowers in small clusters. The flowers fade to light pink with age and bloom mainly in the late spring. There are scattered flowers later in the season. I have grown my plant as a large shrub, but it will climb to about 10 ft if given support and is hardy to USDA zone 5b.

'Lucetta'.

'LUCINDE' (KORtaly).

Breeder: W. Kordes & Sons (Germany, 1988).
Parentage: Unknown.
Class: Shrub.
'Lucinda' opens deep golden yellow and fades to a lighter yellow in time. The flowers are moderately fragrant, large, double and borne singly or in small clusters. The rose reblooms in continuous seasonal flushes. It can be grown as a climber if given support and will reach a height of about 13 ft (4 m).

'LUCY CRAMPHORN, CL.'.

('Maryse Kriloff, Cl.').
Breeder: Michel Kriloff (France, 1984).
Parentage: Sport of 'Lucy Cramphorn' ('Maryse Kriloff').
Class: Climbing Hybrid Tea.
The flowers of this rose are brilliant orange-red, double, large, high-centered and strongly fragrant. They bloom in continual seasonal flushes. The plant has lovely large, dark green, very disease-resistant, shiny foliage. It is hardy to USDA zone 6b, and can be grown as a climber.

'Ludvik Večeřa'.

'LUDVIK VEČEŘA'.

Breeder: Ludvick Večeřa (former Czechoslovakia, 1981).
Parentage: 'Dortmund' x 'Décor'.
Class: Large-Flowered Climber.
The flowers of this rose are medium-sized, double, moderately fragrant and brilliant scarlet-red with ruffled petals that open out flat to show the stamens. They are borne in medium-sized clusters. The plant can be trained as a climber of about 10 ft (3 m).

'Luna-Park'.

'LUNA-PARK'.

Breeder: Paul Croix (France, 1964).
Parentage: 'Gladiator' x unnamed seedling
Class: Large-Flowered Climber.
The flowers of 'Luna-Park' are vermilion, large, double and have one main summer bloom with a few flowers later. It is grown at Roseto Carla Fineschi (Italy).

'Lybelle'.

'LYBELLE'.

Breeder: Noack (Germany, 1984).
Parentage: Unknown.
Class: Large-Flowered Climber.
Deep crimson-red buds open to mid-pink, large-sized, double, lightly fragrant flowers in small clusters. They fade to light pink and open flat in time, nodding a little from their own weight. The plant can be trained as a small climber to about 8 ft (2.5 m).

'LYON ROSE, CL.'.

Breeder: Discovered by Ketten Frères/Bros./Gebrüder (Luxembourg, 1924).
Parentage: Sport of 'Lyon Rose'.
Class: Climbing Hybrid Tea, Climbing Pernetiana.
This rose has double, large, strongly fragrant, high-centered Hybrid Tea style, coral-pink flowers with yellow petal bases. They are borne singly or in small clusters. The heavy flowers tend to hang their heads. They lose their coral color and become light pink with age. The plant has matte, medium green foliage. It can be trained as a climber to about 10 ft (3 m).

'Miss Liberty'.

'MADELINE'. See 'Lunar Mist'.

'Mady'.

'MADY'.

Breeder: Unknown (1925).
Parentage: Unknown.
Class: It has been classed as a Climbing Tea, a Large-Flowered Climber or a Climbing Hybrid Tea by different authorities.
Not much is known about 'Mady's background, as can be seen from the above information. The plant that grows at Sangerhausen has large, double, flowers with quartered petals and an attractive old-fashioned appearance. They are light yellow initially, but soon age to cream and are borne singly or in small clusters. The summer bloom is prolific followed by a few flowers later in the season. The plant has the potential to grow to about 8 ft (2.5 m).

'MAGIC DRAGON'.

Breeder: Ralph S. Moore (United States, 1969).
Introduced in United States by Sequoia Nursery.
Parentage: (0-47-19 x unnamed seedling) x 'Little Buckaroo'.
Class: Climbing Miniature.
'Magic Dragon' has dark red flowers that are small, scentless and mostly carried in large clusters. It blooms in regular seasonal flushes. The plant is healthy, hardy to

'Magic Dragon'.

USDA zone 5b and will grow, in an upright style, to about 10 ft (3 m).

'Magic Meidiland'.

'MAGIC MEIDILAND'.

('Magic Meillandecor', MEIbonrib).
Breeder: Alain Meilland (France, 1992). Introduced in France by SNC Meilland in 1992. Introduced in France by Selection Meilland in 1993.
Parentage: Rosa sempervirens x ('Milrose' x 'Bonica').

Class: Shrub, Ground Cover.

I have seen this rose much used both as a ground cover and as a weeping standard, but it can also be grown as a climber of about 8 ft (2.5 m) in a warm climate. The flowers are mauve-pink with a small white center, small, double, mildly fragrant and borne singly or in small clusters. The rose blooms in continuous seasonal flushes. The plant has healthy, bronze-green foliage.

'Magic Wand'.

'MAGIC WAND'.

Breeder: Ralph S. Moore (United States, 1957).
Parentage: 'Éblouissant' x 'Zee'.
Class: Climbing Miniature.

The flowers of this rose are small, semi-double, deep pink and bloom in continuous seasonal flushes. The plant is healthy and can be trained as a small climber of about 6 ft (1.8 m) in a warm climate.

'Maintower'.

'MAINTOWER'.

Breeder: Christopher H. Warner (United Kingdom, before pre-2007).
Parentage: Unknown.
Class: Large-Flowered Climber.

Brighten a corner of your garden with this beautiful rose. The flowers open from fat buds to form richly fragrant, medium-sized, high-centered, very double orange-red or vermilion flowers held mostly singly or sometimes in small clusters. They bloom in repeated seasonal flushes. The plant can be trained as a medium-sized climber of 8 to 10 ft. (2.5 to 3 m). It can be seen at Sangerhausen.

'MAINZER FASTNACHT, CL.'. See 'Blue Moon, Cl.'.

'MALAGA'.

Breeder: Samuel Darragh McGredy IV (Northern Ireland before pre-1968).
Parentage: ('Hamburger Phoenix' x 'Danse du Feu') x 'Copenhagen'.
Class: Large-Flowered Climber.

The flowers of this rose are large, double, strongly fragrant, deep pink with a touch of coral, high-centered and carried singly or in small clusters. They bloom in continuous seasonal flushes. The foliage is glossy and dark bronze-green. The plant can be trained as a climber of about 10 ft (3 m).

'MALTON' ('Fulgens').

Breeder: Modeste Guérin (Angers) (France, 1828).
Parentage: Unknown.
Class: Hybrid China.

The flowers of this beautiful rose are medium-sized, very double, mildly fragrant, unfading crimson red with a lighter reverse, cupped and quartered with reflexed petals. They are borne singly or in small clusters. There is one main bloom with a few flowers later. The foliage is dark green and glossy. It is somewhat tender so give it frost protection if you are where it may freeze in the winter. The plant will climb to about 10 ft (3 m). This rose is of historical importance as possibly having been one of the parents of the first Hybrid Perpetuals.

'MAMAN COCHET, CL.'

('Pink Maman Cochet, Cl.').
Breeder: Discovered by J. R. Upton (Sr.) (Australia, 1909).
Parentage: Sport of 'Maman Cochet'. There were several sports discovered previously that did not propagate as climbers.

'Maman Cochet, Cl.'

Class: Climbing Tea.

The flowers are medium pink fading from the edges inward to pale pink. They are very large, double, richly fragrant, high-centered and borne singly or in small clusters. The outer petals reflex, forming points to give a star effect, but the inner petals simply roll back. The plant blooms in continuous seasonal flushes. It is a little tender so it will do best in a warm climate of at least USDA zone 7b. With those conditions it will grow to as much as 20 ft (6 m). In a colder climate it may need frost protection.

'MANETTI'.

(Rosa Manetti, 'Rosa x Noisettiana 'Manetti').
Breeder: Giuseppe Manetti (Italy, before 1835).
Parentage: Rosa chinensis x Rosa moschata.
Class: Hybrid Noisette.

This rose was much used as an understock in the 19th century so it is commonly found in places like cemeteries where old roses have been growing for a long time. The attractive flowers are small, semi-double and medium pink with white petal bases and fading to light pink from the petal tips inward. The flowers open out to form nice rosettes that are borne singly or in small clusters. The rose has one fairly long bloom early in the year. The plant can grow to 8 or 10 ft (2.5 or 3 m), has foliage with a blue-green cast and is reported to have few or no prickles. As you might expect with such an old variety, there may be more than one rose being grown under this name.

'MANIPUR MAGIC' ('Virdor').

Breeder: M.S. Viraraghavan (India, 2005).
Introduced in United States by Roses Unlimited in 2005.
Parentage: 'Rêve d'Or' x Rosa gigantea.
Class: Hybrid Gigantea.

This hybrid Gigantea has flowers that are large to very large-sized, very full, mildly fragrant or scentless, light yellow fading to ivory and carried singly or in small clusters. They have one main summer bloom with a scattering of flowers later in the season. The plant has semi-gloss light green foliage. It is somewhat tender and will grow and bloom best in a warm climate of at least USDA zone 7a. It may need frost protection.

'Manita'.

'MANITA' (KORberuhig).

Breeder: W. Kordes & Sons (Germany, 1996).
Parentage: Unknown.
Class: Large-Flowered Climber.

'Manita's flowers are large, semi-double to lightly double, mildly fragrant and medium pink fading to light pink with pale yellow petal bases. They are initially cupped then open out flat with wavy petals and are held singly or in small clusters. They bloom profusely in continuous seasonal flushes. The plant will grow to about 10 to 13 ft (3 to 4 m).

'MÄRCHENLAND'.

Breeder: Mathias Tantau (Germany, 1946).
Parentage: 'Swantje' x 'Hamburg'.
Class: Shrub.

It may be stretching the facts a bit to include this rose as a climber because it will get no taller than 6 or 7 ft (1.8 or 2 m), but it can be trained to a small trellis or pillar where it can add its beauty to the garden. The flowers

'Märchenland'.

are moderately fragrant, lightly double, medium-sized and salmon-pink with yellow-cream petal bases changing to crimson-pink, then to mauve and white with age. The plant blooms profusely in flushes during the flowering season.

'Maréchal Niel'.

'MARÉCHAL NIEL' ('Maréchal Niel').

Breeder: A found rose discovered by Louis Castel (France, 1857). Introduced in France by Eugène Verdier fils aîne in 1864.
Parentage: Seedling of 'Isabella Gray'.
Class: Tea-Noisette, Climbing Tea.
This beautiful Tea-Noisette has flowers that are yellow, very large, very double, strongly fragrant of fruit, globular and high-centered in form and borne singly or in small clusters. The petals roll back at the tips with the outer ones forming points. The rose blooms profusely in repeated flushes throughout the season. The plant has light green, shiny foliage, is shade tolerant, but not rain tolerant or winter hardy and will require frost protection. Under warm conditions it will climb to about 15 ft (4.5 m). Do not confuse this rose with the Hybrid Perpetual of the same name and by the same breeder.

'MARGARET MAE'.

('Pretty in Pink Eden', 'Cyclamen Pierre de Ronsard').
Breeder: Discovered by Reg Tomerlin (before 2015).
Parentage: Sport of 'Eden' ('Pierre de Ronsard').
Class: Large-Flowered Climber.
This is a lovely deep pink sport of the well-known cream and pink 'Eden'. It is identical to the sport parent in all other attributes. The flowers are large, very full and borne mostly singly or sometimes in small clusters. They bloom prolifically in flushes throughout the flowering season. The foliage is medium-sized, semi-glossy and dark green. The plant has a potential height of about 10 ft (3 m). The rose was named in honor of the breeder's mother.

'MARGARET TURNBULL'.

Breeder: Alister Clark (Australia, 1931).
Parentage: Unknown.
Class: Large-Flowered Climber.
The flowers of this rose are soft pink flushed with yellow in the center and are lightly fragrant, semi-double to double and large. They have rolled back petals that add to their charm. They bloom early and abundantly, and then there is a smaller summer flush and a better autumn display. The foliage is rather thinly produced, but is disease resistant. The plant will grow to about 13 ft (4 m).

'MARGO KOSTER, CL.' ('Sunbeam, Cl.').

Breeder: Discovered by Golie (United States, 1962).
Parentage: Sport of 'Margo Koster'.
Class: Climbing Polyantha.
This Climbing Polyantha has flowers that are salmon-pink, semi-double to lightly double, small, scentless, cupped and borne in small to medium-sized clusters. They will fade almost to white if placed in full sun. The rose has good remontancy, blooming in repeating seasonal flushes. The plant is hardy to USDA zone 5b and will grow to about 13 ft (4 m).

'Margot Koster Cl.'.

'MARGUERITE CARELS'.

Breeder: Paul Nabonnand (France, 1922).
Parentage: 'Frau Karl Druschki' x 'General MacArthur'.
Class: Large-Flowered Climber.
The flowers of this lovely rose are medium pink fading to light pink (from outer petals inward), large, double, scented of fruit and globular in shape. The rose blooms generously in repeated seasonal flushes. The flowers are formed in small clusters on long stems, making them good for cutting. The plant can be trained as a climber of about 10 ft (3 m). It can be seen at Sangerhausen (Germany).

'Marguerite Carels'.

'MARGUERITE DESRAYEUX'.

Breeder: Paul & Clément Nabonnand (France, 1906).
Parentage: 'Madame Alfred Carrière' x 'Madame Marie Lavalley'.
Class: Hybrid Noisette.
I failed to see this rose where it grows at Sangerhausen. It is described in the catalogue of their collection as silvery-pink with a darker center, semi-double, large and of climbing height. The plant is thornless and will bloom in repeated seasonal flushes.

'Maria'.

'MARIA'.

Breeder: Franz Wänninger (Germany). Year unknown.
Parentage: Unknown.
Class: Large-Flowered Climber.
The flowers of 'Maria' are large, very full, richly fragrant and yellow with a touch of orange at the bases of the center petals that is sometimes visible as a small center eye. They fade to cream as they age. The plant reblooms well in seasonal flushes and has a potential height of about 12 ft (3.65 m).

'MARIA CALLAS, CL.'
See 'Miss All American Beauty, Cl.'

'MARIE ACCARIE'.

('Mme Marie Accary', 'Marie Accary').
Breeder: Guillot fils (France, 1872).
Parentage: Unknown.
Class: Tea-Noisette.
The softly fragrant, medium-sized, and double flowers are white with tints of coral-pink in the center.

'Marie Accarie'.

'MARIE CLAIRE, CL.'

('Grimpant Marie-Claire', 'Marie-Claire, Cl.').
Breeder: Discovered by Francis Meilland (France, 1944).
Parentage: Sport of 'Marie Claire'.
Class: Climbing Hybrid Tea.
Unfortunately, this striking rose is commercially available only in France. The flowers are brilliant coral-red morphing to orange with age and contrasting with the yellow reverse. They are large, very double, and moderately fragrant. The petals reflex along their sides to become quilled. The rose blooms in continuous seasonal flushes. The plant has shiny, rugose (wrinkled) foliage and will grow to about 10 ft (3 m).

'MARIE NABONNAND'.

(Philippe Pétain, Youri).
Breeder: Clément Nabonnand (France, before 1938).
Parentage: 'Wassili Chludoff' x 'General MacArthur, Cl.'.
Class: Climbing Hybrid Tea.
The flowers of this rose are deep crimson aging to lighter crimson-purple with a small white center and a few small white streaks. They are medium-sized, double, sweetly scented of damask and loosely cupped. The rose blooms prolifically in continuous seasonal flushes. The plant has few thorns, is very disease resistant and has medium gray-green foliage. It can be trained as a shrubby climber to about 10 ft (3 m). 'Noëlla Nabonnand' as sold in the United States may actually be 'Marie Nabonnand'. 'Noëlla Nabonnand' has dark red new growth. 'Marie Nabonnand' has new growth that is light green.

'MARIE PAVIÉ, CL.'

Breeder: Discovered by Georges Bénard (France, 1904).
Parentage: Sport of 'Marie Pavié'.
Class: Climbing Polyantha.
This rose has delicate colors of pale pink fading to white. The flowers are small to medium-sized, double, moderately fragrant, rosettes and are borne in small clusters. The plant is shade tolerant, very disease resistant, hardy to USDA zone 4b, and can be trained as a small climber. There are no public gardens listed for this rose, but the bush form can be seen at Sangerhausen (Germany) as 'Marie Pavic'.

'Marie Pavié, Cl.'

'MARIE ROBERT'.

Breeder: Scipion Cochet (France, 1893).
Parentage: Seedling of 'Isabella Gray'.
Class: Tea-Noisette.
This Tea-Noisette clearly shows its ancestry when it opens with a Tea-like shape. The flowers are large, double, scentless and bright pink. The petal tips soon fade to light pink, but the flowers remain darker in the center and on the petal reverse. When fully opened the flowers develop a rather muddled appearance. The plant will bloom in regular seasonal flushes and will grow to about 10 ft (3 m).

'MARIE VAN HOUTTE, CL.'.

Breeder: Discovered by Thomasville Nursery (United States, 1936).
Parentage: Sport of 'Marie van Houtte'.
Class: Climbing Tea.
The flowers of this rose have an unusual color pattern. They open yellow-cream and soon develop pink petal edges. The pink becomes more extensive as the flower ages until

it is almost entirely pink. The flowers are large, double, moderately fragrant, high-centered and are borne singly (mostly) or in small clusters. They bloom in repeating flushes during the growing season. The plant will grow to about 10 ft (3 m).

'Marie Van Houtte, Cl.'.

'MARIE-ROSE'.

Breeder: Discovered by T. A. Truffaut (France, 1930).
Parentage: Sport of 'Marie-Jeanne'.
Class: Polyantha.
The flowers of 'Marie-Rose' are crimson-pink, large, double, lightly fragrant and borne in large clusters. They rebloom well in continuous seasonal flushes. The plant is almost thornless, has glossy foliage and will grow to about 10 ft (3 m).

'Maritim'.

'MARITIM'.

(RT 01-780, Tan01780, Tanimita, TANmitiram).
Breeder: Hans Jürgen Evers (Germany, 2001).
Parentage: Unknown.
Class: Large-Flowered Climber.
'Maritim' has cerise-pink flowers that are large, double, scentless and with a low dome form. They are borne singly or in small clusters. They bloom prolifically in regular seasonal flushes. The plant has shiny medium green foliage and can be trained as a climber of about 10 ft (3 m).

'MARQUESA DE URQUIJO, CL.'. See 'Pilar Landcho, Cl'.

'MARTHA'.

Breeder: Discovered by H. Knudsen (Denmark, before 1912).
Introduced in Denmark by Zeiner-Lassen & Dithmer in 1912 as 'Martha'.
Parentage: Sport of Zéphirine Drouhin (bourbon, Bizot 1868). The color is paler and more coral-pink than 'Zéphirine Drouhin'.
Class: Bourbon. The paucity of thorns could indicate some Boursault in the ancestry of this rose.
The flowers of 'Martha' are large, double, moderately fragrant and light pink with a touch of coral. They open out to a flat bloom form. They are borne singly (mostly) or in small clusters. The rose is quite floriferous and is remontant in regular seasonal flushes. The plant is almost thornless, hardy to USDA zone 5b and will grow to about 9 ft (2.75 m).

'MARTINE GUILLOT'.

(MASmabay).
Breeder: Dominique Massad (France, 1991). Introduced in France by Guillot/Roseraies Pierre Guillot in 1997.
Parentage: Seed parent: 'New Dawn'. Pollen parent: ['Chaucer' x 'Aloha'] x ['Iceberg' x unnamed seedling].
Class: Shrub. Generosa Collection.
The flowers are double, medium to large-sized, richly fragrant and soft, light coral-buff colored with a cupped bloom form. The outer petals fade to cream and then to ivory, but the center stays darker. The rose blooms in regular flushes throughout the season. The foliage is dark green and glossy. The plant can be pruned and grown as

a shrub or it can be given a low support like a fence or a small trellis and trained as a small climber of about 8 ft (2.5 m).

'Martine Guillot'.

'MARY HART, CL.'

Breeder: Discovered by Western Rose Company (United States, 1937).
Parentage: Sport of 'Talisman'.
Class: Climbing Hybrid Tea.
This rose has crimson petal tips and yellow petal bases with a mix of colors in between. The reverse is light yellow with crimson petal tips. The flowers are semi-double, large, high-centered, strongly fragrant and cupped opening quite flat. There is one main summer bloom with a few flowers later in the season. The plant can be trained as a climber.

'MARYSE KRILOFF, CL.'

See 'Lucy Cramphorn, Cl.'.

'Masquerade, Cl.'

'MASQUERADE, CL.'

(Maskerade, Cl.).
Breeder: Discovered by Charles J. Dillon (United Kingdom, 1958).
Parentage: Sport of 'Masquerade'.
Class: Climbing Floribunda.
This is a sport of a famous rose that was the first cluster-flowered rose to show the unique characteristic, inherited from the China Roses, of becoming darker with age instead of fading. The flowers are initially yellow and age to coral-pink and finally to dark red. They are mildly fragrant, medium-sized, semi-double, cupped and borne singly (mostly) or in small clusters. They bloom in regular flushes throughout the flowering season. The foliage is dark green and disease resistant. The plant is hardy to USDA zone 4b, and is very vigorous, reaching to about 18 ft (5.5 m).

'Mayor of Casterbridge'.

'Masquerade, Cl.'

'MAYOR OF CASTERBRIDGE'.

(AUSbrid, B/20/89).
Breeder: David C. H. Austin (United Kingdom, 1997).
Parentage: 'Charles Austin' x unnamed seedling.
Class: Shrub. English Rose.

This rose is one of Austin's earlier creations. The flowers are very full, medium-sized, lightly fragrant and cup shaped with an outer rim of large petals neatly enclosing a mass of roughly quartered inner petals. They are soft, medium pink with a light pink reverse and bloom in repeated seasonal flushes. The plant is disease resistant and will grow to 8 ft (2.5 m) or more if given support. The rose is named after one of Thomas Hardy's literary characters.

'Max Krause, Cl.'.

'MAX KRAUSE, CL.'.

Breeder: Discovered by Alfredo Moreira da Silva (Portugal, 1940).
Parentage: Sport of 'Max Krause' (Germany, 1930).
Class: Climbing Hybrid Tea.

The flowers of this beautiful rose are fragrant, very large-sized, very full, high-centered and golden yellow flushed with apricot, especially on the petal tips and the petal reverse. They are held singly (mostly) or in small clusters on long stems. The plant has glossy, dark green foliage and will grow to about 8 ft (2.5 m). The climbing form seems to grow only at Sangerhausen.

'Mecklenburg'.

'MECKLENBURG'.

Breeder: Lützow (Germany, 2004).
Parentage: Unknown.
Class: Shrub, Large-Flowered climber.

This is a very pretty rose in the English Rose style. It can be grown as a shrub or can be given support and grown as a small climber of 6 to 8 ft (1.8 to 2.5 m) as it is grown at Sangerhausen. The flowers are fragrant (fruity), very double, large, cupped and sometimes quartered. The color is medium pink fading to light pink and then to almost white. They repeat bloom in regular seasonal flushes.

'Meg'.

'MEG'.

Breeder: Dr. A.C.V. Gosset (United Kingdom U K, 1954).
Parentage: 'Paul's Lemon Pillar' x 'Madame Butterfly'.
Class: Large-Flowered Climber.

'Meg' has flowers that are single or semi-double, very large, strongly fragrant, and apricot-pink with soft yellow petal bases and dark russet-red stamens. There is one main summer bloom with an occasional later repeat. The foliage is semi-glossy and dark green. The plant is very hardy to USDA zone 4b. It can be trained as a climber of 12 to 13 ft (3.65 to 4 m).

'Meilland Décor Arlequin'.

'MEILLAND DÉCOR ARLEQUIN'.

Breeder: Marie-Louise Meilland (France, 1986).
Parentage: [('Zambra' selfed x 'Zambra' selfed) x 'Arthur Bell'].
Class: Shrub.
This is a rose that wants to be noticed. It has flowers that are medium-sized, double, and cupped. The ultra-showy color is brilliant cerise on the petal upper surface and yellow on the reverse side. The blooms are held singly or in small clusters. I have seen it grown as a shrub, a standard and a small climber. It can be seen at Bagatelle Park in France, Roseto Carla Fineschi in Italy and Sangerhausen in Germany.

'MENTOR'.

Breeder: Melvin E. Wyant (United States, 1959).
Parentage: 'Tallyho' x 'New Dawn'.
Class: Shrub, Large-Flowered Climber.
Although this rose is usually thought of as a shrub, I have seen it successfully grown as a small climber at Sangerhausen. The flowers are very fragrant, medium-sized, double and salmon-pink with a darker reverse. The color shifts to regular pink as the flower matures.

'Mentor'.

The plant has dark green, glossy foliage and will grow to about 7 ft. (2 m). The main flowering is early in the season with a few repeats in the fall.

'MERCEDES GALLART'.

Breeder: Blas Munné (Spain, 1930).
Parentage: 'Souvenir de Claudius Denoyel' x 'Souvenir de Claudius Pernet'.
Class: Large-Flowered Climber.
The flowers of this rose open deep pink with small coral-yellow petal bases and gradually change to cerise with age. They are very large, very double and richly fragrant. The rose blooms in continuous seasonal flushes. The plant has glossy foliage and can be trained as a climber. It grows at Sangerhausen (Germany).

'Mercedes Gallart'.

'MESSIRE'.

Breeder: Louis Laperrière (France, 1963).
Parentage: Seedling of 'Danse du Feu'.
Class: Large-Flowered Climber.
'Messire' has bright scarlet-red flowers that are medium-

'Messire'.

sized, semi-double and profusely borne singly or in small clusters. They bloom in repeated seasonal flushes. The plant has bronze-green foliage and will grow to about 10 ft (3 m).

'Messire Delbard'.

'MESSIRE DELBARD'.

(DELsire, Grandessa).
Breeder: G. Delbard (France, 1976).
Parentage: seed parent: 'Danse du Feu' x 'Guinée'.
Pollen parent: ['Ténor' x 'Fugue'] x ['Delbard's Orange Climber' x 'Gloire de Dijon'].
Class: Large-Flowered Climber.
The flowers of this rose are deep crimson-red, scentless, large and double. They are cupped initially and then open out to show the stamens. They are borne singly or in small clusters and bloom in regular seasonal flushes. The plant will grow to about 10 ft (3 m).

'MEVROUW G. A. VAN ROSSEM, CL.'.

('Mrs. G. A. van Rossem, Cl.').
Breeder: Discovered by Jean-Marie Gaujard (France, 1937).
Parentage: Sport of 'Mevrouw G. A. van Rossem'.
Class: Climbing Hybrid Tea.
This rose is basically apricot with a darker bronze-toned reverse, yellow petal bases and outer petals fading to lighter apricot pink, then to pink. Strongly visible red veins run through the petals. The fragrant, large, double flowers bloom in continuous seasonal flushes. The plant will grow to a height of about 12 ft (3.65 m).

'Mevrouw Van Staaten Van Nes, Cl.'.

'MEVROUW VAN STRAATEN VAN NES, CL.'.

('Duchess of Windsor', 'L'Indefrisable', 'Mrs. Van Nes', 'Permanent Wave', 'Van Nes'). 'Permanent Wave' is the registration name.
Breeder: Discovered by Mathias Leenders (Netherlands, 1935).
Parentage: Sport of 'Mevrouw van Straaten van Nes'.
Class: Climbing Floribunda.
This rose lady with the long name has flowers that are crimson-red, large, semi-double, ruffled, open and moderately fragrant. There is excellent rebloom in continuous flushes all during the flowering season. The plant will grow to about 10 ft (3 m).

'Michèle Meilland, Cl.'

'MICHÈLE MEILLAND, CL.'.

(Grimpant Michèle Meilland).
Breeder: Discovered by Francis Meilland (France, 1951).
Parentage: Sport of 'Michèle Meilland'.
Class: Climbing Hybrid Tea.
The opening bud is salmon-colored with flushes of scarlet. The color fades rapidly leaving the outer petals light pink with a hint of lilac and the center petals the original salmon color. The flowers are mildly fragrant, double, large and borne singly or in small clusters. They have long stems which make them good for cutting. The plant can grow to about 12 ft (3.65 m).

'MICHKA'. See 'Garden Sun'.

'MIKADO'.

Breeder: Kiese (Germany, 1913).
Parentage: Unknown.

'Mikado'.

Class: Climbing Hybrid Tea.
The flowers of this rose are medium crimson-pink fading to a lighter mauve-pink color. They are large, semi-double, sweetly scented, and open out flat. They are carried singly or in small clusters. The plant has one main summer bloom with a few repeat flowers later in the season and will grow in an upright manner to about 8 ft (2.5 m) making it a very good pillar rose. It can be observed at Sangerhausen (Germany). There are six different rose varieties listed with this name including a Hybrid Rugosa growing at Sangerhausen, so beware of false friends.

'Milkmaid'.

'MILKMAID'.

Breeder: Alister Clark, introduced by Hazlewood Bros. Pty. Ltd. (Australia, 1925).
Parentage: 'Crépuscule' x unnamed seedling
Class: Tea-Noisette.
Yellow buds open as cream flowers fading to white,

but retain some color in the center for longer. The flowers are fragrant, small to medium-sized and semi-double. They occur singly and in small clusters and bloom once early in the season. They have rather narrow petals that reflex along their sides and they open out almost flat to reveal a big bunch of golden-yellow stamens. The potential climbing height is about 20 ft (7 m).

'Millenium'.

'MILLENIUM'.

Breeder: Heinrich Schultheis (Germany, 2000).
Parentage: Unknown.
Class: Large-Flowered Climber.
'Millenium' has flowers that are light pink, large, very double, lightly fragrant, globular to cupped and borne singly or in small clusters. They fade to pale pink in time. The petals may be quartered. The remontancy is excellent in continuous flushes during the flowering season. The plant has dark green glossy foliage and will grow in a shrubby style to about 16 ft (5 m).

'MINOUCHETTE'.

Breeder: Paul Croix (France, 1970).
Parentage: Unknown.
Class: Large-Flowered Climber.
This rose has medium-sized, semi-double to double, lightly fragrant, light pink flowers borne singly or in small clusters. It is essentially a simple rose that acquires a special beauty when it occurs, as it often does, in sizeable clusters. The flowers rebloom prolifically in continuous seasonal flushes. The plant will climb to about 10 ft (3 m).

'MINUETTE, CL.'.

('La Minuette', 'LAMinuette', 'Minuette', 'Sweetheart').
Breeder: Unknown (Italy, 1980).
Parentage: Sport of 'Minuette'.
Class: Climbing Floribunda.
The flowers of this rose are mildly fragrant, medium-sized, double and cream with deep pink petal borders. They are beautifully shaped in classical high-centered fashion. They repeat in continuous seasonal flushes. The plant can be trained as a modest climber of about 10 ft (3 m).

'Minuette, Cl.'.

'MISS ALL-AMERICAN BEAUTY, CL.'.

('Maria Callas, Cl.', MEIdaudsar).
Breeder: Discovered by Meilland International (France, 1969).
Parentage: Sport of 'Miss All-American Beauty'.
Class: Climbing Hybrid Tea.
This is a beautiful rose, as the name predicts. The flowers are large, full, high-centered, richly fragrant and a lovely deep pink. They are produced singly (mostly) or in small clusters. There is excellent rebloom in continuous seasonal flushes. The plant is heat tolerant and very disease resistant, but not very hardy. It will perform best in a climate of USDA zone 7b or warmer. The plant will grow in a shrubby manner to about 10 ft (3 m).

'Miss All-American Beauty, Cl.'.

'MISS LIBERTY'.

Breeder: Eugene S. "Gene" Boerner (United States, 1956).
Parentage: 'New Dawn' x 'Minna Kordes'.
Class: Large-Flowered Climber.
This rose has deep pink, medium to large-sized, lightly double, strongly fragrant flowers borne singly (mostly) or in small clusters. The plant blooms in continuous seasonal flushes, is well armed with thorns and covered with thick, dark green foliage. It can be expected to grow to 10 to 13 ft (3 to 4 m).

'Miss Liberty'.

'Miss Marion Manifold'.

'MISS MARION MANIFOLD'. ('Marion Manifold').

Breeder: William Jack Adamson (Australia, 1913).
Parentage: Unknown.
Class: Climbing Hybrid Tea, Climbing Hybrid Perpetual.
The opening bud is deep crimson with a hint of scarlet changing to crimson-pink with age. The petal reverse is lighter. The flowers are large, double, moderately fragrant, globular and borne singly (mostly) or in small clusters. There is one main bloom with a few flowers produced later in the season. The plant is nearly thornless and will grow to about 13 ft (4 m).

'Mister Lincoln, Cl.'.

'MISTER LINCOLN, CL.'.

Breeder: Discovered by Ram (Unknown, 1974).
Parentage: Sport of 'Mister Lincoln'.
Class: Climbing Hybrid Tea.
This rose has flowers that are dark, bright red, very large,

'Mlle Cécile Brunner, Cl.'.

double, richly fragrant and high-centered. It blooms in repeated seasonal flushes. The plant has matte, dark green foliage and grows rather stiffly to about 10 ft (3 m).

'Mlle Blanche Lafitte'.

'MLLE BLANCHE LAFITTE'.

Breeder: Henri & Giraud Pradel, père & fils (France, 1851).
Parentage: Unknown.
Class: Bourbon.
The flowers are medium-sized, double, blush pink, long stemmed and formed singly or in small clusters. They bloom in regular seasonal flushes. The plant is a moderate climber, reaching as much as 8 ft (2.5 m) in a warm climate.

'MLLE CÉCILE BRUNNER, CL.'.

('Buttonhole Rose', 'Fiteni's Rose', 'Madame Cécile Brunner, Cl.', 'Mlle Cécile Brunner, Cl.', 'Mignon, Cl.', 'True Friend').
Breeder: Discovered by Franz P. Hosp (United States, 1894). There is also an Australian climbing sport from Richard Ardagh (Australia, 1904).
Parentage: Sport of 'Mlle. or Mme. Cécile Brunner'.
Class: Climbing Polyantha.
The flowers of this famous rose are small, double, and sweetly fragrant like spicy tea. They are light pink and are borne in large clusters. They flower early, but only once except for a few blooms now and then later in the season. The plant is hardy to USDA zone 5b, has matte, dark green foliage and will climb vigorously to about 20 ft (6 m). 'Spray 'Cécile Brünner' ' (AKA 'Everblooming Cécile Brünner' or 'Bloomfield Abundance') will bloom all summer. It resembles 'Cécile Brünner', but it is not related.

'MLLE GENEVIÈVE GODARD'.

Breeder: Antoine Godard (France, 1889).
Parentage: Unknown.
Class: Climbing Tea.
This lovely old Tea has flowers that are medium to large-sized, full, high centered and golden yellow when opening, but morphing to pink with deep pink veining as they age. It repeats well, blooming in constant flushes during the regular flowering season. The plant is vigorous enough to be trained as a climber of about 10 ft (3 m).

'Mlle Mathilde Lenaerts'.

'MLLE MATHILDE LENAERTS'.

Breeder: Antoine Levet, père (France, 1880).
Parentage: Seedling of 'Gloire de Dijon'.
Class: Tea-Noisette.
This rose has flowers that are medium to large-sized, double, fragrant and deep pink with a touch of mauve and with white petal bases. The petal tips are light pink to white. The shape is a shallow cup partially filled with petals turning inward. There is some quartering. The flowers bloom in repeated flushes throughout the flowering season. The plant has dark green matte-surfaced foliage and will climb to an average height.

'MME A. MEILLAND, CL.'.
See 'Peace', Cl.

'MME ABEL CHATENAY, CL.'.

Breeder: Discovered by Charles G. Page (United States, 1917).
Parentage: Sport of 'Madame Abel Chatenay'.
Class: Climbing Hybrid Tea.

'Mme Abel Chatenay, Cl.'.

This climbing Hybrid Tea has medium-sized, double, high-centered pink flowers opening out flat. They have a moderate tea fragrance. They are borne singly (mostly) or in small clusters with long stems that make them good for cutting. The plant has bronze-green foliage, a slight weakness for fungus diseases, and a growth potential of 10 to 13 ft (3 to 4 m). It is not entirely hardy and will grow and bloom best in a climate of USDA zone 7b or warmer.

'Mme Alfred Carriere'.

'MME ALFRED CARRIERE'.

('Madame Alfred Carrière').
Breeder: Joseph Schwartz (France, 1875).
Parentage: Unknown.
Class: Tea-Noisette.
The flowers of this early bloomer are large, very double, fragrant, globular and white to light cream with pink centers. The pink fades to blush in time. The plant is remontant in generous and continuous seasonal flushes. It is drought resistant and shade tolerant, but is susceptible to mildew. It will grow to 10 or 12 ft (3 to 3.65 m) in a temperate climate and to as much as 25 ft (7.6 m) in a warm climate.

'MME AUGUSTE CHOUTET'.

Breeder: Antoine Godard (France, 1901).
Parentage: 'William Allen Richardson' x 'Kaiserin Auguste Viktoria'.
Class: Tea-Noisette.
This rose has very large, double, richly fragrant (tea), buff-yellow flowers with soft orange-yellow centers. In time they fade to pale pink or almost white. The plant can be trained as a moderate climber of about 6 to 8 ft (1.8 to 2.5 m). It is grown only at Sangerhausen (Germany).

'MME AUGUSTE PERRIN'.

Breeder: Joseph Schwartz (France, 1878).
Parentage: Unknown.
Class: Tea-Noisette. Hybrid Noisette (perhaps with some Bourbon or Hybrid Perpetual).
The flowers of this rose are medium-sized, double and light pink with a blush pink to white petal reverse. The large outer petals curve in a little to form a sort of cup for the smaller, quartered inner petals. The flowers bloom in continuous flushes during the flowering season. The plant is moderately vigorous and can be trained as a climber of about 8 ft (2.5 m).

'Mme Bérard'.

'MME BÉRARD'.

Breeder: Antoine Levet (père) (France, 1870).
Parentage: 'Madame Falcot' x 'Gloire de Dijon'.
Class: Tea-Noisette.
The outer petals are pale coral and the center is deeper

coppery-coral. The reverse is darker and pinker. The flowers are medium to large-sized, very double, richly fragrant with inner petals quartered and outer petals reflexed at the tips. The seasonal bloom is in regular flushes. The plant has dark green foliage and will grow to about 10 ft (3 m).

'Mme Butterfly, Cl.'.

'MME BUTTERFLY, CL.'.

Breeder: Discovered by Edward Smith (United Kingdom, 1926).
Parentage: Sport of 'Madame Butterfly' (a sport of 'Ophelia').
Class: Climbing Hybrid Tea.
The flowers of this rose are large, double, fragrant, high-centered and apricot-pink with golden yellow petal bases. The outer petals fade to pale apricot leaving the center a deeper color for longer. There is good rebloom in continuous seasonal flushes. The plant will reach a height of about 10 ft (3 m).

'MME C. LIGIER'.

Breeder: R. Berland (France, 1899).
Parentage: Unknown.
Class: Climbing Tea.
The flowers of this rose are richly fragrant, large, very double, quartered strongly and pink with a darker center. It repeats blooms in regular seasonal flushes. The plant grows enough to be trained as a small climber. The rose by this name grown at Roseraie du Val-de-Marne is incorrect.

'MME CAROLINE KÜSTER'.

Breeder: Jean Pernet (France, 1872).
Parentage: Seedling of 'Le Pactole'.
Class: Tea-Noisette, Tea.
Soft golden yellow aging to light cream, medium to large-sized, double flowers with rolled back petals and a classic Tea rose shape are found here. The flowers are carried singly or in small clusters and bloom early in the season with a few repeats later. The plant will grow in a shrubby manner to about 8 ft (2.5 m) and can be trained as a small climber.

'Mme Caroline Testout, Cl.'.

'MME CAROLINE TESTOUT, CL.'.

('Caroline Testout, Cl.', 'Climbing Caroline Testout', 'Climbing Madame Caroline Testout').
Breeder: Discovered by Prof. J.B. Chauvry (France, 1901).
Parentage: Sport of 'Madame Caroline Testout'.
Class: Climbing Hybrid Tea.
This lovely rose has flowers that are large, double, moderately fragrant, high-centered and pink. The flowers are borne singly or in small clusters. They bloom in continuous flushes during the regular flowering season. The plant will grow to about 10 ft (3 m).

'Mme Creux'.

'MME CREUX'.

Breeder: Antoine Godard (France, 1890).
Parentage: Unknown.
Class: Tea-Noisette.
The flowers are light salmon-pink with a darker pink petal reverse. The petals in the center curl inward and show their pink backs making the flower centers appear pink. The flowers are moderately fragrant, large and double. The plant will grow as a climber to about 10 ft (3 m).

'Mme De Sévigné'.

'MME DE SÉVIGNÉ'.

Breeder: Robert and Moreau (France, 1874).
Parentage: Unknown.
Class: Climbing Bourbon.
The rose grown now is probably not the original rose which was described as being lighter at the edges. The present one is quite an even color. The flowers are large, full, strongly fragrant, and globular, sometimes with quartered petals. The petal tips roll back neatly. The flowers are carried singly or in small clusters. The rose reblooms in continuous flushes during the flowering season and is hardy to USDA zone 5b. The plant will grow to about 10 ft (3 m).

'Mme Driout'.

'MME DRIOUT'.

Breeder: Discovered by J. Thiriat (France, before 1901). Introduced in France by Lucien Bolut in 1903.
Parentage: Sport of 'Reine Marie Henriette'.
Class: Climbing Hybrid Tea. It is sometimes classed as a Climbing Tea even though it is a sport of a Climbing Hybrid Tea.
'Mme Driout' has large, double, light pink flowers with deep crimson-pink stripes instead of the over-all deep crimson-pink flowers of 'Reine Marie Henriette', its sport parent. It is sometimes referred to as 'Reine Marie Henriette Panachée' or 'Striped Reine Marie Henriette'. The plant does best in a warm, dry climate where it is less subject to fungus diseases and to frost damage. It can be trained as a climber of about 10 to 12 ft (3 to 3.65 m).

'MME E. SOUFFRAIN'.

Breeder: Prof. J.B. Chauvry (France, 1897).
Parentage: 'Rêve d'Or' x 'Duarte de Oliveira'.
Class: Tea-Noisette.
The fat buds are deep crimson and the flowers are large, very double and light golden yellow with rosy tints in the center. As the flower ages the petal tips become touched with crimson-mauve and reflex in pointed shapes, resulting in a cactus-like bloom. The nearly thornless plant will grow to about 10 ft (3 m).

'Mme Edouard Herriot, Cl.'.

'MME EDOUARD HERRIOT, CL.'.

('Daily Mail Rose, Cl.').
Breeder: Discovered by Ketten Frères/Bros./ Gebrüder (Luxembourg, 1921).
Parentage: Sport of 'Madame Edouard Herriot'.
Class: Climbing Hybrid Tea.
The opening buds are coral-pink with a deeper coral reverse and yellow petal bases. The coral in the outer petals fades to light pink with age. The flowers are large, lightly double, moderately fragrant, high-centered and borne singly (mostly) or in small clusters. There is a profuse bloom early in the year followed by a few flowers later in the season. The plant has glossy foliage, many thorns, is very vigorous and will climb in a bushy manner to about 15 ft (4.55 m).

'Mme Edouard Herriot, Cl.'.

'MME EMILIE DUPUY'.

('Emilie Dupuy').
Breeder: Antoine Levet (père) (France, 1870).
Parentage: 'Madame Falcot' x 'Gloire de Dijon'.
Class: Tea-Noisette.
The flowers of this rose are light yellow with a deeper yellow center. With age they fade almost to white. The form is large, double and globular. The outer petals reflex at the tip and the inner petals are usually quartered. There is a soft tea-like fragrance. Rebloom is excellent and occurs in steady flushes during the flowering season.

'MME ERNEST CALVAT'.

Breeder: Discovered by Marie-Louise aka Widow Schwartz or La Veuve (France, 1888).
Parentage: Sport of 'Madame Isaac Pereire'.
Class: Climbing Bourbon.
The richly fragrant flowers are very large, very double and mid-pink with yellowish petal bases. The strongly quartered inner petals are packed into a "cup" of larger, lighter colored outer petals. They bloom in regular repeating flushes during the flowering season. Train the canes horizontally for the best flowering. Resist pruning more than a small amount as it can be detrimental. The plant is hardy to USDA zone 5b and will grow to about 8 ft (2.45 m).

'Mme Ernest Calvat'.

'MME GASTON ANNOUILH'.

Breeder: Prof. J.B. Chauvry (France, 1899).
Parentage: Unknown.
Class: Hybrid Noisette.
This rose has wonderfully fragrant flowers. They are medium to large-sized, double and pale yellow fading to cream, then to white, as they age. The petal bases, especially the backs, are subtly nuanced with green. The rose flowers prolifically in repeated flushes during the whole blooming season. The plant will grow with moderate vigor to about 10 ft (3 m).

'MME GRÉGOIRE STAECHELIN'.

('La Belle Espagnole', 'Spanish Beauty').
Breeder: Pedro (Pere) Dot (Spain, 1927).
Parentage: 'Frau Karl Druschki' x 'Château de Clos Vougeot'.
Class: Large-Flowered Climber.
This rose reverses the usual pattern of roses fading with age. The petals become darker with time, resulting in darker outer petals. The reverse is also darker. The flowers are fragrant, large, semi-double to lightly double, ruffled and borne singly or in small clusters. There is a prolific spring or summer bloom with a few flowers opening later in the season. The plant

has dark green, glossy foliage and will reach a height of about 20 ft (6 m).

'Mme Grégoire Staechelin'.

'MME HARDY' ('Félicité Hardy').

Breeder: Julien-Alexandre Hardy (France, 1831).
Parentage: Unknown.
Class: Damask.
'Mme Hardy's flowers are white, medium-sized, double and richly fragrant with beautifully quartered petals centered by a small green pip. The buds have long, feathery calyces. The flowers are once blooming, spring or summer with a few repeat blooms later in the season. The plant is shade tolerant, very disease resistant and very hardy to USDA zone 4b. I think it is more vigorous than is usually stated. Mine grew about 10 ft (3 m) onto a shed in partial shade.

'Mme Hardy'.

'MME HECTOR LEUILLOT'.

Breeder: Joseph Pernet-Ducher (France, 1903).
Parentage: Unknown.
Class: Climbing Hybrid Tea.
The flowers of this rose are described as fragrant, large, very full and light, soft golden yellow with crimson-pink toned centers. The petals sometimes have a quartered pattern. They are borne singly or in small clusters. The rose has one main early bloom with a few repeats later in the season. The plant can be trained as a small climber of about 8 ft (2.5 m). The plant growing at Sangerhausen (shown in the photo) has creamy-buff flowers. Perhaps it is a different variety with the wrong label.

'Mme Hector Leuillot'.

'MME HENRI GUILLOT CL.'.

Breeder: Discovered by Francis Meilland (France, 1942).
Parentage: Sport of 'Madame Henri Guillot'.
Class: Climbing Hybrid Tea, Climbing Pernetiana.
The flowers are deep coral pink with a lighter reverse and flushes of yellow in the center. They are mildly fragrant, very large and semi-double. They are once-blooming early in the season with a few blooms later on. The plant has shiny, dark green foliage and will grow vigorously to about 16 ft (5 m).

'MME HERMANN HAEFLIGER'.

Breeder: Victor Hauser (Switzerland, 1937).
Parentage: Seedling of Rosa foetida bicolor x 'Charles P. Kilham'.
Class: Large-Flowered Climber.
This rose has large, semi-double to lightly double, deep crimson-red flowers with a loose, somewhat ragged

form. It repeats well in continuous flushes during the flowering season. The plant has shiny, dark green foliage and will climb with moderate vigor to about 10 ft (3 m).

'Mme Hermann Haefliger'.

'MME ISAAC PEREIRE'.

('Le Bienheureux de la Salle').
Breeder: Armand Garçon (France, 1881).
Introduced in France by Margottin père & fils in 1881.
Parentage: Unknown.
Class: Bourbon.
This rose is deep pink aging to magenta, wonderfully fragrant of raspberries, very large and very full. The form is cupped with quartered petals. The repeat bloom is good. The plant has large, medium green foliage, is hardy to USDA zone 5b and can be trained as a small climber of 8 to 10 ft (2.5 to 3 m).

'Mme Isaac Pereire'.

'MME JULES BOUCHÉ, CL.'.

Breeder: Discovered by California Roses (United States, 1938).
Parentage: Sport of 'Madame Jules Bouché'.
Class: Climbing Hybrid Tea.
The flowers are, richly fragrant, large and double. The color is cream fading to white at the edges and touched with blush pink in the center when newly opened. The repeat bloom occurs in continuous flushes during the flowering season. The plant can be trained as a climber of about 10 ft (3 m).

'Mme Jules Bouché, Cl.'.

'MME JULES GRAVEURAUX'.

Breeder: Soupert & Notting (Luxembourg, 1900).
Parentage: 'Rêve d'Or' x 'Viscountess Folkestone'.
Class: Climbing Tea.
The older records describe a rose that is light buff-yellow with a darker peach-pink center. They are strongly fragrant, very large and very double. They bloom in regular seasonal flushes. The plant has shiny, light green foliage and will grow vigorously to about 12 ft (3.65 m).

'Mme Jules Graveuraux'.

'MME LAURIOL DE BARNY'.

Breeder: Victor Trouillard (France, 1868).
Parentage: Unknown.
Class: Bourbon.
The flowers of this beautiful Bourbon rose are light pink, richly fragrant, medium to large, double and shallow-cupped with quartered petals. They have one main spring or early summer bloom followed by a few repeats later in the season. The plant is well covered with dark green foliage, hardy to USDA zone 5b and disease resistant. I have seen it growing to about 8 ft (2.5 m) or higher.

'Mme Lauriol De Barny'.

'MME LEON CONSTANTIN'.

Breeder: Joseph Bonnaire (France, 1907).
Parentage: Unknown.
Class: Tea-Noisette.
This Tea-Noisette has fragrant, large, double, pale pink flowers with a hint of salmon in the center. The long buds open to a form typical of the Teas. Blooming is continuous during the flowering season. The plant grows and blooms best in a warm climate. It will reach a height of about 8 ft (2.5 m).

'MME LOUIS HENRY'.

Breeder: Marie Ducher (France, 1879).
Parentage: Unknown.
Class: Tea-Noisette.
The flowers of this rose are medium to large-sized, double and ivory white with a pale yellow center. The form is globular, but the flower opens enough to show a little glimpse of the stamens. The petals sometimes have shallow longitudinal creases. The flowering occurs in continuous flushes of bloom during the regular season. The plant has few thorns and is moderately vigorous, growing to 8 or 10 ft (2.5 or 3 m).

'MME LOUIS LENS, CL.'.

Breeder: Discovered by Victor Lens (Belgium, 1935).
Parentage: Sport of 'Madame Louis Lens'.
Class: Climbing Hybrid Tea.
This rose has flowers that are pure white, large, very double, richly fragrant and high-centered in Hybrid Tea style. The long, strong stems make them good for cutting. They bloom abundantly in continuous flushes throughout the flowering season. The plant can be trained as a climber.

'MME NORBERT LEVAVASSEUR, CL.'.

Breeder: Unknown.
Parentage: Sport of 'Mme Norbert Levavasseur'.
Class: Climbing Polyantha.
This climbing sport of a well-known Polyantha has softly fragrant, small, semi-double, light crimson flowers with white petal bases that tend to develop mauve tones with age. The flowers are cup-shaped with wavy petals and are held in large clusters. They bloom in continuous seasonal flushes.

'MME PIERRE COCHET'.

Breeder: Scipion Cochet (France, 1891).
Parentage: Seedling of 'Rêve d'Or'.
Class: Tea-Noisette.
The fragrant, medium to large flowers open apricot and fade, from the petal tips inward, to cream with a slight apricot tint. The petals fold into points at the tips giving a star-like effect. The flowers are borne singly (mostly) or

in small clusters. Remontancy occurs in continuous flushes during the flowering season. The plant will grow vigorously to 10 or 12 ft (3 or 3.65 m).

'MME PIERRE S. DUPONT, CL.'. See 'Mrs. Pierre S. Dupont, Cl.'.

'MME PIZAY'.

Breeder: C. Chambard (France, 1920).
Parentage: unnamed seedling x 'Madame Mélanie Soupert'.
Class: Climbing Hybrid Tea.
The apricot-colored flowers fade to pale apricot-buff, but remain darker on the petal reverse and in the center. They are very large and double with broad outer petals and bloom in repeated flushes during the flowering season. The almost thornless plant can be trained as a shrubby climber of average height. It seems to grow only at Sangerhausen (Germany).

'Mme Plantier'.

'MME PLANTIER'.

Breeder: Plantier (France, 1835).
Parentage: Usually given as Rosa damascena x Rosa moschata. There may be a Boursault in the ancestry of this rose as evidenced by its relative thornlessness.
Class: Damask, Hybrid Noisette.
The buds are surprisingly deep pink for flowers that open light cream in color and soon fade to white. The flowers are richly fragrant of damask, medium-sized and very full with quartered petals, a green pip in the center and sometimes a button eye. They are borne in large clusters and are once blooming, spring or summer with a few repeats later in the year. This variety is sometimes confused with 'Mme Hardy' which has the same color and form, including the green pip. They can be distinguished by the fact that 'Mme Hardy' is well armed and has large leaves, but 'Mme Plantier's thin canes are almost thornless and have much smaller light green leaves. The plant is very vigorous and will climb to about 12 ft (3.65 m).

'MME ROSE ROMARIN'.

('Rose Romarin').
Breeder: Gilbert Nabonnand (France, 1888).
Parentage: 'Papillon' x 'Chromatella'.
Class: Tea-Noisette.
The flowers of the rose by this name at Roseraie du Val-de-Marne match the older description of being large, semi-double, deep crimson-red and remontant. The plant of this name at Sangerhausen has flowers that are fuller and are pale pink with mauve petal tips. It is undoubtedly an imposter.

'MME SEGOND WEBER, CL.'.

Breeder: Discovered by Richard Ardagh (Australia, 1911).
Discovered by Louis Reymond (France, 1929).
Parentage: Sport of 'Madame Segond Weber'.
Class: Climbing Hybrid Tea.
The flowers are salmon-pink fading to a paler and more true pink color. They are strongly fragrant, high-centered, very large and double with long stems that make them good for cutting. They bloom in regular seasonal flushes. The Reymond sport grows at Sangerhausen (Germany).

'MME SOLVAY'.

Breeder: André Eve (France, 1992).
Parentage: Unknown.
Class: Large-Flowered Climber.
The crimson-pink flowers have streaky white petal bases. They are medium-sized, semi-double and held in large clusters. The petals may reflex along their sides and becoming quilled in the mature flowers. The rebloom is good and occurs in regular seasonal flushes. The plant has excellent disease resistance and may grow to 15 or 16 ft (5 m).

'Mme Solvay'.

'MME TRIFLE'.

Breeder: Antoine Levet (père) (France, 1869).
Parentage: Seedling of 'Gloire de Dijon'.
Class: Tea-Noisette.
The flowers of 'Mme Triffle' are fragrant, very large, very double and light yellow softened with a hint of buff. They fade to cream with age. The floral form is very old-fashioned with folded, quartered petals. They occur singly or in small clusters and rebloom in continuous seasonal flushes. The plant can be trained as a climber of about 10 ft (3 m).

'Mock's Rosa Druschki'.

'MOCK'S ROSA DRUSCHKI'.

Breeder: Adolf Mock (Germany, circa 1935).
Parentage: Sport of 'Frau Karl Druschki', according to Harald Enders, a well-known German rosarian.
Class: Climbing Hybrid Perpetual.
This interesting sport has flowers that are pink, large and double with rolled-back petal tips and are borne singly or in small clusters. They bloom in continuous seasonal flushes. The plant has dark green foliage and will grow to 10 or 12 ft (3 to 3.65 m).

'MOJAVE, CL.'.

Breeder: Discovered by Eric L. Trimper (Australia, 1964).
Parentage: Sport of 'Mojave'.
Class: Climbing Hybrid Tea.
The colors of this rose are quite striking. The flowers open pure, bright apricot with darker veining, fade to lighter apricot and then morph to pink. The color changes start at the petal tips and progress inward producing a multicolored effect. The flower form is large, double, and high-centered. The flowers are grouped singly or in small clusters. There is a rich fragrance. Remontancy is in continuous seasonal flushes. The plant has glossy foliage and will grow to about 10 ft (3 m).

'Mojave, Cl.'.

'MOLINEAUX' (AUSmol).

Breeder: David C. H. Austin (United Kingdom, 1994).
Parentage: 'Graham Thomas' x unnamed seedling.
Class: Shrub, English Rose.
This rose has been in my garden for about 20 years and I still find it very rewarding. The old-fashioned flowers are medium-sized, but their large number of petals makes them seem larger in size. The color is deep yellow and they are softly fragrant. They are borne singly or in small clusters and rebloom in continuous flushes during the flowering season. Given support and good nutrition

'Molineaux'.

the plant will grow enough to be trained as a small climber. Mine has reached about 7 ft (2.13 m). It is hardy down to USDA zone 5b.

'Momo'.

'MOMO'.

Breeder: Werner Noack (Germany, 1994).
Introduced by Noack-Rosen (Germany, 1995).
Parentage: Unknown.
Class: Large-Flowered Climber.

This rose has some of the appearances of a Rambler with its small, double flowers held in large clusters and its shiny, dark green Wichurana-type foliage, but with its excellent reblooming in seasonal flushes and bright red color, it seems to be better placed with the modern climbers. The plant can be trained as a small climber to about 8 ft (2.5 m).

'Mon Amour, Cl.'.

'MON AMOUR, CL.'.

Breeder: Stelvio Coggiatti (Italy, 1966).
Parentage: 'Peace, Cl.' x 'Caprice'.
Class: Climbing Hybrid Tea.
The flowers of this rose are large, double, very fragrant and medium pink with a lighter reverse. They bloom in regular seasonal flushes. The plant has dark green, matte-surfaced foliage and will grow to about 8 ft (2.5 m). I have only seen it at Roseto Carla Fineschi in Italy.

'Mon Jardin et Ma Maison'.

'MON JARDIN ET MA MAISON'.

(MEIchavrin, 'Mon Jardin & Ma Maison').
Breeder: Michèle Meilland Richardier (France, before 1998).
Parentage: ('Margaret Merrril' x 'Bonica') x 'Pascali'.
Class: Large-Flowered Climber, Romantica.
It would be nice to know how this lovely rose got its unusual name which translates as "My Garden and My House". The flowers are very large, very double, mildly fragrant, cupped, quartered and buff-yellow fading to cream. They repeat in continuous seasonal flushes. The plant has glossy, medium green foliage and only grows to about 6 ft (1.8 m), but it is usually described as a climber.

'MONSIEUR DÉSIR'.

Breeder: Jean Pernet père (France, 1888).
Parentage: 'Gloire de Dijon' probably crossed with a Hybrid Perpetual.
Class: Hybrid Noisette.
The flowers of this Noisette are very large, semi-double to lightly double, fragrant and deep crimson-pink with petal tips becoming slightly more mauve with age. The form is cupped with reflexing outer petals. The repeat is very good, occurring in continuous flushes during the flowering season. It is grown at Roseraie du Val-de-Marne and is sold in France and the US.

'Monsieur Rosier'.

'MONSIEUR ROSIER'.

Breeder: Gilbert Nabonnand (France, 1887).
Parentage: Seedling of 'Mademoiselle Mathilde Lenaerts'.
Class: Tea-Noisette.
This rose has flowers that are medium-sized, lightly double and initially cupped, then becoming open and flattened, revealing the stamens. The color is pink with a pale yellow center fading to light pink and a white center. The rose reblooms well in regular seasonal flushes. The plant can be expected to grow to 8 or 10 ft (2.5 to 3 m). I have seen it at Sangerhausen and it is also grown in France.

'Montezuma, Cl.'.

'MONTEZUMA, CL.'.

Breeder: Discovered by Langbecker (Australia, 1960).
Parentage: Sport of 'Montezuma'.
Class: Climbing Grandiflora.
The flowers open deep salmon-pink and fade to lighter pink starting at the outer petals. They are medium to large-sized, double, mildly fragrant or lacking scent, high-centered and borne singly or in small clusters. They repeat well and abundantly in regular seasonal flushes. The plant is heat resistant and disease resistant and can be trained as a climber.

'MOODY DREAM' (MACmoodre).

Breeder: Samuel Darragh McGredy IV (Northern Ireland before 1994).
Introduced by Egmont Roses (New Zealand, 1996).
Parentage: 'Moody Blues' x' Lavender Dream'.
Class: Floribunda, Shrub.
Initially the flowers are deep pink with a touch of mauve, but they age lighter and more mauve with white petal tips. They are small to medium-sized, semi-double, fragrant of musk and borne in large clusters. They repeat bloom in regular seasonal flushes, but are said to be somewhat slow. The plant has glossy foliage and can be trained as a climber of about 10 ft (3 m).

'Moody Dream'.

'MOONLIGHT'.

('Kordes Rose Moonlight', KORklemol).
Breeder: Tim Hermann Kordes (Germany, 1995).
Parentage: (unnamed seedling x 'Lichtkönigin Lucia') x unnamed seedling.
Class: Large-Flowered Climber.
The opening flowers are apricot-yellow fading to cream. The petal tips become touched with pink which gives the impression of an apricot-colored rose from a distance. They are medium-sized, semi-double to lightly double, fragrant (fruity), cupped to flat and borne singly or in small clusters. They hold up well in the rain. The rose is remontant in regular seasonal flushes. The plant has very good disease resistance, glossy, dark green foliage and hardiness to USDA zone 5b. It can be trained as a shrubby climber of 8 to 10 ft (2.5 to 3 m).

'Moonlight' (Kordes).

'MOONLIGHT'.

Breeder: Rev. Joseph Hardwick Pemberton (United Kingdom, 1913).
Parentage: 'Trier' x 'Sulphurea'.
Class: Hybrid Musk
This Hybrid Musk has flowers that are medium to large-sized, semi-double, richly fragrant, cream fading to ivory with a hint of yellow in the center and prominent yellow stamens. They are carried singly or in small clusters. There is one main bloom, spring or summer, with a few repeats later in the season. The plant has glossy, reddish-purple foliage that helps to distinguish it from the very similar 'Trier'. It will grow as a branching climber to 8 or 10 ft (2.5 or 3 m).

'Moonlight' (Pemberton).

'MORGENGRÜSS'.

('Morning Greeting').
Breeder: Reimer Kordes (Germany, 1962).
Parentage: R. Kordesii x 'Kleopatra'.
Class: Hybrid Kordesii.
The buds are yellow with flushes of orange-red and open to flowers that are initially deep salmon with yellow petal bases (the colors of a sunrise), but soon fade to light pink with darker centers. They are strongly fragrant, medium to large-sized, very double with ruffled petals and are borne singly or in small clusters. They are essentially once-blooming, spring or early summer, with scattered flowers later in the season. The plant has glossy, light green foliage and can be trained as a climber of about 13 ft (4 m).

'Morgengrüss'.

'MORGENSONNE 88' (KORhoro).

Breeder: W. Kordes & Sons (Germany, 1988).
Parentage: 'Goldstern' x 'Sämling' (according to HMF member, Rosenfee).
Class: Large-Flowered Climber.
Yellow buds flushed with red open as medium to large-sized, double-strong yellow flowers that fade to cream. Initially they have the form of a well-shaped rosette, but become looser and less organized with age. They are carried singly (mostly) or in small clusters. The rebloom is good and occurs in regular seasonal flushes. The plant has dark green, glossy foliage and has a growth potential of about 10 ft (3 m).

'Morgensonne 88'.

'MORNING DAWN'.

Breeder: Eugene S. "Gene" Boerner (United States, 1955).

'Morning Dawn'.

Introduced in United States by Jackson & Perkins Co. in 1955.
Parentage: Seedling of 'New Dawn' x 'R.M.S. Queen Mary'.
Class: Large-Flowered Climber.
This 'New Dawn' descendant has outer petals of pale silvery pink and darker salmon-pink inner petals. The flowers are large, very full, fragrant and borne singly (mostly) or in small clusters. The outer petals reflex to form points giving the mature flower a star-like appearance. This rose reblooms well in continuous seasonal flushes. The plant has shiny, dark green foliage and can be trained as a climber of about 8 ft (2.5 m).

'Morning Jewel'.

'MORNING JEWEL'.

Breeder: Alexander M. (Alec) Cocker (Scotland, 1968).
Parentage: 'New Dawn' x 'Red Dandy'.
Class: Large-Flowered Climber.

Here is another lovely 'New Dawn' descendant. This one has deep rose-pink flowers with a lighter reverse that are medium to large-sized, semi-double to double and carried singly or in small clusters. They are cupped at first, and then open out flat. The rebloom is excellent and occurs in regular seasonal flushes. The plant has glossy foliage and can be expected to climb to about 10 to 13 ft (3 to 4 m).

'MORNING MAGIC' (Radmor).

Breeder: William J. Radler (United States, 2008).
Introduced in United States by The Conard-Pyle Co. in 2008 as 'Morning Magic'.
Parentage: 'RADdsbs' x 'RADspot'.
Class: Large-Flowered Climber.
This flower has light pink single, medium to large-sized flowers with a delicate appearance. They are initially cupped, but open out quite flat and they are borne singly or in small clusters. The rose reblooms in regular flushes during the flowering season. The plant has blackspot resistant, dark green, semi-glossy foliage and is hardy to USDA zone 5b. It will climb to about 8 ft (2.5 m), enough for training as a pillar rose.

'MORTIMER SACKLER' (AUSorts).

Breeder: David C. H. Austin (United Kingdom, 2002).
Introduced by David Austin Roses Limited (United Kingdom, 2002).
Parentage: Ausmound x unnamed seedling.
Class: Shrub. English Rose.
Deep pink buds open to medium pink flowers that soon fade to light pink. They are also large, very full, fragrant and borne singly or in small clusters. They bloom in continuous seasonal flushes. The plants are almost thornless, have semi-glossy, dark green foliage and are known to grow to about 12 ft (3.65 m).

'MOULIN ROUGE, CL.'

Breeder: Discovered by Ignace Hendrickx (Belgium, before 1956). Introduced by Grandes Pépinières C. de Coninck-Dervaes (Belgium, 1956).
Parentage: Sport of 'Moulin Rouge'.
Class: Climbing Floribunda.
The flowers of this rose are often described as geranium-red or turkey-red, giving a good impression of their strikingly brilliant color. They are medium-

'Moulin Rouge, Cl.'.

sized, double, mildly fragrant and carried in large clusters. They bloom in flushes during the flowering season. The plant grows at Roseraie du Val-de-Marne (France).

'Mount Shasta, Cl.'.

'MOUNT SHASTA, CL.'.

Breeder: Discovered by George Knight & Sons (Australia, 1968).
Parentage: Sport of 'Mount Shasta'.
Class: Climbing Hybrid Tea.
This is a pure white rose except for a touch of light creamy yellow at the petal bases. The flowers are also fragrant, large, very double and are borne singly or in small clusters. They bloom in continuous seasonal flushes. The plant has light green, glossy foliage and will grow in a vigorous, spreading manner to about 16.5 ft (5 m). The sport parent

was named for the snow-capped mountain located in northern California and the name was passed on to the climbing sport.

'Mozart'.

'MOZART'.

Breeder: Peter Lambert (Germany, 1936).
Parentage: 'Robin Hood' x 'Rote Pharisäer'.
Class: Hybrid Musk.
'Mozart' has flowers that are small, single and deep pink with a large white center. They are formed in large clusters and bloom prolifically and repeatedly during the flowering season. The plant will grow in a shrubby manner to about 6 ft (1.8 m) and can be used as a small climber. I trained mine to a 6 ft fence with good results.

'Mrs Aaron Ward, Cl.'.

'MRS AARON WARD, CL.'.

Breeder: Discovered by Alexander Dickson II (United Kingdom, 1922).
Parentage: Sport of 'Mrs. Aaron Ward'.
Class: Climbing Hybrid Tea.
The flowers are large, double, high-centered and mildly fragrant with centers of peach and outer petals lighter peach-buff to cream buff. The petal tips are sometimes scalloped or irregularly shaped. The flowers are usually solitary, but may be grouped into small clusters. There is one main bloom with an occasional repeat later. The plant has glossy foliage and will grow to about 15 ft (4.5 m).

'Mrs Anne Dakin'.

'MRS ANNE DAKIN' ('Anne Dakin').

Breeder: Robert A. Holmes (United Kingdom, before 1972). Introduced in United Kingdom by Albrighton Roses in 1972.
Parentage: Unknown.
Class: Large-Flowered Climber.
Beautiful colors grace this Large-Flowered Climber. The bright coral pink of the ruffled petals gradually changes to yellow at the flower's center matching with the creamy yellow petal backs. The blooms are medium-sized, full and mildly fragrant. They are carried in small clusters. The healthy plant bears deep green glossy leaves and may grow to a height of 10 to 13 ft (3 to 4 m).

'MRS ARTHUR CURTIS JAMES'.

Breeder: Brownell Family (United States, 1933).
Parentage: 'Mary Wallace' x unnamed seedling.
Class: Large-Flowered Climber.
The large, double, very fragrant, golden yellow flowers open out to form a shallow cup that reveals the dark golden stamens. The flowers fade with time to pale yellow, then to light cream. They are carried singly

(mostly) or in small clusters. The main bloom occurs early in the season with a few flowers opening later. The plant can be trained as a climber of moderate size, to about 10 ft. (3 m).

'Mrs Arthur Curtis James'.

'MRS C. V. HAWORTH, CL.'.

Breeder: Discovered by Frank Cant & Sons (United Kingdom, 1932).
Parentage: Sport of 'Mrs. C.V. Haworth'.
Class: Climbing Hybrid Tea.
The flowers of this rose are large, semi-double, high-centered, strongly fragrant and initially deep apricot, then fading to light apricot-cream. The flowers are borne singly or in small clusters. They repeat well in flushes during the whole flowering season. The plant can be trained as a climber of average height. I have seen it only at Sangerhausen (Germany).

'Mrs C. V. Haworth, Cl.'.

'MRS G. A. VAN ROSSEM, CL.'.

See 'Mevrouw G. A. van Rossem, Cl.'.

'MRS HENRY BOWLES, CL.'.

Breeder: Discovered by Dobbie & Co. Ltd. (Scotland, 1929).
Parentage: Sport of 'Mrs. Henry Bowles'.
Class: Climbing Hybrid Tea.
This rose has flowers that have light pink petal tips with darker centers and a darker petal reverse. The petal bases are flushed with salmon-pink. In time, the flowers fade completely to light pink. They are also double, very large-sized, high-centered, richly fragrant and carried singly or in small clusters. The flowers rebloom well in continuous seasonal flushes. The plant can be trained as an average-sized climber. It is grown only at Sangerhausen and is no longer commercially available. The climber and the sport parent are a close match except for height.

'Mrs Henry Bowles, Cl.'.

'MRS. HENRY WINNETT, CL.'.

Breeder: Discovered by Pierre (fils) Bernaix (France, 1930).
Parentage: Sport of 'Mrs. Henry Winnett'.
Class: Climbing Hybrid Tea.
Here is a rose to add color to a dull garden corner with its bright crimson-red, fragrant, large, double, high-centered blooms. They are formed mostly singly, but sometimes occur in small clusters. The flowering is extended by repeated seasonal flushes of bloom. The plant has large, glossy foliage and can be trained as a climber. This is another plant that seems to be grown only at Sangerhausen and is not offered by any commercial establishment.

'Mrs Herbert Stevens, Cl.'.

'MRS HERBERT STEVENS, CL.'.

('Grimpant Mrs. Herbert Stevens').
Breeder: Discovered by Joseph Pernet-Ducher (France, 1922).
Parentage: Sport of 'Mrs. Herbert Stevens'.
Class: Climbing Hybrid Tea.
The flowers of this Climbing Hybrid Tea are large, double, high-centered, fragrant and pure white except for some subtle apricot-buff tones at the base of the petals. The petals reflex strongly at the tips to form points as the flower ages. The flowers are borne singly or in small clusters. There is a good rebloom in regular seasonal flushes. The plant is very vigorous and will climb with flexible canes to about 16 to 20 ft (5 to 6 m).

'MRS HUGH DETTMAN'.

Breeder: Alister Clark (Australia, 1930).
Parentage: Hybrid of Rosa gigantea.
Class: Hybrid Gigantea.
The color of the newly opened flowers is apricot, but it fades quickly to buff tones and finally to pale buff-cream. Their floral form is large, double, fragrant and somewhat loosely arranged petals. There is one main profuse bloom with some repeats later in the season. Colorful hips are formed in the fall. The plant can be trained as a climber and makes a good pillar rose. It will grow and bloom best in a climate of USDA zone 7b or warmer. It is commercially available, but the authenticity of the nursery offering has been questioned.

'MRS NORMAN WATSON'.

Breeder: Alister Clark (Australia, 1930).
Parentage: 'Radiance' x 'Gwen Nash'.
Class: Large-Flowered Climber.
This is a very beautiful rose with deep pink flowers that are large, double and have broad, ruffled petals with squared-off tips bordered by narrow pale pink bands. They only lack fragrance. The rose blooms in repeated flushes during the entire flowering season. The plant has long flower stems that make it good for cutting. It will grow to 10 or 13 ft (3 or 4 m), perfect for an arbor.

'MRS PIERRE S. DUPONT, CL.'.

('Madame Pierre S. Du Pont, Cl.', 'Madame Pierre S. Dupont, Cl.', 'Mrs. P. R. du Pont').
Breeder: Discovered by Verne Stone Hillock (United States, 1933). Discovered by M. J. Benn (Laurel Nursery) (Australia, 1940). There were several other sports discovered later.
Parentage: Sport of 'Mrs. Pierre S. duPont'.
Class: Climbing Hybrid Tea.
The large, lightly double, high-centered, mildly fragrant flowers of this rose are golden yellow at first, and then fade to light lemon yellow. They mature from a cupped form to an open, flattened form that reveals the stamens and is borne singly or in small clusters. The plant has good remontancy, blooming in continuous seasonal flushes. It is covered with glossy foliage and can be trained as a climber to about 16 ft (5 m).

'Mrs Pierre S. Dupont, Cl.'.

'MRS RICHARD TURNBULL'.

Breeder: Alister Clark (Australia, 1945).
Parentage: Hybrid of Rosa gigantea
Class: Hybrid Gigantea.

Very large, single, richly fragrant creamy white flowers open from long, narrow light yellow buds. They are borne singly or in small clusters. The rose is once blooming early in the flowering season. The nearly thornless, almost evergreen plant has been known to climb to as much as 30 to 45 ft (10 to 15 m) although it is usually not that tall. It makes a wonderful display when grown into a sturdy tree.

'Mrs Rosalie Wrinch'.

'MRS ROSALIE WRINCH'.

Breeder: W. & J. Brown (United Kingdom, before pre-1913).
Parentage: 'Frau Karl Druschki' (Hybrid Perpetual) x 'Hugh Dickson'.
Class: Large-Flowered Climber. It is called a Climbing Hybrid Perpetual at Sangerhausen.
This little-known climber has flowers that are large, single (with an occasional extra petal), carried singly or in small clusters and light lavender-pink. The plant will grow, with moderate vigor, to about 8 ft (2.5 m). I have only seen it at Sangerhausen.

'MRS SAM MCGREDY, CL.'.

('Geneviève Genest').
Breeder: Discovered by G. A. H. Buisman (Netherlands, 1937), by A. Guillaud (France, 1938), by Somerset Rose Nursery (United States, 1940), by Western Rose Company (United States, before 1940), by California Nursery Co. (United States, 1941) and by Wilson (New Zealand, 1947).
Parentage: Sport of 'Mrs. Sam McGredy'.
Class: Climbing Hybrid Tea.
The copper-apricot flowers are large, double, fragrant and high-centered with flushes of yellow at the petal bases. The petal tips fade to lighter apricot-pink, but the centers and the petal reverses remain

'Mrs Sam McGredy, Cl.'.

darker. The flowers are held singly or in small clusters. They rebloom in continuous flushes during the flowering season. The plant grows and blooms best in a climate of USDA zone 7b or warmer. In this kind of environment and with good care it will climb to about 20 ft (6 m).

'Mrs Tresham Gilbey, Cl.'.

'MRS TRESHAM GILBEY, CL.'.

Breeder: Discovered by Max Vogel (Germany, 1938).
Parentage: Sport of 'Mrs. Tresham Gilbey'.
Class: Climbing Hybrid Tea.

The flowers are large, double, fragrant and medium pink flushed with coral at the petal bases. They are borne singly (mostly) or in small clusters. There is one main profuse bloom with a few flowers later in the season. The foliage is glossy and light green. The plant can be trained as a climber. It grows only at Sangerhausen (Germany).

'Mrs W. H. Cutbush, Cl.'.

'MRS W. H. CUTBUSH, CL.'.

Breeder: Discovered by W. Paling (Netherlands, 1911).
Parentage: Sport of 'Mrs. W. H. Cutbush' which, in turn, is a sport of 'Madame Norbert Levavasseur'.
Class: Climbing Polyantha.
The flowers of this Climbing Polyantha are medium to large, semi-double, mildly fragrant, deep to light pink with a small white center and are borne in large clusters. The plant reblooms in regular seasonal flushes. The climbing sport grows at Roseraie du Val-de-Marne (France) and the bush form (sport parent) can be seen at Sangerhausen.

'Mrs. W. J. Grant, Cl.'.

'MRS. W. J. GRANT, CL.'.

('Belle Siebrecht, Cl.' is the exhibition name.)
Breeder: Discovered by William Paul (United Kingdom, 1899) and by E. G. Hill (US, 1899).
Parentage: Sport of 'Mrs. W. J. Grant'.
Class: Climbing Hybrid Tea.
This sport of a once very popular Hybrid Tea has large, double, high-centered, fragrant, rose-pink flowers with a globular form. They are borne mostly singly or, occasionally, in small clusters. The rose blooms in continuous seasonal flushes. The plant will climb to about 10 ft (3 m). It does best in a climate of USDA zone 7b or warmer.

'Multiflore De Vaumarcus'.

'MULTIFLORE DE VAUMARCUS'.

Breeder: Menet (Switzerland, 1875).
Parentage: Unknown.
Class: Tea-noisette.
The very fragrant, small to medium-sized, very double light pink flowers with white centers fade quickly to all white. The rather narrow petals open out flat and show the golden yellow stamens. The flowers occur in large clusters and bloom in continuous flushes during the flowering season. The plant is only moderately vigorous, and with much branching, reaches a height of about 8 ft (2.5 m).

'MÜNCHEN'.

Breeder: Wilhelm J. H. Kordes II (Germany, 1940).
Parentage: 'Eva' x 'Réveil Dijonnais'.
Class: Hybrid Musk.
This Hybrid Musk rose has flowers that are large, semi-double, mildly fragrant, and crimson with a small white center almost obscured by the large bunch of golden yellow stamens radiating over it. The flowers are borne

singly or in small clusters and repeat their bloom in continuous seasonal flushes. The plant has glossy, dark green foliage and will grow on arching stems to about 7 ft (2 m), barely enough to be trained as a small climber. It is reported to be quite hardy. Public gardens where this rose is grown are Roseto Carla Fineschi (Italy) and Sangerhausen (Germany).

'München'.

'MÜNCHENER FASCHING'.

Breeder: Reimer Kordes (Germany, 1963).
Parentage: Unknown.
Class: Hybrid Kordesii.
This is a typical Kordesii with the bright red flowers and the dark green shiny leaves inherited from its Wichurana ancestors. The flowers are medium-sized, lightly double and arranged singly or in small clusters. It blooms in repeated seasonal flushes. It can be pruned to grow as a shrub or allowed to grow to 7 or 8 ft (2 to 2.5 m) and trained as a shrubby climber.

'Münchener Fasching'.

'MURMURE'.

Breeder: Paul Croix (France, 1971).
Parentage: 'Luna-Park' x 'Moulin Rouge'.
Class: Large-Flowered Climber
The flowers are very fragrant, medium-sized, semi-double (15 to 20 large petals), brilliant scarlet and are held singly or in small clusters. The very floriferous plant is remontant in multiple flushes of bloom during the regular flowering season and can be trained as a climber of about 10 ft (3 m).

'Mutabilis'.

'MUTABILIS'.

('Butterfly Rose', Rosa chinensis 'Mutabilis', 'Tipo Ideale').
Breeder: Unknown (before 1894).
Parentage: Unknown.
Class: Hybrid China, Bengale.
'Mutabilis' is named for its unusual changes of color associated with its China heritage in which the rose becomes darker with age rather than fading in the usual manner. There is some variability caused by climate, but the usual pattern is for the flowers to open yellow to apricot and become pink, then crimson. Their form is medium-sized and single with petals spread out flat or twisted a little and well spaced. The rose reblooms in regular flushes during the flowering season. The plant has glossy, dark green foliage. It is shrubby, but can be trained as a climber of about 10 ft (3 m). There are other rose varieties grown under this name.

N

'Nice Day'.

'Nachsommer'.

'NACHSOMMER'.

Breeder: Franz Wänninger (Germany, 1988).
Parentage: 'Lawinia' x 'Altenstadt'.
Class: Large-Flowered Climber.
The flowers are bright salmon-pink, mildly fragrant, large, and very double. They are carried singly or in small clusters. They bloom in regular seasonal flushes and form light red hips in the fall. The foliage is glossy. The plant will grow to about 8 ft (2.5 m), enough to train as a small climber.

'Nahéma'.

'NAHÉMA' (DELéri, 'Naema').

Breeder: G. Delbard (France, 1991).
Parentage: 'Grand Siècle' x 'Heritage'.
Class: Large-Flowered Climber.
Medium pink buds open to flowers of the same color, but the outer petals fade quickly to pale pink while the center remains darker. The flowers are medium to large-sized, very full and have a rich, fruity fragrance. The petals may be quartered in old rose style. The flowers are borne singly or in small clusters. The remontancy is very good and occurs in continuous seasonal flushes. The plants have dark green foliage and a climbing habit with a height of about 10 ft (3 m) or more.

'NANCY HAYWARD'.

Breeder: Alister Clark (Australia, 1937). Introduced in Australia by Hazlewood Bros. Pty. Ltd. in 1937 and by T. G. Stewart in 1937.
Parentage: 'Jessie Clark' x unnamed seedling.
Class: Hybrid Gigantea, Large-Flowered Climber.
This Hybrid Gigantea has softly fragrant, single, very large brilliant cerise-pink flowers borne mostly singly or occasionally in small clusters. They open out flat and look almost as if they could fly away. They repeat well in continuous flushes during the flowering season. The plant is very vigorous and will grow to about 16 or 20 ft (5 or 6 m).

'Nardy'.

'NARDY'.

Breeder: Gilbert Nabonnand (France, 1888).
Parentage: Seedling of 'Gloire de Dijon'.
Class: Tea-Noisette.
The flowers are often described as salmon-yellow, but the base color is more buff-yellow with flushes of salmon on the underside of the petals. With age, the color fades to creamy white. The form is very large, double and globular in the early

stages, then it opens out to a slightly more flattened shape as it matures. There is a moderate fragrance. The repeat bloom is prolific and continuous in regular flushes during the flowering season. The plant has slightly mildew prone, large, dark green foliage shaded with a hint of bronze. It will grow to at least 10 ft (3 m) and makes a lovely pillar rose.

'NEERVELT'.

Breeder: Hendrikus Antoni Verschuren (Netherlands, 1910).
Parentage: 'Gloire de Dijon' x 'Princesse de Béarn'.
Class: Tea-Noisette.
The flowers of this rose are bright crimson aging to purple. These are surprisingly vivid colors for a Tea-Noisette, a class noted for softly colored roses. The form is medium to large-sized, double. The flower occurs singly or in small clusters. There is a moderate fragrance. It has very good remontancy in continuous flushes during the flowering season. The plant can be expected to grow to about 10 ft (3 m).

'NEGRESCO'.
See 'Crimson Sky'.

'Neige Rose'.

'NEIGE ROSE'.

Breeder: G. Delbard (France, 1955).
Parentage: Unknown.
Class: Large-Flowered Climber.
The flowers of this rose are large, double, mildly fragrant and deep pink in the center and on the petal reverse. The outer petals are lighter than the center. At first the form is cupped with ruffled petals and later opens out flatter to show the stamens. The flowers are carried singly or in small clusters. The plant will climb vigorously about 10 to 13 ft (3 to 4 m). 'Neige Rose' translates as "Pink Snow", not as "Snow Rose" as sometimes thought.

'New Dawn'.

'NEW DAWN'.

Breeder: Discovered by Somerset Rose Nursery, 1930.
Parentage: Sport of 'Dr. W. Van Fleet'.
Class: Large-Flowered Climber, Hybrid Wichurana.
As a Hybrid Wichurana, 'New Dawn' is included in my book on Ramblers. I am also placing it here because it was considered the first Large-Flowered Climber and, crossed with Hybrid Teas, was the parent of a large number of new, highly regarded Large-Flowered Climbers and other reblooming climbing roses. It was the first rose to be patented. The lovely flowers are medium to large, double, fragrant and light pink. They are borne singly (mostly) or in small clusters. The plant has glossy, dark green foliage and is said to grow to as much as 15 or 16 ft (5 m), a little less than 'Dr W. Van Fleet', its sport parent. It is hardy to USDA zone 5b. Unlike the once-blooming 'Dr. W. Van Fleet', it repeats.

'NEW DAWN RED'.
See 'Étendard'.

'NEW DAWN ROUGE'.
See 'Étendard'.

'NEW YEAR, CL.' (BURyear).

Breeder: Joe Burks (United States, 1995).
Introduced in United States by Certified Roses in 1995 as 'New Year'.
Parentage: Sport of 'New Year'.

'New Year, Cl.'.

Class: Climbing Grandiflora.

Here is a rose to enjoy greatly, although it may clash with your pink roses. It is bright orange-yellow with a hint of bronze, reddish stamens and a touch of red-orange to the outer petals. The flowers are medium-sized, semi-double to lightly double, mildly fragrant and carried singly (mostly) or in small clusters. The form is cupped opening to flat with age. The rebloom occurs in continuous seasonal flushes. The plant has glossy, dark green foliage, a bushy form and will grow to about 8 ft (2.5 m).

'New Yorker, Cl.'.

'NEW YORKER, CL.'.

Breeder: Eugene S. "Gene" Boerner (United States, 1951).
Parentage: Sport of 'New Yorker' (Boerner, Hybrid Tea, 1947).
Class: Climbing Hybrid Tea.

The flowers of 'New Yorker' are large, double, high-centered, and richly fragrant with a fruity scent and bright scarlet-red color that fades very little. They are borne singly (mostly) or in small clusters. The rose is remontant in regular flushes during the flowering season.

'NICE DAY'.

(CHEWsea, Patio Queen).
Breeder: Christopher H. Warner (United Kingdom, 1992).
Parentage: 'Seaspray' x 'Warm Welcome'.
Class: Climbing Miniature, Climbing Patio Rose.

The outer petals of this rose are medium salmon-pink and the inner ones are lighter salmon-yellow with dark golden salmon petal bases. The flowers are sweetly fragrant. The form is a small, double, open and orderly rosette and the flowers are borne singly or in small clusters. They rebloom in continuous seasonal flushes. The plant has glossy, medium green foliage, very few thorns and can be trained as a bushy small climber of about 8 ft (2.5 m).

'Night Light'.

'NIGHT LIGHT' (POUllight).

Breeder: Niels Dines Poulsen (Denmark, 1982).
Parentage: 'Westerland' x 'Pastorale'.
Class: Large-Flowered Climber.

The fragrant flowers open deep yellow with touches of crimson-red on the petal tips. They become progressively more crimson with age until the entire flower has changed color. The flower form is medium to large-sized, double and borne singly or in small clusters. There is one main bloom with a few flowers produced later in the season. The plant has healthy, shiny, dark green foliage, plentiful thorns and will grow in a bushy manner to at least 8 ft (2.5 m). It is hardy to USDA zone 5.

'Night Owl'.

'NIGHT OWL'.

Breeder: Tom Carruth (United States, 2005).
Parentage: ('International Herald Tribune' x seedling of Rosa soulieana) x [('Sweet Chariot'× 'Blue Nile') x 'Rosy Outlook'].
Class: Large-Flowered Climber.
This is a special plant for those of us who love roses in the dark red and purple colors. The flowers open deep wine-red and become purpler with age, contrasting perfectly with the yellow stamens and enlivened by the white eye and the white streaks that run through some of the petals. They are large, single to semi-double, fragrant with a spicy scent and are held in large clusters. They bloom in continuous seasonal flushes. The plant is almost thornless, has semi-glossy, grey-green foliage and will grow to 12 or 14 ft (3.65 to 4.25 m).

'Nina Weibull, Cl.'.

'NINA WEIBULL, CL.'.

Breeder: Unknown.
Parentage: Sport of 'Nina Weibull'.
Class: Climbing Floribunda.
The flowers are dark red, scentless, medium-sized, double rosettes that are formed in large clusters. There is one prolific spring or summer bloom with a few flowers later in the season. The plant is very disease resistant, has few thorns and will grow in a bushy manner to about 10 ft (3 m). It is quite hardy.

'Niphetos, Cl.'.

'NIPHETOS, CL.'.

Breeder: Discovered by Williams & Co. Keynes (United Kingdom, 1889).
Parentage: Sport of 'Niphetos'.
Class: Climbing Tea.
Pale yellow buds open to pure white flowers with a hint of light apricot in the center. They are richly scented, medium to large-sized, double and globular in shape. They bloom in repeated flushes during the flowering season. The plant can be trained as a branching climber of 12 to 15 ft (3.65 to 4.25 m). Niphetos means falling snow in Greek and alludes to the white flowers.

'NOËLLA NABONNAND'.

Breeder: Paul Nabonnand (France, 1901).
Parentage: 'Reine Marie Henriette' x 'Bardou Job'.
Class: Climbing Tea.
The flowers of 'Noëlla Nabonnand' are crimson-purple, very large, semi-double to double, richly fragrant with a cupped form that opens to show the stamens. The petal bases are white with small streaks radiating out. The petal reverse is lighter and becomes progressively whiter

toward the petal bases. The rose blooms in continuous seasonal flushes. The plant will grow vigorously to as much as 16 ft (5 m). 'Noëlla Nabonnand' in commerce in United States may actually be 'Marie Nabonnand'. 'Noëlla Nabonnand' has dark red new growth whereas 'Marie Nabonnand' has light green new growth. This helps to distinguish them.

'Noëlla Nabonnand'.

'Norwich Pink'.

'NORA CUNNINGHAM'.

('Nora Cunningham').
Breeder: Alister Clark (Australia, 1920).
Parentage: Seedling of 'Gustav Grünerwald'.
Class: Large-Flowered Climber.
This rose has flowers that are large, semi-double, moderately fragrant, cupped and mid-pink with white petal bases and dark reddish stamens. They are borne singly (mostly) or in small clusters. There is one main bloom with some repeats later in the season. The plant has light green, rugose foliage and a tendency to get blackspot. It will grow to about 12 ft (3.65 m).

'NORMANDIE'.
See 'Laura Ford'.

'NORTHERN LIGHTS'.
See 'Flamenco'.

'NORWICH PINK'.

Breeder: Reimer Kordes (Germany, 1962).
Parentage: Unknown.
Class: Hybrid Kordesii.
The flowers of 'Norwich Pink' are large, semi-double, moderately fragrant and deep cerise-pink fading in time to bright medium pink. The form is flat and open. There is one main bloom with a few flowers later in the season. The plant has dark green, shiny foliage and will grow, with much branching, to about 10 ft (3 m).

'NORWICH SALMON'.

Breeder: Reimer Kordes (Germany, 1962).
Parentage: Unknown.
Class: Hybrid Kordesii.
This rose has flowers that are medium-sized, double, moderately fragrant and soft salmon-pink with yellow petal bases and a lighter reverse. They fade in time to pink petals and white petal bases. The petals reflex at the tips to form points, giving the flower a star-like appearance. The flowers are formed in small to medium clusters. They bloom in continuous seasonal flushes. The plant has dark green, shiny foliage and can be trained as a climber of about 10 ft (3 m).

'NOZOMI'.

('Heideröslein', 'Heideröslein-Nozomi').
Breeder: Dr. Toru Onodera (Japan, 1968).
Parentage: 'Fairy Princess' x 'Sweet Fairy'.
Class: Miniature, Cl.
The flowers are small, single, cupped to flat in form, light pink and grouped in large clusters. There is one main bloom with a few repeats later in the season. The plant has small, glossy foliage, is very hardy to USDA zone 4b, very disease resistant and can be trained as a climber of about 6 ft (1.8 m). It was named for the breeder's niece who, sadly, was a casualty of World War II at the age of four.

'NUAGE PARFUMÉ'

See 'Fragrant Cloud, Cl.'.

'Nubian'.

'NUBIAN'.

Breeder: Bobbink & Atkins (United States, 1937).
Parentage: Unknown.
Class: Large-Flowered Climber/Climbing Hybrid Tea.
The flowers of 'Nubian' are large, double, high-centered and globular, richly fragrant, dark crimson-red and are held singly or in small clusters. The rose has one main bloom followed by a few repeats later in the season. The plant will grow to 8 or 10 ft (2.5 or 3 m), perfect for a pillar.

'Nur Mahál'.

'NUR MAHÁL'.

Breeder: Rev. Joseph Hardwick Pemberton (United Kingdom, 1923).
Parentage: 'Château de Clos Vougeot' x unnamed seedling.
Class: Hybrid Musk.
This rose has medium-sized, semi-double, crimson flowers with a musky fragrance. The flowers open out flat as they mature and they are carried in large clusters. They are fully remontant with continuous flushes of bloom during the season. The plant is almost thornless and will grow in a shrubby fashion to about 10 ft (3 m).

'Nymphenburg'.

'NYMPHENBURG'.

Breeder: Reimer Kordes (Germany, 1954).
Parentage: 'Sangerhausen' x 'Sunmist'.
Class: Hybrid Musk, Shrub.
The opening flowers are salmon-pink with yellow petal bases. This lovely color ages to light pink, then to nearly white. They are semi-double to lightly double, large and cupped to flat in form. They are borne in medium clusters. The rose reblooms well in repeated flushes during the flowering season and can be trained as a climber of about 10 ft (3 m).

'NYMPHE'.

Breeder: Robert Türke (Germany, 1910). Introduced by Koyer & Klemm (Germany, 1910).
Parentage: 'Mignonette' (Polyantha) x 'Maréchal Niel' (Tea-Noisette).
Class: Climbing Tea.
The flowers of 'Nymphe' are lightly fragrant, medium-sized, double and white with flushes of light yellow in the center. The floral form is globular. The roses are carried singly (mostly) and in small clusters. The plant has medium green, glossy foliage and will grow to at least 10 ft (3 m). There is one main bloom early in the season with a few flowers opening later.

'Oscar Chauvry'.

'OBÉLISQUE' (DELmot).

Breeder: G. Delbard (France, 1967).
Parentage: 'Spectacular' x ('Orange Triumph' x 'Floradora').
Class: Large-Flowered Climber.
The flowers of this rose are medium to large, semi-double, lightly scented, globular in shape and orange-pink with copper overtones. They are borne in large clusters. The rose is fully remontant, blooming in repeated flushes during the flowering season. The plant has shiny medium green foliage flushed with bronze tones and will grow to about 10 ft (3 m).

'Obélisque'.

'ODETTE JOYEUX'.

Breeder: Marcel Robichon (France, 1959).
Parentage: 'Lady Sylvia' x unnamed seedling.
Class: Large-Flowered Climber.
'Odette Joyeux' has large to very large, double, richly scented, and orange-pink flowers with a cupped, globular bloom form. They are borne singly (mostly) or in small clusters and bloom prolifically in repeated flushes during the flowering season. The plant has glossy foliage and will grow to about 12 or 13 ft (3.65 to 4 m).

'OH WOW'.
See 'Purple Splash'.

'OKLAHOMA, CL.'.

Breeder: Discovered by Herbert C. Swim (United States, 1965), O. L. "Ollie" Weeks (United States, 1965), A. Ross & Son/Ross Roses (Australia, 1972).
Parentage: Sport of 'Oklahoma'.

'Oklahoma, Cl.'.

Class: Climbing Hybrid Tea.
This rose has lovely dark red flowers that are sweetly scented, double, large and high-centered in Hybrid Tea style. They rebloom well in seasonal flushes. The plant has dark green, matte foliage, is very disease resistant, but may burn if exposed to strong sunlight. It is not hardy and must be protected from frost. It will grow to about 10 ft (3 m) and can be trained as a climber. Sadly, this rose is close to becoming extinct. 'Oklahoma', the sport parent, is identical to the climbing sport except for the height of the plant.

'Old Blush, Cl.'.

'OLD BLUSH, CL.'.

('Climbing Old Blush' 'Climbing Parson's Pink China', 'Point Stewart Climbing China').
Breeder: Unknown (1752).
Parentage: Sport of 'Old Blush'.
Class: Climbing China, Found Rose.
This climbing sport of 'Old Blush' has flowers that are semi-double to double, medium-sized, pink and held singly or in small clusters. Initially cupped and orderly, it ages to a loose, spreading form. There is one prolific bloom followed by a few repeats later in the season. The plant is remarkably vigorous, reportedly growing to about 33 ft (10 m).

'Olive'.

'OLIVE' (HARpillar).

Breeder: Harkness (United Kingdom, 1982).
Parentage: (['Vera Dalton x 'Highlight'] x Seedling) x 'Dublin Bay'.
Class: Shrub, Large-flowered Climber.
The flowers are large, double, mildly scented of spice and fire engine red that doesn't fade or become more blue. The outer petals are sometimes ruffled. The flowers are borne singly (mostly) or in small clusters. The plant has glossy foliage and will grow with some branching to about 10 ft (3 m). It can be trained as a climber or grown as a shrub.

'OLYMPIC GOLD'.

See 'Goldener Olymp'.

'OPALINE'.

See 'Coraline'.

'Open Arms'.

'OPEN ARMS'.

(CHEWpixcel, 'Coral Seas').
Breeder: Christopher H. Warner (United Kingdom, 1995).
Parentage: 'Mary Sumner' x 'Laura Ashley'.
Class: Climbing Miniature, Patio Rose.
'Open Arms' has flowers that are small, semi-double and light coral pink with petal bases flushed with light yellow. With age the whole bloom fades to white. The form is shallowly cupped, opening to flat and revealing large bunches of golden yellow stamens. The flowers are borne in large clusters. There is one main bloom with a few flowers opening later in the season. The plant is clothed with very small, shiny dark green foliage and can be trained as a climber of about 8 ft (2.5 m) or used as a ground cover.

'OPHELIA, CL.'.

Breeder: Discovered by Alexander Dickson II (United Kingdom, 1920).
Parentage: Sport of 'Ophelia'.
Class: Climbing Hybrid Tea.
The opening bud is salmon-pink with a yellow flush at the petal bases. The outer petals and inner petal tips fade quickly

to pale pink, then to white leaving the salmon color longer in the center. The flowers are richly scented, large, double and well shaped with high centers like a Hybrid Tea. They are borne mostly singly, but sometimes in small clusters. The plant reblooms in continuous flushes during the flowering season. It is very vigorous and can be trained as a climber to as much as 20 ft (about 6 m).

'Ophelia, Cl.'.

'ORANGE BEAUTY'.

Breeder: Frank Raffel (United States, 1961).
Parentage: 'Little Darling' x 'Gertrude Raffel'.
Class: Climbing Floribunda.
Indeed, this is a beauty! The flowers are large, semi-double to double, lightly scented and coral orange with a darker reverse and lighter coral petal bases, all fading eventually to pale peach. The flowers open out flat to reveal large bunches of golden yellow stamens and are held in large clusters. They bloom in continuous seasonal flushes. The plant can be trained as a climber of about 8 ft (2.5 m).

'Orange Beauty'.

'ORANGE DAWN'.

(CHEworangedawn, 'Sundancer').
Breeder: Christopher H. Warner (United Kingdom, 2006).
Parentage: 'Dawn Chorus' x unnamed seedling'
Class: Large-Flowered Climber.
The flowers of 'Orange Dawn' have salmon outer petals and salmon-orange inner petals with flushes of yellow at the petal bases. The reverse is deep yellow. They are large, double, lightly scented, remontant and borne in small clusters. The plant has medium green foliage and can be grown as an 8 to 10 ft (2.5 to 3 m) pillar rose or trained on a small trellis.

'Orange Elf'.

'ORANGE ELF'.

Breeder: Ralph S. Moore (United States, 1959).
Parentage: 'Golden Glow' x 'Zee'.
Class: Climbing Miniature.
This little rose has small, double, mildly scented flowers that open light orange with flushes of pink on the outer petal tips and bright yellow petal bases. The whole flower fades to light yellow. It is remontant in repeated seasonal flushes. The plant can be trained as a small climber.

'ORANGE EVERGLOW'.

Breeder: Brownell Family (United States, 1942).
Parentage: Sport of 'Copper Glow'.
Class: Large-Flowered Climber.
The flowers of this rose are intensely fragrant, medium to large, lightly double, high-centered and orange-colored (aging to lighter orange). The plant will reach a height of up to 20 ft (6 m). Blooming is mainly for a couple of weeks early in the season. This rose differs from 'Copper

'Orange Everglow'.

Glow', its sport parent, only in having a little deeper and more pure orange color.

'Orange Sensation, Cl.'.

'ORANGE SENSATION, CL.'.

Breeder: Unknown.
Parentage: Sport of 'Orange Sensation'.
Class: Climbing Floribunda.
The flowers are medium-sized, lightly double, mild to moderately fragrant, with a flat form and very bright orange flushed red on the petal tips and yellow on the petal bases. They bloom in repeated flushes during the flowering season. The plant can be trained as a climber of about 10 ft (3 m). The nonclimbing sport parent is identical except for height.

'Orange Triumph, Cl.'.

'ORANGE TRIUMPH, CL.'.

Breeder: Discovered by Mathias Leenders (Netherlands, 1945). Discovered by W. Koopmann (Germany, 1948).
Parentage: Sport of 'Orange Triumph'.
Class: Climbing Polyantha.
In spite of the name, the flowers of this rose are more scarlet or vermilion than orange. They are also small-sized, semi-double, fragrant and cupped in form. The blooms are borne singly or in small clusters and repeat in continuous seasonal flushes. The plant can grow to about 10 ft (3 m) and makes a good pillar rose.

'ORANGE VELVET'.

Breeder: J. Benjamin Williams (United States, 1986).
Parentage: 'Tropicana, Cl.' x 'Swarthmore'.
Class: Large-Flowered Climber.
The flowers of this rose are lightly scented of damask, large, double and high-centered in Hybrid Tea style, but opens flatter with age. The color is soft orange-red (vermilion)

with a lighter reverse. In time, the orange tones fade and the petals become more pink. The plant will grow as a vigorous climber to 10 or 12 ft (3 or 3.65 m).

"Orange Velvet'.

'ORANGEADE, CL.'.

('Climbing Orangeade').
Breeder: Discovered by Waterhouse (United Kingdom, 1964).
Parentage: Sport of 'Orangeade'.
Class: Climbing Floribunda.
This rose has bright orange-red (vermilion) flowers that are large, semi-double and mildly fragrant. They are remontant in regular seasonal flushes. The plant has dark green foliage that is reported to be susceptible to blackspot. It is quite bushy, but, with proper pruning, can be trained as a small climber.

'Orangeade, Cl.'.

'ORANGES 'N' LEMONS'.

(MACoranlem, 'Papagena').
Breeder: Samuel Darragh McGredy IV (before 1989).
Parentage: 'New Year' x ('Freude' x unnamed seedling).
Class: Hybrid Tea.
This striking rose will certainly get garden visitors' attention with its orange and yellow striped flowers. They are medium to large-sized, double, mildly scented (fruity), borne singly or in small clusters and remontant in continuous seasonal flushes. It will grow and bloom best in a USDA zone climate of 7b or more. The plant is armed with thorns, clothed with dark green foliage and, although classed as a Hybrid Tea, it can be trained as a 10 ft (3 m) climber.

'Oranges 'N' Lemons'.

'ORCHID MASTERPIECE, CL.'.

Breeder: Discovered by G. Buckner.
Parentage: Sport of 'Orchid Masterpiece'.
Class: Climbing Hybrid Tea.
This climbing rose has flowers that are large, very full, fragrant and soft orchid in color. The petals are gently ruffled. The plant has dark green foliage and will reach a height of about 8 ft (2.5 m), enough to be grown as a small pillar rose. It is presently grown only in private gardens and is no longer commercially available. The sport parent, 'Orchid Masterpiece', is identical except for height.

'Orfeo'.

'ORFEO'.

Breeder: Jan Leenders (Netherlands, 1963).
Parentage: 'Curly Pink' x 'Guinée'.
Class: Large-Flowered Climber.
'Orfeo' has large, double, high-centered, moderately fragrant, repeat-blooming, deep, bright crimson-red flowers. The petals are strongly reflexed, forming broad points at the petal tips and giving the flowers an old rose look. The plant can be trained as a 10 to 15 ft (3 to 4.5 m) climber.

'Orientale'.

'ORIENTALE'.

Breeder: Marcel Robichon (France, 1944).
Parentage: 'George Dickson' x 'Mrs. Pierre S. duPont'.
Class: Climbing Hybrid Tea.
The flowers are large, double, moderately scented, high-centered and deep pink. The petals may be roughly quartered. This rose is remontant and will grow and bloom best in a USDA zone 8 or warmer climate. The plant has glossy foliage and will grow on long, arching stems to about 10 ft (3 m).

'Oscar Chauvry'.

'OSCAR CHAUVRY'.

Breeder: Prof. J. B. Chauvry (France, 1900).
Parentage: Seedling of 'Elise Heymann'.
Class: Tea-Noisette.
The fragrant, medium to large-sized, double flowers are light pink with a hint of mauve. The mauve becomes more pronounced as the flower ages and fades to a very pale color. The form is cupped with petals reflexed at the tips. The flowers are held singly or in small clusters and bloom in regular seasonal flushes. Expect moderate vigor with growth to about 8 ft (2.5 m).

'Otto Hermann'.

'OTTO HERMANN'.

Breeder: Bernhard Bührmann (Germany, 2009).
Parentage: Unknown.
Class: Large-Flowered Climber.
This lovely rose has flowers that are large, very double and light pink. The buds open in a globose shape and then expand into an open cup tightly packed with small, quartered petals in the style of an old-fashioned rose. The blooming is repeated in multiple flushes throughout the season. The plant can be trained as a moderately vigorous climber of about 8 to 10 ft (2.5 to 3 m).

P

'Pink Perpetue'.

'PALAIS ROYAL'. See 'White Eden'.

'Paname'.

'PANAME'.

Breeder: Delbard-Chabert (France, 1959).
Parentage: 'Spectacular' x unnamed seedling.
Class: Large-Flowered Climber.
'Paname' has flowers that are large, double, mildly scented, deep pink tinted with a little salmon and some yellow flushes at the petal bases. The buff-yellow reverse contrasts attractively with the pink although it becomes pinker with age. The flowers are globular in shape at first, then open out flat to show the stamens and are borne singly or in small clusters. There is one main bloom with a few flowers produced later in the season. The rose can be trained as a shrubby climber to about 10 ft (3 m).

'Papa Gontier, Cl.'.

'PAPA GONTIER, CL.'.

Breeder: Discovered by Franz Hosp (United States, 1898), Chevrier (France, 1903), and Chase Nursery Company (United States, 1905).
Parentage: Sport of 'Papa Gontier'.
Class: Climbing Tea.
The flowers of this rose are large-sized, semi-double to barely double, moderately fragrant (tea) and crimson-pink with light yellow flushes at the petal bases. The petals become strongly quilled with age to give a star-burst effect. The flowers are borne mostly singly or sometimes in small clusters and bloom in repeated seasonal flushes. The plant has dark green foliage, is shade tolerant and will grow to about 12 ft (3.6 m).

'Papa Meilland, Cl.'.

'PAPA MEILLAND, CL.'.

('Grimpant Papa Meilland', MEIsarsar).
Breeder: Discovered by Les Stratford (Australia, 1970).
Parentage: Sport of 'Papa Meilland'.
Class: Climbing Hybrid Tea.
The flowers are large, double, richly fragrant (old rose), high-centered in Hybrid Tea style, but opening flat enough to reveal the stamens. The color is very dark red with almost no fading. The flowers are mostly borne singly, but sometimes in small clusters as well. Flowering is remontant in repeated seasonal flushes. The plant has glossy, dark green foliage and a potential height of about 13 ft (4 m).

'PAPI DELBARD'.

Breeder: G. Delbard (France, before 1992).
Parentage: Unknown.
Class: Large-Flowered Climber.

'Papi Delbard'.

The flowers of 'Papi Delbard' are scented of rose, very large and very double with a cupped old-rose form. The color is apricot that fades to pink from the outer petals inward and then to almost white with the center retaining its color longer. The flowers are borne singly or in small clusters and bloom in continuous seasonal flushes. The plant can be trained as a climber of about 10 ft (3 m).

'Papillon'.

'PAPILLON'.

Translation: Butterfly.
Breeder: Gilbert Nabonnand (France, 1878).
Parentage: Unknown.
Class: Tea-Noisette.
The softly fragrant, medium-sized, semi-double flowers are warm coppery pink at first with lighter centers punctuated by big bunches of golden-yellow stamens. The petal reverse is rose pink. The petals twist as the flower matures and opens up so that the outer petals resemble the wings of a butterfly (a papillon in French). The flowers are borne in medium clusters and repeat bloom in flushes during the flowering season. The plant will grow to about 16 ft (5 m). Etienne Bouret notes that a plant at Val-de-Marne has flowers that are too full to be authentic.

'Paprika'.

'PAPRIKA'.

(Gavroche, MEIriental).
Breeder: Alain Meilland (France, 1995).
Parentage: ('Centenaire de Lourdes' x 'Picasso') x 'Sparkling Scarlet'.
Class: Large-Flowered Climber.
'Paprika' has flowers that are medium-sized, single, scentless, and bright vermilion-red with a lighter petal reverse. They are borne singly or in small clusters and rebloom in repeated seasonal flushes. The plant has glossy, dark green foliage and will grow to about 10 ft (3 m). There are other roses with the same name.

'PARADE'.

Breeder: Gene Boerner (United States, 1953).
Parentage: Seedling of 'New Dawn' x 'World's Fair, Cl.'.
Class: Large-Flowered Climber.
'Parade' has inherited many of 'New Dawn's fine attributes such as excellent remontancy in repeating seasonal flushes, old-rose type flowers, a lovely damask fragrance and good disease resistance. The flowers are medium to large, double, deep pink, have a cupped form and are borne singly or in small clusters. The plant has dark green glossy foliage and will grow to 10 or 12 ft (3 or 3.65 m).

'Parade'.

'PARADISE, CL.'.

Breeder: Discovered by O. L. "Ollie" Weeks (United States, 1980).
Parentage: Sport of 'Paradise'.
Class: Climbing Hybrid Tea.
The flowers of this rose are large, double, lightly scented, high-centered and light mauve with deep, bright crimson-pink petal tips developing with age, especially in a warm, sunny climate. The mauve fades almost to white. The flowers are carried singly or in small clusters and are remontant in repeating seasonal flushes. The plant is clothed with glossy, dark green foliage. It is very vigorous and reportedly will grow to at least 16 ft (5 m). It will grow and bloom best in a climate of USDA zone 7b or warmer.

'Paradise, Cl.'.

'PARFUM ROYAL, CL.' (ADAmuging).

Breeder: Discovered by Michel Adam (France, before 2012).

'Parfum Royal, Cl.'.

Parentage: Sport of 'Parfum Royal'.
Class: Climbing Hybrid Tea.
This beautiful rose has flowers that are richly fragrant (fruity), very large, double and medium pink with yellow petal bases and petal reverse side. As the bloom ages it fades to mauve-pink and white. The floral form is cupped at first then opens out to a low dome. The arrangement of the flowers is single or small clusters. They are remontant in regular seasonal flushes. The plant is clothed with dark green, shiny foliage. It is quite vigorous, reaching a height of about 16 ft. (5 m). It is commercially available in Europe.

'Parkdirektor Riggers'.

'PARKDIREKTOR RIGGERS'.

Breeder: Reimer Kordes (Germany, 1957).
Parentage: Rosa kordesii x 'Our Princess'.
Class: Hybrid Kordesii.
These flowers are medium-sized, semi-double, scentless to mildly scented and deep bright vermilion with a few

small white flecks in the centers. The color fades little or not at all and doesn't acquire blue tones like many red roses do. The flowers are borne in large clusters which add to their splendid showiness and they rebloom in continuous seasonal flushes. The plant has glossy, dark green foliage and can be trained as a climber of 13 to 16 ft (4 to 5 m).

'PARKFEUR'.

Breeder: Rudolf Geschwind (former Austria-Hungary, before pre-1905).
Parentage: R. lutea 'bicolor' x Rosa canina L.
Class: Hybrid Foetida.
This rose has medium-sized, single to semi-double and bright scarlet flowers. The color is enhanced by golden-yellow stamens. The flowers are borne singly or in small clusters and bloom once early in the season with a few later additions. The plant is almost thornless, very hardy (USDA zone 4b) and can be trained as a climber to at least 20 ft (6 m).

'Parure d'Or'.

'PARURE d'OR'.

Breeder: G. Delbard (France, 1965).
Parentage: ('Queen Elizabeth' x 'Provence') x (Seedling of 'Sultan' x 'Madam Joseph Perraud').
Class: Large-Flowered Climber.
The flowers are medium-sized, semi-double, lightly scented and a striking color combination of bright golden yellow with crimson petal edges. The stamens, revealed by the open flower form, are a perfect match with golden yellow anthers and crimson filaments. The flowers are carried in small clusters and rebloom in repeating seasonal flushes. The plant has dark green, glossy foliage and will grow to about 12 ft (3.65 M).

'Pas de Deux'.

'PAS DE DEUX' (POUlhult).

Breeder: Poulsen Roser A/S (Denmark).
Parentage: Unknown.
Class: Climber, Courtyard Collection.
'Pas de Deux' has flowers that start with deep yellow-apricot buds, open as yellow flowers and fade to white. They are scented of wild rose, medium-sized, semi-double and borne in medium clusters. The plant is disease resistant, shade tolerant and grows to 10 or 12 ft (3 or 3.65 m). Courtyard roses, like this one, won't overwhelm a small garden.

'PASADENA TOURNAMENT, CL.'.

('Red 'Cécile Brunner, Cl.').
Breeder: Discovered by Edward E. Marsh (United States, 1946).
Parentage: Sport of 'Pasadena Tournament'.
Class: Climbing Floribunda, Climbing Polyantha.
The flowers of this rose are small to medium-sized, double, richly fragrant and cerise-red. When they open out fully a touch of white can be seen in the center. The heritage of 'Cecile Brunner' is revealed in the scrolled, high-centered "sweetheart buds". The rose is remontant in regular seasonal flushes. The plant is very vigorous and can be trained as a large climber. The sport parent of this rose is officially classed as a Floribunda even though it is the offspring of a Polyantha.

'Pasadena Tournament, Cl.'.

'PASCALI, CL.'.

Breeder: Discovered by Anderson, 1968.
Parentage: Sport of 'Pascali'.
Class: Climbing Hybrid Tea.
This climbing sport of 'Pascali' has beautifully shaped, large, double, high-centered, fragrant, ivory-white flowers with soft coral centers. They occur singly or in small clusters and rebloom in regular seasonal flushes. The plant is very vigorous and may grow to as much as 16 or 20 ft (5 or 6 m). It will bloom and grow best in a climate of USDA zone 7b or warmer.

'Pascali, Cl.'.

'PAUL LÉDÉ, CL.'.

(Monsieur Paul Lédé, Cl.).
Breeder: Discovered by Low & Co. (20th century) (United Kingdom, 1913).
Parentage: Sport of 'Monsieur Paul Lédé'.
Class: Climbing Hybrid Tea.
'Paul Lédé, Cl.' has medium to large-sized, double, apricot-pink flowers. They are strongly scented of tea. The outer petals fade to pale apricot while the center remains darker. The outer petals reflex with age, giving the outer petals pointed tips. There is a main bloom early in the season with a few flowers produced later. The plant will climb vigorously to about 15 ft (4.5 m).

'Paul Lédé Cl.'.

'PAUL'S LEMON PILLAR'.

('Lemon Pillar', 'Mrs. John Whicher').
Breeder: George Paul (United Kingdom, 1915).
Parentage: 'Frau Karl Druschki' x 'Maréchal Niel'.
Class: Large-Flowered Climber.
The flowers are large, full, fragrant (lemon) and creamy-white with light lemon-yellow centers. They are borne mostly singly or in small clusters. There is one main flush of bloom with scattered flowers later. The plant will grow from 10 to 15 ft (3 to 4.5 m).

Paul's Lemon Pillar'.

'PAVILLON DE PRÉGNY'.

Breeder: Guillot père (France, 1863).
Parentage: Unknown.
Class: Hybrid Noisette. Not typical in appearance. Perhaps part Bourbon or Hybrid Perpetual.
The flowers are fragrant, very full, medium-sized and deep mauve-pink with a white reverse. The petals sometimes curl over in the center giving the flower the appearance of having a white eye. The deep color fades to light mauve, then almost to white as the flowers age. They are borne singly or in small clusters. Remontancy is very good, occurring in continuous flushes during the flowering season. This rose is a moderate climber of about 8 ft (2.5 m).

'Pax'.

'PAX'.

Breeder: Rev. Joseph Hardwick Pemberton (United Kingdom, 1918).
Parentage: 'Trier' x 'Sunburst'.
Class: Hybrid Musk.
'Pax' has medium to large-sized, semi-double, white flowers held in large clusters. They open out flat to show the golden stamens in the center. There is good rebloom in regular seasonal flushes. The plant will grow to about 8 ft (2.5 m) and can be trained as a climber on a small trellis or fence.

'PAXTON'.

('Sir Joseph Paxton').
Breeder: Jean Laffay (France, 1852).
Parentage: Unknown.
Class: Climbing Bourbon.
The flowers of this rose are deep pink, large, double, fragrant and held singly or in small clusters. They are sometimes roughly quartered and the petals reflex along their sides to become loosely quilled with age. They bloom in continuous seasonal flushes. The plant is well armed and will grow to about 8 ft (2.5 m). It is hardy to USDA zone 5b.

'Peace, Cl.'.

'PEACE, CL.'.

('Gioia, Cl.', 'Gloria Dei, Cl.', 'Madame A. Meilland, Cl.')
Breeder: Discovered by Lee A. Brady (United States, 1949).
Parentage: Sport of 'Peace'.
Class: Climbing Hybrid Tea.
This climbing sport of one of the world's most loved roses has very large, double, high-centered, fragrant yellow flowers with pink petal edges. The colors are fairly strong at first, then they fade somewhat and acquire a soft pastel appearance as they mature. The flowers are borne singly or in small clusters. They are fully remontant in regular seasonal flushes. The plant is a vigorous climber, reaching as much as 20 ft (6 m).

'PEAUDOUCE'.
See 'Elina'.

'PEARLY GATES' (WEKmeyer).

Breeder: Discovered by Lawrence E. Meyer (United States, 1999).
Parentage: Sport of 'America'.
Class: Large-Flowered Climber.
Unlike 'America', its deep salmon-pink parent, 'Pearly Gates' has light peach-pink flowers that fade from the outer petals inward to blush pink and then almost to white while the center retains the color longer. Other than color, the roses are identical. The flowers are medium to large, double,

'Pearly Gates'.

high-centered, fragrant and are borne singly or in small clusters. They bloom in repeated seasonal flushes. The plant is disease resistant and quite hardy. It can be used as a climber of 10 or 12 ft (3 or 3.65 m) or pruned and used as a shrub.

'Pegasus'.

'PEGASUS' (AUSmoon).

Breeder: David C. H. Austin (United Kingdom, 1995).
Parentage: 'Graham Thomas' x 'Pascali'.
Class: Shrub, English Rose.
'Pegasus' is classed as a shrub, but it can be trained as a lovely climber of about 8 ft (2.5 m) if given support, a moderate-to-warm climate and good nutrition. The medium to large-sized, generously full apricot flowers have a cupped, quartered old-fashioned form. As they age the flowers fade to creamy white from the outer petals inward. They are borne singly or in small clusters and rebloom in regular flushes all during the flowering season. The plant is shrubby, almost thornless and is hardy down to USDA zone 5b.

'PELÉ'.

Breeder: Frank A. Benardella (United States, 1979).
Introduced in United States by Co-Operative Rose Growers as 'Pelé'.
Parentage: Unknown.
Class: Large-Flowered Climber.
The opening buds of this rose already have outer petals that are faded to creamy-white while the center is bright salmon-pink, a lovely contrast. Fading continues until almost the entire rose is creamy-white. The floral form is large and double and held on long stems, making the flowers suitable for cutting. The rose is fully remontant in seasonal flushes and moderately fragrant. It can be trained as a small climber of about 8 ft (2.5 m).

'Pelé'.

'PENELOPE'.

Breeder: Rev. Joseph Hardwick Pemberton (United Kingdom, 1924).
Parentage: 'Ophelia' x unnamed seedling.
Class: Hybrid Musk, Shrub.
'Penelope' has flowers that are large, semi-double, fragrant and pink with yellow petal bases. The colors fade quickly to white, giving the overall impression of a white rose. The flowers are carried in large clusters and rebloom in continuous seasonal flushes. Orange hips will form in the fall if the rose is not deadheaded. The plant is drought resistant, hardy and shade tolerant, but is sensitive to pruning. It has small, dark green, semi-glossy foliage and will grow in a bushy manner to about 8 ft (2.5 m).

'Penelope'.

bloom in continuous seasonal flushes. The plant has glossy, dark green foliage, is disease resistant and can be trained as a climber of about 8 ft (2.45 m).

'PENNY LANE'.

(HARdwell, HARwell).
Breeder: Harkness (United Kingdom, 1998).
Parentage: 'Anne Harkness' x 'New Dawn'.
Class: Large-Flowered Climber.
'Penny Lane' has much to recommend it. The flowers are large, very double, strongly scented and bicolored with honey-apricot centers and pale honey-blush outer petals. They bloom prolifically early in the season with a scattering of flowers later. The plant has small-sized, medium green glossy foliage. It is hardy to USDA zone 5b and rain tolerant and has a potential growth of about 15 ft (4.55 m), a perfect height for an arbor.

'Penny Lane'.

'PENNANT'.

Breeder: Alister Clark (Australia, 1941).
Parentage: 'Flying Colors' x 'Lorraine Lee'.
Class: Hybrid Gigantea, Large-Flowered Climber.
The flowers of 'Pennant' appear very much like those of a typical Tea in accordance with the class of the majority of its progenitors, especially through the 'Lorraine Lee' line. The genetic inheritance from Rosa gigantea is revealed in the vigor of the plant. The flowers are fragrant, double, medium-sized and have 'Lorraine Lee's rich, glowing pink. They are once blooming early in the season. The nearly thornless plant will grow vigorously to about 20 ft (6 m).

'PENNIES FROM HEAVEN'.

(WEKwapunk).
Breeder: Tom Carruth (United States, 2006).
Parentage: 'What a Peach' x 'Easy Going'.
Class: Climbing Miniature.
The name of this rose refers to the unusual coppery-orange color of the newly opened flowers. Unfortunately, as the flowers age they acquire a dull lavender tone and lose much of their appeal except as a novelty. The flowers are small, semi-double, very mildly scented and borne in small clusters. They

'PERLA ROSA, CL.'.

Breeder: Pedro Dot (Spain, 1947).
Parentage: Sport of 'Perla Rosa'.
Class: Climbing Miniature.
The flowers of this pretty rose are small, very full and light pink. They repeat in regular seasonal flushes. The sepals are beautifully foliate. The plant can be grown as a small climber of about 40 inches (1 meter). It does well in a large pot with a support for climbing.

'PERLE DES BLANCHES'.

Breeder: François Lacharme (France, 1872).
Parentage: 'Mademoiselle Blanche Lafitte' x 'Sapho'.

Class: Bourbon, Hybrid Noisette.
The buds of this rose have crimson tipped outer petals, but the opened flower is creamy white, sometimes with a light pink flush, and fades to pure white. It is also medium-sized, double, globular and old fashioned in form, very mildly scented and carried in small clusters. It is a continuous bloomer in regular seasonal flushes. The plant is quite vigorous, growing to a maximum of about 15 ft (4.55 m) and can be trained to cover an arbor or a portion of a fence.

'Perle Des Blanches'.

'PERLE DES JARDINS, CL.'.

Breeder: John Henderson (United States, 1890).
Parentage: Sport of 'Perle des Jardins'.
Class: Climbing Tea.
This Climbing Tea has flowers that are large, very double, strongly scented and lemon yellow fading from the petal tips inward. The flowers have an old-fashioned shape. The outer petals fold back forming points and the numerous inner petals fold inward and are roughly quartered. They are borne singly or in small clusters, bloom in repeating seasonal flushes and are identical with the flowers of the nonclimbing form of this rose. The plant has the potential to climb to about 15 ft (4.55 m).

'PERNILLE POULSEN, CL.'.

Breeder: Discovered by Niels Dines Poulsen (Denmark, 1980).
Introduced by Vilmorin-Andrieux (France, 1980).
Parentage: Sport of 'Pernille Poulsen'.
Class: Climbing Floribunda.

'Pernille Poulsen, Cl.'.

The flowers of this rose are large, semi-double, moderately fragrant, medium salmon-pink and are borne in large clusters. They have a continuous flowering pattern in regular seasonal flushes. The plant has dark green, glossy leaves and will climb 16 to 20 ft (5 to 6 m).

'PERPETUALLY YOURS'.

(Canterbury, HARfable).
Breeder: Harkness (United Kingdom, 1999).
Parentage: Unknown.
Class: Large-Flowered Climber.
This is a light yellow rose fading to creamy-white with flowers that are medium-sized, very full with an old fashioned quartered form and carried singly or in small clusters. The flowering repeats well in regular seasonal flushes. The plant climbs to 10 or 16 ft (3 to 5 m).

'Perpetually Yours'.

'Peter Frankenfeld, Cl.'.

'PETER FRANKENFELD, CL.'.

Breeder: Discovered by Les C. Allen (Australia, before 1975).
Parentage: Sport of 'Peter Frankenfeld'.
Class: Climbing Hybrid Tea.
This rose shows its Hybrid Tea heritage with large, double, high-centered, deep rose-pink flowers borne mostly singly or sometimes in small clusters. They are mildly fragrant and repeat well in regular seasonal flushes. The plant has medium green foliage and can be grown as a fairly vigorous climber. It will grow and bloom best in a USDA zone 7b climate or warmer. The climbing sport has become quite rare and seems to be grown only in a few private gardens. It is identical to the non-climbing version except for height.

'Phare'.

'PHARE' (DELgo).

Breeder: Delbard-Chabert (France, 1961).
Parentage: 'Spectacular' x ('Floradora' x unnamed seedling).
Class: Large-Flowered Climber.
This striking rose attracts much attention in the garden with its deep bright vermilion, medium-sized, double, small-clustered flowers. As the flowers fade they lose some of the orange tones and become redder. The long stems make these flowers good for cutting. They rebloom regularly in flushes during the flowering season. The plant is clothed with glossy, dark green foliage and has a potential height of about 10 ft (3 m).

'Picture, Cl.'.

'PICTURE, CL.'.

Breeder: Discovered by Herbert C. Swim (United States, 1942).
Parentage: Sport of 'Picture'.
Class: Climbing Hybrid Tea.
This climbing Hybrid Tea has medium-sized, double, moderately fragrant flowers that are light pink with a touch of coral. The petal bases are yellow. The flowers fade to true pink and then acquire a touch of mauve. They are borne singly or in small clusters and bloom in flushes during the flowering season. The plant is quite vigorous, growing to as much as 15 ft (4.55 m). The flowers and foliage are identical to those of the sport parent.

'PIERRE DE RONSARD'.

('Eden', 'Eden Rose 85', MEIviolin).
Breeder: Jacques Mouchotte (France, before 1985).
Parentage: 'Music Dancer' x 'Pink Wonder, Cl.'.
Class: Large-Flowered Climber.
This is many people's favorite climbing rose. The old fashioned flowers are large, very double, fragrant and cream with crimson-pink petal edges. The inner petals are more crimson-pink than the outer ones. The flowers are borne singly or in small clusters. Rebloom occurs in continuous flushes during the flowering season. The plant has semi-

glossy dark green foliage, is hardy to USDA zone 5b, heat and rain tolerant and will climb to about 12 ft (3.65 m). 'Pretty in Pink Eden' is a deep pink sport. 'White Eden' is a pale pink sport that fades to white.

'Pierre De Ronsard'.

'PILAR LANDECHO, CL.'.

('Marquesa de Urquijo, Cl.').
Breeder: Folgado, 1954.
Parentage: Sport of 'Pilar Landecho'.
Class: Climbing Hybrid Tea.

The outer petals are yellow touched with splashes of crimson. The inner petals have a slight reddish cast overlaying the yellow that gives the impression of orange. The flowers are fragrant, large and double with reflexing outer petals. They rebloom in continuous seasonal flushes. The plant is almost thornless, clothed with bronze-green foliage and will climb to an average height for a modern climber.

'Pilar Landecho, Cl.'.

'PILLAR OF GOLD'.
See 'E. Veyrat Hermanos'.

'PIÑATA' ('Fure-Daiko').

Breeder: Seizo Suzuki (Japan, 1978).
Parentage: ('Joseph's Coat' x 'Arlene Francis') x (['Goldilocks' x 'Golden Scepter'] x 'Sarabande').
Class: Large-Flowered Climber.

This colorful rose opens brilliant yellow and quickly starts morphing to vermilion from the petal tips inward with the petal bases remaining yellow. The color is best in cool weather. The flowers are medium-sized, semi-double to double, mildly fragrant and borne singly or in small clusters. They rebloom in continuous seasonal flushes. The plant is shade tolerant, somewhat lacking in disease resistance and a little tender. It has the potential to reach a height of 8 to 10 ft (2.45 to 3 m).

'Piñata'.

'PINK ABOVE ALL'.
See 'Star Performer'.

'PINK ANGEL'.

('Angel Pink', MORgel).
Breeder: Ralph S. Moore (United States, 1987).
Introduced by The Uncommon Rose (United States, 2005) as 'Angel Pink'.
Parentage: 'Little Darling' x 'Eleanor'.
Class: Climbing Miniature.

The flowers open soft medium coral and become pinker with age. They are small, double, mildly fragrant and high-centered aging to flat. Rebloom occurs in continuous seasonal flushes. The plant can be grown as a climber of 6 to 8 ft (1.8 to 2.5 m).

'PINK ARCTIC'.
See 'Show Garden'.

'PINK CLOUD'.

Breeder: Eugene S. "Gene" Boerner (United States, 1952).
Parentage: 'New Dawn' x Seedling of 'New Dawn'.
Class: Large-Flowered Climber.
This rose is grown in many European gardens, especially in France, so it seems very strange that it is almost unknown in the United States, the land of its origin. 'New Dawn', as both parent and grandparent, has given it much beauty. The flowers are medium to large-sized, double, fragrant and a lovely deep shade of pink. They are borne in medium to large clusters and rebloom in continuous flushes during the flowering season. The plant has dark green, glossy foliage and will climb to 10 or 12 ft (3 or 3.65 m).

'Pink Cloud'.

'PINK CLOUDS'.

Breeder: Ralph S. Moore (United States, 1956).
Introduced in United States by Sequoia Nursery, Moore Miniature Roses.
Parentage: 'Oakington Ruby' x Rosa multiflora.
Class: Climbing Miniature.
The flowers are single, small, very fragrant and deep pink. They are once blooming and will form hips. Cuttings taken from this plant root very easily. For this reason and for its hardiness, it is used as a rootstock, especially for miniature roses and minifloras. It can also be grown as a climber of about 8 to 10 ft (2.45 to 3 m).

'PINK DON JUAN'.

Breeder: Discovered by Brian Nelson (United States, 1996).

'Pink Don Juan'.

Parentage: Sport of 'Don Juan'.
Class: Large-Flowered Climber.
'Pink Don Juan' has flowers that are large instead of very large like those of 'Don Juan'. They are semi-double rather than fully double and, as the name implies, they have morphed from red to pink. There is a strong fragrance. The rose is remontant in continuous seasonal flushes. The plant will grow to about 10 ft (3 m).

'Pink Grootendorst'.

'PINK GROOTENDORST'.

Breeder: Discovered by F. J. Grootendorst (Netherlands, 1923).
Parentage: Sport of 'F. J. Grootendorst'.
Class: Hybrid Rugosa.
The flowers of this Hybrid Rugosa are mildly fragrant, small, double and light pink. They are cup-shaped and carried in large clusters. Their most distinguishing characteristic is the presence of serrations at the tips of the petals, giving them a carnation-like appearance. They bloom in continuous

seasonal flushes. The plant has typical wrinkled Rugosa-style leaves, is hardy to USDA zone 4b and is best in a cool or moderate climate. It will grow to about 7 ft (2 m) in height and can be trained as a small, shrubby climber.

'Pink Ocean'.

'PINK OCEAN' (HAVink).

Breeder: Verschuren (Netherlands, 1980).
Parentage: 'Pink Showers' x 'Alexander'.
Class: Climbing Hybrid Tea.
The flowers of 'Pink Ocean' are richly fragrant, large, full and high-centered like a Hybrid Tea. Initially they are coral-pink, but become more pink with age as the coral fades. The rose is remontant in continuous seasonal flushes. The plant can be grown as a climber of about 8 ft (2.5 m).

'Pink Peace, Cl.'.

'PINK PEACE, CL.' (MEIbilsar).

Breeder: Discovered by Meilland International (France, 1968).
Parentage: Sport of 'Pink Peace'.
Class: Climbing Hybrid Tea.
Two different hybrids of 'Peace' were crossed to produce 'Pink Peace', the sport parent of this rose, so 'Pink Peace, Cl.' is a close descendant of 'Peace', not a sport. The flowers are still very similar to those of 'Peace' except for the color which is medium pink rather than yellow with pink petal edges. They are very large, very full, richly fragrant and borne mostly singly, but sometimes in small clusters as well. The rose blooms in continuous flushes throughout the flowering season. The plant will grow to about 10 ft (3 m). This rose is seldom grown now and could easily become extinct.

'Pink Perpetue'.

'PINK PERPETUE'.

Breeder: Charles Walter Gregory (United Kingdom, 1965).
Parentage: 'Spectacular' x 'New Dawn'.
Class: Large-Flowered Climber.
This rose has deep pink buds and medium-sized, semi-double to lightly double, lightly scented, medium pink flowers with a deep pink petal reverse that soon fades to a lighter color. The petals have rounded tips and are arranged in a regular, open form. The flowers are borne in small to medium clusters and rebloom in continuous flushes during the flowering season. The plant has a potential of about 10 ft (3 m) in height and makes a good pillar rose.

'Pink Rover'.

'PINK ROVER'.

Breeder: William Paul (United Kingdom, 1891).
Parentage: Unknown.
Class: Climbing Hybrid Tea or Climbing Bourbon.
The flowers are richly fragrant, large, double and light pink with darker centers. The floral form is globular at first, then opens out in a cupped, old-fashioned shape with quartered petals. It is very remontant in continuous seasonal flushes. The plant is very hardy down to USDA zone 4a.

'Pink Showers'.

'PINK SHOWERS'.

Breeder: Verschuren (Netherlands, 1974).
Parentage: 'Carla' x 'Golden Showers'.
Class: Large-Flowered Climber.
'Pink Showers' has flowers that are semi-double and medium to large-sized. The color is coral-pink with white petal bases fading to light pink and white. The wide-petaled flowers change shape with aging from cupped to flat and show a central bunch of stamens with reddish filaments. They are grouped in small clusters. The plant will grow sufficiently to be trained as a small climber.

'PINK WONDER, CL.'.

('Kalinka, Cl.', MEIhartforsar).
Breeder: Discovered by Marie-Louise Meilland (France, 1976).
Parentage: Sport of 'Pink Wonder'.
Class: Climbing Floribunda.
The medium to large-sized, richly fragrant, double flowers are pink at the edges and coral-pink in the centers. There is a flush of yellow at the petal bases. The rose reblooms in continuous seasonal flushes. The plant is almost thornless, has large glossy foliage and can be trained as a climber of 10 to 13 ft (3 to 4 m).

'Pink Wonder, Cl.'.

'PINOCCHIO, CL.'.

('Rosenmärchen, Cl.')
Breeder: Discovered by John Parmentier Roses (NY) (United States, 1951).
Parentage: Sport of 'Pinocchio'.
Class: Climbing Floribunda.
This rose has flowers that open light pink with coral-pink centers and soft yellow petal bases. As they age they become flushed with deeper pink at the petal edges. Some clones are more yellow than others. The flowers are small to medium-sized, lightly double, fragrant and borne in small clusters. They bloom in continuous flushes during the flowering season. The plant will grow to 10 or 13 ft (3or 4 m).

'Pinocchio, Cl.'.

'PIRATE' (CROastrali).

Breeder: Paul Croix (France, before 2011).
Parentage: Unknown.
Class: Large-Flowered Climber.
The flowers are large, double, mildly fragrant and white with deep red stripes and many small red flecks. When first opened the floral form is high-centered. With maturity it becomes a flattened rosette. The flowers are held singly or in small clusters and repeat their bloom in regular seasonal flushes. The plant can be trained as a climber of about 8 ft (2.5 m).

'Pirate'.

'PIROUETTE' (POULyc003).

Breeder: L. Pernille Olesen and Mogens Nyegaard Olesen (Denmark, 2002).
Parentage: 'Bonica '82' x unnamed seedling.
Class: Climber, Shrub. Courtyard Collection.
The opening buds are coral except for the tips of the outer petals that have already faded to pink. As the flowers age, the coral fades and the pink takes over. The center and the petal bases retain the coral the longest. The flowers are small, very double, old-fashioned quartered rosettes borne singly or in small clusters. They rebloom in regular seasonal flushes. There is little if any fragrance. The plant has thorns, glossy medium green foliage and will climb in a bushy style to about 8 ft (2.5 m).

'Plaisanterie'.

'PLAISANTERIE' (LENtrimera).

Breeder: Louis Lens (Belgium, 1996).
Parentage: 'Trier' x 'Mutabilis'.
Class: Hybrid Musk.
The newly opened flowers are yellow with pink petal tips. They age to pink with a touch of mauve, then to pale pink. These are colors similar to those of the parent, 'Mutabilis', but softer. Their form is single, small and flat. They are borne in large clusters. They bloom in continuous seasonal flushes. The plant is disease resistant, armed with thorns, clothed with semi-glossy foliage and can be trained as a bushy climber of about 10 ft (3 m).

'PLAYGIRL, CL.' (MORclip).

Breeder: Discovered by Ralph S. Moore (United States, 1993).
Parentage: Sport of 'Playgirl'.

'Playgirl, Cl.'.

Class: Climbing Floribunda.
This showy rose has medium to large-sized, single, ruffled, deep pink flowers with a touch of lavender added as the flowers age. There is little if any fragrance. The abundant stamens have golden-yellow anthers and red filaments. The flowers are held singly or in small clusters. Rebloom occurs in continuous seasonal flushes. The plant has dark green, glossy foliage, very few thorns and will grow to about 12 ft (3.65 m) in height. This rose is seldom grown now and is hard to find.

'Polareis'.

'POLAREIS'.

('Polar Ice', 'Polarisx', 'Ritausma', STRonin).
Breeder: Dr. Dzidra Alfredovna Rieksta (Latvia, 1963).
Parentage: Rosa rugosa var. plena x 'Abelzieds'.
Class: Hybrid Rugosa.
This rose has medium to large, lightly double, fragrant pink flowers with creamy white petal bases. They soon fade to nearly white. The flowers are borne singly or in small clusters. The main bloom is early in the season with some repeat flowering in the fall. The plant is very disease resistant, very cold hardy to USDA zone 3b and has beautiful thick dark green rugose foliage. It can be trained as a small shrubby climber of about 7 ft (2.15 m).

'Polka'.

'POLKA'

('Lord Byron', MEItosier, 'Polka 91', 'Scented Dawn', 'Twilight Glow').
Breeder: Jacques Mouchotte (France, before 1991).
Parentage: (Meipaisar x 'Golden Showers') x 'Lichtkönigin Lucia'.
Class: Large-Flowered Climber.
The flowers are large to very large-sized, double and richly fragrant of old rose. Their color is apricot fading to light apricot-pink. The petals are beautifully ruffled in old rose style and some clones have scalloped petal tips as well. They bloom in continuous seasonal flushes. The plant is hardy (USDA zone 5b), very disease resistant, armed with large thorns and can be trained as a climber of about 12 ft (3.65 m).

'POMPON DE PARIS, CL.'.

('Rouletti, Cl.).
Breeder: Discovered by Unknown (1839).
Parentage: Sport of 'Pompon de Paris', the first miniature. 'Pompon de Paris' is thought by some people to be identical to 'Rouletii'.
Class: Climbing Miniature, China.
The flowers are small, double, mildly fragrant, pink and are borne in small clusters. They are not exciting, but they put on a great show by blooming profusely early in the season.

There is a sparse scattering of repeat blooms later in the fall. The plant will grow and bloom best in a warm climate where it is capable of growing to 12 ft (3.65 m).

'POPPY FLASH'. See 'Rusticana, Cl.'.

'Porthos, Cl.'.

'PORTHOS, CL.' (LAPadsar).

Breeder: Discovered by Bois (before 1976).
Parentage: Sport of 'Porthos'.
Class: Climbing Floribunda.
This rose has a bold character with its bright, true red flowers and their upright growth. They are medium-sized, double and held singly or in small clusters. There is good rebloom in repeating flushes. The plant has glossy, dark green foliage and can be trained as a climber of about 12 ft (3.6 m).

'PORTLANDIA' (CLEzap).

Breeder: John Clements (United States, 2002).
Parentage: Unnamed seedling x 'Golden Celebration'.
Class: Large-Flowered Climber.
Initially the flowers are apricot with yellow petal bases, but as they age the apricot turns to pink and fades to a paler tone. The centers retain the bright, warm colors for the longest time. The flower form is medium to large-sized, very double with flowers grouped singly or in small clusters. They are remontant in continuous flushes during the flowering season. The plant has dark green, sturdy foliage, is hardy to USDA zone 5b and will reach a height of about 10 ft (3 m).

'President Herbert Hoover, Cl.'.

'PRESIDENT HERBERT HOOVER, CL.'.

Breeder: Discovered by Benjamin R. Cant & Sons (United Kingdom, 1937).
Parentage: Sport of 'President Herbert Hoover'.
Class: Climbing Hybrid Tea.
This beautiful Climbing Hybrid Tea has flowers that are large, semi-double to lightly double and golden yellow changing to pink with sun exposure. The change occurs from the petal tips inward, giving a two-toned appearance. There is a moderate fragrance. The flowers are carried singly (mostly) or in small clusters and rebloom in continuous seasonal flushes. The plant has shiny foliage, is resentful of much pruning and benefits from dry, warm weather. It can be trained as a climber of about 15 to 16 ft (4.5 to 5 m).

'Président Léopold Senghor, Cl.'.

'PRÉSIDENT LÉOPOLD SENGHOR, CL.'.

Breeder: Discovered by Meilland International (France, 1982).
Parentage: Sport of 'Président Léopold Senghor'.
Class: Climbing Hybrid Tea.
The flowers are very large, double, high-centered and dark velvety crimson-red. They bloom generously in repeated flushes during the flowering season. The lovely dark color causes the flowers to burn easily with exposure to hot sun. The plant has glossy, dark green foliage and will flower and grow best in a USDA zone 7b or warmer climate. It has the potential to grow to about 10 ft (3 m).

'Président Vignet, Cl.'.

'PRÉSIDENT VIGNET, CL.'.

Breeder: Discovered by Max Vogel (Germany, 1942).
Parentage: Sport of 'Président Vignet'.
Class: Climbing Hybrid Tea.
This is a showy climbing Hybrid Tea with large, double, high-centered, mildly scented, deep crimson flowers. The petals are softly ruffled and the color fades little, but becomes more cerise with age. The flowers, which are produced mainly singly, but sometimes in small clusters, are long-stemmed and good for cutting. They rebloom well in seasonal flushes. The plant will reach a height of about 8' (2.45 m).

'PRETTY IN PINK EDEN'.
See 'Margaret Mae'.

'Pretty Pink'.

'PRETTY PINK' (BARprett).

Breeder: Vittorio Barni (Italy, 1992).
Parentage: Unknown.
Class: Large-Flowered Climber.
This climber has flowers that are lightly fragrant, medium-sized, semi-double and deep, glowing pink fading with age to a light pink. They are carried in small clusters and are fully remontant. The plant has shiny, dark green foliage, good disease resistance and the potential to be trained as a climber of about 8 ft (2.5 m). There are two other roses by this name that I know of. One is a climber by John Patterson that doesn't seem to exist anywhere and the other is a lovely Hybrid Musk by Louis Lens that isn't tall enough to use as a climber.

'PRIDE OF REIGATE, CL.'.

Breeder: Discovered by Max Vogel (Germany, 1941).
Parentage: Sport of 'Pride of Reigate' (in turn, a sport of 'Comtesse d'Oxford').
Class: Climbing Hybrid Perpetual.
The flower is initially large, double, high-centered and crimson with some white stripes and a multitude of small white streaks. It fades to a soft pink and becomes flattened. The flowers are mostly held singly, but may be seen in small clusters. There is one main bloom early in the season with a few flowers later. The plant is almost thornless and will grow in a bushy style to about 10 ft (3 m).

'PRIDE OF VENUS'.

('Elfe' 'Francine Jordi', 'L'Alcazar', TANelfe).
Breeder: Hans Jürgen Evers (Germany, before 2000).

'Pride of Venus'.

Parentage: Unknown.
Class: Large-Flowered Climber.
'Elfe' has light yellow flowers slightly nuanced with green that fade to cream, often with quartered petals. They have a mild fruity scent, large, are very full and borne in small clusters. They repeat well in continuous seasonal flushes. The canes will grow to a height of about 10 ft (3 m).

'Prince Igor, Cl.'.

'PRINCE IGOR, CL.'.

('Gpt. Prince Igor', MEIgosar).
Breeder: Discovered by Meilland International (France, 1985).
Parentage: Sport of 'Prince Igor'.
Class: Climbing Floribunda.
The orange bud opens bright yellow with orange-red petal tips and becomes progressively more deep vermilion-red with age. The petal reverse is yellow. The flower form is double and small to medium-sized. There is a fruity scent. The rebloom occurs in continuous flushes during the flowering season. The climbing plant can only be seen at Roseraie du Val-de-Marne (France) and Roseraie François Mitterand (France).

'PRINCE STIRBEY'.

Breeder: Joseph Schwartz (France, 1871).
Parentage: Unknown.
Class: Climbing Hybrid Perpetual.
According to earlier records, this rose has flowers that are large, double and light pink or flesh pink. It blooms in flushes throughout the flowering season. 'Prince Stirbey' at Sangerhausen and in commerce is definitely a darker color (light crimson) and is thought to possibly be 'Ulrich Brunner Fils'. It is also listed as growing at Roseraie du Val-de-Marne (France).

'Prince Stirbey'.

'PRINCEPS'.

Breeder: Alister Clark (Australia, 1942).
Parentage: Unknown.
Class: Large-Flowered Climber.
The flowers are fragrant, semi-double to lightly double, large and deep crimson with a lighter reverse. The petals are lightly ruffled at the tips. This is essentially a once-blooming rose, but there are reports of a few flowers produced in the fall in warm climates. The plant will grow to at least 12 ft (3.65 m).

'PRINCESS D'ORANGE'.

See Princess van Orange.

'PRINCESS MARGARET OF ENGLAND, CL.'.

(MEIistasar, 'Princesse Margaret d'Angleterre, Cl.').
Breeder: Discovered by Meilland International (France, 1969).
Introduced in France by URS (Universal Rose Selection)-Meilland in 1969 as 'Princess Margaret of England, Cl.'.
Parentage: Sport of 'Princess Margaret of England'.
Class: Climbing Hybrid Tea.
The flowers of this rose, opening from long, pointed buds, are softly scented, large, double, high-centered and much the same pink as the rose's grandparent, 'Queen Elizabeth'. They bloom in continuous flushes during the flowering season. The plant will grow and bloom best in a climate of USDA zone 7b or warmer.

'Princess May'.

'PRINCESS MAY'.

Breeder: William Paul (United Kingdom, 1893).
Parentage: Seedling of 'Gloire de Dijon'.
Class: Tea-Noisette.
I have seen 'Princess May' only at Sangerhausen (Germany). It has large, double, fragrant, globular, light pink flowers arranged singly or in small clusters. It is once blooming with a few flowers produced in the fall. The plant is almost thornless and will grow to about 10 ft (3 m).

'PRINCESS OF ORANGE'. See 'Princess van Orange'.

'PRINCESS SIBILLA DE LUXEMBOURG'. See 'Stormy Weather'.

'Princess Van Orange'.

'PRINCESS VAN ORANGE'.

('Gloria Mundi, Cl.', 'Princess d'Orange', 'Princess of Orange', 'Princesse d'Orange', 'Prinses van Oranje').
Breeder: Discovered by de Ruiter (Netherlands, 1929) and Victor Lens (Belgium, 1933, as 'Gloria Mundi, Cl.').
Parentage: Climbing sport of 'Gloria Mundi'.
Class: Climbing Polyantha.
'Gloria Mundi', the sport parent of this rose, was a famous orange-scarlet sport of the crimson-colored 'Superba', also known as 'Superb' (polyantha, De Ruiter, 1927). The new, unique color was caused by a spontaneous genetic change that codes for a high production of the pigment pelargonin, a phenomenon not known before 1929. All previous red roses were in the crimson range of red. 'Gloria Mundi' has passed on its bright orange-red flowers to 'Princess van Orange'. This rose also has flowers that are large, double, carried in large clusters and bloom in continuous seasonal flushes. The foliage is glossy and light green. There is some tendency to mildew. The plant can be trained as a small climber of about 8 ft (2.5 m).

'PRINCESSE DE MONACO, CL.'.

Breeder: Discovered by Unknown.
Parentage: Sport of 'Princesse de Monaco'.
Class: Climbing Hybrid Tea.
This is a very pretty rose with large, double, high-centered cream-colored flowers with pink edges. As the flower matures the cream fades to white creating an even greater contrast. There is a mild fragrance. The flowers are borne singly or in small clusters and rebloom in regular seasonal flushes. The plant has dark green shiny foliage and can

be trained as a climber of about 15 ft (4.5 m). It is very disease resistant.

'Princesse De Nassau'.

PRINCESSE DE NASSAU'.

('Autumnalis', Rosa moschata 'Autumnalis').
Breeder: Jean Laffay (France, before pre-1828).
Parentage: Unknown.
Class: Noisette.
Coral-pink buds open to light yellow blooms that fade to white with yellow centers. The flowers are small to medium-sized, lightly double and flat in form. The rose blooms late and continues until fall. The plant will grow to a height of 8 to 10 ft (2.5 to 3 m) in a warm environment.

'PRINCESSE D'ORANGE'.
See 'Princess van Orange'.

'PRINCESSE MARGARET D'ANGLETERRE, CL.' See 'Princess Margaret of England, Cl.'

'PROBUZENI'.
See 'Awakening'.

'PROFESSOR DR HANS MOLISCH'.

Breeder: Arpad Mühle (Romania, 1923).
Parentage: Unknown.
Class: Large-Flowered Climber, Climbing Hybrid Tea.
The pink buds have foliate sepals, an old rose characteristic. They open to form large, double, light pink flowers that are grouped singly or in small clusters. There is one main prolific bloom with a scattering of flowers later. The plant is well armed with thorns, has broad leaves and will grow to about 8 ft (2.5 m).

'Professor Dr Hans Molisch'.

'PROFESSOR ERICH MAURER'.

Breeder: Hugo Tepelmann (Germany, 1939).
Parentage: Unknown.
Class: Large-Flowered Climber.
The flowers of this rose are large, double and deep pink with lighter petal bases and reverses. The petals have a quartered pattern. There is a mild fragrance. The outer petals reflex to form points. The plants have dark green, matte-surfaced foliage and a climbing potential to about 8 ft (2.5 m). The rose grows at Sangerhausen (Germany) and seemingly nowhere else.

'Professor Erich Maurer'.

'PROSPERITY'.

Breeder: Rev. Joseph Hardwick Pemberton (United Kingdom, 1919).
Parentage: 'Marie-Jeanne' x 'Perle des Jardins'.
Class: Hybrid Musk.
This is an all-round good garden rose. The buds are pale pink, the pretty flowers are creamy white with yellow centers and there may be touches of blush pink on the petal tips. The flowers are small to medium-sized, double, fragrant and are carried in large clusters. The repeat bloom occurs in continuous flushes during the flowering season. The plant has glossy, dark green foliage, is disease resistant and shade tolerant and has a height potential of about 10 ft (3 m). 'Pink Prosperity' is a sport with pink flowers that fade to blush-pink. The other characteristics are identical to those of 'Prosperity'.

'Prosperity'.

'PROUD BRIDE'.

Breeder: Discovered by Ingwer J. Jensen (Germany, 1992)
Parentage: Sport of 'Charles Austin'.
Class: Shrub, English Rose.
The floral form of this new attractive addition to the English Rose group is the same at that of 'Charles Austin', the sport parent. The flowers are medium to large, very double and borne singly or in small clusters at the ends of the canes. The color is apricot-pink in the newly opened bud and shifts to lavender tones as it ages rather than to apricot-yellow like the parent. The plant can be pruned and kept as a shrub or supported and allowed to climb in a bushy manner to 8 or 10 ft (2.5 or 3 m). Expect several flushes of bloom. It is grown as a climbing rose at Sangerhausen.

'Proud Bride'.

'Puerta Del Sol'.

'PUERTA DEL SOL' (DELglap).

Breeder: G. Delbard (France, 1971).

Parentage: ('Queen Elizabeth' x 'Provence') x ('Michèle Meilland' x 'Bayadère')
Class: Large-Flowered Climber.
The mildly fragrant flowers open golden yellow, and then develop peach flushes on the petal tips. With aging they fade and finally become almost white. The flower form is medium to large-sized, double and borne singly (mostly) or in small clusters. The rose reblooms in continuous seasonal flushes. The plant will grow to about 10 ft (3 m).

'PURPLE SKYLINER' (Franwekpurp).

Breeder: Frank R. Cowlishaw (United Kingdom, 2002).
Parentage: Unknown.
Class: Large-Flowered Climber.
The flowers of this climber are fragrant, small to medium-sized, semi-double and purple with some narrow white streaks mostly running down the petal centers. The petal bases are white resulting in a small white center that is revealed when the flower is mature. The flowers are borne in medium to large clusters and bloom in continuous seasonal flushes. The plant can be trained as a climber of about 10 ft (3 m) or pruned and grown as a shrub. It is disease resistant.

'Purple Splash'.

'PURPLE SPLASH'.

('Oh Wow!' Wekspitrib).
Breeder: Tom Carruth (United States, 2009).
Parentage: 'Soaring Spirits' x' Rhapsody in Blue'.
Class: Large-Flowered Climber.
This rose is guaranteed to get your attention with its broad white and deep purple stripes, each interrupted by narrow streaks of the alternate color. The flowers are medium to large-sized, semi-double and held in medium to large clusters. There is little or no fragrance. The flowers rebloom in repeating seasonal flushes if deadheading is performed well since hips are formed regularly. The plant is very disease resistant, heat tolerant and is quite hardy. It has shiny, medium green leaves and will grow to about 10 to 13 ft (3 to 4 m). The rose is too newly introduced at this writing to have become established in any public gardens.

'Queen of Hearts'.

'Quadra'.

'QUADRA' (J.F. Quadra).

Breeder: Dr. Ian S. Ogilvie and Dr. Felicitas Svejda (Canada, 1981).
Parentage: [('Queen Elizabeth' x 'Arthur Bell') x ('Simonet Double Red' x 'Von Scharnhorst')] x [(R. kordesii x ('Red Dawn' x 'Suzanne')) x ('Red Dawn' x 'Suzanne')].
Class: Hybrid Kordesii.
'Quadra' has flowers that are well shaped, medium to large-sized, double, cupped and quartered in old-rose style, and dark red with a lighter reverse. They are quite similar to some of the Austin roses. They are held singly (mostly) or in small clusters and bloom in continuous seasonal flushes. The plant has dark green glossy foliage, is unusually hardy (USDA zone 3b), very disease resistant and has the potential to grow to about 8 ft (2.5 m). It can be used as a climber or pruned and grown as a shrub. It is grown in many gardens in Canada and some in Scandinavia and other areas with cold winters.

'QUEEN ELIZABETH, CL.'.

Breeder: Discovered by Dorothy S. Whisler (United States, 1957).
Parentage: Sport of 'Queen Elizabeth'.
Class: Climbing Hybrid Tea.
Even without sporting to a climbing form this rose grows tall enough to train as a small climber. The climbing sport has flowers identical to the sport parent. They are large, double, high-centered like a Hybrid Tea, fragrant and medium pink. They occur singly or in small clusters. The rose has one main bloom with a scattering of later

'Queen Elizabeth, Cl.'.

flowers unlike the bush form which blooms in repeated flushes. The plant is almost thornless, has shiny dark green foliage and grows vigorously to 16 to 20 ft (5 to 6 m).

'Queen of Hearts'.

'QUEEN OF HEARTS'.

Breeder: Alister Clark (Australia, 1919).
Parentage: 'Gustav Grünerwald' x 'Rosy Morn'.
Class: Climbing Hybrid Tea.
The older references refer to this rose as having semi-double flowers. The rose grown today has flowers that are double, large, globular in shape, strongly fragrant and medium pink fading to light pink. It blooms in continuous seasonal flushes. The plant has dark green foliage and will reach a height of 10 to 12 ft (3 to 3.5 m). The plant grown today may not be the original rose.

'QUICK SILVER' (KORpucoblu).

Breeder: W. Kordes & Sons (Germany, before 2014).
Introduced in Germany by W. Kordes' Söhne (Retail) in 2015.
Parentage: Unknown.
Class: Large-Flowered Climber.
This is a beautiful new rose from the well known Kordes Nursery. The flowers are softly fragrant, large, very double and a true, deep lavender color in the center and with lighter outer petals. They are well shaped with reflexed petal tips. The plant has dark green, matte-surfaced foliage and potential growth to 7 or 8 ft (2 to 2.5 m).

R

'Ruth Alexander'.

'RADAR, CL.'.

Breeder: Discovered by the Barni Nursery (Italy) and introduced by Meilland (France, 1959).
Parentage: Unknown.
Class: Climbing Hybrid Tea.
The flowers of this rose are very fragrant, large, very double and a color best described as vermilion. This rose is not as remontant as its sport parent and only has one main bloom with a few flowers later in the season. The plant will grow to about 8 to 10 ft (2.5 to 3 m).

'Radiance, Cl.'.

'RADIANCE, CL.'.

Breeder: Discovered by W. D. Griffing (United States, 1927) and by H. J. Catt (Australia, 1928).
Parentage: Sport of 'Radiance'.
Class: Climbing Hybrid Tea.
'Radiance', the sport parent of this rose was a famous Hybrid Tea created early in the last century and the first in line of a large family of roses all related by genetic sporting. 'Radiance, Cl.' has flowers identical to those of its parent. They are large, double, globose in shape and light pink with a medium pink reverse. Because the petals are slow to open fully, only the darker petal reverses are visible in the center of the flower, giving it the appearance of being darker than the edges. The rose reblooms in continuous seasonal flushes. The plant is quite vigorous and can be expected to grow to about 15 ft (4.5 m).

'RAGTIME' (POUltime).

Breeder: L. Pernille Olesen and Mogens Nyegaard Olesen (Denmark, 1991).
Introduced by Poulsen Roser A/S (Denmark, 2000).
Parentage: 'Morning Jewel' x unnamed seedling.
Class: Large-Flowered Climber. Courtyard Rose.
This rose has flowers that are mildly scented, medium-sized, semi-double, gently ruffled and deep pink with a lighter petal reverse. The petals reflex at the tips to give a rolled-back look. The rose blooms in continuous flushes all during the flowering season. The plant has dark green, shiny foliage, is disease resistant and can be trained as a climber of about 10 ft (3 m).

'RAINBOW'S END, CL.'.

(SAVaclend).
Breeder: Discovered by Sue O'Brien (United States, 1998). Introduced by Nor' East Miniature Roses (United States 1998).
Parentage: Sport of 'Rainbow's End'.
Class: Climbing Miniature.
'Rainbow's End, Cl.' is a complete rainbow when seen in full bloom. The flowers open bright yellow, then starting inward at the petal tips, the color shifts through orange, vermilion, scarlet and crimson. The entire flower becomes crimson-red before fading to light pink. There is a mild fragrance. The flower form is small, double, high-centered and the flowers are born singly or in small clusters. The rose blooms prolifically in continuous seasonal flushes. The plant has glossy, small, dark green foliage and is generally disease resistant, but is said to be susceptible to blackspot. It will grow to about 12 ft (3.65 m).

'Ramblin' Red'.

'RAMBLIN' RED' (RADramblin).

Breeder: William J. Radler (United States, 2001).
Parentage: 'Razzle Dazzle' x 'Henry Kelsey'.
Class: Large-Flowered Climber.

The flowers of this rose are medium-sized, double, bright red, mildly fragrant and are borne singly or in small clusters. There is one main bloom early in the season with scattered flowers produced later and hips following. The plant has plentiful, dark green glossy foliage, is hardy to USDA zone 3b, and will climb to about 10 ft (3 m). It is mostly grown in Canada and the colder parts of the United States and is commercially available there.

'RAMBLING ROSIE'.

(HORcojasper, HORjasper, TG2752).
Breeder: Colin P. Horner (United Kingdom, 2001).
Introduced by Warner's Roses (United Kingdom, 2005).
Parentage: 'Super Excelsa' x ('Baby Love' x 'Golden Future').
Class: Climbing Miniature.
This pretty climber will brighten your spirits as well as your garden. The flowers are bright red with pure white petal bases that form a small white ring around the stamens. They are semi-double, small, mildly scented and grouped in large clusters. The petals are beautifully ruffled. The repeat bloom is excellent and occurs in repeated seasonal flushes. The plant has shiny, medium green foliage and can be expected to grow to about 12 ft (3.65 m).

'Ramira'.

'RAMIRA'.

('Agatha Christie', KORmeita).
Breeder: W. Kordes & Sons (Germany, 1988).
Parentage: Unknown.
Class: Large-Flowered Climber.
'Ramira', or 'Agatha Christie' as it is more often known, has beautiful large, double, mildly scented, high-centered,

'Ramira'.

rich coral pink flowers that occur singly or in small clusters. There is one prolific bloom early in the flowering season with a few flowers later. The plant has shiny dark green foliage, is disease resistant and grows to about 10 ft (3 m). 'Agatha Christie' was named for a famous British mystery story writer.

'Rapture, Cl.'.

'RAPTURE, CL.'.

Breeder: Dixie Rose Nursery, 1933.
Parentage: Sport of 'Rapture' which was a sport of 'Mme. Butterfly'.
Class: Climbing Hybrid Tea.
Rapture, Cl. is a sport of 'Rapture', a Hybrid Tea that sported from 'Madame Butterfly' and belongs to a well-known family of Hybrid Teas from the early 20th Century that started with 'Ophelia'. It has coral-pink flowers with yellow petal bases. The flower form is medium-sized, lightly double and high-centered. The flowers are grouped singly or in small clusters and they are moderately fragrant. The rose blooms in continuous flushes during the flowering season. The plant will climb to about 10 ft (3 m).

'Raspberry Cream Twirl'.

'RASPBERRY CREAM TWIRL'.

(AM 811, Colibri 2010, 'Colibri Farbfestival', 'Ines Sastre', MEITaratol).
Breeder: Alain Meilland (France, before 2010).
Parentage: 'Deborah' x ('Sorbet Fruité, Cl.' x 'Bonica '82').
Class: Large-Flowered Climber.
This rose has medium to large-sized, very double, scentless, deep raspberry-pink flowers with white stripes which are interrupted by numerous narrow raspberry-pink stripes and streaks. The raspberry color fades to pale lavender with age. The bloom form is deeply cupped and may show some quartering and the flowers are held singly or in small clusters. The rose repeat blooms in flushes during the flowering season. The plant has shiny, dark green foliage, few thorns and will grow to about 12 ft (3.65 m).

'RAYMOND CHENAULT'.

Breeder: Reimer Kordes (Germany, 1960).
Parentage: Rosa kordesii x 'Montezuma'.
Class: Hybrid Kordesii.
The flowers are medium-sized, semi-double, lightly to moderately scented and scarlet-red. They change to more of a crimson hue as they age. They are held in large clusters and have one main bloom with occasional repeats. The flowers are slightly wavy and open out flat to show the stamens. The plant is cold hardy and can be expected to reach a height of 12 to 13 ft (3.65 to 4 m).

'Raymond Chenault'.

'REBECCA'S CHOICE' (Virchoice).

Breeder: M. S. Viraraghavan (India, 2012). Introduced in Europe in 2012 by La Roseraie du Désert. It was named for Becky Hook, co-owner of this nursery.
Parentage: 'Mrs. B.R. Cant' x Rosa gigantea.
Class: Hybrid Gigantea.
The flowers of this Hybrid Gigantea are pale pink, large, single, moderately scented and are borne singly or in small clusters. The large, rounded petals may have mucronate tips (sharp projections). Rebloom is good, occurring in continuous flushes during the flowering season. The plant has attractive large, shiny dark green foliage, is well armed with thorns and will grow to about 10 ft (3 m).

'Red Cascade'.

'RED CASCADE'.

(82-68-5, MOORcap).
Breeder: Ralph S. Moore (United States, 1976).
Parentage: 0-47-19 x 'Magic Dragon'.
Class: Climbing Miniature, Patio Rose.
'Red Cascade' has crimson-red, small, double mildly fragrant flowers borne singly or in small clusters. They repeat bloom very well in regular seasonal flushes. The plant is very disease resistant and is hardy to USDA zone 5b. The very flexible canes facilitate its use as a ground cover, an easily trained climber, a cascading container or hanging basket plant and an excellent weeping standard. The canes will grow to about 8 ft (2.45 m).

'RED CECILE BRUNNER'.
See 'Pasadena Tournament, Cl.'.

'RED EDEN.
See 'Eric Tabarly'.

'Red Empress'.

'RED EMPRESS'.

('Impératrice Rouge', 'Robur').
Breeder: Charles Mallerin (France, 1956).
Parentage: ('Holstein' x 'Décor') x ('Holstein' x 'Décor').
Class: Large-Flowered Climber.
The flowers of this rose are red, as the name promises, richly scented, large, double and borne singly (mostly) or in small clusters. The floral form is long stemmed and high-centered like a Hybrid Tea. There is a generous bloom early in the season with scattered flowers appearing later. The plant will grow vigorously to about 16 ft (5 m).

'Red Explorer'.

'RED EXPLORER'.

Breeder: Discovered by Antoine Penny (France, 1928).
Parentage: Sport of 'Miss Edith Cavell'.
Class: Climbing Polyantha.
The crimson flowers have dark shading. They are small,

double, lightly scented and grouped in medium to large clusters. They bloom in regular seasonal flushes. The plant can be trained as a climber of 10 to 12 ft (3 to 3.6 m) and will look much like a Rambler with its small flowers.

'RED FRAME'.
See 'Commandant Cousteau, Cl.'

'RED FLARE'.

Breeder: Ada Mansuino (Italy, 1954).
Introduced by Jackson & Perkins Co. (United States 1954).
Parentage: 'Reine Marie Henriette' x seedling of 'Paul's Scarlet Climber'.
Class: Large-Flowered Climber.
This rose has large, double, fragrant, cup shaped, crimson-red flowers borne singly or in small clusters. They fade just a little. There is one main profuse bloom early in the season with occasional flowers produced later. The plant has glossy, dark green foliage and will grow to about 10 ft (3 m).

'Red Flare'.

'RED FOUNTAIN'.

Breeder: J. Benjamin Williams (United States, 1975).
Parentage: 'Don Juan' x 'Blaze'.
Class: Large-Flowered Climber.
'Red Fountain's flowers are dark, brilliant red and occur singly or in small clusters. They hold their color quite well. Their form is medium-sized, double, sometimes roughly quartered and high-centered on opening, but becomes cupped with maturity. They are scented with a typical rose fragrance and rebloom in continuous flushes during the flowering season. The plant can be expected to reach a height of about 14 ft (4.25 m).

'Red Fountain'.

'RED GROOTENDORST'.
See 'F. J. Grootendorst'.

'RED NEW DAWN'.
See 'Étendard'.

'Red Parfum'.

'RED PARFUM'.

Breeder: André Eve (France, 1972).
Parentage: Unknown. The shiny leaves suggest Rosa wichurana as an ancestor, possibly by way of Kordesii.
Class: Large-Flowered Climber.
The flowers of this rose are bright red, medium-sized, double, richly fragrant and borne singly or in small clusters. They bloom in repeating flushes during the flowering season. The plant has glossy medium green leaves and will grow to a height of 10 to 13 ft (3 to 4 m).

'RED PIERRE'.
See 'Eric Taberly'.

'Red Queen, Cl.'.

'RED QUEEN, CL.'.
Breeder: Reimer Kordes (Germany, 1968).
Parentage: Sport of 'Red Queen'.
Class: Climbing Hybrid Tea.
This is a first-quality climbing red rose. The flowers are large, double and brilliant crimson-red. There is a light fragrance. The floral form is high-centered and has an exhibition shape. The long stems make it ideal as a cut flower. It is borne singly and in small clusters and is remontant in repeated flushes during the whole flowering season. The plant has glossy, medium green foliage and will grow to about 8 ft (2.5 m). 'Red Queen', the sport parent, is identical except for height.

'Red Talisman, Cl.'.

'RED TALISMAN, CL.'.
Breeder: Unknown.
Parentage: Probably a sport of 'Red Talisman' which, in turn, is a sport of 'Talisman'.
Class: Climbing Hybrid Tea.
The flowers of this rose are large, double, fragrant and crimson with a flush of warmer color at the petal bases. Fading produces more cerise tones. The rose reblooms in continuous flushes throughout the flowering season. The plant is very vigorous and may reach a height of about 20 ft (6 m).

'RED WAND'.
Breeder: Ralph S. Moore (United States, 1964).
Parentage: (0-47-19 x 'Orange Triumph') x unnamed seedling. 0-47-19 = Rosa wichurana x 'Floradora'.
Class: Climbing Miniature.
This Climbing Mini has small, double, deep crimson-pink flowers with an open cup shape. They are borne singly or in small clusters and bloom in continuous flushes during the whole flowering season. The plant has small, medium green, somewhat glossy foliage and will grow to 4 or 5 ft (1.2 or 1.5 m). It is perfect for planting in a pot and training to a small trellis.

'REDGOLD, CL.'.
(DICorsar, 'Rouge et Or, Cl.').
Breeder: Discovered by Les Stratford (Australia, 1970).
Parentage: Sport of 'Redgold'.
Class: Climbing Floribunda.
The flowers of 'Redgold' are medium to large-sized, very double, mildly scented and golden yellow with narrow red petal tips. The rose blooms in flushes during the flowering season. The plant is moderately vigorous and can be trained as a climber of about 10 ft (3 m).

'REINE MARIA PIA'.
Breeder: Joseph Schwartz (France, 1880).
Parentage: Seedling of 'Gloire de Dijon'.
Class: Climbing Tea.
This rose has flowers that are large, double and deep crimson-pink with lighter pink petal tips and reverses. The flowers are deeply cupped and only show the petal upper surface in the center. This makes the centers appear darker than the outer edges. The flowers are borne singly or in small clusters. The rose is remontant in continuous seasonal flushes. It can be expected to climb to about 15 to 16 ft (4.5 to 5 m).

'Reine Marie Pia'.

'REINE MARIE HENRIETTE'.

Breeder: Antoine Levet (père) (France, 1878).
Parentage: 'Madame Bérard' x 'Général Jacqueminot'.
Class: Climbing Hybrid Tea. It is sometimes described as a Climbing Tea.

In the past, both 'Parade' (United States) and 'Noella Nabonnand' (Australia) have been sold as this rose. The flowers of the correct variety should be broadly cupped, sometimes quartered, large, double, richly fragrant and bright cerise-red. They become more magenta with age. The form is not high-centered, but rather like that of an old rose. The rose is remontant in continuous seasonal flushes. The plant is almost thornless, has dark green foliage and can be trained as a moderate climber of about 12 ft (3.65 m).

'REINE OLGA DE WÜRTTEMBERG'.

('Herzogin Olga v. Württemberg').
Breeder: Gilbert Nabonnand (France, 1881).
Parentage: Unknown.
Class: Hybrid Noisette.

The flowers of this rose are medium to large-sized, semi-double, loosely formed, fragrant and bright cerise-red. They develop more blue tones with age. The foliage is glossy, large and medium green. The plant has one main summer bloom with a scattering of flowers in the fall. It can be trained as a climber of about 13 ft (4 m). The rose was named for a queen of a historical kingdom of Germany.

'RÊVE D'OR'.

('Condesa da Foz', 'Golden Chain').
Breeder: Jean-Claude Ducher (France, 1869).
Parentage: Seedling of 'Madame Schultz'.
Class: Noisette, Tea-Noisette.

Growing next to an entry door, this rose has provided me with much enjoyment over many years. The flowers are soft yellow-apricot fading to pale buff yellow, but darker and more apricot in the center. Their form is medium to large-sized, double, fragrant and globular opening into a flattened cup with reflexed outer petals. They are borne singly or in small clusters and bloom in repeating flushes throughout the flowering season. The plant has deep green, glossy foliage. It is healthy and surprisingly hardy for a Noisette. Mine has survived many years of winter freezes with little or no dieback. It will grow to about 10 ft (3 m) in a cool climate like mine in the Pacific NW or as much as 18 ft (5.5 m) in a warm climate.

'Rêve d'Or'.

'RÉVEIL DIJONNAIS'.

Breeder: Emmanuel Buatois (France, 1931).
Parentage: 'Eugène Fürst' x 'Constance'. The pollen parent is a third-generation descendant of Rosa foetida.
Class: Climbing Pernetiana, Large-Flowered Climber.

'Rêveil Dijonnais'.

This very garden-worthy rose has large, semi-double, fragrant, cerise-red flowers with large yellow centers and a yellow reverse. They are borne singly or in small clusters. Réveil translates as "wake up" and this rose with its striking colors is a real wakeup call. There is one main bloom with an occasional production of later flowers. The plant is quite vigorous and will reach a height of about 12 ft (3.6 m).

'Rhapsody In Blue'.

'RHAPSODY IN BLUE'.

(FRAntasia).
Breeder: Frank R. Cowlishaw (United Kingdom, before 1999).
Parentage: ('Summer Wine' x 'International Herald Tribune') x [('Blue Moon' x 'Montezuma') x ('Violacea' x 'Montezuma')].
Class: Shrub.
The flowers open soft purple and change to slate blue with age. They have a small white eye and may show a few white streaks. Their form is medium-sized, semi-double and opens out flat. They are scented of spice and are produced in large clusters. They bloom in continuous seasonal flushes. The plant has glossy, light green foliage and is healthy overall, but somewhat inclined to blackspot. It can be pruned and grown as a shrub or given support and grown as a climber. It does best in cool climates where it will grow to about 8 ft (2.45 m).

'Rhonda'.

'RHONDA'.

Breeder: Jack Lissemore (United States, 1968).
Parentage: 'New Dawn' x 'Spartan'.
Class: Large-Flowered Climber.
The flowers are medium pink brightened by a slight touch of coral. Their form is medium to large, double, high-centered in Hybrid Tea style and sometimes quartered as well. They have a mild fragrance. The flowers are arranged singly or in small clusters and are mainly summer blooming with a few flowers opening in the fall. The plant has dark, glossy, disease-resistant foliage is hardy to USDA zone 4b and will grow to about 10 ft (3 m).

'RICHMOND, CL.'.

Breeder: Discovered by Alexander Dickson II (United Kingdom, 1912).
Parentage: Sport of 'Richmond'.
Class: Climbing Hybrid Tea.
This Climbing Hybrid Tea has flowers that are medium to large, lightly double, scented of damask and bright crimson. They bloom in repeating seasonal flushes and are borne mostly singly, but may occur in small clusters. They tend to burn in the hot sun so they will do best in cooler climates or in partial shade. The plant can be trained as a climber of about 10 ft (3 m).

'Richmond, Cl.'.

'RIMOSA, CL.'. See 'Gold Badge, Cl.'.

'RINGLET'.

Breeder: Alister Clark (Australia, 1922).
Parentage: 'Ernest Morel' x 'Betty Berkeley'.
Class: Large-Flowered Climber.
I find it hard to believe that this dainty, pastel rose is the offspring of a Tea and a Hybrid Perpetual, but that is what the records show. The flowers are small to medium-sized, single, richly fragrant and white with pink petal tips. They are borne in small clusters and bloom in continuous flushes during the flowering season. The plant is almost thornless and can be trained as a climber of about 10 ft (3 m) or can be pruned and grown as a shrub.

'RIO RITA'.

Breeder: Discovered by Elmer's Nursery (United States, 1935).
Parentage: Sport of 'E. G. Hill'. Another sport discovered by G. Marlin (Australia, 1942) is called 'E. G. Hill, Cl.'. They appear to be identical.
Class: Climbing Hybrid Tea.
The flowers are deep scarlet-pink, very large, double and high-centered. The warm, scarlet color becomes closer to pure pink in the mature flower. There is a rich fragrance of damask. The rose blooms in flushes throughout the season. The foliage is glossy. This rose will form a climber of average size.

'RITTER VON BARMSTEDE'.

Breeder: Reimer Kordes (Germany, 1959).
Parentage: Unknown.
Class: Hybrid Kordesii.
The flowers of this rose are small to medium-sized, semi-double to double, light crimson-pink with white petal bases and a lighter reverse and are carried in large clusters. They have a light citrus scent. The plant has dark green, glossy foliage and will grow to 10 or 15 ft (3 to 4.5 m).

'Ritter Von Barmstede'.

'RIVERS' GEORGE IV'.

('George IV', 'King George IV').
Breeder: Thomas Rivers (United Kingdom, circa 1817).
Parentage: Unknown.

Class: Hybrid China. Perhaps a hybrid with a Damask. The double, medium-sized flowers open red, then soon evolve to crimson and then become purpler as they age. They are said to be mildly fragrant, but I can detect very little scent. The Loubert Nursery in France reports a height of 3 to 5 ft (1 to 1.5 m), but the plant growing on a pillar at the Roseto Carla Fineschi in Italy is at least 12 ft (3.65 m) tall. The nearly thornless canes are clothed with dark-green, shiny foliage.

'Rivers' George IV'.

'ROBERT LÉOPOLD'.

Breeder: Paul Buatois (France, 1941).
Parentage: Unknown.
Class: Climbing Moss.
Climbing mosses are not common, but this rose has virtues in addition to rarity. The buds are attractively mossed. The flowers are fragrant, medium-sized, full with a globular form and salmon-pink with crimson-pink petal edges. They are carried singly (mostly) or in small clusters. The plant is heavily armed with thorns. It has the potential to grow to about 10 ft (3 m).

'Robert Léopold'.

'Roberta Bondar'.

'ROBERTA BONDAR'.

Breeder: Joyce L. Fleming (Canada, 1987).
Parentage: 'King's Ransom' x 'Buff Beauty'.
Class: Large-Flowered Climber.
This rose is strongly influenced by its yellow Hybrid Tea seed parent, 'King's Ransom'. The flowers are medium-sized, double, moderately fragrant, high-centered like a Hybrid Tea and medium yellow. They are borne singly or in small clusters and bloom in continuous seasonal flushes. The plant has semi-glossy, dark green foliage and will grow to about 8 ft (2.5 m). It is hardy to USDA zone 5b.

'Robusta'.

'ROBUSTA'.

(KORgosa, 'Kordes Robusta').
Breeder: Reimer Kordes (Germany, 1979).
Parentage: Seedling x Rosa rugosa.
Class: Hybrid Rugosa.
This rose has large, single, lightly scented, scarlet-red

flowers becoming more purple with age. They are borne mostly singly or occasionally in small clusters and repeat in continuous flushes during the flowering season. The plant is very susceptible to black spot, but is healthy otherwise. It is shade and heat tolerant and is hardy down to USDA zone 4b. The foliage is dark green and shiny and the canes have many very sharp thorns. Many sources consider it to be a tall shrub, but there are reports of it growing to at least 8 ft (2.5 m).

'ROCKETEER'

See 'Rosalie Coral'.

'Romance'.

'ROMANCE'.

Breeder: Discovered by George Beckwith & Son (United Kingdom, 1933).
Parentage: sport of 'Isa'.
Class: Climbing Hybrid Tea.
Who wouldn't like to have romance in their garden? You could with this lovely rose, but it is no longer in commerce and is grown only at Sangerhausen (Germany). The flowers are medium-sized, semi-double with an open form, strongly fragrant and pink fading to light pink. They are remontant in continuous seasonal flushes. The plant will climb to about 10 ft (3 m).

'ROSABELLE'.

Breeder: François-Georges-Léon Bruant (France, before pre-1899).
Parentage: 'Fortune's Double Yellow' x 'Madame de Tartas'.
Class: Climbing Tea. Sometimes classed as a Noisette.
'Rosabelle' has fragrant (tea), large, double, light pink flowers with a darker reverse. They are borne singly or in small clusters. The shape is that of a typical Tea and seems to have little or no influence from 'Fortune's Double Yellow', a Climbing China. There is one main bloom early in the season with a few repeats later in the season. The plant has shiny, dark green foliage and will climb to about 12 ft (3.65 m).

'ROSALIE CORAL'.

(CHEWallop,' Rocketeer', 'Rosilia').
Breeder: Christopher H. Warner (United Kingdom, before 1991).
Parentage: ('Elizabeth of Glamis' x ['Galway Bay' x 'Sutter's Gold']) x 'Anna Ford'.
Class: Climbing Miniature.
The flowers of this pretty, brightly colored rose are more orange than coral. They have yellow petal bases and reverses. They are small to medium-sized, semi-double, mildly fragrant and bloom well in regular seasonal flushes. The plant has small, shiny, medium green foliage and can be trained as a small climber of about 7 ft (2 m). The only public garden where the rose grows is Sangerhausen (Germany) where it is listed as 'Rosilia'. Warner created another rose in 2012 with the name 'Rosilia'. It is a more modern climber with crimson-red and white flowers.

'Rosalie Coral'.

'ROSANNA'.

(KO 93/2046-01, KORhokhel, 'La Vanoise Parc National').
Breeder: Reimer Kordes (Germany, 1993. Introduced by Kordes & Sons, 2006).
Parentage: Unknown.
Class: Large-Flowered Climber.
The later version of Kordes' 'Rosanna' can be distinguished from the earlier variety by its lack of fragrance, deeply cupped flowers and less vigor. The salmon-pink color is very similar to the color of the earlier variety. The flowers are large, full and are borne in small clusters. They rebloom in repeated seasonal flushes. The plant has shiny, medium green foliage and can be trained a climber of about 10 ft (3 m).

'Rosanna'.

'ROSARIO' (TANoras).

Breeder: Hans Jürgen Evers. Intro. by Rosen Tantau (Germany, 1993).
Parentage: Unknown.
Class: Large-Flowered Climber.
'Rosario' is a good choice for someone wanting a small pink climber. The rose opens with pale pink outer petals and deep pink centers giving a pretty bicolor effect which fades in time to nearly white. The flower form is small to medium-sized and double with beautifully ruffled petals. There is a moderate fragrance. The flowers are borne singly or in small clusters and bloom in regular seasonal flushes. The plant has shiny, dark green foliage with good disease resistance. It will grow to roughly 7 or 8 ft (2 or 2.5 m).

'Rosario'.

'ROSARIUM UETERSON'.

(KORtersen, 'Seminole Wind', 'Uetersen').
Breeder: Reimer Kordes (Germany, 1977).
Parentage: 'Karlsruhe' x unnamed seedling. 'Karlsruhe' is a Hybrid Kordesii.
Class: Large-Flowered Climber.
This is one of my favorites of all times. The flowers are double with ruffled petals, very full, deep pink with a hint of coral and are carried in large clusters. There is a mild fragrance. Most of the flowers are produced early in the

'Rosarium Ueterson'

season, a real show, with a scattered opening later. The plant has shiny, medium green foliage and is hardy to USDA zone 4b. It will reach a height of about 12 ft (3.65 m).

'Rose Céleste'.

'ROSE CÉLESTE' (DELroceles).

Breeder: G. Delbard (France, 1979).
Parentage: ('Queen Elizabeth 'x 'Provence') x ('Sultane' x 'Madam Joseph Perraud').
Class: Large-Flowered Climber.
This rose has flowers that are large, semi-double to lightly double, moderately fragrant, cupped (opening wide) and light pink with a hint of coral and darker centers. They are borne singly or in small clusters and are fully remontant in seasonal flushes. The plant is disease resistant, but not tolerant of much hot sun exposure. It can be trained as a climber to about 10 ft (3 m).

'ROSE DE TOLBIAC' (KORcaseipp).

Breeder: Thomas Proll (Germany, 1998). Introduced in Germany by W. Kordes' Söhne in 2013.
Parentage: 'Caramella' x 'Sebastian Kneipp'.
Class: Large-Flowered Climber.
The flowers, which open from deep scarlet buds, are medium to large-sized, very double and medium salmon-pink fading from the outer petals inward to a lighter color and becoming more true pink. The form is old fashioned with ruffled, quartered petals. The flowers are carried singly or in small clusters. The plant can be trained as a small climber of about 7 ft (2 m) suitable for growing on a low fence or on a small trellis. Tolbiac was the Roman name of Zülpich in Germany.

'Rose Gaujard, Cl.'.

'ROSE GAUJARD, CL.'.

Breeder: Discovered by Nagashima (Japan, 1964).
Parentage: Sport of 'Rose Gaujard'.
Class: Climbing Hybrid Tea.
This Hybrid Tea sport has flowers that are predictably high-centered in typical Hybrid Tea style. They are also very full, large, mildly fragrant, broad-petaled and cerise-pink with very light, almost white reverses and petal bases. This creates a striking two-toned effect. The plant has dark green, glossy foliage and will climb to as much as 12 ft (3.65 m).

'Rose Marie, Cl.'.

'ROSE MARIE, CL.'.

Breeder: Discovered by Pacific Rose Company (United States, 1927), Low & Co. (United Kingdom, 1935) and others.
Parentage: Sport of 'Rose Marie'.
Class: Climbing Hybrid Tea.
The flowers of this sport of a once-famous Hybrid Tea open deep cerise-pink and then fade to a lighter pink with time.

They are large, double, richly fragrant, grouped singly or in small clusters and high-centered like a Hybrid Tea. They bloom in flushes during the flowering season. The plant will grow to about 10 ft (3 m).

'ROSEMARY, CL.'.

Breeder: Discovered by Dingee & Conard (United States, 1920).
Parentage: Sport of 'Rosemary', E. G. Hill, 1907.
Class: Climbing Hybrid Tea.
The blooms of this old pink rose are very full, very large, mildly scented and deeply cupped—not the usual high-centered shape for this rose class. The plant can be expected to grow to about 10 ft (3 m).

'Rosendorf Schmitshausen'.

'ROSENDORF SCHMITSHAUSEN'.

Breeder: Alexander M. (Alec) Cocker (Scotland, 1977).
Parentage: Unknown.
Class: Large-Flowered Climber.
This fine rose from Alec Cocker has medium to large-sized, very double, high-centered, lightly scented, dark, true red flowers. It is borne mostly singly or occasionally in small clusters and is very remontant with continuous flushes of bloom during the flowering season. The plant has glossy foliage and has a potential height of about 12 to 16 ft (3.5 to 5 m).

'Rosenfest'.

'ROSENFEST'.

Breeder: Anni Berger (former East Germany, pre-1981). Introduced by GPG Roter Oktober (former East Germany, 1981).
Parentage: 'Dortmund' seedling x Seedling.
Class: Large-Flowered Climber.
'Rosenfest' is only medium-sized and single to semi-double, but because of the lovely deep scarlet to crimson color, the large clusters and the prolific and continuous seasonal bloom, it makes an exceptionally decorative addition to the garden. It is also fragrant. The plant is hardy to USDA zone 4b and will grow to about 10 ft (3 m).

'ROSENGARTEN ZWEIBRÜCKEN'.

(CHEwpurplex).
Breeder: Christopher H. Warner (United Kingdom, before 2009).
Parentage: Unknown.
Class: Large-Flowered Climber.
The flowers are medium-sized (8 cm), semi-double to double, cupped strongly scented and dark purple-red before fading to deep violet. They are borne singly or in small clusters. The plant can be trained as a climber of about 10 ft (3 m).

'Rosenholm'.

'ROSENHOLM' (POUlover).

Breeder: L. Pernille Olesen and Mogens Nyegaard Olesen (Denmark, 1994).
Parentage: Unknown.
Class: Large-Flowered Climber, Courtyard Collection.
Small, semi-double, soft light-pink ruffled blooms in very large clusters hanging gracefully from the longer canes make this rose exceptionally attractive. The plant is healthy and tough having survived many years of neglect on a distant fence. It can be expected to climb to about 10 ft (3 m). I think it should be grown more often.

'ROSENMÄRCHEN'. See 'Pinocchio'.

'Roseraie De La Haÿ'.

'ROSERAIE DE LA HAŸ'.

('Old Rosemary').
Breeder: Jules Gravereaux (France, 1901).
Parentage: Seedling of Rosa rugosa 'Rubra'.
Class: Hybrid Rugosa.
The flowers are very fragrant (clove-like), large, lightly double and crimson becoming more lavender with age. The floral form is open and flattened and the arrangement is solitary or small clusters. There is one main bloom early in the season with a few flowers opening later. The plant is very hardy (USDA 4a), very disease resistant and drought resistant. It has a shrubby habit, but can be trained as a climber of 10 to 12 ft (3 to 3.65 m).

'ROSILIA' (Warner, pre-1991). See 'Rosalie Coral'.

'Rostock'.

'ROSTOCK'.

Breeder: Wilhelm J. H. Kordes II (ca. 1918 - 1955) (Germany, 1937).
Parentage: 'Eva' x 'Louise Catherine Breslau'.
Class: Hybrid Musk.
'Rostock' has very large, double, mildly fragrant, apricot-pink flowers with a flush of yellow at the petal bases. As the flowers age they become more pink and then pale lavender-pink. They rebloom well in seasonal flushes. The maximum height of the plant is about 10 ft (3 m).

'ROSY MANTLE'.

Breeder: Alexander M. (Alec) Cocker (Scotland, 1968).
Parentage: 'New Dawn' x 'Prima Ballerina'.
Class: Large-Flowered Climber.
The flowers of this rose are very large, double, fragrant and medium pink with a hint of coral. Their form is more high-centered than you would expect in a Large-Flowered Climber and is a trait inherited from the pollen parent, 'Prima Ballerina', a Hybrid Tea. The rose is remontant in seasonal flushes. The plant has dark green glossy foliage and will

'Rosy Mantle'.

grow to about 10 ft (3 m). It will perform best in a climate of USDA zone 7b or warmer.

'ROTE FLAMME'.

Breeder: Reimer Kordes (Germany, 1967).
Parentage: Unknown.
Class: Hybrid Kordesii, Large-Flowered Climber.
The flowers are dark red with a bit of white at the petal bases. They are medium to large, double, scentless, and are formed singly or in small clusters on pendant lateral canes. They bloom generously early in the season with scattered flowers opening later. The plant has glossy, dark green foliage and will reach a height of about 13 ft (4 m).

'Rote Flamme'.

'ROTFASSADE' (Noaroca, TG2468).

Breeder: Noack (Germany, 1997).
Parentage: 'Pink Flower Carpet' x unnamed seedling.
Class: Climbing Floribunda.
This cheerful rose has flowers that are mildly fragrant, small to medium-sized, semi-double and bright red. They are borne singly or in small clusters and bloom in regular seasonal flushes. The plant has plentiful dark green, glossy foliage and can be trained as a climber of about 10 ft (3 m).

'Rotfassade'.

'ROUGE ET OR, CL.'. See 'Redgold, Cl.'.

'Rouge Meilland, Cl.'.

'ROUGE MEILLAND, CL.'.

('Happiness, Cl.').
Breeder: Discovered by Francis Meilland (France, 1954).
Parentage: Sport of 'Rouge Meilland', (Hybrid Tea, Meilland, 1949).
Class: Climbing Hybrid Tea.
The flowers are initially bright red, but fade to more crimson, starting with the outer petals. They are mildly fragrant, very large, double and cupped with ruffled petal tips. There is very good rebloom in repeated seasonal flushes. The plant will grow to about 10 ft (3 m) and will look beautiful on a small trellis or pillar.

'ROUGE PIERRE DE RONSARD'.
See 'Eric Taberly'.

'ROULETTI'.
See 'Pompon de Paris'.

'Roundlay, Cl.'.

'ROUNDELAY, CL.'.

Breeder: Discovered by Langbecker (Australia, before 1965).
Parentage: Sport of 'Roundelay'.
Class: Climbing Grandiflora.
The newly opened dark red flowers are high-centered, but become quite flat as they mature. They are medium to large-sized, very full, fragrant and occur singly or in small clusters. The rose blooms in repeated flushes during the flowering season. The plant has disease resistant, dark green, shiny, fragrant foliage and will grow 12 or 13 ft (3.6-4 m).

'ROVILLE' (Evero).

Breeder: André Eve (France, 2002).
Parentage: Unknown.
Class: Large-Flowered Climber.
I had the privilege of seeing this pretty rose in the breeder's lovely private garden soon after it was created. The flowers are medium to large-sized, single and cerise-pink with white petal bases. Stamens with red filaments provide an interesting contrast. The flowers are carried mostly singly or occasionally in small clusters. The plant is quite vigorous, showing growth to as much as 16 ft (5 m).

'Roville'.

'Roxane, Cl.'.

'ROXANE, CL.' (LAPdalsar).

Breeder: Discovered by Robert Laperrière (France, 2000).
Parentage: Sport of 'Roxane'.
Class: Climbing Hybrid Tea.
The flowers of this striking climber are large, very double, high-centered, cluster flowered and light golden yellow with coral-red petal edges. As the flower matures the yellow fades to ivory and the red becomes more crimson. The rose is remontant in continuous seasonal flushes. The plant will achieve a height of 10 to 13 ft (3 to 4 m).

'ROYAL AMERICA'.

Breeder: Discovered by Curt Cooper (1995).
Parentage: Sport of 'America'.
Class: Large-Flowered Climber.

The flowers of this sport of the salmon-pink 'America' are cream fading to ivory. The fading starts at the outer petals leaving the center darker. Like 'America', they are borne mostly singly, or occasionally in small clusters, and bloom in flushes during the whole season. The plant is very disease resistant and is quite hardy. It may reach a height of about 12 ft (3.65 m) and can be grown on pillars, arbors and fences or it can be pruned lower and grown as a shrub. It is still in commerce in the United States.

'Royal Gold'.

'ROYAL GOLD'.

Breeder: Dr. Dennison H. Morey (United States, 1957).
Parentage: 'Goldilocks, Cl.' x 'Lydia'.
Class: Large-Flowered Climber.
This rose is one of a series of beautiful climbing roses by Dr. Morey, all with "Royal" included in their names. The flowers are large, double, fragrant and deep golden-yellow with an initial high-centered Hybrid Tea form that opens flat with maturity and reveals the stamens with their striking red filaments. They are carried singly or in small clusters and repeat their bloom in seasonal flushes. The plant has the potential to grow to about 10 ft (3 m).

'ROYAL LAVENDER'.

Breeder: Dr. Dennison H. Morey (United States, 1961).
Parentage: 'Lavender Queen' x 'Amy Vanderbilt'.
Class: Large-Flowered Climber.
The flowers are medium-sized, double, sweetly fragrant and lavender-pink with a slightly darker reverse. They occur singly or in small clusters and repeat their bloom in continuous flushes during the flowering season. The flowers on the Sangerhausen plants look fuller than those of the plants from Vintage Gardens in California, perhaps just a clonal difference. The plant will grow vigorously to about 13 ft (4 m).

'Royal Lavender'.

ROYAL PAGEANT'.
See 'Della Balfour'.

'ROYAL SHOW' (MEIrasimac).

Breeder: Meilland International (France, 1983).
Parentage: Unnamed seedling x LAVjune ('June Laver') is as stated, but it seems odd that a very small yellow rose could be the parent of a large, red climber. An error?
Class: Shrub.
The bright vermilion-red flowers are double, medium-sized and lack fragrance. They are arranged in medium-sized clusters. The plant has dark green foliage and is described on Help Me Find as growing to less than 8 ft (2.5 m), but there are reports of it growing much taller. The Sangerhausen Rosen-Datenbank states 350cm (11.5 ft), enough to train as a climber.

'Royal Sunset'.

'Royal Show'.

'ROYAL STAR AND GARTER' (FRYbizzy).

Breeder: Gareth Fryer (United Kingdom, 2000).
Parentage: Unknown.
Class: Large-Flowered Climber.
For many years I have enjoyed the beautiful big pink Hybrid Tea-style flowers of this rose in my garden. They are high-centered and coiled when first opened, then they flatten out to show the stamens. There is a little fading, outer petals first. The rose has a main bloom early in the season with some repeats later. It will form hips if not deadheaded. My plant has never quite reached 10 ft (3 m).

'Royal Star and Garter'.

'ROYAL SUNSET'.

Breeder: Dr. Dennison H. Morey (United States, 1960).
Parentage: 'Sungold' x 'Sutter's Gold'.
Class: Large-Flowered Climber.
Another lovely royal creation by Morey with large, double, fragrant apricot flowers produced singly (mostly) or in small clusters. The floral form is cupped, sometimes with a button eye. The rose repeats in continuous seasonal flushes. It is quite vigorous and may reach a height of 15 ft (4.5 m).

'ROZÁLIA'.

Breeder: Gergely Márk (Hungary).
Parentage: 'Kõrösi Csoma Sándor emléke' x 'Sutter's Gold, Cl.'
Class: Large-Flowered Climber.
I was surprised to discover this beautiful rose that I had never heard of before at Sangerhausen. Gergely Márk's roses are only just becoming known as they much deserve. The flowers of this variety are medium to large-sized, double, mildly fragrant, high-centered and orange-pink fading to golden yellow. They are borne singly or in small clusters. There is one main flush of bloom early in the season with scattered flowers later.

'Rozália'.

'RUBIS'.

Breeder: Charles Mallerin (France, 1948).
Parentage: Unknown.
Class: Large-Flowered Climber.
The deep, bright red flowers of 'Rubis' are large, double and richly scented. The flowering may be remontant.

The rose can be observed at Roseraie du Val-de-Marne (France), Roseto Carla Fineschi (Italy) and Sangerhausen (Germany).

'Rubis'.

'RUBY PENDANT'.

Breeder: Leslie E. (Gene) Strawn (United States, 1979).
Parentage: ('Lotte Günthart' x 'Salvo') x 'Baby Betsy McCall'.
Class: Climbing Miniature.
This pretty rose seems to not be well known in spite of its excellent attributes. The mildly fragrant, mauve flowers are an exhibition-quality Hybrid Tea type with high centers that open out into well-formed rosettes. They bloom in repeating flushes during the flowering season. The plant is disease resistant and will grow to about 7 ft (2 m). It can be seen at Elizabeth Park Rose Garden (Connecticut) and San Jose Heritage Rose Garden (California).

'Ruby Pendant'.

'Rudolfina'.

'RUDOLFINA'.

Breeder: Vojtech Benetka (Czech Republic, 2002).
Parentage: 'Flammentanz' x L83 (AgCan).
Class: Large-Flowered Climber.
This lovely rose from the Czech Republic has medium to large-sized, double, cup shaped, deep pink flowers born in medium clusters. They are slow to fade. There is a generous bloom early in the season with no repeats. The plant can be expected to reach a height of 10 to 13 ft (3 to 4 m). It is grown at Arboretum Borova hora (Slovakia) and Sangerhausen (Germany).

'Rusticana, Cl.'.

'RUSTICANA, CL.'.

(MEIlénasar, 'Poppy Flash, Cl.').
Breeder: Discovered by Francesco Giacomo Paolino (France, 1975).
Parentage: sport of Rusticana.

Class: Climbing Floribunda.
The flowers are medium-sized, double, mildly fragrant or scentless, vermilion to orange and are formed singly or in small clusters. They repeat bloom in flushes during the flowering season. The plant can be trained as a small climber of about 10 ft (3 m). The plant grows at Bagatelle Park (France), Roseraie du Val-de-Marne (France) and Roseto Carla Fineschi (Italy).

'RUTH ALEXANDER'

Breeder: Rena E. Wilber (United States, 1937).
Parentage: 'Myra' (Wilber, 1926) x 'Constance Casson'.
Class: Large-Flowered Climber.
The flowers of this rose are large, semi-double, strongly fragrant and salmon colored with yellow petal bases. The stamens have red filaments that give a nice touch of contrast at the flower's centers. There is one flush of bloom early in the season with no repeat. The plant is healthy, has dark green glossy foliage and can be grown as a small climber that will reach about 10 ft in height. It was created close to where I live in the Pacific Northwest area of the United States. It is no longer in commerce, but can be seen at Soos Creek Botanical Garden in Seattle, Washington.

'Ruth Leuwerick, Cl.'.

'RUTH LEUWERICK, CL.'.

Breeder: Kamio (1972).
Parentage: Sport of 'Ruth Leuwerick'.
Class: Climbing Floribunda.
This rose will brighten the garden with its medium-sized, double, very fragrant, bright scarlet flowers. The floral form is open and flattened and the petals are scalloped and gently ruffled. The flowers are carried singly or in small clusters. They bloom in regular seasonal flushes. The plant has bronze-green foliage and can be grown as a shrubby, moderate-sized climber. I have seen it at several French gardens including Roseraie du Val-de-Marne.

S

'Soaring Spirits'.

'Sabrina'.

'SABRINA'. (AM116, MEIptorius).

Breeder: Meilland International (France, before 2012).
Introduced in Germany by BKN Strobel in 2012.
Introduced in France by Meilland Richardier in 2017.
Parentage: Unknown.
Class: Large-Flowered Climber.
Sabrina has flowers that are medium to large-sized, very double, quartered, initially deeply cupped, then open and shallowly cupped. The color can be described as cream or pale apricot with darker apricot centers. The floral arrangement is single or small clusters. The flowers repeat their bloom in regular seasonal flushes. The plant has dark green, glossy foliage and will reach a height of about 8 ft (2.5 m).

'Safrano'.

'SAFRANO'.

Breeder: Beauregard (France, 1839).
Parentage: 'Parks' Yellow Tea-scented China' x unknown (Sometimes said to be 'Jaune Desprez').
Class: Tea
'Safrano' was one of the most popular roses of its day and even more important as the early progenitor of a multitude of roses. The flowers are medium to large-sized, semi-double to double, fragrant and yellow-apricot, sometimes with flushes of pink on the outer petals. They are borne singly and repeat bloom in seasonal flushes. They are most attractive before they fully open. The plant is hardier than might be expected of a Tea, but will do best in a moderate to warm climate. It can be trained as a climber to about 8 ft (2.5 m).

'Salammbô'.

'SALAMMBÔ'.

Breeder: G. Delbard (France, before 1990).
Parentage: [('Dame du Feu' X 'Guinée') X ('Tenore' X 'Fugue') X ('Grimpant Delbard' X 'Gloire de Dijon')] X ('Rouge Meilland' X 'Soraya').
Class: Large-Flowered Climber.
The flowers of this Large-Flowered Climber look like Hybrid Tea flowers with their high centers. They are large-sized, double, moderately fragrant, dark red and are borne singly or in small clusters. Their long stems and their classical beauty make them good for cutting. The plant will grow as a climber to about 10 ft (3 m).

'SALITA' (Kormorlet).

Breeder: W. Kordes & Sons (Germany, 1987).
Parentage: Unknown.
Class: Large-Flowered Climber.
'Salita' has medium to large-sized, double, scentless, Hybrid tea-style, brilliant orange-red flowers carried singly or in small clusters. It is very decorative and

blooms in flushes during the whole flowering season. The plant has glossy foliage and grows to about 8 ft (2.5 m). It makes a good pillar rose.

'Salita'.

'SALLY HOLMES'.

Breeder: Robert A. Holmes (United Kingdom, 1976).
Parentage: 'Ivory Fashion' x 'Ballerina'.
Class: Hybrid Musk.
This Hybrid Musk has flowers that are single, medium to large-sized and mildly fragrant. They are coral-pink when they first open and fade to white. The individual flowers are carried in large clusters and repeat their bloom in seasonal flushes. The plant is almost thornless, bushy, clothed with dark green glossy leaves and will grow to about 10 ft (3 m). It is hardy down to USDA zone 5b and does especially well in my moist, mildly cool Pacific Northwest climate.

'Sally Holmes'.

'SANTA ANITA, CL.'.

Breeder: Howard & Smith (United States, 1946).
Parentage: Unknown. Perhaps sport of 'Santa Anita' (Hybrid Tea, Howard, 1932).
Class: Climbing Hybrid Tea.
The flowers are fragrant, deep pink, medium to large-sized, double and high-centered. They bloom in continuous seasonal flushes. The rose is grown at Sangerhausen and nowhere else that I know of. It is not commercially available.

'SANTA CATALINA'.

Breeder: Samuel Darragh McGredy IV (1970).
Parentage: 'Paddy McGredy' x 'Heidelberg'.
Class: Large-Flowered Climber.
The flowers are medium to large-sized, semi-double and mildly fragrant. They are medium coral-pink with a touch of yellow at the center when first opened and the outer petals have dark pink tips. The flowers soon fade to light pink and open out flat. They are borne singly or in small clusters and bloom in continuous seasonal flushes. The plant has shiny dark green leaves. It is grown at Bagatelle Park (France), Les Chemins de la Rose (France), Roseto Carla Fineschi (Italy) and Roseraie du Val-de-Marne (France).

'Santa Catalina'.

'SANTANA' (TANklesant).

Breeder: Mathias Tantau, Jr. (1912 - 2006) (Germany, 1985).
Parentage: Unknown
Class: Large-Flowered Climber.
'Santana' has vermilion, medium to large, semi-double to lightly double, mildly fragrant flowers borne singly and in small clusters. The bloom is remontant. The plant can be trained as a climber to about 10 ft (3 m).

'Santana'.

'SARABANDE, CL.' (MEIhandsar).

Breeder: Discovered by Meilland International (France, 1968).
Parentage: Sport of 'Sarabande'.
Class: Climbing Floribunda.
The flowers of this climbing Floribunda are large, single to semi-double, mildly scented and bright vermilion. They are cupped at first and then open out flat. They are borne singly or in small clusters and are fully remontant in seasonal flushes. They will set hips if not deadheaded. The plant has semi-glossy foliage and will grow to about 10 to 12 ft (3 to 3.6 m).

'Sarabande, Cl.'.

'SAROLT'.

Breeder: Gergely Márk (Hungary).
Parentage: Seedling of 'Grimpant Delbard'.
Class: Large-Flowered Climber.
'Sarolt' is a beautiful, but little-known rose from a Hungarian breeder. It has scarlet-red flowers that are medium to large-sized, double, high-centered like a Hybrid Tea and little if any fragrance. There is one main bloom with a few flowers opening later in the season. The disease resistant plant has glossy, medium green foliage and will climb to about 10 ft (3 m).

'Sarolt'.

'SCENT FROM ABOVE'.

(CHEWgoldtop).
Breeder: Christopher H. Warner (United Kingdom, 2005).
Introduced by Jackson & Perkins (Wholesale) (United States, 2005).
Parentage: 'Laura Ford' x 'Amanda'.
Class: Large-Flowered Climber.
This is a very pretty rose with flowers that are large, double, fragrant of licorice and soft golden yellow fading to cream, outer petals first. The form, on opening, is coiled and high-centered, much like that of a Hybrid Tea. In maturity, the flowers open out widely with reflexed petals and show the golden stamens. They are borne singly or in small clusters and repeat in regular flushes during the flowering season. The foliage is dark green, glossy and resistant to mildew. The plant is capable of growth to about 10 ft (3 m).

'Scent From Heaven'.

'SCENT FROM HEAVEN'.

('Barbara Ann', CHEwbabaluv, CHEwbabluv).
Breeder: Christopher H. Warner (United Kingdom, before 2012).
Introduced in United Kingdom by Cants of Colchester Ltd. in 2016.
Parentage: Unknown.
Class: Large-Flowered Climber.
'Scent From Heaven' is strongly fragrant as the name predicts. The flowers are medium-sized, lightly double. They are peach-colored on the outer petals and orange on the inner petals. The mature floral form is open with a clear view of the stamens and very little reflexing of the petals. This rose is remontant in regular seasonal flushes. The plant has glossy, dark green foliage and will climb vigorously to about 20 ft (6 m).

'Scepter'd Isle'.

'SCEPTER'D ISLE'.

(AUSland, O/18/89, TG2049).
Breeder: David C. H. Austin (United Kingdom, 1989).
Introduced by David Austin Roses Limited (United Kingdom, 1997).
Parentage: 'Wife of Bath' x 'Heritage'.
Class: Shrub.
The flowers are very fragrant (myrrh), medium-sized, double and deeply cupped with pink centers and pale pink outer petals. They are borne singly or in small clusters and rebloom in regular seasonal flushes. The plant is disease resistant and fairly hardy, but may require frost protection in anything less than a USDA zone 6 climate. It has good heat tolerance and will grow best in a warm climate where it will reach a height of 7 to 8 ft, enough to be trained as a small climber.

'SCHLÖSSER'S BRILLANT, CL.'.
See Detroiter, Cl.

'SCHLOSS BAD HOMBURG'.
See 'Ali Baba'.

'Schloss Dryburg'.

'SCHLOSS DRYBURG'.

Breeder: Anni Berger (1904 - 1990) (East Germany, pre-1969).
Introduced by GPG Roter Oktober, Bad Langensalza (East Germany, 1969).
Parentage: Unknown.
Class: Climbing Hybrid Tea.
The lightly fragrant flowers of this variety are large, double and deep golden yellow which fades very little. They are

arranged singly or in small clusters. There is one main bloom early in the season with a few flowers produced later. The plant is armed with large thorns, is somewhat disease prone and will reach a height of 8 to 10 ft (2.5 to 3 m).

'Schloss Seusslitz'.

'SCHLOSS SEUSSLITZ'.

Breeder: Ernst Dechant (Germany, 1933).
Parentage: 'Frau Karl Druschki' x 'Harisonii'.
Class: Large-Flowered Climber.
The flowers are sweetly fragrant, medium sized, semi-double and cream with yellow centers aging to ivory and light yellow. At first they are deeply cupped, and then they open out to reveal the stamens. They are borne singly or in small clusters. There is one main bloom with very little repeat. The plant is very hardy to USDA zone 4b, well armed with straight thorns, healthy except for a little black spot and will grow to about 10 ft (3 m).

'SCHLOSSER'S BRILLANT'.
See 'Detroiter, Cl.'.

'SCHNEEWALZER'.

('Schneewalzer 87', 'Snow Waltz', TANrezlaw, 'Valse des Neiges').
Breeder: Hans Jürgen Evers (Germany, 1987). Tantau.
Parentage: Unknown.
Class: Large-Flowered Climber.
'Schneewalzer' has very large, double, fragrant, high-centered, pale lemon-yellow flowers with pale pink centers. They soon fade to ivory-white, outer petals first. They are carried singly or in small clusters. They bloom in repeated flushes during the flowering season. The plant has dark green, glossy foliage, a bushy habit and expected growth to about 10 ft (3 m).

'Schneewalzer'.

'SCHNEEWITTCHEN, CL.'.
See 'Iceberg, Cl.'.

'School Girl'.

'SCHOOL GIRL'.

('Schoolgirl').
Breeder: Samuel Darragh McGredy IV (Northern Ireland, 1964).
Parentage: 'Coral Dawn' x 'Belle Blonde'
Class: Large-Flowered Climber.
The large, lightly double, strongly fragrant, apricot flowers with a darker reverse soon start to fade, starting at the outer petals, to light apricot-pink. They are borne singly (mostly) or in small clusters. The mature flower

form is flat. The two-color effect produced by the fading is enhanced by the colorful stamens with red filaments. The rose has one main flowering with an occasional flower opening later. The plant is well armed, has dark green, glossy foliage and will grow to roughly 10 or 15 ft (3 or 4 m).

'SCHWANENSEE'. See 'Swan Lake'.

'Schwarzer Samt'.

'SCHWARZER SAMT'.

Breeder: VEG (S) Baumschulen, Dresden (East Germany, 1969).
Parentage: 'Alain' x 'Oskar Scheerer'.
Class: Hybrid Kordesii.
The medium-sized, semi-double, scentless, very dark velvety red flowers have an open bloom form and are carried in medium-sized clusters on a moderately vigorous plant that will get to about 10 ft (3 m). It is useful for training on small trellises, pillars and arbors or it can be pruned and grown as a shrub.

'Schweizer Grüss, Cl.'.

'SCHWEIZER GRÜSS, CL.'.

Breeder: Discovered by P. Münster (Germany, pre-1958).
Parentage: Sport of Schweizer Gruss (Mathias Tantau, Jr., pre-1951).
Class: Climbing Floribunda.
This rose seems to only grow at Sangerhausen where I saw it on my last visit. It has flowers that are medium-sized, semi-double and dark red. They are arranged in small, rather dense clusters. The floral form is open to reveal the stamens and the petals are softly ruffled. This rose is remontant in regular seasonal flushes of bloom. The plant will reach a height of about 8 ft (2.5 m).

'Scorcher'.

'SCORCHER'.

Breeder: Alister Clark (Australia, 1922).
Parentage: Thought by some to be 'Madame Abel Chatenay' x Unknown (perhaps Rosa moyesii). The parentage is uncertain.
Class: Large-Flowered Climber.
'Scorcher' has large, semi-double, mildly fragrant, crimson-red flowers with white petal bases. They bloom profusely early in the season, but have little or no repeat later. The plant has large, medium green, rugose foliage and can be trained as a climber to a height of about 10 ft (3 m).

'SCOUT'S HONOUR'. See 'Full Moon Rising'.

'SECRET GARDEN MUSK CLIMBER'.

Breeder: A found rose discovered by Joyce Demits (United States, before 1993).

Parentage: Unknown.
Class: Hybrid Musk, Large-Flowered Climber.
The flowers are rather ordinary in appearance—white, single and medium-sized. The wonderful strong, clove-like fragrance is the feature that has made it so appealing. The flowers are carried singly or in small clusters and bloom in continuous seasonal flushes. The plant has matte-surfaced, medium green foliage, is said to be disease resistant and fairly hardy and will grow vigorously to about 10 ft (3 m) or even more in a warm climate.

'Sénateur Amic'.

'SÉNATEUR AMIC'.

Breeder: Paul Nabonnand (France, 1924).
Parentage: Rosa gigantea x 'General MacArthur'.
Class: Hybrid Gigantea.
The flowers of 'Sénateur Amic' are large, semi-double, cupped and deep crimson-pink. They are once-blooming early in the season. The plant is very vigorous and may grow to 32 ft (almost 10 m). Roses in commerce by this name may be imposters with double flowers.

'SÉNÉGAL'.

Breeder: Charles Mallerin (France, 1944).
Parentage: Seedling of 'Guinée' seedling.
Class: Large-Flowered Climber.
This striking black-red rose has flowers that are medium to large-sized, double, high-centered and richly fragrant. There is a main bloom early in the season with a very few flowers produced later. The plant is very vigorous and can reach at least 16 ft (5 m).

'Sénégal'.

'SENSASS DELBARD'.

(DELmoun, 'Sensass').
Breeder: G. Delbard (France, 1974).
Parentage: ('Danse du Feu' x 'Floradora' seedling) x Seedling of 'Ténor'.
Class: Large-Flowered Climber.
The flowers of this rose are large, double, scentless, cupped and bright scarlet-red that becomes more crimson with age. The flowers are borne singly or in small clusters and repeat in continuous seasonal flushes. The plant can be trained as a small climber of about 10 ft (3 m).

'SEPPENRADER ELFE'.

Breeder: Ewald Scholle (Germany, 1975).
Parentage: Unknown.
Class: Hybrid Kordesii.
The flowers of the rose growing at Sangerhausen (Germany) are medium-sized, double, mildly scented and light yellow. The plant will grow to about 8 ft, (2.5 m), enough for a small pillar rose. Sangerhausen is the only public garden where this rose is said to grow and the only place I have seen it.

'SETINA'.

('Climbing Hermosa', 'Hermosa, Cl.', 'Hermosa Grimpant').
Breeder: Discovered by Peter Henderson (United States, 1879).
Parentage: Sport of 'Hermosa' (bourbon, Marchesseau, 1832).
Class: Climbing Bourbon, Climbing China.
'Setina' is a lovely old variety that has medium to large,

'Setina'.

double, light pink flowers with a deeply cupped, globular bloom form that opens out to a shallow cup as it matures. There is a moderate fragrance. The repeat bloom is good and occurs in seasonal flushes. The plant will do best in a moderate to warm climate of at least USDA zone 7b. It is fairly vigorous and can be expected to grow to about 13 ft (4 m).

'Shadow Dancer'.

'SHADOW DANCER'.

(MORstrort).
Breeder: Ralph S. Moore (United States, 1998).
Parentage: 'Dortmund' x seedling of 'Dortmund'.
Class: Large-Flowered Climber.
The flowers of this unusual rose are medium to large, semi-double, mildly scented and deep crimson interrupted by pale pink and white stripes. Most of the petals are broad and gently wavy, but a few in the center are small and tend to curl tightly over the stamens. The flowers are produced singly or in small clusters and bloom generously in regular seasonal flushes. The plant has medium green, shiny foliage and grows to about 10 ft (3 m). It is hardy to USDA zone 5b and is very disease resistant.

'Shenandoah'.

'SHENANDOAH'.

Breeder: J. H. Nicolas (United States, 1934).
Parentage: Étoile de Hollande x Schoener's Nutkana.
Class: Large-Flowered Climber, Hybrid Nutkana.
The flowers are very fragrant, large, semi-double and crimson becoming more cerise with age. They open widely to reveal the stamens. They bloom only once in late spring or early summer. The plant has large, glossy foliage and the potential to reach a height of about 10 ft (3 m). It now grows only in Europe and is commercially available there. Shenandoah is a river and also the title of a beautiful old sea chanty.

'Shirpa'.

'SHIRPA'.

Breeder: André Eve (France, 1976).
Parentage: Unknown.
Class: Large-Flowered Climber.
The medium to large flowers are semi-double to lightly double, cup-shaped and salmon-pink with yellow petal bases. The foliage is dark green and matte surfaced. The plant will grow to 10 to 13 ft (3 to 4 m).

'SHOGUN'.

('Constanze', 'Tanugosh').
Breeder: Hans Jürgen Evers (Germany, before 2000). Tantau.
Parentage: Unknown.
Class: Large-Flowered Climber.
The flowers are initially deep pink with a hint of coral, a lighter reverse and yellow petal bases. They become lighter and truer pink with age. There is a light scent. The flower form is medium to large-sized, double, high-centered in Hybrid Tea style and borne singly or in small clusters. The rose blooms in continuous seasonal flushes. The plant has glossy, medium green foliage and can be expected to reach a height of 10 to 13 ft (3 to 4 m).

'Shot Silk, Cl.'.

'SHOT SILK, CL.'.

Breeder: Discovered by George Knight & Sons (Australia, 1931) and by Low & Co. (United Kingdom, 1935).
Parentage: Sport of 'Shot Silk'.
Class: Climbing Hybrid Tea, Climbing Pernetiana.
This rose is named for a fabric, popular in my childhood, which was woven of two different thread colors to make it look iridescent. The flowers are richly fragrant, medium-sized and double. They are deep pink with yellow petal bases on first opening and become lighter and more mauve-pink with maturity. The remontancy is good and occurs in repeated seasonal flushes. The plant has shiny, dark green foliage, few thorns and a height potential of about 10 to 16 ft (3 to 5 m). My plant is probably the Knight variety from Vintage Gardens. It survived a winter with a low temperature of 0 degrees, Fahrenheit.

'Show Garden'.

'SHOW GARDEN'.

('Everblooming Pillar No. 82', 'Pink Arctic').
Breeder: Brownell Family (United States, 1954).
Parentage: Unnamed seedling x 'Queen o' the Lakes'.
Class: Large-Flowered Climber.
'Show Garden' is one of the Brownell Family's Sub-Zero roses that is hardy enough for USDA zone 4b. The flowers are lightly scented, medium to large, double and, although they are high-centered at the opening bud stage, they later show a flattened shape and an almost imbricated arrangement of petals with a glimpse of the stamens. The color is deep pink with a touch of yellow in the center, fading a little and becoming more mauve in time. The plant can be trained as a short climber of about 8 ft (2.5 m).

'SHOW GIRL, CL.'.

Breeder: Discovered by Chaffin (1949) and introduced in the United States the same year by Armstrong Nursery.
Parentage: Sport of 'Show Girl'.
Class: Climbing Hybrid Tea.
This rose has flowers that are large, double, fragrant, pink and borne singly (mostly) or in small clusters. They become darker with age. Long stems make the flowers good for cutting. The rose blooms in continuous seasonal flushes. The plant is said to grow to as much as 15 ft (4.5 m).

'Show Girl, Cl.'.

'SHROPSHIRE LASS'.

Breeder: David Austin.
Parentage: 'Madame Butterfly' x 'Madame Legras de St. Germain'.
Class: English Rose, Shrub.

The flowers of this rose are large, lightly scented, single to semi-double and coral-pink, but fading to lighter and more mauve. The flowers are borne singly and in small clusters and are rather delicate in overall appearance. The rose is once blooming, an unusual feature for a David Austin variety. It is quite vigorous and makes a good pillar rose. There are reports of it achieving a height of at least 12 ft (3.6 m). It is also hardy with a cold tolerance down to USDA zone 5b.

'Shropshire Lass'.

'Sif'.

'SIF'.

Breeder: Arne Lundstad (Norway, 1960).
Parentage: 'Traumland' (Tantau, 1958) x 'Royal Gold'.
Class: Large-Flowered Climber.

'Sif' has medium to large, semi-double to lightly double, scentless, cupped, apricot flowers with yellow centers. The color shifts to more pink with age. There is good rebloom. The plant can be trained as a 10 or 12 ft (3 or 3.6 m) climber.

'Silver Jubilee, Cl.'.

'SILVER JUBILEE, CL.'.

Breeder: Discovered by Anne G. Cocker (Scotland, 1983).
Parentage: Sport of 'Silver Jubilee' (Cocker, 1978).
Class: Climbing Hybrid Tea.

This rose has lightly fragrant, large, double, high-centered, salmon-pink flowers that become pinker and darker at the outer petal tips. The reverse is darker, also. I have only seen the climber at the Royal National Rose Society's garden (St. Albans, United Kingdom).

'SIR GEORGE WATT'.

(VIRwatt).
Breeder: M.S. Viraraghavan (India, 2008).
Introduced by Roses Unlimited (United States, 2008).
Parentage: 'Rêve d'Or' x R. gigantea.
Class: Hybrid Gigantea.
This beautiful Hybrid Gigantea is named for Sir George Watt, a medical doctor who discovered Rosa gigantea in India in the late 1800s. It has flowers that are softly fragrant, medium to large and light yellow with outer petals fading to cream or white. The flowers are borne singly or in small clusters and are fully remontant in repeated flushes during the flowering season. The plant has glossy, medium-green foliage and will climb to about 20 ft (6 m).

'SIR HENRY COLLETTE'.

(VIRcollette).
Breeder: M.S. Viraraghavan (India, 2008).
Parentage: 'Rêve d'Or' x R. gigantea.
Class: Hybrid Gigantea.
The flowers of this rose are softly fragrant, large, double, cream and shaped in classical Tea rose style. They are carried singly or in small clusters and are remontant. The plant has glossy, medium green leaves composed of typical long, drooping Gigantea leaflets. It is very vigorous and can be expected to climb to about 20 ft (6 m).

'SIR JOHN MILLS'.

Breeder: Bred by Amanda Beales (United Kingdom, 2006).
Parentage: 'Armada' x 'Westerland'.
Class: Large-Flowered Climber.
This very attractive rose has fragrant, medium-sized, double, pink flowers that fade to light pink, outer petals first. This gives them the appearance of light pink flowers with a darker pink center. They are borne mostly singly and occasionally in small clusters. There is good bloom in repeated flushes throughout the flowering season. The plant has glossy, dark green foliage and can reach a height of about 8 ft (2.5 m).

'SIR JOSEPH PAXTON'.

('Paxton').
Breeder: Jean Laffay (France, 1852).
Parentage: Unknown.
Class: Climbing Bourbon.
This climbing Bourbon has large, double, richly fragrant, deep pink flowers that become lighter and more crimson with age. They may be roughly quartered and are borne singly or in small clusters. There is good rebloom in repeating flushes during the flowering season. The plant is well armed and will grow to about 10 ft (3 m).

'Sir Joseph Paxton'.

'SIROHI SUNRISE'.

(Virgiant).
Breeder: M.S. Viraraghavan (India, 2005).
Parentage: 'Brown Velvet' x ('Carmosine' x Rosa gigantea).
Class: Hybrid Gigantea, Large-Flowered Climber.
The flowers of this rose are mildly fragrant, large, double and bright coral-pink. They are well shaped with large outer petals. They are produced singly (mostly) or in small clusters and are remontant. The plant has typical Gigantea foliage with large, glossy, medium green leaves. It can be trained as a small climber of about 8 ft (2.5 m) or grown as a shrub.

'SISSI, CL.'.
See 'Blue Moon, Cl.'.

'SKY TOWER'.

(Somskywer).
Breeder: Rob Somerfield (New Zealand, 2002).
Parentage: 'Strawberry Ice' x 'Hot Chocolate'.
Class: Large-Flowered Climber.
The pretty flowers of this rose are medium to large-sized, semi-double to double and medium pink fading to pale pink from the petal tips inward. The petal reverses are a deeper color. The ruffled petals open widely to

show the stamens which are enhanced by the light yellow-cream petal bases. There is no fragrance. The flowers are borne in large clusters and bloom in regular flushes during the flowering season. The plant has glossy, dark green foliage and will grow to about 10 ft (3 m).

'SKY'S THE LIMIT'.

(WEKprimsoul).
Breeder: Tom Carruth (United States, 2005).
Parentage: 'Princess Marianna' x Hybrid of R. soulieana
Class: Large-Flowered Climber.
Here is another rose with a novel name to remind the reader that it can be used as a climber. It has medium-sized, lightly double, soft yellow flowers that fade to cream, then to ivory white. The petals are slightly ruffled and have a fruity fragrance. The flowers are borne in medium clusters and have one main season of bloom early in the season with a few scattered flowers produced later. The foliage is medium green and glossy. Weeks, the grower, reports that it should reach heights of 10 to 14 ft (3 to 4.3 m). That is a respectable height, but not quite sky high.

'Sky's The Limit'.

'SLEIGH BELLS, CL.'.

Breeder: Discovered by Miriam Wilkins (United States, 1995).
Parentage: Sport of 'Sleigh Bells'.
Class: Climbing Hybrid Tea.
This white climbing rose has flowers that are large, full, cupped and richly fragrant. The white is softened by the pale yellow centers. There is very good rebloom in regular flushes during the flowering season. The plant has dark green, glossy foliage and will grow to about 10 ft (3 m). It has become very rare and is no longer in commerce.

'Sleigh Bells, Cl.'.

'Smiley Face'.

'SMILEY FACE'.

('Happiness', MEIlaclost).
Breeder: Alain Meilland (France, pre-2010).
Parentage: 'Clos Fleuri Jaune' x 'Follette'.
Class: Large-Flowered Climber.
I agree that this is a happy rose. The flowers are single to semi-double, large to very large, fragrant and deep, bright yellow fading to light yellow, petal tips first. The form is cupped at first, then opening out flat to show the stamens. There is very good rebloom in regular flushes during the flowering season. The plant has disease resistant, medium green, glossy foliage and growth to about 10 to 12 ft (3 to 3.65 m).

'SNOW GOOSE'.

(AUSpom).
Breeder: David C. H. Austin (United Kingdom, 1997).
Parentage: Unknown.
Class: Large-Flowered Climber.
The flowers of 'Snow Goose' are small, lightly double with narrow petals and pale yellow fading to pure white. They have a mild musky fragrance. Rebloom is good. The plant has few thorns and will grow to about 10 ft (3 m) according to the breeder.

'Snow Goose'.

'SNOWBIRD, CL.'.

Breeder: Discovered by Weeks (United States, 1949).
Parentage: Sport of 'Snowbird'.
Class: Climbing Hybrid Tea.
The flowers of 'Snowbird, Cl.' are fragrant of tea, large and very double. The opening bud is high-centered, but becomes more like an old-fashioned form when fully opened. The color is white with a pale yellow center. They are produced singly or in small clusters on short lateral canes along the main canes. The rebloom is in continuous flushes during the flowering season. The plant will grow vigorously to about 10 to 12 ft (3 to 3.65 m).

'Snowbird, Cl.'.

'SOARING SPIRITS'.

Breeder: Tom Carruth (United States, 2004).
Parentage: 'Berries 'n' Cream' x 'Fourth of July'.
Class: Large-Flowered Climber.
This lovely rose has deep pink and cream stripes with the cream merging into yellow centers. The floral form is large, single blooms held in large clusters. They are mildly fragrant. The rose blooms in continuous flushes throughout the flowering season. The plant has glossy, light green foliage and will grow to about 8 ft (2.5 m). The rose commemorates the people who lost their lives in the Twin Towers attack on 9/11/2001.

'Soaring Spirits'.

'SOCIAL CLIMBER'.

(JACweave).
Breeder: Dr. Keith W. Zary (United States).
Parentage: Unknown.
Class: Large-Flowered Climber.

'Social Climber'.

This rose has flowers that are deep pink fading lighter, large, double and scented of spice. It is classed as a Large-Flowered Climber, but the flowers are very much in the high-centered, Hybrid Tea mold. As they mature, they become open cup shaped and reveal their stamens. They are carried singly or in small clusters and bloom in continuous flushes during the flowering season. The plant is hardy to USDA zone 5b and will grow to about 10 ft (3 m).

'Softee, Cl.'.

'SOFTEE, CL.'.

Breeder: Discovered by Falk Hannemann (Australia, 1992).
Parentage: Sport of 'Softee'.
Class: Climbing Miniature.
The flowers of this little climber are small, double and fragrant. The buds are yellow, but the flower starts to fade to cream and then to white as it opens. The yellow remains longer on the petal bases and the center petals and finally fades almost completely. The petals are rather narrow and may have mucronate tips. The form is open and flat with petals neatly imbricated. The mature flower has somewhat the appearance of a double daisy. The flowers are borne singly (mostly) or in small clusters. The rose blooms in repeated seasonal flushes. The plant is disease resistant, nearly thornless, has foliage that is semi-glossy, medium green and small and will grow to about 5 ft (1.5 m).

'Soirée Du Bonheur'.

'SOIRÉE DU BONHEUR'.

(CROest).
Breeder: Paul Croix (France, 1993).
Parentage: Unknown.
Class: Climber. (Shrub per ARS)
Here's another winner for Paul Croix. The flowers are mildly fragrant, semi-double, medium-sized and pink with a touch of apricot. They fade to pale pink, then to white. The floral form is an open cup. They are arranged singly or in small clusters on a plant that will grow to 8 or 10 ft (2.5 or 3 m). The rose can be seen at Roseto Carla Fineschi (Italy) and Roseraie du Val-de-Marne (France).

'SOLDIER BOY'.

Breeder: Edward Burton Le Grice (United Kingdom, 1953).
Parentage: Unnamed seedling x 'Guinée'.

'Soldier Boy'.

Class: Large-Flowered Climber.
This rose has the beauty of simplicity. The flowers are single, medium to large-sized, mildly scented and pure bright scarlet with contrasting straw-yellow stamens. They are borne singly or in small clusters. There is one main bloom followed by a few flowers later. The plant is known to grow to 10 to 12 ft (3 to 3.65 m).

'Soleil d'Orient'.

'SOLEIL D'ORIENT'.

Breeder: J.B. Croibier & Fils (France, 1935).
Parentage: 'Frau Karl Druschki' x 'Madame Edouard Herriot'.
Class: Climbing Hybrid Tea.
'Soleil d'Orient' has lightly double, large, very fragrant warm pink flowers with yellow petal bases. The large outer petals reflex to form pointed tips, creating a star-burst effect. They are once-blooming early in the season with a few flowers usually produced later. The plants have glossy, dark green foliage and can be trained to climb to about 10 ft (3 m).

'Soleil Levant, Cl.'.

'SOLEIL LEVANT, CL.'.

Breeder: André Hendrickx (France, before 1956).
Introduced in France by Grandes Roseraies du Val de la Loire (France, 1956).
Parentage: 'Spectacular' x unnamed seedling.
Class: Large-Flowered Climber.
The flowers of this rose are scentless, single, medium-sized, open formed and strongly orange. There is nothing subtle about this color. The flowers are borne singly or in small clusters. They rebloom in regular seasonal flushes. The plant can be trained as a moderate-sized climber. It is grown at Bagatelle Park (France), Roseraie du Val-de-Marne (France), Roseto Carla Fineschi (Italy) and Sangerhausen (Germany).

'SOLFATARE'.

('Augusta').
Breeder: Joseph Boyeau (France, 1843).
Parentage: Seedling of 'Lamarque'.
Class: Tea-Noisette.

'Solfatare'.

This rose has large, double, lightly scented, buff-yellow flowers that are borne singly or in small clusters. The form is cupped initially, and then becomes flattened with maturity. They have excellent remontancy, blooming in continuous flushes during the flowering season. The plant has the potential to grow to 10 to 13 ft (3 to 4 m). The name of this rose is sometimes spelled 'Solfaterre', but that spelling more properly belongs to a lemon-yellow found rose.

'Solitaire, Cl.'.

'SOLITAIRE, CL.'.

Breeder: Discovered by Ronald Earnshaw (1997).
Parentage: Sport of 'Solitaire' (Hybrid Tea, McGredy).
Class: Climbing Hybrid Tea.
The fragrant light yellow flowers of this Climbing Hybrid Tea have pink petal edges and a flush of pink in the center. The floral form is high-centered when opening, then unfolds as a medium to large low-domed rosette. The flowers are arranged singly and in small clusters. They repeat very well in regular seasonal flushes. The plant can be trained as a moderately vigorous climber of about 10 ft (3 m).

'Solo'.

'SOLO'.

Breeder: Mathias Tantau, Jr. Germany, 1956).
Parentage: 'Crimson Glory' x unnamed seedling.
Class: Large-Flowered Climber.
Here is another beautiful bright crimson-red climbing rose. The flowers are mildly fragrant, large, double and high-centered in Hybrid Tea style and are borne singly or in small clusters. They repeat very well in continuous flushes during the flowering season. The plant has dark green, strongly textured foliage and will grow to 13 to 16 ft (4 to 5 m).

'Sombreuil'.

'SOMBREUIL'.

('Colonial White').
Breeder: Unknown (circa-1940).
Parentage: 'New Dawn' x 'Madam Hardy'.
Class: Large-Flowered Climber.
Do not confuse this rose with Mlle. de Sombreuil, a Tea. Also note that ARS has ruled that the name 'Colonial White' should no longer be used for this rose. Both the registration name and the exhibition name are 'Sombreuil'. The flowers are creamy-white, large, very full, fragrant and formed as a flattened rosette with orderly imbricated petals. It blooms in repeated flushes during the flowering season. The plant can be trained as a climber of 10 to 13 ft (3 to 4 m). It is widely grown in the United States and Europe and is also commercially available.

'Sommergold'.

'SOMMERGOLD'.

Breeder: Noack (Germany, before pre-2012).
Parentage: Unknown.
Class: Large-Flowered Climber.
This rose has flowers that are fragrant (lemon-scented), medium-sized, very double and bright golden-yellow fading to cream. The form is globular on opening and then the flower spreads out flat in an imbricated pattern with the stamens visible in the center. The flowers occur singly and in small clusters. The foliage is dark green and shiny. The plant has the potential to grow to about 10 ft (3 m). It is remontant in regular seasonal flushes.

'Sonia, Cl.'.

'SONIA, CL.'.

('Grimpant Sonia Meilland', MEIhelvetsar, 'Sonia Meilland, Cl.', 'Sweet Promise, Cl.').
Breeder: Discovered by Marie-Louise (Louisette) Meilland (France, 1976).
Parentage: Sport of 'Sonia'.
Class: Climbing Hybrid Tea.
'Sonia, Cl.' is one of the Meilland family's best productions by way of 'Sonia', the sport parent, one of the world's most loved Hybrid Teas (Meiland, 1974). The lovely coral-pink flowers are large, double and have a rich fruity fragrance. They are high-centered at first, then become flattened as they open and sometimes show quartered petals. They are carried singly or in small clusters. The rose is mainly once blooming early in the season with a few scattered flowers later. The plant has dark green, glossy foliage and will reach a modest height of about 10 ft (3 m).

'Sophie's Perpetual'.

'SOPHIE'S PERPETUAL'.

('Bengal Centifolia', 'Dresden China').
Breeder: Unknown (pre-1922). An unknown rose found in an old garden and reintroduced by Humphrey Brooke (United Kingdom, 1960).
Parentage: Unknown.
Class: Bourbon Hybrid, China. Perhaps a Bourbon-China hybrid.
The flowers of this lovely old rose are very fragrant, medium-sized, lightly double and light pink flushed with deeper cerise on the outer petals and petal tips. The floral form is globular and the flowering is remontant in continuous seasonal flushes. The plant has dark green foliage and few thorns, does best in a warm climate and will grow to at least 8 ft (2.5 m). It makes a nice pillar rose. It can be seen at Cranford Rose Garden (New York), Les Chemins de la Rose (France), Mottisfont Abbey (United Kingdom), Roseto Carla Fineschi (Italy), San Jose Heritage Rose Garden (California) and Sangerhausen (Germany).

'SORAYA, CL.'.

(Grimpant Soraya, MEIjenorsar, Mejenorsar).
Breeder: Discovered by Vittorio Barni (Italy, before pre-1960).
Parentage: Sport of 'Soraya'.
Class: Climbing Hybrid Tea.
The flowers of this rose are double, large, mildly fragrant and bright, deep orange-red. The reverse is a little darker and slightly more crimson. The floral form is cupped and the stems are long. The rose

'Soraya, Cl.'.

repeats well in regular flushes during the flowering season. The plant has healthy, glossy foliage and can be expected to grow to 10 or 13 ft (3 or 4 m). 'Soraya', the sport parent of this rose was named for Empress Soraya, the last empress of Iran.

'Sorbet'.

'SORBET'.

Breeder: Meilland International (France, 1993).
Parentage: Unknown.
Class: Large-Flowered Climber.
'Sorbet' has richly fragrant, large, double, medium pink

flowers touched with yellow at the petal bases. They fade to light pink, outer petals first, giving a bicolor effect. The sepals have pectinate edges. The rose blooms in continuous flushes during the flowering season. The plant is moderately vigorous and can be trained as a climber to about 8 ft (2.5 m).

'Sorbet Fruité, Cl.'.

'SORBET FRUITÉ, CL.'.

(MEIhestries).
Breeder: Meilland International (France, 2001).
Introduced in France by Selection Meilland in 2001 as 'Sorbet Fruité'. ARS has added the term "Climbing".
Parentage: Unknown.
Class: Climbing Floribunda.
This rose has flowers with red-orange and yellow stripes. This striking color combination soon fades to pink and cream. The stripes vary in size. Some are merely streaks and others involve entire petals. The flowers are large, lightly double, have a cupped form and are held singly or in small clusters. They bloom in flushes during the regular flowering season. The plant will reach a height of about 8 ft (2.5 m) and can be trained as a climber.

'SOURIRE D'ORCHIDÉE'.

(CROchetdit).
Breeder: Paul Croix (France, pre-1985).
Parentage: Seedling of 'Age Tendre'.
Class: Large-Flowered Climber.
Bright pink buds open to form light lavender-pink flowers that soon fade to white. They are fragrant, medium-sized, semi-double and grouped in small clusters. They rebloom in continuous flushes during the flowering season. The plant has glossy, light green foliage and can be trained as a small, shrubby climber to about 8 ft (2.5 m).

'Sourire d'Orchidée'.

'SOUVENIR DE CLAUDIUS DENOYEL'.

('Denoyel').
Breeder: C. Chambard (France, 1920).
Parentage: 'Château de Clos Vougeot' x 'Commandeur Jules Gravereaux'.
Class: Climbing Hybrid Tea.
The flowers of this rose are very fragrant, large, double and bright crimson with flushes of scarlet in the centers. They are borne singly (mostly) or in small clusters and repeat very well in regular flushes during the flowering season. The plant will grow, in a much branching fashion, to about 12 ft (3.65 m).

'Souvenir de Claudius Denoyel'.

'SOUVENIR DE CLAUDIUS PERNET, CL.'.

Breeder: Discovered by Western Rose Co. (US, 1925), Johann Schmidt (Germany, 1932) and Gaujard (France, 1933).

Parentage: Sport of 'Souvenir de Claudius Pernet'.
Class: Climbing Hybrid Tea, Climbing Pernetiana.
This rose produces beautiful very large, double, high-centered, fragrant, medium yellow flowers in solitary blooms or sometimes in small clusters. They fade to ivory as they age. Rebloom is in regular seasonal flushes. The plant is armed with thorns, has glossy foliage and will grow to about 10 ft (3 m).

'Souvenir de Claudius Pernet, Cl.'.

'SOUVENIR DE GEORGES PERNET, CL.'.

Breeder: Discovered by Joseph Pernet-Ducher (France, 1927).
Parentage: Sport of 'Souvenir de Georges Pernet'.
Class: Climbing Hybrid Tea (Pernetiana).
The flowers are richly fragrant, large, very full, globular in form and deep crimson-pink with flushes of yellow on the petal bases. They repeat well in regular seasonal flushes. The plant is well armed and will grow to about 10 ft (3 m).

'Souvenir de Georges Pernet, Cl.'.

'Souvenir de la Malmaison, Cl.'.

'SOUVENIR DE LA MALMAISON, CL.'.

Breeder: Charles Bennett (United Kingdom, 1892).
Parentage: Sport of 'Souvenir de la Malmaison'.
Class: Climbing Bourbon.
This truly lovely rose is widely grown and much admired. The flowers are light pink, large, full, fragrant of tea and have large outer petals that reflex slightly across the tips. They form a shallow cup that holds the smaller, quartered, darker inner petals. The flowers are held singly or in small clusters. They rebloom in continuous flushes during the flowering season. The plant is shade tolerant, hardy to USDA zone 5b and is known to grow to as much as 16 to 20 ft (5 to 6 m).

'Souvenir de Lucie'.

'SOUVENIR DE LUCIE'.

Breeder: Marie-Louise Schwartz (France, 1893).
Parentage: Unknown.
Class: Noisette.

I have seen a rose by this name in several European gardens including Roseraie du Val-de-Marne and Sangerhausen. In the United States it grows at San Jose Heritage Rose Garden. John Hook, who has a rose nursery in France, has stated on the Help Me Find website that he believes the rose at Sangerhausen to be incorrect and the one at Val-de-Marne to be the right one. His photographs of the rose at Val-de-Marne seem to match the description best. The flowers are medium-sized, double and pink with a lighter center. They don't have the mauve tones of the Sangerhausen rose and they look more like a Noisette should look.

'Souvenir du Dr. Jamain'.

'SOUVENIR DE MADAME JOSEPH MÉTRAL'.

('Souvenir de Madame J. Métral', 'Souvenir de Madame Métral').
Breeder: Alexandre Bernaix (France, 1882).
Parentage: 'Madame Bérard' x 'Eugène Fürst'.
Class: Tea-Noisette.

The flowers of this rose are large, double and deep pink changing with age to a more cerise hue. The reverse is crimson-cerise. The plant is moderately vigorous and can be trained as a climber of about 8 to 10 ft (2.5 to 3 m).

'Souvenir de Madame Leonie Viennot'.

'SOUVENIR DE MADAME LEONIE VIENNOT'.

Breeder: Alexandre Bernaix (France, 1898).
Parentage: 'Gloire de Dijon' x unknown seedling.
Class: Tea-Noisette.
This rose has large, double, pink flowers with a touch of apricot, a lighter reverse and flushes of yellow at the petal bases. They become pinker with time and fade to almost white starting at the outer petals and leaving the center darker for a longer time. They have a tea scent. There is one main bloom early in the flowering season with an occasional repeat later. The plant will grow to 10 to 12 ft (3 to 3.65 m) and will do best in USDA climate zone 7b or warmer.

'Souvenir de Némours'.

'SOUVENIR DE NÉMOURS'.

Breeder: Hervé (France, 1869).
Parentage: Unknown.
Class: Climbing Bourbon.
This attractive Climbing Bourbon has medium-sized, double, medium pink flowers with a lighter reverse. They bloom in continuous flushes throughout the flowering season. The plant is known to grow to about 10 ft (3 m).

'Souvenir de Pierre Dupuy'.

'SOUVENIR DE PIERRE DUPUY'.

Breeder: Antoine Levet (père) (France, 1876).
Parentage: Seedling of 'Général Jacqueminot'.
Class: Climbing Hybrid Perpetual.
The flowers of this old rose are fragrant, large, double and dark crimson-red, one of my favorite rose colors. The floral form is globular and the petals are quartered. The flowers are borne singly or in small clusters. They bloom profusely early in the season and produce an occasional flower later. The plant can be trained as a climber of about 10 ft (3 m).

'Souvenir de Pierre Notting, Cl.'.

'SOUVENIR DE PIERRE NOTTING, CL.'.

Breeder: Discovered by Frank Cant (United Kingdom, 1913).
Parentage: Sport of 'Souvenir de Pierre Notting'.
Class: Climbing Tea.
The flowers are large, very double and apricot fading to very pale apricot. The centers fade more slowly remaining darker than the outer portion and the petal bases are lightly flushed with yellow. The petals may show some quartering. There is a tea rose fragrance. The flowers are carried singly or in small clusters and bloom in continuous seasonal flushes.

'Souvenir du Docteur Jamain'.

'SOUVENIR DU DOCTEUR JAMAIN'.

Breeder: François Lacharme (France, 1865).
Parentage: 'Général Jacqueminot' x 'Charles Lefebvre'.
Class: Climbing Hybrid Perpetual.
This lovely rose from times long past has fragrant, medium-sized, double, cupped dark crimson-red flowers that become purpler with age. It has very good remontancy with flowers blooming in repeated flushes during the flowering season. The flowers tend to fade in the sun so a partially shady location is best for color. The almost thornless plant is hardy to USDA zone 4b and can be trained as a small climber of about 10 ft (3 m). I once grew a plant of this rose next to Clematis 'Niobe' with a truly serendipitous effect.

'SOUVENIR OF WOOTTON, CL.'.

Breeder: Discovered by Thomas Butler (United States, 1899).
Parentage: Sport of 'Souvenir of Wootton'.
Class: Climbing Hybrid Tea.

The parents of 'Souvenir of Wootton' were 'Bon Silène' (a Tea) and 'Louis van Houtte' (a Hybrid Perpetual). This made it a Hybrid Tea in the original fashion. The climbing sport is one of the earliest Climbing Hybrid Teas. The flowers of both the bush and climbing forms of this rose are richly fragrant, very large, double and crimson with flushes of purple. The color fades to crimson-pink starting at the petal tips. The form is an open cup, sometimes with quartered petals. The flowers are borne singly or in small clusters. The rose has several flushes of bloom each season with the first being the most prolific. The plant grows to about 10 ft (3 m).

'Souvenir of Wootton, Cl.'.

'SPANISH BEAUTY'.
see 'Madame Grégoire Staechelin'.

'Sparkling Scarlet'.

'SPARKLING SCARLET'.

('Iskra', MEIhaiti, MEIhati).
Breeder: Meilland International (France, before 1969).
Parentage: 'Danse des Sylphes' x 'Zambra'.
Class: Climbing Floribunda.
The flowers of 'Sparkling Scarlet' are a little more orange than true scarlet and are perhaps better described as vermilion. They are medium-sized, semi-double and are said to have a light fruity scent which I cannot detect. They bloom in continuous seasonal flushes. The plant can be trained as a moderate climber of about 10 ft (3 m).

'SPARTAN, CL.'.

Breeder: Discovered by Reimer Kordes (Germany, 1960).
Parentage: Sport of 'Spartan' (Boerner, 1955).
Class: Climbing Floribunda.
'Spartan, Cl.' has flowers that are medium to large-sized, double, high-centered and deep coral. They open out to show the imbricated petals and a small view of the stamens. The floral arrangement is mostly solitary, but sometimes in small clusters. The rose is remontant in continuous seasonal flushes. The plant has glossy, dark green foliage and can be expected to reach a height of about 13 to 16 ft (4 to 5 m).

'Spartan, Cl.'.

'SPECTACULAR'.

('Danse du Feu').
Breeder: Charles Mallerin (France, 1953).
Parentage: 'Paul's Scarlet Climber' x seedling of Rosa multiflora.
Class: Large-Flowered Climber.

This attractive climbing rose has weakly scented, medium to large-sized, lightly double vermilion flowers aging to crimson with nuances of purple. They are borne singly or in small clusters. The flowering occurs in regular seasonal flushes. The plant is well armed, has glossy, dark green foliage, susceptibility to blackspot and potential growth to about 12 ft (3.65 m). 'Spectacular' has sported several times to produce roses of different colors. 'Amazone' is red and otherwise identical to 'Spectacular'. It grows at Vrijbroek Park (Belgium). 'Anne Jackson' is deep pink and is thought to be a sport or an offspring. It may be extinct.

'Spectacular'.

'SPEK'S YELLOW, CL.' See 'Golden Scepter, Cl.'.

'SPICE SO NICE'.

(WEKwesflut).
Breeder: Tom Carruth (United States, 2002).
Parentage: 'Westerland' x 'Flutterbye'.
Class: Large-Flowered Climber.
Large, double apricot flowers with yellow petal bases and reverse. The petal tips become more crimson with time. There is a pronounced spicy fragrance. The floral arrangement is single or in small clusters and

'Spice So Nice'.

the rose reblooms well in continuous seasonal flushes. The shrubby plant has glossy, dark green foliage and will reach about 12 ft (3.65 m) in height.

'Spirit of Freedom'.

'SPIRIT OF FREEDOM'.

(AUSbite).
Breeder: David Austin (United Kingdom, 2002).
Parentage: unnamed seedling x 'Abraham Darby'.
Class: Shrub (English Rose).
The flowers of this English Rose are soft, light pink becoming more lilac with age. They are large, very double and form in small clusters. Rebloom is in regular flushes during the flowering season. The outer petals form a cup around the smaller quartered inner petals, a feature found in other Austin roses. The plant has semi-glossy, dark green foliage and is reported to grow to 8 or 10 ft (2.5 or 3 m).

'ST. ELIZABETH OF HUNGARY'.

('Árpád-házi Szent Erzsébet emléke', 'Heilige Elisabeth', 'Szent Erzsébet emléke').
Breeder: Gergely Márk (Hungary, 1988).
Parentage: 'Queen Elizabeth' x 'Excelsa'.
Class: Shrub, Large-Flowered Climber.
This is a lovely rose from a little known, but talented Hungarian breeder. The flowers are pink nuanced with lavender, medium-sized, double with an old rose form and are borne singly or in small clusters. They repeat in continuous flushes during the flowering season. The plant has glossy, medium green foliage and can be trained as a branching, shrubby climber of about 10 ft (3 m). It is hardy to USDA zone 5b, is drought resistant and disease resistant.

'ST. SWITHUN'.

(AUSwith, 'Saint Swithun').
Breeder: David Austin.
Parentage: 'Mary Rose' x ('Chaucer' x 'Conrad Ferdinand Meyer').
Class: Shrub, English Rose.
This rose with the ecclesiastical name has medium-sized, very double, musk-scented light pink flowers that fade to blush pink. They are borne mostly singly, but sometimes in small clusters. The plant is often described as a shrub, but it can be trained to grow as a very attractive climber of about 8 ft (2.5 m).

'STAIRWAY TO HEAVEN'.

(JACetima).
Breeder: Dr. Keith W. Zary (United States, 2002).
Parentage: 'Dynamite' x 'Dream Weaver'.
Class: Large-Flowered Climber.
The medium to large-sized, double, lightly fragrant, deep scarlet-red flowers fade to lighter crimson-red with age. They open out widely and the outer petals reflex at the tips, finally forming points. They are held singly or in small clusters and rebloom in regular seasonal flushes. The plant, which is susceptible to mildew, will grow to about 12 ft (3.5 m).

'STAR PERFORMER'.

('Pink Above All', 'Pink Keops', 'CHEWpearl').
Breeder: Christopher H. Warner (United Kingdom, 1998).
Parentage: 'Laura Ford' x 'Congratulations'.

'Stairway To Heaven'.

Class: Climbing Miniature, Mini-Flora.
Even before I saw the registration name, CHEwpearl, this rose reminded me of a pearl. The pink color is very soft and the petals seem to have a pearl-like glow. The flowers are small, double and are carried in large clusters. They rebloom very well in regular seasonal flushes. The attractive, disease-resistant foliage is small, dark green and glossy, there are few thorns and the growth is to about 7 ft (2 m).

'STEFANOVITCH'.

('Lemania, Cl.', 'Stephanovitch').
Breeder: Discovered by Francis Meilland (France, 1943).
Parentage: Sport of 'Lemania', a Hybrid Tea.
Class: Climbing Hybrid Tea.
This is a very fragrant, very dark, velvety black-red rose with very large, double, high-centered flowers in the Hybrid Tea mold of 'Lemania', its sport parent. It blooms in flushes during the flowering season. The plant has long stems that make it good for cutting. It is well armed and will grow to about 10 ft (3 m). The climber can be seen at Sangerhausen.

'Stefanovitch'.

'STERLING SILVER, CL.'.

Breeder: Discovered by Hiroshi Miyawaki (Japan, 1963).
Parentage: Sport of 'Sterling Silver'.
Class: Climbing Hybrid Tea.
This rose is even more beautiful as a climber than as a bush. The flowers are large and double with a coiled, elevated center in Hybrid Tea Style and a soft lavender color. The flowers are held singly or in small clusters. There is a rich fruity fragrance. There is one main bloom early in the season with occasional flowers produced later. The plant has few thorns and dark green, glossy foliage. It is said to grow best in a warm climate of at least USDA zone 7b and it needs frost protection in a cold one. The potential height is about 10 ft (3 m).

'STORMY WEATHER'.

('Orafantanov', 'Princess Sibilla de Luxembourg').
Breeder: Pierre Orard (France, before 2006).
Parentage: 'Heart 'n' Soul' x 'Rhapsody in Blue'.
Class: Large-Flowered Climber.
This is an excellent dark purple rose except for its modest height of about 8 ft (2.5 m) maximum. The flowers have a nice spicy fragrance and are large, lightly double, arranged in large clusters and have an open cupped form. They are deep, rich purple lighted up at the petal tip with flushes of crimson. The reverse and the center are lighter and silvery. The light center is almost obscured by the large bunch of golden yellow stamens. The flowers rebloom in continuous seasonal flushes. The plant has plentiful dark green, matte foliage. It is widely available commercially.

'Stormy Weather'.

'STRAWBERRY HILL'.

(AUSrimini).
Breeder: Bred by David C. H. Austin (United Kingdom, 2001).
Parentage: Unknown.
Class: English Rose.

'Strawberry Hill'.

This rose produces medium to large-sized, double, rose pink flowers with a lovely cupped old-fashioned quartered form. They are richly fragrant of myrrh. The flowers are carried singly or in small clusters. They bloom in regular flushes during the flowering season. The plant has glossy, dark green foliage and can be trained as a small climber of about 8 ft (2.5 m). It is commercially available from many sources in Europe, the United States and Canada.

'Studienrat Schlenz'.

'STUDIENRAT SCHLENZ'.

Breeder: Peter Lambert (Germany, 1926).
Parentage: 'Mrs. Aaron Ward' x 'Frau Karl Druschki'.
Class: Large-Flowered Climber, Climbing Hybrid Tea.
This rose is the result of a cross between a Hybrid Tea and 'Frau Karl Druschki', Peter Lambert's famous Hybrid Perpetual. The rose's climbing vigor is part of the Druschki heritage. The attractive flowers are very large, double, mildly fragrant and pink with flushes of yellow at the center and a darker reverse. In time, the pink fades to almost white. The flowers are borne singly or in small clusters and have one long, single bloom in spring or early summer. The plant has glossy, dark green foliage and can be trained as a small climber to about 8 ft (2.5 m).

'SULTANE, CL.'.

Breeder: Unknown.
Parentage: Sport of 'Sultane' (Meilland, 1946).
Class: Climbing Hybrid Tea.
This rose has flowers that are fragrant, large, double and vermilion-red with a golden yellow reverse. The petal tips become pinker with age and the petals become quilled, giving the flower a dahlia-like appearance. The plant is grown at Sangerhausen and is for sale in France and Germany.

'Sultane, Cl.'.

'SUMMER WINE'.

(KORizont).
Breeder: Reimer Kordes (Germany, 1985).
Parentage: 'Coral Dawn' x seedling.
Class: Large-Flowered Climber.
This rose has well-shaped single to semi-double, medium to large-sized flowers. The buds are coral, but the flowers open coral pink with pale yellow-cream petal bases and become more pink and lighter with age. The stamens with their red filaments contrast beautifully with the colors of the petals. There is a strong fragrance. The rose has one prolific spring or early summer bloom with occasional flowers produced later. The plant will grow to about 12 or 14 ft (3.5 or 4.5 m). My two plants cover the entry arbor for the formal rose garden.

'Summer Wine'.

'SUNBLEST, CL.'. See 'Landora, Cl.

'SUNDANCER'.

(CHEworangedawn, 'Orange Dawn').
Breeder: Christopher H. Warner (United Kingdom, 2006).
Parentage: 'Dawn Chorus' x unnamed seedling.
Class: Large-Flowered Climber.
'Sundancer' has apricot-yellow flowers with crimson flushes on the outer petals. The form is double, medium-sized with flowers borne singly or in small clusters. The plant has medium green foliage and will grow to about 8 ft (2.5 m) or more.

'SUNDAY BEST'.

Breeder: Alister Clark (Australia, 1924).
Parentage: Seedling of 'Frau Karl Druschki'.
Class: Hybrid Perpetual.
The flowers of 'Sunday Best' are single to barely semi-double, medium-sized, mildly fragrant and light red fading to crimson-pink with white centers. They are borne singly or in small clusters. The plant is armed with good-sized thorns and has light green, rugose foliage. It has a growth potential of about 10 to 12 ft (3 to 3.5 m).

'Sunday Best'.

'Sun Flare, Cl.'.

'SUN FLARE, CL.'.

(BURyellow, JAClem, 'Sunflare, Cl.', 'Yellow Blaze').
Breeder: Discovered by William Warriner (United States, 1987) and by Joe Burks (United States, 1987). Exhibition name for both clones is 'Sun Flare'.
Parentage: Sport of 'Sun Flare'.
Class: Climbing Floribunda.
The mildly fragrant flowers are large, double and pure, deep yellow slowly fading to cream. The form is initially cupped, and then opens flat to show the broad petals and the central bunch of stamens. They are carried singly or in small clusters and bloom in continuous flushes during the flowering season. The plant is armed with thorns, has glossy, dark green foliage and will grow to about 12 ft (3.5 m).

'SUNNY SOUTH'.

Breeder: Alister Clark (Australia, 1918).
Parentage: 'Gustav Grünerwald' x 'Betty Berkeley'.
Class: Large-Flowered Climber, Shrub.
The large, single to semi-double, very fragrant flowers are crimson-pink with a touch of mauve at the petal tips and lighter, with a flush of yellow, at the center. As they mature, they fade to light pink, white and a hint of yellow and the broad petals open out fully to show the stamens. The flowers rebloom in regular seasonal flushes. The plant is almost thornless, has dark green, semi-glossy foliage and will grow to about 8 ft (2.5 m).

'SUNRISE'.
See 'Freisinger Morgenröte'.

'SUNSPRITE, CL.'.

Breeder: Discovered by Henry Kroeger (United States, 1989).
Parentage: Sport of 'Sunsprite'.
Class: Climbing Floribunda.

This is the rose you will be happy to see on a dull day with its cheerful, deep yellow flowers. They are richly fragrant, medium-sized, double and borne singly (mostly) or in small clusters. The rebloom is excellent in seasonal flushes. The form is high-centered like the rose's Floribunda parent with a little twist to the petals that adds to the charm. The plant has semi-glossy, light green foliage and a potential for growth of about 10 ft (3 m).

'Sunsprite, Cl.'.

'SUNSTAR, CL.'.

Breeder: Discovered by Alexander Dickson II (United Kingdom, 1925).
Parentage: Sport of 'Sunstar' (Hybrid Tea, Dickson, 1921)
Class: Climbing Hybrid Tea.

The flowers of 'Sunstar, Cl.' are fragrant, medium-sized, semi-double and yellow with coral-pink flushed petal tips. The coral hue is replaced with crimson as the flower fades. They are borne mostly solitary, but sometimes in small clusters and are known to rebloom in continuous flushes during the flowering season. The plant can be expected to grow to about 10 ft (3 m).

'Sunstar, Cl.'.

'SUPER STAR, CL.'.
See 'Tropicana, Cl.'.

'Surpassing Beauty of Woolverstone'.

'SURPASSING BEAUTY OF WOOLVERSTONE'.

('Woolverstone Church Rose').
Breeder: Original unknown. Discovered by Humphrey Brooke (United Kingdom, before pre-1973). Reintroduced by Peter Beales Roses (United Kingdom, 1980).
Parentage: Unknown.

Class: Hybrid Perpetual, Large-Flowered Climber.
When the rose was taken from the Woolverstone Church at Suffolk, England in 1993, it was already at least 100 years old. The Hybrid Perpetual-style flowers are dark crimson and become darker with age instead of fading as most roses do. They are fragrant, medium-sized and very full and are borne singly or in small clusters. They have one main period of bloom early in the season with a few flowers produced later. The plant can be grown as a climber of about 10 to 12 ft (3 to 3.5 m).

'Suspense, Cl.'.

'SUSPENSE, CL.'.

Breeder: Meilland International (France, 1960).
Parentage: Sport of 'Suspense'.
Class: Climbing Hybrid Tea.
This climbing sport of 'Suspense' has flowers that are large, double and bright scarlet-red with a yellow reverse accented by red petal tips. In cool weather the color is pinker. The form is high-centered and classical Hybrid Tea shaped. The rose is borne singly or in small clusters and blooms in continuous flushes during the flowering season. The plant has glossy, dark green foliage and will grow to about 10 ft (3 m). It will grow and bloom best in a warm climate, at least USDA zone 7b.

'SUTTER'S GOLD, CL.'.

Breeder: Discovered by O. L. Weeks (United States, circa 1950).
Parentage: Sport of 'Sutter's Gold'.
Class: Climbing Hybrid Tea.
Vermilion buds open to golden-yellow flowers that soon develop crimson flushes on the broad, reflexing outer petal tips. They are large, double, high-centered, very fragrant and are borne singly (mostly) or in small clusters. The rose has one main flush of bloom with flowers produced occasionally after that. The plant has the potential to grow to about 12 ft (3.5 m).

'Sutter's Gold, Cl.'.

'Swan Lake'.

'SWAN LAKE'.

('Schwanensee').
Breeder: Samuel Darragh McGredy IV (1961).
Parentage: 'Memoriam' x 'Heidelberg'.
Class: Large-Flowered Climber.
'Swan Lake' has very large, double, high-centered white flowers with pink centers. The pink fades to white when they are mature and open with reflexed petals. The flowers occur singly or in small clusters and bloom in regular seasonal flushes. The plant is armed with thorns, has semi-glossy, dark green foliage and will grow to about 12 ft (3.5 m).

'SWEET SULTAN'.

Breeder: S. Eacott (United Kingdom, 1958).
Parentage: 'Independence' x 'Honour Bright'.
Class: Climbing Hybrid Tea.
This unusual and beautiful rose has richly fragrant, large, single deep dark red flowers. The petal tips are almost black. The color is set off by a large bunch of golden yellow stamens in the center. It is fully remontant in regular seasonal flushes. It will grow sufficiently to be trained as a small climber. A plant grows at Sangerhausen. It is sold in France and Germany.

'Sylt'.

'SYLT'.

(KORylt).
Breeder: Reimer Kordes (Germany, 1980).
Parentage: Rosa kordesii x unnamed seedling.
Class: Hybrid Kordesii.
The flowers are mildly fragrant, single to semi-double, medium to large-sized and dark red. They are borne singly or in small clusters. The plant has medium, dark green foliage and if given support can be trained as a small climber of about 8 ft (2.5 m). It is also useful as a ground cover.

'SYMPATHIE'.

Breeder: Reimer Kordes (Germany, 1964).
Parentage: 'Wilhelm Hansmann' x 'Don Juan'.
Class: Kordesii, Large-Flowered Climber.
This rose has very fragrant, large, lightly double bright red flowers arranged singly or in small clusters. It reblooms very well in continuous flushes during the flowering season. The plant is cold hardy, has thick, dark green foliage and will grow to at least 16 ft (5 m). You will probably want to plant a bush or shrub rose in front of it since the lower parts of the canes tend to become bare. The long stems make the flowers good for cutting.

'Sympathie'.

'SZENT ERZSEBET'.

See 'St. Elizabeth of Hungary'.

T

'Twilight Mist'.

'TAHITIAN MOON'.

(BAloon).
Breeder: Ping Lim, (United States, 1996).
Parentage: R871 x 'Aspen'.
Class: Large-Flowered Climber, Shrub.
The flowers are beautifully formed yellow, medium-sized rosettes filled to very double with quartered petals. They fade to cream as they age. The mildly fragrant flowers are borne singly or in small clusters and bloom in continuous flushes during the flowering season. The plants have glossy, dark green foliage and can be trained as climbers of about 10 ft (3 m).

'Talisman, Cl.'.

'TALISMAN, CL.'.

Breeder: Discovered by Western Rose Company (United States, 1930). Discovered by Dixie Rose Nursery (United States, 1932).
Parentage: Sport of 'Talisman' (Hybrid Tea, Montgomery Co., 1929).
Class: Climbing Hybrid Tea.
This climbing sport of an old and highly regarded Hybrid Tea has medium, semi-double to lightly double high-centered scarlet flowers with golden-yellow petal bases and reverse. There is a rich fragrance. The flowers are borne mostly singly or occasionally in small clusters. The plant is almost thornless, has light green foliage and a growth potential of about 20 ft (6 m).

'TANTAU'S TRIUMPH, CL.'.

Breeder: Discovered by Europa Rosarium, Sangerhausen (East Germany, 1957).
Parentage: Sport of 'Tantau's Triumph'.
Class: Climbing Floribunda.

'Tantau's Triumph, Cl.'.

It is considered by some authorities to be a Climbing Polyantha, but there seem to be no Polyanthas in its ancestry. The flowers of this rose are mildly fragrant, medium-sized, semi-double and scarlet with a white eye. They are cupped initially, and then open widely to show the stamens with their red filaments. The flowers are born singly or in small clusters and rebloom in regular seasonal flushes.

'TARZAN'.

Breeder: G. Delbard (France, 1955).
Parentage: Unknown.
Class: Large-Flowered Climber.
I haven't seen this rose and there is very little information about it in the rose literature. The flowers are very fragrant, double and medium red. The floral form is cupped. It has one main bloom early in the year with a few flowers formed in the fall. It seems to grow only at Roseraie du Val-de-Marne in France and is not commercially available.

'TASOGARE, CL.'.

Breeder: Discovered by Kenji Inoue (Japan, 1996).
Parentage: Sport of 'Tasogare'.
Class: Climbing Floribunda.
The flowers are mildly fragrant, medium-sized, semi-double and mauve with white petal bases and an occasional white stripe. The floral form is open and flattened with a full display of the yellow stamens and the floral arrangement is single or small clusters. There is one main bloom early in the season and an occasional repeat later. The plant has glossy, dark green foliage and will grow to about 8 ft (2.5 m).

'Tasogare, Cl.'.

'TASSIN, CL.'.

Breeder: Discovered by Moreira da Silva (Portugal, circa 1950).
Parentage: Sport of 'Tassin' (Meilland, France, 1942).
Class: Climbing Hybrid Tea.

The richly fragrant, large, double, dark scarlet-red roses with blackish overtones look almost like they are made of velvet. The form is high-centered, exhibition-quality Hybrid Tea. The rose blooms in repeated seasonal flushes, but it is not a prolific bloomer. Tassin is a small town near Lyon where the Meilland Nursery was once located.

'Tassin, Cl.'.

'Tchin-Tchin, Cl.'.

'TCHIN-TCHIN, CL.'.

('Grimpant Tchin-Tchin', MEIchansosar).
Breeder: Discovered by Meilland International (France, 1995).
Parentage: Sport of 'Tchin-Tchin'.
Class: Climbing Hybrid Tea.

This orange-red rose makes a wonderful display with its prolific bloom and brilliant color. The flowers are mildly fragrant, medium to large-sized, double and high-centered. They occur mostly in small clusters and bloom in continuous flushes during the flowering season. The plant likes warm weather and will do best in a USDA zone climate of 7b or warmer.

'Teasing Georgia'.

'TEASING GEORGIA'.

(AUSbaker, P/27/88, TG2476).
Breeder: David Austin.
Parentage: 'Charles Austin' x unnamed seedling.
Class: Shrub, English Rose.

Here is another excellent Austin rose that can be pruned as a shrub or trained as a climber of about 8 ft (2.5 m). The flowers are medium to large, very double, fragrant and golden-yellow with a hint of apricot at the center. The outer petals fade quickly to cream and as the flower ages the inner petals also fade. The flowers are borne singly or in small clusters and rebloom in regular flushes during the flowering season. The plant has dark green, semi-glossy foliage and grows in a shrubby manner. It is hardy to USDA zone 5b.

'Te Awamutu'.

'TE AWAMUTU'.

'Big John' is sometimes given as a synonym, but this is controversial.
Breeder: Pat Stephens (New Zealand, 1985).
Parentage: 'Strawberry Ice' x unnamed seedling.
Class: Hybrid Tea. It has also been classed as a Large-Flowered Climber and described as a pillar rose in the rose literature.
This is a very tall-growing bush rose that can be trained as a shrubby climber of about 8 ft (2.5 m). The flowers, which are quite beautiful, are large, double and white with cerise petal tips and are arranged in medium to large clusters. I could not detect a scent. The foliage is dark green and glossy. Hopefully, it will find its way into commerce.

'TEIDE'.

('Teide, Cl.').
Breeder: Pedro (Pere) Dot (Spain, 1948).
Parentage: 'Texas Centennial' x 'Guinée'.
Class: Climbing Hybrid Tea.

'Teide'.

The flowers of 'Teide' are medium-sized, double, high-centered and crimson pink. The petal tips reflex strongly giving the flowers a rolled-back look. Sangerhausen is the only garden where I have seen this rose and it seems to not be in commerce any longer.

'TEMPO'.

(JACclop).
Breeder: William A. Warriner (United States, 1975).
Parentage: 'Ena Harkness, Cl.' x unnamed seedling.
Class: Large-Flowered Climber.
The flowers are large, double, mildly fragrant and dark crimson-red. The sepals have long, drawn-out tips (acuminate) and add to the beauty of the opening buds. There is one main flowering season early in the season with occasional flowers produced later. The plant is moderately vigorous and can be trained as a climber of about 8 ft (2.5 m).

'TEMPTATION'.

Breeder: Martin R. Jacobus (United States, 1950).
Introduced in United States by Bobbink & Atkins in 1950
Parentage: Unknown.
Class: Large-Flowered Climber.
Here is another lovely rose that is becoming very rare and could easily become extinct. The well-formed flowers are fragrant, medium to large-sized, very double, globular in form with quartered petals and deep crimson-pink. The plant has glossy, medium green foliage, a branching habit and a growth potential of 13 to 16 ft (4 to 5 m).

'Tender Night, Cl.'.

'TENDER NIGHT, CL.'.

(MEIlaursar, 'Florian, Cl.').
Breeder: Discovered by Marie-Louise (Louisette) Meilland (France, 1976).
Parentage: Sport of 'Tender Night'.
Class: Climbing Floribunda.
The Floribunda-style flowers are mildly fragrant, medium to large-sized, double and pure, brilliant red. They are borne singly or in small clusters and bloom in seasonal flushes. The plant has semi-glossy foliage and will grow to about 10 ft (3 m).

'Ténor'.

'TÉNOR'.

(DELcap).
Breeder: Delbard-Chabert (France, 1963).
Parentage: Unknown.
Class: Large-Flowered Climber.
This rose is very showy with its semi-double, medium-sized, scentless, brilliant red flowers displayed in large clusters. Initially cupped, they open out and roll back their petal tips as they mature to reveal a small white eye with a bunch of golden-yellow stamens in the center. The flowers rebloom in seasonal flushes. The plant has glossy, dark green foliage and will grow to about 10 ft (3 m).

'Tess of the D'Urbervilles'.

'TESS OF THE D'URBERVILLES'.

(AUSmove)
Breeder: David Austin pre-1997.
Parentage: 'The Squire' x unnamed seedling.
Class: Shrub, English Rose.
I have enjoyed this lovely crimson rose in my garden for many years and regard it as one of David Austin's best roses. It has an old rose fragrance and large, very double old fashioned style flowers with quartered petals. They are produced singly or in small clusters and rebloom in continuous flushes during the regular flowering season. The plant is armed with thorns and has medium green, semi-glossy foliage. It will grow, in a bushy manner, to about 8 ft (2.5 m).

'Texas Centennial, Cl.'.

'TEXAS CENTENNIAL, CL.'.

Breeder: Discovered by George Washington Weaver (United States, 1942).
Parentage: Sport of 'Texas Centennial'.
Class: Climbing Hybrid Tea.
'Texas Centennial', the sport parent of this beautiful rose, was a sport of 'President Herbert Hoover'. The colors have changed from orange and crimson to soft pink touched with coral and crimson. The pattern of lighter petals in the center and a lighter reverse has been inherited intact along with flowers that are large, fragrant and double and are borne singly or in small clusters. The rose is fully remontant in regular flushes during the flowering season. It grows to about 12 ft (3.5 m) and makes a beautiful climber for an arbor or a trellis placed against a wall.

'THE ADJUTANT, CL.'.

Breeder: Unknown.
Parentage: Sport of 'The Adjutant'.
Class: Climbing Hybrid Tea.
The flowers of this rose open from long, pointed buds. They are large, semi-double, high-centered, richly fragrant and a beautiful vermilion color. They are borne singly or in small clusters and bloom in continuous seasonal flushes. The plant has dark green foliage and will climb to an average height of about 10 ft (3 m).

'THE ALBRIGHTON RAMBLER'.

(AUSmobile).
Breeder: David C. H. Austin (United Kingdom, before 2013).
Parentage: Unknown.
Class: Large-Flowered Climber.
The flowers are semi-double, medium-sized and light pink fading to blush pink. The broad outer petals form a cup around the numerous small, quartered inner petals with visible stamens when the flower is fully opened. There is an old rose fragrance. The plant is disease resistant, has dark green semi-glossy foliage and makes an excellent climber of 10 to 12 ft (3 to 3.5 m).

'The Alexandra Rose'.

'THE ALEXANDRA ROSE'.

(AUSday). Named for a favorite charity.
Breeder: David Austin (United Kingdom, 1992).
Parentage: ('Shropshire Lass' x 'Shropshire Lass') x 'Heritage'.
Class: Shrub, English Rose.
The flowers of this unusual rose are fragrant of musk, small to medium-sized, single and have coral-pink petal tips with yellow centers. The coral hue shifts to pink and then all fades to almost white as the flower ages. The flowers are produced singly or in small clusters. They rebloom in continuous flushes during the flowering season. The plant is very disease resistant and has the potential to grow in a shrubby style to about 8 ft (2.5 m). It is hardy to USDA zone 5b.

'THE DARK LADY'.

(AUSbloom, 'Dark Lady').
Breeder: David Austin (United Kingdom, pre-1991).
Parentage: 'Mary Rose' x 'Prospero'.
Class: Shrub, English Rose.
I have grown this rose for about 25 years and it is one of my favorite Austins. It is as beautiful now as when

'The Dark Lady'.

it was first planted. Now, as I write, it is October in the Pacific Northwest and the plant is still filled with lovely fragrant, dark red old-rose style flowers. They are medium-sized, very full and arranged mostly singly or in small clusters. They bloom prolifically in flushes all during the flowering season. My plant has dark green foliage and grows to about 8 ft with support and good care. It has survived zero-degree temperatures during a winter cold spell.

'The Doctor, Cl.'.

'THE DOCTOR, CL.'.

Breeder: Dyess, Reliance Rose Nursery (United States, 1950).
Parentage: Unknown.
Class: Climbing Hybrid Tea.
The large, double, high-centered bloom is initially deep, warm pink with a small flush of yellow at the petal bases. The form is initially cupped and as the flowers mature they open out widely and shift in color to a more mauve-pink hue. They have a deep, rich fragrance. The rose is remontant in seasonal flushes and it will climb vigorously to 10 or 12 ft (3 or 3.5 m). I can't find any public gardens that grow the climber. It is available from one nursery in England.

'The Generous Gardener'.

'THE GENEROUS GARDENER'.

(AUSdrawn).
Breeder: David Austin (United Kingdom, 2002).
Parentage: 'Sharifa Asma' x unnamed seedling.
Class: Shrub, English Rose.
This rose has large, very full, light pink flowers with broad outer petals and a center filled with rather narrow ones. They occur singly or in small clusters. There is a very strong old rose fragrance with nuances of musk and myrrh. The rose has one main bloom in spring or early summer with a few flowers appearing later. The plant is plentifully provided with dark green, glossy foliage and will reach to about 10 to 12 ft (3 to 3.5 m).

'THE IMPRESSIONIST'.

(CLEpainter).
Breeder: John Clements (United States US, 2000).

Parentage: 'Graham Thomas' x 'Distant Drums'.
Class: Large-Flowered Climber. Heirloom Roses describes this rose as an English-style rose.
This attractive rose has large, very full, golden yellow to orange flowers grouped singly or in small clusters and scented of myrrh. The flowers fade in time to light coral pink and then to white. The form is an orderly rosette, the center filled with small petals. The plant will grow vigorously to about 12 ft (3.5 m). It is hardy to USDA zone 5b.

'The Impressionist'.

'THE LADY OF THE LAKE'.

(AUSherbert).
Breeder: Bred by David C. H. Austin (United Kingdom, before 2014).
Parentage: Unknown.
Class: English Rose.
This new Austin rose has fragrant, small to medium-sized, semi-double, light, warm pink flowers fading to white. They open widely to show the bunch of golden yellow stamens in the center. They are borne singly or in small clusters and bloom in flushes during the flowering season. The plant has foliage with a bronze green hue and will climb to about 12 ft (3.5 m).

'THE PILGRIM'.

(AUSwalker, 'Gartenarchitekt Günther Schulze').
Breeder: David Austin (United Kingdom, pre-1991).
Parentage: 'Graham Thomas' x 'Yellow Button'.
Class: Shrub, English Rose.
The flower are medium-sized, very full, mildly fragrant (spicy) and yellow fading from the outer petals inward. They are borne singly (mostly) or in small clusters. The

'The Pilgrim'.

form is a low-domed rosette with broad outer petals and small inner petals that are reflexed along the sides and roughly quartered. The rose reblooms in seasonal flushes. The plant is hardy to USDA zone 5b and is said to be somewhat susceptible to mildew, but healthy otherwise. It is known to grow to about 10 ft (3 m).

'The Prince's Trust'.

'THE PRINCE'S TRUST'.

('Baikal', HARholding, 'Prince's Trust', 'Red Sox').
Breeder: Harkness (United Kingdom, 2002).
Parentage: Unknown.
Class: Large-Flowered Climber.
The flowers are medium-sized, lightly double, mildly fragrant and bright crimson-red. They are produced singly or in small clusters. The plant has glossy, dark green foliage, excellent disease resistance and will grow to about 12 ft (3.5 m). It is hardy to USDA zone 5b.

'THE QUEEN ALEXANDRA ROSE, CL.'.

('Rankende The Queen Alexandra Rose'). Rankende means climbing in German.
Breeder: Discovered by Lindecke (Germany, 1929) and by Harkness (United Kingdom, 1931).
Parentage: Sport of 'The Queen Alexandra Rose'.
Class: Climbing Hybrid Tea, Climbing Pernetiana.
The flowers of this rose are mildly fragrant, large, full and light scarlet-red with a golden yellow reverse. Since the flowers are deeply cupped, the reverse sides of the petals are visible inside the reflexing outer petals and form a strong contrast and an unusual color effect. There is a good rebloom in regular seasonal flushes. The plant has the potential to grow to about 10 ft (3 m).

'THE SCHOFIELD ROSE'.
See 'Jacob's Ladder'.

'THE WEDGEWOOD ROSE'.

(AUSjosiah).
Breeder: David Austin (United Kingdom, 2009).
Parentage: Unknown.
Class: Shrub, English Rose.
The flowers of this rose are medium to large-sized, very full, fragrant (clove and fruit), rose-pink with a lighter reverse and the floral form is deeply cupped and the petals have mucronate (sharply projecting) tips. The flowers are borne singly or in small clusters and they rebloom in continuous flushes during the flowering season. The plant has dark green glossy foliage and will grow to about 8 ft (2.5 m).

'THÉO'.

(EVEthau).
Breeder: Jérôme Rateau (France, 2005).
Introduced in France by André Eve/Roses Anciennes André Eve in 2011 as 'Théo'.
Parentage: 'Coraline' x 'Étude'.
Class: Large-Flowered Climber.
'Théo' has flowers that are fragrant, medium-sized, very double, pink and held singly or in small clusters. They bloom prolifically in repeated seasonal flushes. The floral form is that of an old fashioned rose. The plant is hardy, disease resistant and will climb vigorously to about 16 ft (5 m).

'Théo'.

'THISBE'.

Breeder: Rev. Joseph Pemberton (United Kingdom 1918).
Parentage: 'Marie-Jeanne' x 'Perle des Jardins'. Thought by some authorities to be a sport of 'Daphne'.
Class: Hybrid Musk.
'Thisbe' has small to medium-sized, double, very fragrant (musk), yellow-buff flowers in a flat rosette form. They are borne singly or in small clusters and rebloom in regular seasonal flushes. The plant has semi-glossy, light green foliage and will grow to 7 or 8 ft (2 or 2.5 m).

'Thisbe'.

'THREE WEDDINGS'.

Breeder: Ruth Pallek (Canada, 2003).
Parentage: Unknown.
Class: Large-Flowered Climber.
This very attractive rose has fragrant, medium-sized, very

full, cream flowers with broad crimson petal edges which are made more visible by the reflecting of the tips. The flowers are borne singly or in small clusters and bloom in continuous seasonal flushes. The plant can be trained as a climber of about 8 or 10 ft (2.5 or 3 m).

'Tiffany, Cl.'.

'TIFFANY, CL.'.

Breeder: Discovered by Robert V. Lindquist (United States, 1958).
Parentage: Sport of 'Tiffany'.
Class: Climbing Hybrid Tea.
This is a sport of one of our loveliest Hybrid Teas. It has flowers that are very large, very full, strongly fragrant, high-centered and rose pink, becoming more apricot toward the center, and blending in with the yellow petal bases. They are borne singly or in small clusters and rebloom in regular seasonal flushes. The rose can be expected to grow to 10 or 13 ft (3 or 4 m).

'Times Past'.

'TIMES PAST'.

(HARhilt).
Breeder: Harkness (United Kingdom, 2001).
Parentage: 'City of London' x 'Heritage'.
Class: Large-Flowered Climber.
'Times Past' has very double, large, light pink flowers borne singly or in small clusters. The outer petals of the old rose style flowers reflex at the tips and the smaller inner petals fold inward slightly along the centers. The flowers rebloom in flushes during the flowering season. The plant will grow to as much as 12 ft (3.5 m).

'Tip Top, Cl.'.

'TIP TOP, CL.'.

Breeder: Discovered by Mathias Tantau, Jr. (Germany, 1963).
Parentage: Sport of 'Tip Top'.
Class: Climbing Floribunda.
The coral-pink flowers have a lighter reverse, are mildly fragrant, large, semi-double, cupped and are carried singly or in small clusters. The plant will grow to about 8 ft and makes a lovely pillar rose. I have seen it at Roseto Carla Fineschi (Italy) and Sangerhausen (Germany). It grows at Bagatelle Park (France) as well.

'TONNER'S FANCY'.

Breeder: Alister Clark (Australia, 1928).
Parentage: Seedling of Rosa gigantea x unnamed seedling.
Class: Hybrid Gigantea, Large-Flowered Climber.
There are two clones that exist with this name. The so-called "Thelangerin Tennis Court Rose" or simply the Thelangerin clone is now thought to be the authentic

variety. The flowers are fragrant, large, double and creamy white with a pale pink center that fades as the flower ages. They have a globular form that opens to become a flattened cup with stamens visible in the center. They are borne singly (mostly) or in small clusters. The plant is almost evergreen, has Gigantea type foliage and will grow to 15 to 16 ft (4.5 to 5 m). The Glenara clone has similar characteristics, but is pinker and more double and has a less attractive floral form. Both clones are once-blooming early in the flowering season.

'Too Hot To Handle'.

'TOO HOT TO HANDLE'.

('Heinrich Siesmayer', MACloupri).
Breeder: Samuel Darragh McGredy IV (1987).
Parentage: 'Waiheke' x 'Eyeopener'.
Class: Large-Flowered Climber.
The flowers are medium-sized, lightly double, mildly fragrant and bright vermilion. They are borne in large clusters. There is one main bloom early in the season with an occasional repeat later in the year. The plant has glossy, dark green plentiful foliage and will grow to about 10 ft (3 m). It seems to be grown only in private gardens.

'TOP OF THE WORLD'.

(WEKwoagorol).

'Top of the World'.

Breeder: Christian Bédard (United States, pre-2013).
Northland Rosarium thinks it was Carruth.
Parentage: ('Work of Art' x 'Goldmarie') x 'Rosy Outlook').
Class: Miniature Climber.
This pretty, colorful rose has small to medium-sized, double, mildly fragrant (fruit, tea) bright orange flowers with yellow petal bases and reverse. They are borne singly and in small clusters and rebloom in continuous flushes during the flowering season. The small foliage is semi-glossy. The plant has the potential to grow to about 10 ft (3 m).

'Torch'.

'TORCH'

('Torch, Cl.').
Breeder: De Ruiter (Netherlands, 1942).
Parentage: Unknown.
Class: Climbing Polyantha.
Here's a rose to liven up a dull corner of the garden. The semi-double flowers are small, mildly fragrant and somewhere

between orange and vermilion with a small white eye. They are borne singly or in small clusters. There is one plentiful bloom in spring or summer with a few flowers later in the year. The plant has glossy, dark green foliage and the potential to grow to about 8 ft (2.5 m).

'Tour Eiffel 2000'.

'TOUR EIFFEL 2000'.

(DELrugro, 'Eiffel Tower 2000', 'Eiffelturm 2000').
Breeder: G. Delbard (France, 1998).
Parentage: Unknown.
Class: Large-Flowered Climber.
The flowers of this rose are semi-double, large and vermilion-red. The form is an open cup with ruffled petals and the flowers are carried in small to medium-sized clusters. The plant will grow to about 10 ft (3 m). It can be seen at Bagatelle Park (France), Roseto Carla Fineschi (Italy) and Sangerhausen (Germany).

'Tradescant'.

'TRADESCANT'.

(AUSdir).
Breeder: David Austin (United Kingdom, pre-1992).
Parentage: 'Prospero' x ('Charles Austin' x 'Gloire de Ducher').
Class: Shrub, English Rose.
Black-red buds open to medium-sized, very full, fragrant (old rose), dark crimson flowers with blackish and purple flushes. They become darker with age. The form is cupped with the broad outer petals forming an enclosure for the numerous smaller, quartered inner petals. The plant is hardy to USDA zone 5b and is fairly heat tolerant although the dark petal color may cause the flowers to burn. The plant is often described as being compact, but like many Austins, it can be trained as a small climber of about 8 ft (2.5 m).

'Tradition'.

'TRADITION'.

(KORkeltin, 'Tradition 95').
Breeder: W. Kordes & Sons (Germany, 1995).
Parentage: Unknown.
Class: Large-Flowered Climber.
In my own garden this is one of my best performing and most beautiful climbing red roses. It has mildly fragrant, medium-sized, semi-double, bright true red flowers borne mostly in medium to large clusters. They rebloom in continuous seasonal flushes that don't end until the first frost. The plant has glossy, dark green foliage and can be trained as a climber of average height to about 10 to 12 ft (3 to 3.5 m). Kordes produced an earlier rose, a Hybrid Tea, named 'Tradition' that is not related to the rose presented here.

'TRAVERSER'.

Breeder: Alister Clark (Australia, 1928).
Parentage: Hybrid of Rosa gigantea.
Class: Hybrid Gigantea.
'Traverser' has flowers that are softly fragrant, large, semi-double and yellow fading to cream except for the centers which remain yellow to the end. They are carried singly or in small clusters and bloom early in the flowering season. The plant has healthy foliage and will grow to at least 20 to 25 ft (6 to 8 m). It must be grown in a warm, frost-free climate. A rose that is similar to the descriptions of the original variety still grows at Glenara, Clark's old home, but it is not certain that it is authentic.

'Triomphe Des Noisettes'.

'TRIOMPHE DES NOISETTES'.

Breeder: Jean Pernet (père) (France, 1887). There was an earlier rose by the same name (Prevost, France, before 1826).
Parentage: 'Général Jacqueminot' x 'Ophirie'.
Class: Noisette.
The flowers of this early variety are large, lightly double, very fragrant and dark crimson-pink fading to a lighter color with age. They are borne singly or in small clusters and bloom continuously during the flowering season. The plant will reach a height of about 10 ft (3 m) and makes a good pillar rose.

'Triomphe Orléanais Cl.'.

'TRIOMPHE ORLÉANAIS CL.'.

Breeder: Eugène Turbat & Compagnie (France, 1922).
Parentage: Sport of 'Triomphe Orléanais'.
Class: Climbing Polyantha.
This rose has lightly scented, semi-double, small to medium-sized, deeply cupped crimson flowers fading to medium pink. They are large for a Polyantha. They are borne in large clusters and are not remontant. The rose can be observed at Roseraie du Val-de-Marne (France) and Roseto Carla Fineschi (Italy).

'TROPICAL LIGHTNING'.

Breeder: Pierre Orard (France, pre-2011).
Parentage: ORAstricap x (MEIronsse × HARzazz).
Class: Large-Flowered Climber. Shrub.
The strikingly attractive flowers are large, semi-double to lightly double and striped alternately with yellow-cream and dark red-orange nuanced with taupe. The centers are flushed with yellow. The visual effect is unusual. The foliage is large, dark green and glossy. The plant will grow to 8 or 10 ft (2.5 to 3 m) in a warm climate, but will remain a shrub in a cool one. At this writing it is grown mainly in private gardens, but it is commercially available in Europe and the United States.

'Tropicana, Cl.'.

'TROPICANA, CL.'.

(TANgosar, TANgostar, 'Super Star, Cl.').
Breeder: Discovered by Eugene Boerner (United States, 1971).
Parentage: Sport of 'Tropicana'.
Class: Climbing Hybrid Tea.
This offspring of a famous Hybrid Tea has very fragrant (fruity), large to very large, double, bright vermilion flowers with flushes of salmon on the reverse. They are borne singly or in small clusters and rebloom in regular seasonal flushes. The plant is quite vigorous and will climb to about 10 to 13 ft (3 to 4 m).

'TROPIQUE'.

(DELjis).
Breeder: G. Delbard (France, 1956).
Parentage: Unknown.
Class: Large-Flowered Climber.
The colorful flowers of 'Tropique' are medium to large, double, bright scarlet-red and are borne in small-sized clusters. They have one main bloom early in the season with scattered flowers produced later. The plant has glossy dark green foliage and will reach to about 12 ft (3.5 m).

'Tropique'.

'Trumpeter, Cl.'.

'TRUMPETER, CL.'.

Breeder: Unknown.
Parentage: Sport of 'Trumpeter' (McGredy, Floribunda).
Class: Climbing Floribunda.
This climbing form of a well-known Floribunda has mildly fragrant, medium to large-sized, double strikingly brilliant vermilion flowers borne singly or in small clusters. It blooms in continuous seasonal flushes. The plant has glossy, dark green foliage and can be trained as a climber of about 10 ft (3 m).

'TWIST'.

('POUlstri')
Breeder: Bred by L. Pernille and Mogens Nyegaard Olesen (Denmark, 1993).
Parentage: Unnamed seedling x 'Queen Margrethe'.
Class: Large-Flowered Climber, Patio Rose, Cl. (Courtyard Rose).
The unique flowers are large, double and deep pink with white streaks, stripes and patches. There is little, if any, fragrance. They are borne singly or in small clusters and rebloom in regular seasonal flushes. The plant is prickly, has glossy, medium green foliage and will grow in a bushy style to about 7 ft (2 m).

'TYRELLE'.

Breeder: Introduced in United States by Nor' East Miniature Roses in 2008.
Parentage: Sport of 'Jeanne Lajoie'.
Class: Climbing Miniature.
This is a very pretty Climbing Miniature with lightly scented, small to medium-sized, double white flowers formed like an open cup with imbricated petals centered by golden-yellow stamens. The plant has somewhat shiny, dark green foliage and will grow to about 10 ft (3 m), tall for a Climbing Miniature.

'TZIGANE, CL.'.

Breeder: Discovered by Lagoona Nursery (Australia, 1958).
Parentage: Sport of 'Tzigane'.
Class: Climbing Hybrid Tea.
This very ornamental rose has flowers that are large, full, softly fragrant and deep, warm vermilion-pink with a light yellow reverse. They are well formed in classical, high-centered Hybrid Tea style and are borne singly or in small clusters. The rose is fully remontant, blooming prolifically in regular seasonal flushes.

'Ulrich Brunner Fils'.

'Uetersener Klosterrose'.

'UETERSENER KLOSTERROSE'.

Breeder: Hans Jürgen Evers (Germany, 2006).
Parentage: Unknown.
Class: Large-Flowered Climber.
This "cloister" rose from 'Uetersen' has fragrant, large, deeply cupped, double cream-colored flowers carried singly or in small clusters. The flower center is deeper colored, sometimes yellow or yellow flushed with pink. The plant can be trained as a small climber of about 10 ft (3 m).

'Ulmer Münster'.

'ULMER MÜNSTER'.

(KORtello).
Breeder: Reimer Kordes (Germany, 1982).
Parentage: 'Sympathie' x 'Sympathie'.
Class: Shrub, Climber.
The flowers are mildly fragrant, large, double and shallowly cupped with ruffled petals. The color is brilliant dark scarlet at first and then it becomes more crimson as the flowers age. The individual flowers are arranged singly or in small clusters. It is classed as a Shrub, but in a warm climate this rose can be trained as a much-branching climber of about 8 ft. (2.5 m). I saw it growing this way at the Roseto Carla Fineschi in Italy.

'Ulrich Brunner Fils'.

'ULRICH BRUNNER FILS'.

('Ulrich Brunner').
Breeder: Antoine Levet (père) (France, 1881). Introduced by Hazlewood Bros. (Australia, before pre-1911).
Parentage: Seedling of 'Paul Neyron'.
Class: Hybrid Perpetual.
This beautiful old rose is widely grown and sometimes can be seen trained as a climber of about 8 ft (2.5 m). It is used as a pillar rose at Sangerhausen. The richly fragrant flowers are large, very double and cerise pink. They have a cupped floral form. The blooming is remontant in regular seasonal flushes. The plant has few thorns. Long stems make it a good source of cut flowers.

'Viking Queen'.

'Valenciennes'.

'VALENCIENNES'.

('Valenciennes, Cl.').
Breeder: Marcel Robichon (France, 1959).
Parentage: 'Paul's Scarlet Climber' x unnamed seedling.
Class: Large-Flowered Climber.
This brilliant deep red rose has mildly fragrant, medium-sized, semi-double flowers borne singly or in small clusters. They become more crimson with age. The stamens are color matched with red filaments. The flowers are remontant in continuous seasonal flushes. Glossy dark green foliage adorns the plant which will grow to about 15 ft (4.5 m).

'Valentine's Day'.

'VALENTINE'S DAY'.

(Wekamrav).
Breeder: Tom Carruth (United States 2004).
Parentage: 'Amalia' x 'Raven'.
Class: Large-Flowered Climber, Mini-Flora.
The flowers are mildly fragrant, medium-sized, full, cupped with reflexing petals and deep, brilliant red. They are produced in medium to large clusters and bloom in regular seasonal repeating flushes. The plant has glossy, dark green foliage and will climb to about 10 ft (3 m). I wonder why this rose is classed as a Mini-Flora with flowers of this size and a plant this tall.

'Vanity'.

'VANITY'.

Breeder: Rev. Joseph Pemberton (United Kingdom, 1920)
Parentage: 'Château de Clos Vougeot' x unnamed seedling.
Class: Hybrid Musk.
'Vanity' is one of the best of Pemberton's Hybrid Musks. The flowers are fragrant (musk), medium-sized, semi-double, deep pink with lighter centers and are borne in large clusters. Rebloom occurs in regular seasonal flushes. The plant will grow in a bushy manner to about 10 ft (3 m).

'VARIEGATA DI BOLOGNA'.

Breeder: Massimiliano Lodi (Italy, before 1909).
Parentage: Unnamed seedling x 'Pride of Reigate'.
Class: Hybrid Perpetual, Bourbon.
Although this rose is usually described as a Bourbon, it is probably best classed as a Hybrid Perpetual like its pollen parent which it resembles strongly. The flowers are very fragrant, large, very full, globular and white with cherry-red stripes and small streaks. The inner petals may be roughly quartered. The flowers are borne singly (mostly) or in small clusters during a spring or summer bloom. There is only an occasional flower produced later in the season. The rose is

'Variegata Di Bologna'.

known to sport to a solid purple form generally known as 'Purpurea di Bologna' which resembles 'Comtesse D'Oxford' and also 'Victor Emmanuel'. Some DNA study is needed here. The plant is hardy, healthy except for a susceptibility to blackspot and will grow to about 10 ft (3 m) under favorable conditions.

'Vicomtesse Pierre Du Fou'.

'VICOMTESSE PIERRE DU FOU'.

Breeder: Joseph Sauvageot (France, 1923).
Parentage: 'L'Idéal' (Noisette) x 'Joseph Hill' (Hybrid Tea).
Class: Large-Flowered Climber, Tea-Noisette.
The flowers of this rose are large, double, very fragrant (tea rose) and deep coral pink with petal bases flushed yellow on first opening. The color shifts to more true pink, then crimson-pink and fades as the flower matures. The petals reflex at the tips and form a partially quartered pattern. The flowers are carried singly or in small clusters and bloom in regular seasonal flushes. The plant is very vigorous and can be expected to grow to 15 to 20 ft (4.5 to 6 m).

'VIKING QUEEN'.

Breeder: R.A. Phillips (United States, 1963).
Parentage: 'White Dawn' x 'L.E. Longley'.
Class: Large-Flowered Climber.
The strongly fragrant flowers are large, double and pink. The color is darkest in the center. They are initially high-centered like a Hybrid Tea, but open to more old-fashioned flowers with reflexed and quartered petals. The individual blooms are borne singly or in small clusters. The rose reblooms in seasonal flushes. It has glossy, dark green, blackspot-resistant foliage, hardiness to USDA zone 5b and will climb to about 12 ft (3.5 m).

'Viking Queen'.

'VILLE DE PARIS, CL.'.

Breeder: Discovered by John A. Armstrong (United States, 1935).
Introduced in Australia by Hazlewood Bros. Pty. Ltd. in 1938.
Parentage: Sport of 'Ville de Paris'.
Class: Climbing Pernetiana.
The flowers of this rose are faintly scented, large, semi-double to double and medium golden-yellow fading to light creamy yellow. The stamens have filaments with pink bases. The floral form is globular at first, and then it becomes a shallow cup, often with uneven or slightly crumpled petals. The rose reblooms well in repeated seasonal flushes. The plant has glossy foliage with flushes of red-bronze. The climbing sport is grown at the Roseto Carla Fineschi (Italy) and the bush sport parent can be seen at Bagatelle Park (France) and San Jose Heritage Rose Garden (California).

'Virgo, Cl.'.

'VIRGO, CL.'.

Breeder: Discovered by Ignace Hendrickx (Belgium, before 1957).
Parentage: Sport of 'Virgo'.
Class: Climbing Hybrid Tea.
This elegant Climbing Hybrid Tea has mildly fragrant, large-sized, double, high-centered, pure white flowers carried singly or in small clusters. The rose reblooms in regular seasonal flushes. The plant has dark green foliage and will reach a height of about 10 ft (3 m).

'Voie Lactée, Cl.'.

'VOIE LACTÉE, CL.'.

Translation: 'Milky Way, Cl.'.
Breeder: Marcel Robichon (France, 1950).
Parentage: 'Frau Karl Druschki' x 'Julien Potin'.
Class: Climbing Hybrid Tea.
This very fragrant rose has flowers that are large, double, high-centered and creamy white. They are deeply cupped which causes them to open poorly in wet weather. They are borne singly or in small clusters. The rose reblooms in continuous seasonal flushes. The plant has dark green, glossy foliage and will grow to about 10 to 13 ft (3 to 4 m).

W

'Westerland'.

'WALTER C. CLARK'.

Breeder: William Paul and Son (United Kingdom, 1917).
Parentage: Unknown.
Class: Hybrid Tea.
The flowers are very fragrant, large, double and dark red becoming more cerise with age. The large petals reflex loosely along the center line and give the flowers a somewhat ragged appearance. They bloom in regular flushes during the flowering season. The plant is hardy to USDA zone 4a. It can be trained as a small climber as can be seen at Sangerhausen.

'Walter C. Clark'.

'WALTHAM CLIMBER NO. 1'.

Breeder: William Paul (United Kingdom, 1885).
Parentage: Seedling of 'Gloire de Dijon'.
Class: Tea-Noisette.
This Noisette from long ago has richly fragrant, medium to large-sized, double, deep crimson-pink flowers with a lighter and slightly more purple reverse and with an old-fashioned form. They are borne singly or in small clusters and rebloom in regular seasonal flushes. They were considered a real novelty when first introduced because of the combination of the remontancy and the

'Waltham Climber No.1'.

deep, bright color. The plant is nearly thornless and can be trained as a climber of about 8 to 10 ft (2.5 to 10 m). It will grow and bloom best in a warm climate. I have seen it only at Roseraie du Val-de-Marne (France).

'WALTHAM CLIMBER NO. 2'.

Breeder: William Paul (United Kingdom, 1885).
Parentage: Seedling of 'Gloire de Dijon'.
Class: Tea-Noisette.
This version of the Waltham series is very similar to the first with very fragrant, double flowers arranged singly (mostly) or in small clusters, remontant in regular seasonal flushes, but with a slightly deeper color and a large size. The plant is nearly thornless and will grow to about 8 to 10 ft (2.5 to 3 m). 'Waltham Climber No. 3' is now extinct.

'Waltham Climber No. 2'.

'WARM WELCOME'.

Breeder: Christopher Warner (United Kingdom, 1992).

Parentage: ['Elizabeth of Glamis' x ('Galway Bay' 'Sutter's Gold)] x 'Anna Ford'.
Class: Climbing Miniature.
'Warm Welcome' has mildly fragrant (spicy), small, single to semi-double, orange flowers with golden yellow petal bases. The petals have rather pointed tips and this is accentuated by the reflexing of the tips to form strong points and to give a star-like shape to the flower. The flowers rebloom in repeated flushes during the flowering season. The plant is very disease resistant and can be grown as a small climber to about 7 ft (2.15 m).

'Warm Welcome'.

'WATER MUSIC'.

Breeder: Ronald Bell (Australia, 1982).
Parentage: 'Handel' x unnamed seedling.
Class: Large-Flowered Climber, Climbing Floribunda.
The flowers have gently ruffled silvery white petals with crimson-pink edges and flushes of cream in the centers. They are mildly fragrant, medium-sized, semi-double to lightly double and are borne singly or in small clusters. There is one main bloom early in the season with a scattering of flowers later. The plant is well armed with thorns, has glossy, dark green foliage and will grow to about 8 ft (2.5 m).

'WEISSE AUS SPARRIESHOOP'.

('White Sparrieshoop').
Breeder: Discovered by Reimer Kordes (Germany, 1962).
Parentage: Sport of 'Sparrieshoop'.
Class: Climbing Floribunda.
Except for the white color this rose is identical to 'Sparrieshoop', the pink sport parent. The flowers are richly fragrant, single, medium-sized and form a shallow, open cup centered by a big bunch of yellow stamens. They rebloom in regular seasonal flushes. The plant can be trained as a climber of about 8 ft.

'Weisse New Dawn'.

'WEISSE NEW DAWN'.

('New Dawn White', 'White New Dawn').
Breeder: Discovered by Walter Berger (Germany, 1959).
Parentage: Sport of 'New Dawn'.
Class: Large-Flowered Climber.
This sport of the famous 'New Dawn' is very similar to its parent except for the color which looks like a faded version of 'New Dawn', having white outer petals and a light pink center. They both have flowers that are fragrant, and medium-sized, semi-double to double and are borne singly (mostly) or in small clusters. There is one main bloom early in the season with some scattered flowers later. The plant has glossy, dark green foliage and is said to grow to as much as 15 or 16 ft (5 m).

'WEISSE WOLKE'.

(KORstacha, 'Nuage Blanc', 'White Cloud').
Breeder: W. Kordes & Sons (Germany, 1993).
Parentage: Unknown.
Class: Large-Flowered Climber.
'Weisse Wolke' has large, very fragrant, semi-double, pure white flowers that are initially cupped, but open widely to show their stamens as they mature. They are borne singly or in small clusters. There is a prolific bloom, a white cloud of flowers, early in the season with an occasional repeat later. The plant is very vigorous and will climb to as much as 25 ft (7.6 m).

'Weisse Wolke'.

'WELLS' CLIMBER'.

('Wells' Pink and White Climber').
Breeder: Verlie W. Wells, Jr. (United States, 1995).
Parentage: Unknown.
Class: Large-Flowered Climber.
I wonder why this beautiful rose isn't grown more often. It has large, double, crimson-pink flowers with a lighter reverse that is almost white and a perfectly formed, high-centered Hybrid Tea shape. The flowers are carried singly or in small clusters. There is a main summer bloom with a few flowers produced later in the season. The plant has shiny, dark green foliage and will climb to 10 or 12 ft (3 to 3.65 m).

'Wells' Climber'.

'Wendy Cussons, Cl.'.

'WENDY CUSSONS, CL.'.

Breeder: Discovered by Follen (United Kingdom, before 1967).
Parentage: Sport of 'Wendy Cussons'.
Class: Climbing Hybrid Tea.
This lovely rose has very fragrant, large, double, high-centered, deep crimson pink flowers. The outer petals reflex to form points creating a star-like effect in mature flowers. The plant has dark green, glossy foliage and will climb to about an average height of 10 ft (3 m).

'Wenlock'.

'WENLOCK'.

(AUSwen).
Breeder: David Austin.
Parentage: 'The Knight' x 'Glastonbury'.
Class: Shrub, English Rose.
The flowers of 'Wenlock' are scented of old rose, large,

very double and crimson fading to more cherry tones with aging. The flowering repeats in regular flushes during the season. The plant has semi-glossy, very disease resistant, dark green foliage. It is hardy to USDA zone 5b and can be trained as a climber of about 8 ft (2.5 m) in a warm climate or as a shrub in a cool climate.

'Wenzel Geschwind, Cl.'.

'WENZEL GESCHWIND, CL.'.

Breeder: Discovered by Max Vogel (Germany, 1940).
Parentage: Sport of 'Wenzel Geschwind'.
Class: Climbing Hybrid Tea.
This rose has large, double, fragrant dark crimson-red flowers with flushes of purple and a lighter reverse. It is remontant in continuous seasonal flushes. The plant will grow to about 10 ft (3 m) in a much branching manner.

'WERNER DIRKS'.

Breeder: Wilhelm J. H. Kordes II (Germany, 1937).
Parentage: 'Mrs. Pierre S. Dupont' x 'Daisy Hill' (Hybrid Macrantha).
Class: Large-Flowered Climber.
The buds are pink, but this color is found on the guard petals only, so the flowers open ivory colored with cream centers. They are fragrant, large, double high-centered and open enough at maturity to show a glimpse of the stamens. The plant has rugose, dark green foliage and can be trained as a small climber of about 8 ft (2.5 m).

'Werner Dirks'.

'WESTERLAND'.

(KORlawe, KORwest).
Breeder: Reimer Kordes (Germany, 1969).
Parentage: 'Friedrich Wörlein' x 'Circus'.
Class: Shrub, Climbing Floribunda.
The flowers open large, double and deep apricot from buds of the same color. There are flushes of yellow in the centers. As they age the flowers fade and acquire more of a pink hue on the petal tips and the centers become more cream. The flower form is a shallow cup with ruffled petals. There is a spice-like fragrance. The flowers are borne singly or in small clusters and are remontant in regular seasonal flushes. The healthy plant has dark green foliage, is hardy to USDA zone 5b and will climb to as much as 12 ft (3.65 m).

'Westerland'.

'Westfalenpark'.

'WESTFALENPARK'.

(Chevreuse, KORplavi).
Breeder: W. Kordes & Sons (Germany, 1986).
Parentage: Unnamed seedling x 'Las Vegas'.
Class: Large-Flowered Climber.
Apricot buds open to golden yellow flowers enlivened by a slight touch of apricot. The flowers are fragrant, large, double and are borne singly or in small clusters. They bloom in continuous seasonal flushes. The plant can be grown as a small climber of about 8 ft (2.5 m).

'Whiskey Mac, Cl.'.

'WHISKEY MAC, CL.'.

(ANDmac, 'Whiskey, Cl.').
Breeder: Discovered by Anderson Rose Nursery (Scotland, 1985).
Parentage: Sport of 'Whiskey Mac'.
Class: Climbing Hybrid Tea.
This rose is a climbing sport of one of the most famous Hybrid Teas. The flowers are large, double, high-centered, richly fragrant and bronze-yellow lightly touched with apricot. They bloom generously in repeated flushes during the flowering season. The plant has healthy, glossy, dark green foliage and grows vigorously.

'White Cap'.

'WHITE CAP'.

(Everblooming Pillar No. 3).
Breeder: Brownell (United States, 1954).
Parentage: Unnamed seedling x 'Break O'Day, Cl.'
Class: Large-Flowered Climber.
'White Cap' has large, very double, very fragrant white flowers with creamy yellow centers. The petals may show some quartering, but it is not a prominent feature like the reflexing petals with their rolled-back look. The flowers are borne singly or in small clusters and rebloom in continuous seasonal flushes. The plant is hardy to USDA zone 5b and will climb to about 10 ft (3 m).

'WHITE COCKADE'.

Breeder: Alec Cocker (Scotland, 1969).
Parentage: 'New Dawn' x 'Circus'.
Class: Large-Flowered Climber.
'White Cockade' has medium to large-sized, double, fragrant, white flowers with cream-colored centers. The form is cupped and somewhat flattened. They are borne singly or in small clusters. The rose has one main bloom early in the season with a scattering of flowers later. It is moderately vigorous and can be trained as a climber of about 10 ft (3 m) or grown as a shrub with a little pruning.

'White Cockade'.

'WHITE DAWN'.

Breeder: L. E. Longley (United States US, 1949)
Parentage: 'New Dawn' x 'Lily Pons'.
Class: Large-Flowered Climber.
The flowers of this rose are fragrant, medium-sized, double and pure white with a touch of cream or creamy yellow in the center backing up the large bunch of yellow stamens. The form is an open, shallow cup. The flowers are arranged in medium clusters and have one main bloom early in the season with a few repeat flowers later. The plant has glossy, dark green foliage, hardiness to USDA zone 5b and growth to about 12 ft (3.5 m). This offspring of 'New Dawn' should not be confused with 'Weisse New Dawn', a white sport of 'New Dawn'.

'White Dawn'.

'WHITE EDEN'.

('Blanc Pierre de Ronsard', 'MElviowit', 'Palais Royal').

'White Eden'.

Breeder: Discovered by Alain Meilland (France, 1999).
Parentage: Sport of 'Pierre de Ronsard'.
Class: Large-Flowered Climber. Romantica.
The flowers of this climbing sport are identical to its sport parent except for the color which starts out ivory white with pink centers instead of cream with pink petal edges. They soon fade to pure white except for a small flush of pink around the stamens. They are large, very double in a cupped, old-fashioned form and are borne singly or in small clusters. There is a mild fragrance. The rose has one main bloom early in the season with some scattered repeats later and makes a lovely pillar rose of about 10 ft (3 m) that is well clothed with shiny, dark green foliage.

'White Grootendorst'.

'WHITE GROOTENDORST'.

('Grootendorst White').

Breeder: Discovered by Paul Eddy (United States, 1962).
Parentage: Sport of 'Pink Grootendorst'.
Class: Hybrid Rugosa.
The flowers of this Hybrid Rugosa are identical to 'Pink Grootendorst' except for color. The flowers are fragrant, small, double and white. They are cup-shaped and carried in large clusters. Their most distinguishing characteristic is the presence of serrations at the tips of the petals, giving them a carnation-like appearance. They bloom in continuous seasonal flushes. The plant has typical wrinkled Rugosa-style leaves, is hardy to USDA zone 4b, is best in a cool or moderate climate and will grow to about 7 ft (2 m) in height. It can be trained as a small, shrubby climber.

'WHITE MAMAN COCHET, CL.'.

Breeder: Discovered by George Knight & Sons (Australia, 1907).
Parentage: Sport of 'White Maman Cochet'.
Class: Climbing Tea.
The flowers are very large, double, high-centered and creamy-white with pink tips on the outer petals and a light flush of yellow at the center. They have a pronounced tea-like scent. They are remontant in continuous flushes during the flowering season. The plant will grow from 10 to 12 ft (3 to 3.5 m) in height.

'WHITE NEW DAWN'.
See 'Weisse New Dawn'.

'WHITE NIGHTS'.

('Armorique Nirpaysage', POUlaps).
Breeder: L. Pernille and Mogens Nyegaard Olesen (Denmark, 1985).
Parentage: Unnamed seedling x 'Kalahari' (McGredy, 1965, Hybrid Tea).
Class: Climbing Hybrid Tea, Shrub (Courtyard Collection).
'White Nights' has very fragrant flowers that open light yellow and fade to white, starting at the outer petals and leaving the center the deeper color. They are large, double, high-centered and are subtended by sepals with extended tips. They are borne singly (mostly) or in small clusters and rebloom in seasonal flushes. The plant has glossy, dark green foliage and, with support, the ability to climb to about 10 ft (3 m).

'WHITE SPARRIESHOOP'.
See 'Weisse aus Sparrieshoop'.

'WHITE STAR'.

(HARquill).
Breeder: Harkness (United Kingdom, pre-2008).
Parentage: Unknown.
Class: Climber.
Here is a lovely white climber to lighten up the garden. The flowers are fragrant, medium-sized (8 cm average), semi-double (15 petals) and arranged in small clusters. The blooming is prolific, prolonged and is remontant in seasonal flushes. The plant can be trained as a climber of about 8 ft (2.5 m). It makes a good pillar rose.

'WIESENBURGER PARKPRINZESSCHEN'.

Breeder: Krietsch (Germany, pre-2010). Introduced by Baumschule Graeff (Germany, 2010).
Parentage: Unknown.
Class: Large-Flowered Climber.
The flowers of this rose are large-sized, double, very fragrant, high-centered and pink with yellow-apricot petal bases and flushes of those colors on the petal backs. The floral form is very beautiful with large, softly reflexing petals. It grows only at Sangerhausen and a few private gardens. The Sangerhausen database simply lists it as a tall climber.

'Wiesenburger Parkprinzesschen'.

'WILHELM'.

('Skyrocket').
Breeder: Wilhelm J. H. Kordes II (Germany, 1934).
Parentage: 'Robin Hood' x 'J. C. Thornton'

Class: Hybrid Musk.
This is a very good rose to use as a small climber or a large shrub where a bright spot is needed in the garden. The flowers are medium-sized, lightly double and deep brilliant red with white petal bases and a few white streaks. The flower form is an open cup with a large bunch of golden yellow stamens in the center. The flowers are carried singly or in small clusters and bloom in continuous seasonal flushes. The foliage is large, glossy and medium green. The rose has the potential to grow to about 8 ft (2.5 m).

'WILHELM HANSMANN'.

Breeder: Wilhelm J. H. Kordes II (Germany, 1955).
Parentage: ('Baby Château' x 'Else Poulsen') x R. kordesii.
Class: Hybrid Kordesii.
The flowers of this showy rose are mildly fragrant, medium-sized, semi-double and dark glowing red with small touches of white in the centers. The flower form is an open cup with gently wavy petals. They are borne in large clusters. There is one main bloom early in the season with a few flowers opening later. The foliage is dark green and glossy and the plant grows to about 15 ft (4.5 m).

'WILLIAM ALLEN RICHARDSON'.

('Altaville Saffron Noisette', 'W. A. Richardson').
Breeder: Marie aka Veuve (aka Widow Schwarz or La Veuve) Ducher (France, 1875).
Introduced in France by Veuve Ducher in 1878.
Parentage: Seedling of 'Rêve d'Or'.
Class: Tea-Noisette.
This offspring of 'Reve d'Or' is equally as lovely as its sport parent rose. The flowers are fragrant (tea), medium-sized, double and several shades of golden yellow and apricot that age to white. The centers fade last. The petals have a distinctive way of folding along the mid-line and rolling back along the sides to create a starburst effect. The flowers are borne singly (mostly) or in small clusters and bloom in continuous seasonal flushes. The plant is almost thornless, has dark green, glossy foliage and will climb to about 12 ft (3.5 m). It will grow and bloom best in a USDA zone climate of 7b or warmer.

'William Morris'.

'WILLIAM MORRIS'.

(AUStir, AUSwill, N/75/88).
Breeder: David Austin (United Kingdom, 1987).
Parentage: 'Abraham Darby' x seedling.
Class: Shrub, English Rose.
The flowers are formed on a familiar old-fashioned pattern often found in Austin roses. The larger outer petals fit together closely to form a cup around the smaller, quartered inner petals. The flowers are very fragrant, medium-sized, very double and soft apricot which, in time, fades and becomes pinker. They are arranged singly or in small clusters and bloom in repeated seasonal flushes. The plant has semi-glossy, dark green foliage and will grow to about 8 ft (2.5 m). It is somewhat susceptible to rust, but is healthy otherwise.

'Willowmere, Cl.'.

'William Allen Richardson'.

'WILLOWMERE, CL.'.

Breeder: Discovered by Louis Mermet (France, 1924).
Parentage: Sport of 'Willowmere'.
Class: Climbing Hybrid Tea, Climbing Pernetiana.
The flowers of this climbing sport are lightly fragrant, medium to large-sized, double, high-centered and apricot-pink with yellow petal bases. They fade very slowly, but become more pink with time, starting at the outer petals. They bloom in regular seasonal flushes. The plant has light green, glossy foliage, is almost thornless and will grow to an average size of about 10 ft (3 m).

'WINDING ROAD'.

(TALroad).
Breeder: Pete & Kay Taylor (United States, 2003).
Parentage: 'Nicole' x 'Chelsea Belle'.
Class: Climbing Miniature.
This rose has medium-sized, double, white flowers with red edges. There is no fragrance. The flowers are carried singly or in small clusters and bloom in continuous seasonal flushes. The plant has semi-glossy, dark green foliage and will grow to about 7 ft (2 m).

'Winifred Coulter, Cl.'.

'WINIFRED COULTER, CL.'.

Breeder: Discovered by Jarvis (Unknown, circa 1968).
Parentage: Sport of 'Winifred Coulter'.
Class: Climbing Floribunda.
'Winifred Coulter' has medium-sized, lightly double, mildly fragrant, crimson flowers with white petal bases and a white reverse. The flowers open out flat at maturity. They bloom in regular seasonal flushes. The plant is quite vigorous and will climb to about 15 ft (4.5 m).

'WINNER'S CIRCLE'.

(RADwin) Winsom
Breeder: William Radler (United States, 1997).
Parentage: RADliv x RADkoswe.
Class: Large-Flowered Climber.
This beautiful rose has medium to large-sized, single, dark red flowers carried in large clusters and produces hips in the fall. There is little if any fragrance. Rebloom occurs in regular seasonal flushes. The plant has very healthy dark green, semi-glossy foliage, is hardy to USDA zone 5b and will grow to about 8 ft (2.5 m). It makes a lovely pillar rose.

'Winsome'.

'WINSOME'.

Breeder: Dobbie & Co. Ltd. (Scotland, 1931).
Parentage: Unknown.
Class: Climbing Hybrid Tea.
'Winsome' has large, double, crimson-pink flowers carried singly or in small clusters. The petals are large and loosely held which gives the flowers a windblown look. The weight of the large flowers causes them to nod. There is a main bloom early in the season with an occasional repeat later. The plant is known to grow to about 8 or 10 ft (2.5 or 3 m).

'WOBURN ABBEY, CL.'.

Breeder: Discovered by S. Brundrett & Sons (Australia, 1972).
Parentage: Sport of 'Woburn Abbey'.
Class: Climbing Floribunda.
The flowers are mildly fragrant, medium to large-sized, double and orange with yellow centers and lighter, yellow-orange reverses. As the flower ages the orange hue shifts to crimson-pink. The flowers are borne in small to medium clusters. The plant will climb to about 15 ft (4.5 m).

'Woburn Abbey, Cl.'.

'WOLLERTON OLD HALL'.

(AUSblanket).
Breeder: David Austin (United Kingdom pre-2011).
Parentage: Unknown.
Class: Shrub, English Rose.
The flowers of this rose are medium-sized, full and very soft, light apricot in color. They fade in time to cream. The form is much like that of 'Jude the Obscure'. It is deeply cupped, almost closed, and remains so as the flower ages. There is a floral fragrance. The rose reblooms in regular, continuous seasonal flushes. The plant is almost thornless and, if given support, will climb to about 8 ft (2.5 m).

'WOOLVERSTONE CHURCH ROSE'.
see 'Surpassing Beauty of Woolverstone'.

Y

'Yellow Charles Austin'.

'YELLOW CHARLES AUSTIN'.

(Ausling, AUSyel).
Breeder: David Austin.
Parentage: Sport of 'Charles Austin'.
Class: Shrub. English Rose.
The flowers are very fragrant, medium to large-sized and double with reflexing outer petals and quartered inner petals. They open deep golden-yellow and fade to light yellow. The rose blooms in flushes during the flowering season, especially if pruned regularly. The plant can be pruned and grown as a shrub or given support and grown as a climber of 10 to 12 ft (3 to 3.5 m) in a warm to moderate climate.

'Yellow Charles Austin'.

'YELLOW ROMANTICA'. See 'Lunar Mist'.

'Yellow Sweetheart'.

'YELLOW SWEETHEART'.

Breeder: Ralph Moore.
Parentage: Seedling of 'Étoile Luisante' x 'Goldilocks'.
Class: Climbing Floribunda.
This is one of Ralph Moore's few non-miniature roses. The flowers are very fragrant, medium to large-sized, double, light yellow and borne in large clusters. The rose reblooms in continuous seasonal flushes. The plant is almost thornless and will climb to about 12 ft (3.5 m).

'Yellowhammer, Cl.'.

'YELLOWHAMMER, CL.'.

Breeder: Francois Dorieux I (France, 1976).
Parentage: Unknown. Probably a sport of 'Yellowhammer'.
Class: Climbing Floribunda.
The flowers of 'Yellowhammer, Cl.' are fragrant, medium-sized, lightly double and golden yellow that fades slowly. They are borne in small clusters and bloom in repeated seasonal flushes. The plant has dark green glossy foliage and climbs to about 10 ft (3 m).

'YOUNG VENTURER, CL.'.

Breeder: Gianfranco Fineschi (Italy, 1984).
Parentage: Sport of 'Young Venturer'.
Class: Climbing Floribunda.
This climbing floribunda has very fragrant, large, double, apricot-colored flowers that bloom in continuous flushes during the flowering season. The plant has dark, green, glossy foliage and can be trained as a climber to about 10 ft (3 m).

'Young Venturer, Cl.'.

'YVES PIAGET, CL.'.

(KEltsupiatsu).

Breeder: Discovered by Keisei Rose Nursery (Japan, 2005). Introduced by Meilland Richardier (France, 1916).

Parentage: Sport of 'Yves Piaget'.

Class: Climbing Hybrid Tea.

This climbing sport is identical to its sport parent except for height. The flowers are very fragrant, very large, very double and deep pink fading to light pink. The floral form is globular and the arrangement is single or small clusters. There is one main bloom spring or summer with a few flowers opening in the fall. The plant has semi-glossy foliage and will grow to about 10 ft (3 m).

'Yves Piaget, Cl.'.

Z

'Zéphirine Drouhin'.

'Zambra, Cl.'.

'ZAMBRA, CL.'.

(MEIalfisar).
Breeder: Meilland International (France, 1969).
Parentage: Sport of 'Zambra' (Floribunda. Meilland, France, 1960)
Class: Climbing Floribunda.
'Zambra, Cl.' has flowers that are fragrant, medium-sized, semi-double and medium orange. The petals have streaks of yellow, yellow-orange bases and sometimes have flushes of orange-red on the tips of the outer petals. The flowers, which bloom continuously in seasonal flushes, open out flat and reveal large clusters of stamens in their centers. The plant is said to have moderate growth and to be suitable as a pillar rose.

'Zenith'.

'ZENITH'.

(DELzen).
Breeder: G. Delbard (France, 1982).
Parentage: ('Spectacular' x seedling of 'Ténor') x ('Floradora' x 'Incendie').
Class: Large-Flowered Climber.
'Zenith' has medium-sized, semi-double, vermilion flowers with a flattened, open form. They are borne singly or in small clusters. The plant has a potential height of about 8 ft (2.5 m).

'Zéphirine Drouhin'.

'ZÉPHIRINE DROUHIN'.

('Charles Bonnet').
Breeder: Bizot (France, 1868).
Parentage: Unknown.
Class: Climbing Bourbon. A Boursault ancestor may be indicated by the lack of thorns.
The flowers are medium to large-sized, double, very fragrant, medium cerise-pink and are carried singly or in small clusters. They are early bloomers and continue blooming in flushes the rest of the flowering season. The plant is hardy to USDA zone 5b, has few thorns, matte, light green foliage and will grow to a height of 12 to 15 ft (3.5 to 4.5 m).

'ZORBA'.

(POULyco08).
Breeder: L. Pernille and Mogens Nyegaard Olesen (Denmark, 1992).
Parentage: Seedling x 'Aspen'.
Class: Large-Flowered Climber. Courtyard rose.
The buds and opening flowers are apricot, but quickly fade to golden yellow and then more slowly to cream. The flowers are small-sized and double with an open, flat form. The petals have the distinctive feature of mucronate tips (little points). There is little or no fragrance. The plant has glossy, dark green foliage and can be trained as a small climber of about 7 to 8 ft (2 to 2.5 m).

'Zweibrücken'.

'ZWEIBRÜCKEN'.

Breeder: Wilhelm J. H. Kordes II (Germany, 1955).
Parentage: Rosa kordesii x 'Independence'.
Class: Hybrid Kordesii.
This rose has softly fragrant, large, semi-double, dark crimson-red flowers with small white petal bases borne in large clusters. There is one main bloom early in the season with a scattering of flowers later. The shrubby plant has dark green, glossy foliage and can be trained as a climber of about 10 ft (3 m). It is grown at Sangerhausen (Germany).

SUGGESTED READING LIST

Allison, S., *Climbing and Rambling Roses*, Moa Beckett, New Zealand, 1993.

Austin, D. & Beales, P., *Botanica's Roses: The Encyclopedia of Roses*, Koneman, 2005.

Austin, D., *Climbing and Rambling Roses*, Garden Art Press, 2016.

Austin, D., *Shrub Roses and Climbing Roses*, Antique Collector's Club Dist., U.K., 2007.

Austin, D., *The English Roses*, Timber Press, 2005.

Beales, P., *Classic Roses*, Henry Holt and Co., New York, 1997.

Beales, P., *Visions of Roses*, Little Brown, London and Bulfinch, New York, 1996.

Chapman, L., Drage, N., Durston, D., Jones, J., Merrifield, H. and West, B., *Tea Roses*, Rosenberg, 2008.

Dean, J., Storm, L., Vierra, B., *Field Report of Rose Characteristics, An Innovative Approach to the Documentation of Old Roses*, Private Pub.,2002. For purchasing information, e-mail: storm@caltel.com.

Dickerson, B. C., *Old Roses: The Master List*, iUniverse, Inc., New York, 2007.

Dickerson, B. C., *Roll Call: The Old Rose Breeder*, Author's Choice Press, USA, 2000.

Dickerson, B. C., *The Old Rose Advisor*, Timber Press, Portland, Oregon, 1992.

Dobson, P. R., & Schneider, P., Combined Rose List. *Hard to Find Roses and Where to Find Them*, published annually. See www.combinedroselist.com for purchasing information.

Fagan, G., *Rose of the Cape of Good Hope*, Private Publication, 1988.

Fearnley-Whittingstall, J., *Rose Gardens*, Chatto & Windus, London, 1989.

Griffiths, T., *My World of Old Roses*, Whitcoulls, 1986.

Harkness, J., *Roses*, J. M. Dent & Sons, London, 1978.

Harkness, J., *Makers of Heavenly Roses*, Souvenir Press, London, 1985.

Horst, R. and Cloyd, R., *Compendium of Rose Diseases and Pests*, 2nd Ed., APS Press, 2007.

Howells, J., *The Rose and the Clematis*, Garden Art Press, 1996.

Krüssmann, G., *Roses*, Timber Press, Oregon, 1982. Completely revised and updated from the German edition, *Rosen, Rosen, Rosen*, 1974. Translated by Gerd Krüssmann and Nigel Raban.

LeRougetel, H, *A Heritage of Roses*, Unwin Hyman, London, 1989.

Lord, T., *Designing With Roses*, Frances Lincoln, 1999.

Phillips, R. and Rix, M., *Random House Book of Roses*, Random House, 1988.

Quest-Ritson, C. and Quest-Ritson, B., *American Rose Society Encyclopedia of Roses: The Definitive A to Z Guide*, DK Pub., New York, 2003.

Quest-Ritson, *Climbing Roses of the World*, Timber Press, Oregon, 2003.

Scannielo, S., *A Year of Roses*, Cool Springs Press, USA, 2006.

Scannielo, S., and Bayard, T., *Climbing Roses*, Macmillan, USA,1994.

Scannielo, S., *Jackson and Perkins Rose Companions*, Cool Springs Press, USA, 2005.

Scannielo, S., *Roses of America*, Henry Holt, New York, 1990.

Schneider, P., *Right Rose, Right Place*, Storey Publishing, USA, 2009.

Thomas, C., *In Search of Lost Roses*, Summit, New York, 1989.

Thomas, G. S., *Climbing Roses, Old and New*, J. M. Dent & Sons, London, 1979.

Thomas, G. S., *The Graham Stuart Thomas Rose Book*, John Murray, London,1994.

Warner, C., *Climbing Roses, Their Care and Cultivation* (Illustrated Monographs), Weidenfeld Nicolson Illustrated, 1990.

Young, M., Shorr, P., Baer, R., *Modern Roses 12*, American Rose Society, USA, 2007.

Zimmerman, Paul, *Everyday Roses*, The Taunton Press, USA.

SOME USEFUL WEBSITES

Help Me Find Roses.
www.helpmefind.com/rose

Garden Web.
www.gardenweb.com

Rose Gardening World.
www.rosegardeningworld.com

Integrated Pest Management of Roses.
www.gardening.cornell.edu/factsheets/ecogardening/ipmrose.html

Rose Hybridizer's Assoc.
www.rosebreeders.org

World Federation of Rose Societies.
www.worldrose.org

Heritage Rose Foundation.
www.heritagerosefoundation.org

The Heritage Roses Group.
www.heritagerosesgroup.org

PHOTO CREDITS

All photos are by Anne Belovich except the following:

Andrew Hornung:
'Ali Baba', 'Commandant Cousteau, Cl.', 'Nieborgs Nr. 221'.

Europa Rosarium, Sangerhausen, Germany:
'Agnes', 'Allen's Fragant Pillar', 'Amélie Gravereaux',' Ards Pillar', 'Arthur Bell', 'Banzai 83', 'Beauty Fairy', 'Belinda', 'Belkanto', 'Blue Moon', 'Break O'Day', 'Capitaine Soupa', 'Carla', 'Charlotte Armstrong', 'Château de Clos Vougeot', 'Cognac', 'Colonia', 'Elli Knab, Cl.', 'Golden Ophelia, Cl.', 'Ivory Fashion, Cl.', 'Jackie, Cl.', 'Kordes Perfecta, Cl.'', 'Lal, Cl.', 'Mary Hart, Cl.', 'Maryse Kriloff, Cl.', 'Max Krause, Cl.', 'Mevrouw G. A. van Rossem, Cl.', 'Mme Henri Guillot, Cl.',' Mme Segond Weber, Cl.', 'Mrs Henry Winnett, Cl.', 'Pompon de Paris, Cl.', 'Santa Anita, Cl.', 'The Adjutant, Cl.', 'Virgo, Cl.', 'Comte de Torres', 'Concerto', 'Coquette des Blanches', 'Countess of Stradbroke', 'Curiosity', 'Dearest', 'Dr Domingos Pereira', 'Duquesa de Peñaranda', 'E. G. Hill', 'Eclipse', 'Effective', 'Emilie Dupuy', 'Exploit', 'Gardejäger Gratzfeld', 'General-Superior Arnold Janssen', 'Glory of Waltham', 'Grand Mère Jenny', 'Gribaldo Nicola', 'Hermann Löns', 'James Sprunt', 'Josephine Baker', 'Kaiserin Friedrich', 'Kathleen', 'Kimono', 'Lemon Queen',' Libertas', 'Louis Pajotin', 'Mainzer Fastnacht', 'Marie Accarie', 'Maritim', 'Mme Auguste Choutet', 'Mme Auguste Perrin', 'Mme Norbert Levavasseur', 'Mojave', 'Monsieur Rosier', 'Moonlight', 'Moulin Rouge', 'Mrs W. H. Cutbush', 'Mrs W. J. Grant', 'Multiflore de Vaumarcus', 'Nardy, 'Nur Mahal', 'Orange Elf', 'Oscar Chauvry', 'Polareis', 'Princesse de Nassau', 'Red Queen', 'Rina Herholdt', 'Robusta', 'Rosalie Coral', 'Royal Show', Show Girl', 'Souvenir de Nemours', 'Souvenir de Pierre Dupuy', 'Studienrat Schlenz', 'Sultane', 'Sunstar', 'Suspense', 'Tassin', Torch', Wiesenburger Parkprinzesschen', 'Winsome', 'Wrams Gunnarstorp', 'Zweibrücken'.

Harald Enders:
'Alain, Cl.' (Roth Clone), 'Albert Poyer', 'Apotheker Georg Höfer', 'Belkanto', 'Böhms Climber', 'Brindis', 'Cathrine Kordes', Chatter, Cl. 'Comtesse de Noghera', 'Čsl Legie', 'Dr Renata Tyršová', 'Edda', 'Fashionette, Cl.', 'Floradora', 'Fürst Bismarck', 'Gardejäger Gratzfeld', 'Geschwinds Gorgeous', 'Glarona', 'Holstein', 'Honor Bright', 'Kaiser Wilhelm' (Drögemüller), 'Los Angeles, Cl,', 'Louis Barbier', 'Max Krause', 'Mrs Tresham Gilbey, Cl.', 'New Yorker, Cl.', 'Orangeade', 'Professor Dr Hans Molisch', 'Professor Erich Maurer', 'Rosalie Coral', 'Sif', 'Soldier Boy', 'Soleil d'Orient', 'Studienrat Schlenz', 'Sunstar', 'Teide', 'Texas Centennial, Cl.', 'Tropique', 'Walter C. Clark', 'Winsome'.

Steve Jones:
'Betty Uprichard', 'Black Boy', 'Blackberry Nip', 'Black Tea', 'Blessings', 'Captain Hayward', 'Cherry Vanilla', 'Christine, Cl.', 'Circus, Cl.', 'Colcestria' (distant), 'Condesa de Sastigo', 'Conquistador', 'Etoile de Hollande', 'Duchesse de Brabant, Cl.', 'George Dickson, Cl.', 'Geschwind's Gorgeous', 'Golden Glow', 'Goldmarie, Cl.', 'Independence Day, Cl.',' Josephine Bruce, Cl.', 'La France, Cl.', 'Lady X', 'Laurent Carle, Cl.', 'Mady', 'Mercedes Gallart', 'Mikado', 'Minuette, Cl.', 'Mister Lincoln, Cl.', 'Mme Abel Chatanay Cl,', 'Mount Shasta', 'Niphetos, Cl.', 'Orange Sensation, Cl.', Orangeade, Cl.', 'Papa Gontier, Cl.', 'Pink Wonder, Cl.', 'President Leopold Senghor, Cl.', 'President Vignet, Cl.', Queen of Hearts', 'Sakuragasumi, Cl.', 'Sarabande Cl.', 'Schneewalzer', 'Softee, Cl.', 'Soldier Boy', 'Sonia Meilland', 'Soraya, Cl.', 'Spek's Yellow', 'Tasogare, Cl,, Te Awamutu Centennial', 'Teide', 'The Doctor', 'Yametsu-Hime, Cl.', 'Yves Piaget, Cl.'

Susan Feichtmeir:
'Dixieland Linda'.